The Funding of Political Parties

This book explores the problems associated with regulating the funding of political parties and election campaigns in a timely assessment of a topic of great political controversy.

From interest in Barack Obama's capacity to raise vast sums of money, to scandals that have rocked UK and Australian governments, party funding is a global issue, reflected in this text with case studies from Australia, Canada, New Zealand, the United Kingdom, and the United States. Taking an interdisciplinary approach with leading scholars from politics, geography and law, this text addresses key themes: contributions, spending controls, the role of broadcasters and special interests, and the role of the state in funding political parties. With regulatory measures apparently unable to change the behaviour of parties, why have existing laws failed to satisfy the demands for reform, and what kind of laws are necessary to change the way political parties behave? *The Funding of Political Parties: Where Now?* brings fresh comparative material to inform this topical and intractable debate, and assesses the wider implications of continuing problems in political funding.

This book will be of interest to students and scholars of political science, political theory, policy and law.

Keith D. Ewing has been Professor of Public Law at King's College London since 1989, having previously taught at the universities of Edinburgh and Cambridge.

Jacob Rowbottom is a Lecturer at the Faculty of Law, University of Cambridge and Fellow of King's College, University of Cambridge.

Joo-Cheong Tham is an Associate Professor at the Melbourne Law School, Australia.

Routledge Research in Comparative Politics

1 **Democracy and Post-communism**
Political change in the post-communist world
Graeme Gill

2 **Sub-state Nationalism**
A comparative analysis of institutional design
Edited by Helena Catt and Michael Murphy

3 **Reward for High Public Office**
Asian and Pacific Rim States
Edited by Christopher Hood and B. Guy Peters

4 **Social Democracy and Labour Market Policy**
Developments in Britain and Germany
Knut Roder

5 **Democratic Revolutions**
Asia and Eastern Europe
Mark R. Thompson

6 **Democratization**
A comparative analysis of 170 countries
Tatu Vanhanen

7 **Determinants of the Death Penalty**
A comparative study of the world
Carsten Anckar

8 **How Political Parties Respond to Voters**
Interest aggregation revisited
Edited by Kay Lawson and Thomas Poguntke

9 **Women, Quotas and Politics**
Edited by Drude Dahlerup

10 **Citizenship and Ethnic Conflict**
Challenging the nation-state
Haldun Gülalp

11 **The Politics of Women's Interests**
New comparative and international perspectives
Edited by Louise Chappell and Lisa Hill

12 **Political Disaffection in Contemporary Democracies**
Social capital, institutions and politics
Edited by Mariano Torcal and José Ramón Montero

13 **Representing Women in Parliament**
A comparative study
Edited by Marian Sawer, Manon Tremblay and Linda Trimble

14 **Democracy and Political Culture in Eastern Europe**
Edited by Hans-Dieter Klingemann, Dieter Fuchs and Jan Zielonka

15 **Social Capital and Associations in European Democracies**
A comparative analysis
Edited by William A. Maloney and Sigrid Roßteutscher

16 **Citizenship and Involvement in European Democracies**
A comparative analysis
Edited by Jan van Deth, José Ramón Montero and Anders Westholm

17 **The Politics of Foundations**
A comparative analysis
Edited by Helmut K. Anheier and Siobhan Daly

18 **Party Policy in Modern Democracies**
Kenneth Benoit and Michael Laver

19 **Semi-Presidentialism Outside Europe**
A comparative study
Edited by Robert Elgie and Sophia Moestrup

20 **Comparative Politics**
The principal-agent perspective
Jan-Erik Lane

21 **The Political Power of Business**
Structure and information in public policymaking
Patrick Bernhagen

22 **Women's Movements**
Flourishing or in abeyance?
Edited by Marian Sawer and Sandra Grey

23 **Consociational Theory**
McGarry and O'Leary and the Northern Ireland conflict
Edited by Rupert Taylor

24 **The International Politics of Democratization**
Comparative perspectives
Edited by Nuno Severiano Teixeira

25 **Post-communist Regime Change**
A comparative study
Jørgen Møller

26 **Social Democracy in Power**
The capacity to reform
Wolfgang Merkel, Alexander Petring, Christian Henkes and Christoph Egle

27 **The Rise of Regionalism**
Causes of regional mobilization in Western Europe
Rune Dahl Fitjar

28 **Party Politics in the Western Balkans**
Edited by Věra Stojarová and Peter Emerson

29 **Democratization and Market Reform in Developing and Transitional Countries**
Think tanks as catalysts
James G. McGann

30 **Political Leadership, Parties and Citizens**
The personalisation of leadership
Edited by Jean Blondel and Jean-Louis Thiebault

31 **Civil Society and Activism in Europe**
Contextualizing engagement and political orientation
Edited by William A. Maloney and Jan W. van Deth

32 **Gender Equality, Citizenship and Human Rights**
Controversies and challenges in China and the Nordic countries
Edited by Pauline Stoltz, Marina Svensson, Zhongxin Sun and Qi Wang

33 **Democratization and the European Union**
Comparing Central and Eastern European post-Communist countries
Edited by Leonardo Morlino and Wojciech Sadurski

34 **The Origin of Electoral Systems in the Postwar Era**
A worldwide approach
Krister Lundell

35 **The Globalization of Motherhood**
Deconstruction and reconstructions of biology and care
Edited by Wendy Chavkin and JaneMaree Maher

36 **Parties, Elections, and Policy Reforms in Western Europe**
Voting for social pacts
Kerstin Hamann and John Kelly

37 **Democracy and Famine**
Olivier Rubin

38 **Women in Executive Power**
A global overview
Edited by Gretchen Bauer and Manon Tremblay

39 **Women and Representation in Local Government**
International case studies
Edited by Barbara Pini and Paula McDonald

40 **The Politics of Charity**
Kerry O'Halloran

41 **Climate Policy Changes in Germany and Japan**
A path to paradigmatic policy change
Rie Watanabe

42 **African Parliamentary Reform**
Edited by Rick Stapenhurst, Rasheed Draman and Andrew Imlach with Alexander Hamilton and Cindy Kroon

43 **The Politics of International Law and Compliance**
Serbia, Croatia and The Hague tribunal
Edited by Nikolas Rajkovic

44 **The Funding of Political Parties**
Where now?
Edited by Keith D. Ewing, Jacob Rowbottom and Joo-Cheong Tham

The Funding of Political Parties

Where now?

Edited by Keith D. Ewing, Jacob Rowbottom and Joo-Cheong Tham

Routledge
Taylor & Francis Group
LONDON AND NEW YORK

First published 2012 by Routledge

2 Park Square, Milton Park, Abingdon, Oxfordshire OX14 4RN
711 Third Avenue, New York, NY 10017

Routledge is an imprint of the Taylor & Francis Group, an informa business

First issued in paperback 2018

British Library Cataloguing in Publication Data
A catalogue record for this book is available from the British Library

Library of Congress Cataloging in Publication Data
The funding of political parties: where now?/edited by Keith D. Ewing, Jacob Rowbottom and Joo-Cheong Tham.
p. cm. – (Routledge research in comparative politics; 44)
Includes bibliographical references and index.
1. Campaign funds. 2. Campaign funds–Law and legislation. 3. Political parties–Law and legislation. 4. Campaign funds–Great Britain. 5. Campaign funds–Law and legislation–Great Britain. 6. Political parties–Law and legislation–Great Britain. I. Ewing, Keith. II. Rowbottom, Jacob. III. Tham, Joo-Cheong.
JF2112.C28F86 2011
324.7'8–dc22

2011013526

ISBN: 978-0-415-58001-4 (hbk)
ISBN: 978-1-138-37694-6 (pbk)

Typeset in Times
by Wearset Ltd, Boldon, Tyne and Wear

Contents

Contributors

Ingrid van Biezen is Professor of Comparative Politics at Leiden University, the Netherlands.

Keith D. Ewing is Professor of Public Law at King's College London, England.

Colin Feasby is a Partner at Osler, Hoskin & Harcourt LLP.

Justin Fisher is Professor of Political Science and Director of the Magna Carta Institute at the University of Brunel, England.

Andrew Geddis is a Professor at the Faculty of Law, University of Otago, Dunedin, New Zealand.

Navraj Singh Ghaleigh is a Lecturer at the School of Law, University of Edinburgh, Scotland.

Richard L. Hasen is Professor of Law at UC Irvine School of Law, USA.

Ron Johnston is Professor of Geography at the School of Geographical Sciences, University of Bristol, England.

Graeme Orr is an Associate Professor at TC Beirne School of Law, the University of Queensland, Australia.

Stephanie Palmer is a Senior Lecturer at the Faculty of Law, University of Cambridge, Fellow of Girton College Cambridge, and barrister at Blackstone Chambers, London, England.

Charles Pattie is a Professor at the Department of Geography, University of Sheffield, England.

Jacob Rowbottom is a Lecturer in Law at the University of Cambridge and Fellow of King's College, Cambridge, England.

Joo-Cheong Tham is an Associate Professor at the Faculty of Law, University of Melbourne, Australia.

1 Introduction

Keith D. Ewing, Jacob Rowbottom and Joo-Cheong Tham

Following the UK General Election in 2010, the Coalition Agreement between the Liberal Democrat and the Conservative Parties pledged to 'pursue a detailed agreement on limiting donations and reforming party funding in order to remove big money from politics'. Shortly after coming into office, the new government referred the issue of party funding to the Committee on Standards in Public Life (CSPL), the recommendations of which are likely to form the basis of legislative proposals.

This is not the first time that the CSPL has been asked to look at political finance, as its 1998 report formed the basis of the Political Parties, Elections and Referendums Act 2000. The latter was a landmark piece of legislation which gave the UK system for funding politics its biggest overhaul since 1883. While the Act has had a number of successes, most notably introducing a regime of transparency in political donations, that latter success inevitably also exposed additional problems that needed to be addressed.

The problem of party funding

The legislation of 2000 was itself the child of a decade of controversy surrounding political funding which had dogged the Major government since 1992. These controversies related to secret funding, foreign donations and escalating campaign costs. Controversy also followed the New Labour government, with the Ecclestone donation of £1 million in 1997 embroiling the government in difficulty of its own making from its earliest days. The Ecclestone donation was controversial because it became associated with a change of policy on the part of the government.

Having been enacted in the shadow of the latter donation, the 2000 Act did not deal with it directly, concentrating on the transparency and source of donations rather than their amount (though it did require shareholder approval for corporate donations). Nor did the 2000 Act otherwise resolve the problem of party funding which continued to generate controversy, with claims being made that donors were buying privileges, a claim given fresh impetus during the cash for honours affair in 2005–2006.

It has to be said, however, that it is easier to make claims of impropriety than to substantiate them. None of the major so-called scandals led to a prosecution or conviction, even though the cash for honours affair was by no means the end of it, with the Labour Party and Labour politicians in particular haunted by the Act during the period that Brown was prime minister, as discussed by Navraj Ghaleigh in Chapter 9. The continuing concerns did, however, lead to a number of high-profile police inquiries, while the continuing discomfort led to a number of inconclusive reports addressing the question of further funding reform.

The problem of party funding is by no means unique to the United Kingdom, as revealed by developments in the United States, where the cost of 'democratic' politics is very high. Attempts in the US to secure legislation to address the problems have met with extreme difficulty as there is no consensus about the nature of the problem or the means needed to address it, and the Supreme Court has consistently used its powers to strike down legislation which it perceives as restricting free speech.

It is true that some commentators take great inspiration from the efforts of President Obama to raise vast sums of money through smaller donations, given mainly as a result of internet targeting of voters. But as Rick Hasen points out below, these same commentators overlook the fact that George W. Bush did much the same, and that Obama also generated large sums of money from traditional sources, that is to say, special interests. The idea that Obama offers a solution to the British problem is implausible, and it remains to be seen how much he is able to garner in small donations when he runs for a second term.

In the meantime, the 2010 US congressional campaigns have been a sobering experience for those intoxicated by the belief that the solution to party funding is for political parties and candidates to raise money in 'small sums' from 'small people'. There we see familiar concerns about 'special interests' pouring money into the process, especially following the Supreme Court's protection of corporate election spending in *Citizens United*, discussed by Stephanie Palmer in Chapter 10. There is no sign that business as usual will not continue to be the order of the day.

Addressing the problem

When designing a regulatory framework, there is a need to protect political freedoms that are also a central feature of a democracy. The emphasis placed on these goals varies from country to country, with each different jurisdiction designing regulatory frameworks in different ways to fit with its own political culture and constitutional values. These clearly include the right to free speech, which is essential to the conduct of elections. Without free speech there can be no free elections.

The concern with the US position, however, is the treatment by the Supreme Court of money as speech, and the failure on the part of the Court to accept the need to reconcile freedom of speech with other essential pre-conditions of free and fair elections. These include ensuring that everyone has an equal opportunity to participate in the process, as well as fair competition among the different parties representing major stands of opinion.

The difficulty with party funding reform is not only that the objectives are thus contested, but that the politics are uncertain as a result. As in the United States, political funding reform in the UK has also been difficult to secure on the basis of all-party consensus, which some would contend is an essential constitutional pre-condition for reform. That difficulty was seen in 2005–2006, when attempts by a retired civil servant to broker reforms collapsed in a spirit of mutual distrust and recrimination.

The current political climate will prove to be as a great a challenge for any agreement on reform. The 2010 General Election may have been one of the most closely fought in recent years, but the spending in the campaign was notably uneven among the parties. The Electoral Commission reported that the Conservative Party spent £16.7 million on its campaign, while the Labour Party spent £8 million and the Liberal Democrats spent £4.8 million.

The asymmetries continue to be found in the organisation of the parties and the sources of income, with the Conservatives relying on individuals and companies for donations, and Labour gaining a substantial amount of funds from trade unions. In this context, any attempt to adjust the rules on donations and election spending could result in an advantage for one party. With the stakes so high in the current political environment, consensus will be hard to come by.

For some, the asymmetries go deeper still, As discussed by Rowbottom, Ewing and Tham in Chapters 2, 3, and 4, there is a danger that party funding reform has implications not only for party funding, but also for party organisation and structure. This is a particular problem in the United Kingdom (though it is by no means unique to the United Kingdom) because of the nature of the party organisations.

Methods of regulation

It is not only uncertain objectives and intractable politics that make this such a difficult area for regulation. There is also the problem of different regulatory methods and techniques. One starting point is to look at the source of the funds, at where the candidates and parties get their money from, and how much is given by each source. Along these lines, scandals following large political donations have been a regular feature in UK politics, with much recent attention focusing on the role of wealthy individuals, companies or interest groups in bankrolling the leading political parties.

But although it is tempting to impose the 'blunt instrument' approach of legally imposed contribution caps, there may be problems with such a strategy. At what level should a cap be set without giving one party an advantage over another? How could it be done consistently with the need to respect the diverse party structures and forms of organisation? Although desirable in principle, can it be made to work in practice, or is the temptation for evasion too great and effective enforcement impossible?

This leads some to suggest that the focus should be on spending, with tight limits to reduce the demand for money, so-called demand side solutions. This may take the form of general limits (say on all forms of election activity by parties and candidates), or segmental limits (say on parts of election action). The latter might take the form a ban on the use of billboards for example, and thereby significantly reduce costs at a stroke of the parliamentary pen.

Although spending in British elections is dwarfed by spending levels elsewhere, there are still frequent concerns that elections are becoming too costly. But while further spending regulation is also tempting, there are problems here as well. At what point does the spending level need to be set to be effective? Are there not also problems of evasion and enforcement here too? If these can be avoided only by a cap on all party spending (general as well as election spending), have we not reached the stage where the state is too intrusive, and freedom of association too heavily compromised?

The other concern relating to both contributions to and expenditures by political parties is that if we regulate too tightly, there is a danger that we simply drive the money elsewhere. It will not go away but will end up in even murkier places that are even harder to regulate, partly because it is being spent by bodies and people not subject to the same legal and public scrutiny as political parties, and partly because the claims based on free speech will be harder to ignore. Nevertheless, tight regulation of political parties suggests that we at least need to be prepared to contemplate the tight regulation of others.

The list of others includes (but is not confined to) the media, whose influence over political debate, for example, can sometimes be subject to controversy. The connection between the mass media is most obviously symbolised in Italy by Silvio Berlusconi, the country's biggest media mogul and longest serving post-war prime minister. Such an overlap in personnel is unusual, but more common is the close connection between those in office and those owning the media. Rupert Murdoch's frequent contact with governments in the UK and the consequent opportunities for lobbying the government is an obvious reminder that media ownership brings the potential to influence.

Structure of the book

Above are some of the underlying concerns and issues dealt with in this book, which brings together a range of different scholars to examine the workings of a number of systems of political finance from a range of different perspectives. While the majority of contributions to this volume look at the United Kingdom, there are contributions from United States, Canada, Australia, and New Zealand, which draw on the experience of related problems in the various countries.

The volume not only brings together scholars from a range of jurisdictions, but also includes contributions from political scientists as well as lawyers. These contributions look at the developments in campaigning in practice, to investigate how well the regulations fulfil their goals, and look also at the impact of money on electoral success. These perspectives provide a valuable resource both in terms of the rationales for regulating political finance and the design of those laws.

Contributions

The first theme of this volume looks at the questions concerning political contributions. In Chapter 2, Jacob Rowbottom examines the role of institutional donations in British politics. While British political parties have long depended on companies and trade unions as a stable source of funds, their continuing role has proved to be a stumbling block for further reform. Rowbottom looks at the existing regulation of institutional donations, and considers the options for a regulatory framework which applies similar requirements to all institutions.

In Chapter 3, Keith Ewing looks at the role of trade unions in financing political parties. In this, he examines the extensive legal framework that regulates trade union donations and independent campaigns. Ewing argues that trade union activity provides a channel for grassroots participation and calls for the protection of the autonomy of such activity instead of an increase in the levels of regulation. These themes are developed in Chapter 4 by Joo-Cheong Tham, who emphasises the need for an approach to contributions which avoids a one-dimensional approach to the question.

Expenditures

The second theme to be addressed in the volume is political spending. In Chapter 5, Keith Ewing and Jacob Rowbottom examine the operation of the national spending limits in British elections. In this chapter, the authors note that, within the existing system, a significant disparity in election spending exists between the major parties. While the regulations also cap spending by independent actors, relatively few organisations appear to be regulated by these provisions according to the records with the Electoral Commission. The growth of independent electoral expression on the internet is also identified as a potential challenge for the regulatory authorities. In the following two chapters, the focus turns to election spending at the local level.

In Chapter 6, Professors Johnston and Pattie review the controls imposed on local level campaigning in Britain. While much attention is paid to national political expenditures, they note spending at the local level is increasingly important – a finding that has not been lost on British political parties that have invested in marginal constituencies in recent campaigns. This study on local spending is therefore a welcome contribution and highlights an often overlooked area. Johnston and Pattie outline the various patterns in local spending, and show the shortcomings of the existing legislation. They explain how the British laws have been drafted in a way that provides much scope for higher local spending to take place outside the controls imposed on candidates.

Based on empirical work, in Chapter 7 Professor Justin Fisher explains how local campaigning in Britain has experienced a shift away from volunteer-based activities and towards capital intensive methods. This is explained on account of the decline in available volunteers and also the decrease in the cost of some of the expense-incurring activities. Fisher also finds that the impact of money on electoral success should not be simply assumed, that much depends on the way the money is spent, and any advantages secured can be challenged by opponents through free campaigning. For these reasons, he argues for caution before extending controls on local spending.

The role of other actors

The third theme to be addressed is the problem of 'other actors'. The term 'other actors' is used broadly to refer to those other than parties and candidates. In Chapter 8, Andrew Geddis looks at the role of the media. While not participants in the election directly nor formally part of the campaign machinery, the mass media nevertheless play a crucial role in shaping the campaign, by helping to decide which issues will be most salient, through their own commentary and critique, and by providing a platform to certain parties and candidates.

A second key actor in the regulation of party funding is the regulator established to ensure that the law is complied with. This is the subject of Chapter 9, by Navraj Ghaleigh, which looks at the enforcement activities of the Electoral Commission. The Commission had a rocky start and has been heavily criticised in the past, though it appears now to be much more sure footed in the discharge of its responsibilities. This seems unlikely to be as a result of the ill-conceived changes to its composition in 2009.

As already mentioned, a third key actor is the judiciary, who have the capacity to make or break any regulatory system. In Chapter 10, Stephanie Palmer looks at the legal challenges to controls on the media that are imposed during election campaigns. Surveying the recent cases in the US, the UK and the European Court of Human Rights, Palmer notes the devloping legal trends, in particular in relation to the right to freedom of expression, in the different jurisdictions.

Lessons from other countries

In the penultimate section (Part IV), we examine the lessons to be learned from other countries. Chapter 11 by Ingrid van Biezen focuses on two aspects of state intervention in party politics – regulation of party activity and the public funding of political parties. Drawing upon comparative data relating to European democracies, van Biezen argues that both types of intervention are a vital element of how political parties in these countries have strengthened their linkages with the state, a development that increasingly reflects the view of political parties as public utilities

In Chapter 12, the focus turns to a national study of the Canadian system, sometimes held up as a model for others to follow, and particularly in the United Kingdom in light of Canada being a parliamentary democracy on the Westminster model. Here, Colin Feasby shows how the regulatory framework has been subject to a number of legal challenges, as the courts have become battlegrounds on which disputes about the uncertain principles and objectives of party funding legislation are now fought. Like all party funding regimes, it is unclear how easily the Canadian system can be successfully transplanted elsewhere.

An important feature of the Canadian system, however, is the extent to which the parties are now heavily dependent on State funding. This is one of several features addressed by Rick Hasen in Chapter 13 in his insightful account of the US system. Voluntary public funding was introduced for presidential elections, but has now been largely displaced by private funding, by which it is greatly outstripped. Hasen also examines the role of new campaigning and funding techniques.

Party funding and party regulation

Finally, in Part V, Graeme Orr deals in Chapter 14 with the overlapping issue of public funding and State regulation of party funding. Public funding of political parties is an issue that is touched upon by a number of the chapters, and is almost certainly an issue that will be addressed by the Committee on Standards in Public Life. There are, however, a number of problems. The first is practical. Can the State make the public funding of political parties a priority at a time of budget cuts, and if so how much should be provided?

In addressing the question of public funding, Graeme Orr addresses yet another difficulty, this time relating to the conditions under which any such funding should be provided. If the State is to fund political parties in the interests of democracy, does the State have an interest in demanding that parties should be organised and governed in accordance with democratic principles, and if so, what are these principles? It remains to be seen whether any government in the present climate would be willing to adopt a system in which parties are given money without something in return.

Conclusion

It remains to be seen also whether the current review by the CSPL initiated by the government will prompt any significant change. The Committee is considering imposing limits on political donations, expanding state support for political parties, and adjusting the spending controls during elections. Having regulated three national general elections and numerous elections to the other bodies over the last decade, it is clear that the time is right for an assessment of the legal framework. But, as already indicated, there are a number of serious obstacles to be overcome: a lack of consensus about the purpose of reform, the nature of party organisation and structure, the political positions of the political parties, a lack of certainty about regulatory method, the consequences and implication of heavy-handed regulation, to say nothing of the current economic climate, which has implications for this area of activity as with all others.

It would certainly be surprising if the government were to make new spending commitments on behalf of political parties at a time of public spending cuts. Perhaps the best that can be done is to recognise that having started on a process of reform in 2000, we have embarked upon a process of continual reform and renewal. Transparency is not an end in itself but a requirement that reveals problems where people are unprepared to moderate their behaviour. Perhaps the best we can do also is to recognise that there is no single solution to the problem of party funding, but a series of options which, if adopted, will benefit one party more than another. Above all, perhaps the best we can do is to recognise that change can best take place incrementally, dictated by the organisational and institutional structures of the system in which they are to operate. There is no magic bullet.

Part I

The role of contribution caps

2 Institutional donations to political parties

Jacob Rowbottom[1]

Controversies about the funding of political parties in Britain have often centred on money given by wealthy individuals. The 'cash for peerages' affair in 2006 concerned loans and donations to parties from individuals who were later nominated for honours. Newspaper headlines often focus on the large sums given by individuals, two such examples being Sir Paul Getty's £5 million donation to the Conservative Party in 2001 and Lord David Sainsbury's four donations to the Labour Party of £2 million or more each.[2] The fears that very rich people might be able to buy influence or shape the course of an election has provided much of the impetus for reform and calls for a cap on political donations. The donations from individuals are, however, just one dimension of the issue. Institutions, such as companies, pressure groups and trade unions, have long been a major source of funds for British political parties and also a source of controversy. In the 2010 General Election, debates on party funding centred on donations made by institutions rather than individuals, with much attention being given to Lord Ashcroft's role in funding the Conservative Party through his company, Bearwood Corporate Services, and the trade union Unite's role as the Labour Party's largest donor.[3]

At the time of writing the Conservative/Liberal Democrat Coalition Government has promised further reforms to the system of party funding. If such reforms are pursued, the role of institutions in financing political parties should be considered. Most notably, if a cap is imposed on the amount that a person can donate to a party, the question will arise as to whether that cap should also apply to donations from companies, trade unions and other institutions.[4] While it is accepted here that some reform is desirable, it will be argued that, by giving money, some institutions can be an important vehicle for participation in British democracy. Other institutions, however, may act as a conduit for wealthy individuals and organisations. To consider these issues, this chapter will look at the role of institutional donations and how different considerations may apply to different types of institution.

Institutional funding of political parties

Institutional donations have traditionally played an important role in funding British political parties. Companies and trade unions have been a major source of funds for the two main parties, with the former more commonly associated with the Conservative Party and the latter with Labour. The extent of the parties' reliance on institutions can be seen from the Electoral Commission's register of donations to political parties, which divides the sources of funds into categories including individuals, companies, trade unions, unincorporated associations and public funds.[5] The discussion will focus on the three main national political parties and Figures 2.1–2.3 show the total value of donations from those categories received by the parties each year since the Electoral Commission began recording donations in 2001. While these figures include only donations above a certain threshold and do not include other sources of income (such as a party's investments), it provides a general indication of the parties' reliance on different types of donor. Figures 2.1–2.3 illustrate how the parties rely on a mixture of individual and institutional donations, and how the proportion varies with each party.

Figure 2.1 shows that trade unions have consistently been the largest category of donor to the Labour Party (with donations from individuals as the second largest category). Figure 2.2 illustrates the changes in sources of Conservative Party funding. From 2004 onwards the Conservatives received more donations from individuals than any other category of donor (in 2002 and 2003, public funds had been the largest category). However, institutional donations have also been a significant source of funds for the Conservative Party, with companies being the second largest source of funding from 2006–2010. In 2006, the total value of company donations to the Conservative Party was not far from the total

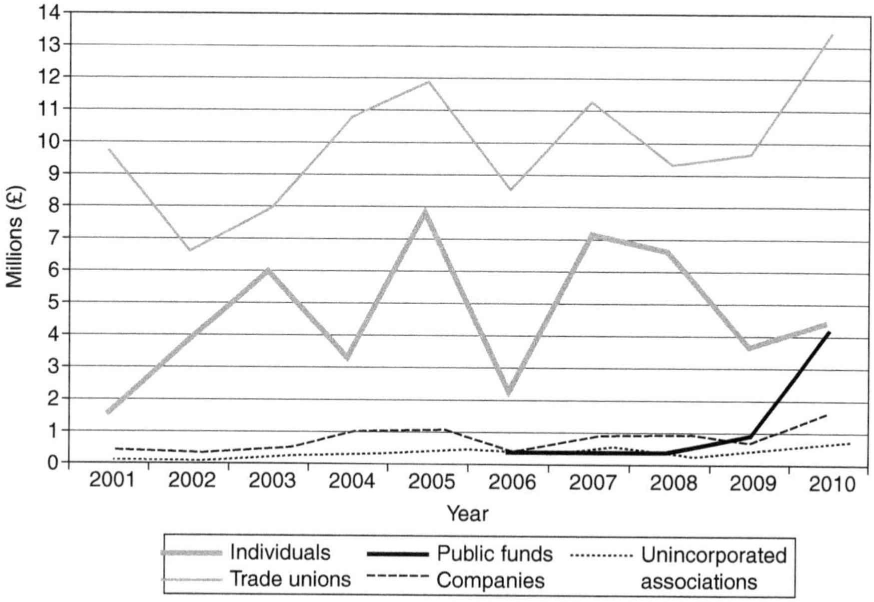

Figure 2.1 Donations to the Labour Party.

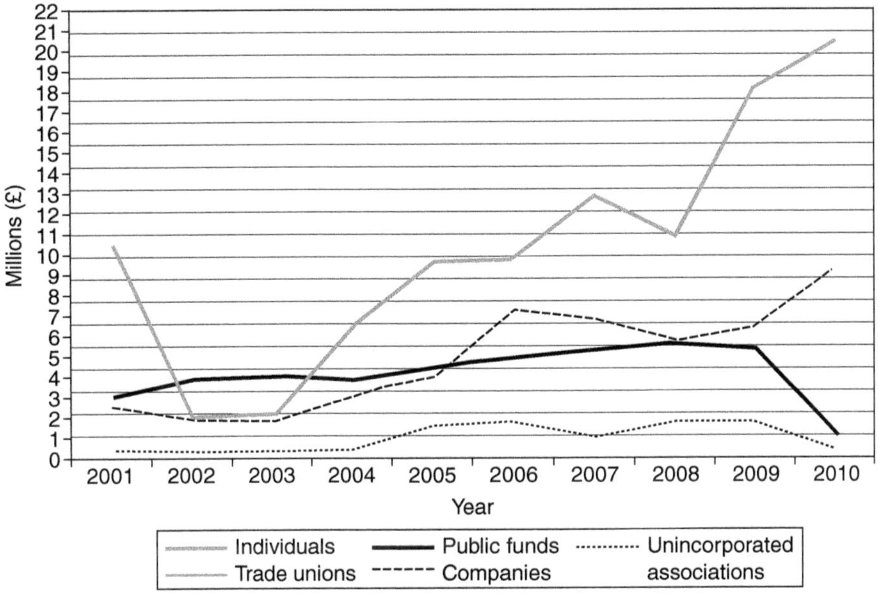

Figure 2.2 Donations to the Conservative Party.

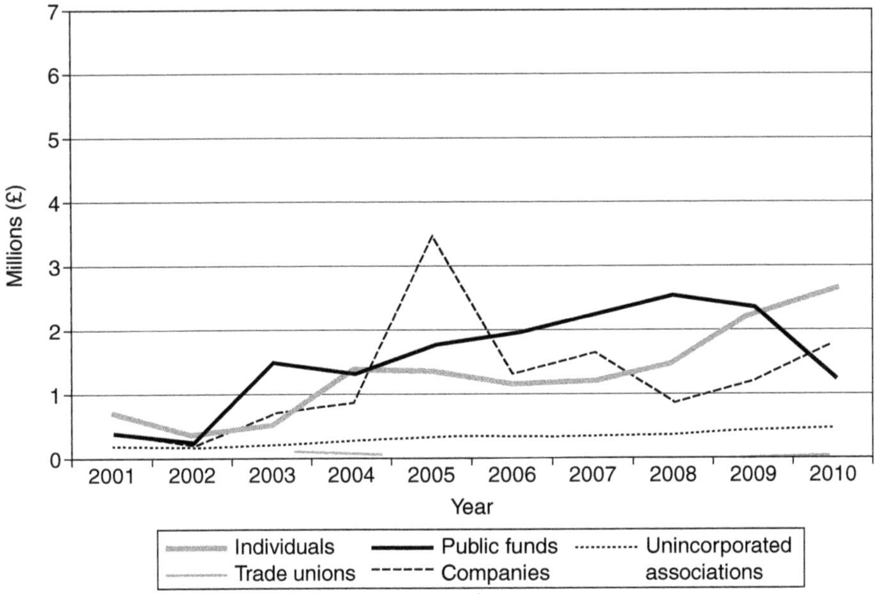

Figure 2.3 Donations to the Liberal Democrats.

amount given by individuals. Figure 2.3 shows the Liberal Democrats' reliance on a combination of individuals, companies and public funds, though its donation income is substantially smaller than that of the other two parties.

Several points can be drawn from the data. The first is that institutional donations are a major source of funding for all political parties. Without resources from companies, trade unions or other associations, there would be a substantial shortfall in political parties' funds. A second point is that the balance between individual, institutional and public funds varies from party to party, with Labour relying more heavily on institutions, the Conservatives more recently relying on individuals and the Liberal Democrats varying between the sources of funds. A third point is that when looking specifically at institutional donations, the types of institution that give the most varies from party to party. Unsurprisingly, this confirms the trend of trade unions giving to Labour and a greater proportion of company donations going to the Conservatives. These differences emphasise the political interests at stake when reforming party funding. If the law were reformed to allow only donations from individuals and banned institutional donations, this would, at the time of writing, give the Conservatives a funding advantage. By contrast, if a low donation limit were to be introduced to individuals, but a more generous limit applied to trade unions, the reform would benefit the Labour Party. Given these strategic implications, it is unsurprising that the role of institutional donations was one factor which prevented the major political parties coming to an agreement on a donation limit of £50,000 when Sir Hayden Phillips reviewed party funding in 2007.[6] Finally, the statistics underline the importance of public funds for opposition political parties, which in 2003 was the largest category of donor for both the Conservative Party and the Liberal Democrats.

The categorisation of the sources of funding given above is not watertight and the difference between individual and institutional donations may be hard to draw in some cases. For example, while the newspapers have paid much attention to Lord Ashcroft's role in funding the Conservative Party, the bulk of these donations have been made by the company Bearwood Corporate Services, rather than by Ashcroft as an individual. Similarly, while the Liberal Democrats gained much attention for receiving financial support from businessman Michael Brown, the donations of £2.4 million were made by Brown's company, 5th Avenue Partners. In these examples, the donations were made by an institution, a company, rather than by an individual. However, where the institution is so closely associated with a particular individual or where an individual effectively controls the institution, the difference between individual and institutional donations may be of little significance.

Institutional donations in a reformed system of party funding

The figures above reveal the level of reliance on institutional funds and the political interests at stake when reforming the system. The central question to be considered here is what role institutions should play in a reformed system of party funding. To address this, the discussion will examine several goals of reform and how institutional donations may relate to those goals.

The first and most common rationale for regulating political donations is a concern with actual or perceived corruption. The term 'corruption' implies a departure from some ideal standard of politics. While there is debate about what those ideal standards are, it is generally accepted that political favours should not be bought by giving money to a political party (or to anyone else). While laws against practices such as bribery, which involves direct exchanges of money for favours, criminal law offences are not as easy to establish and the perception of corruption may linger even where there is little hard evidence of politicians being 'bought'. A cap on donations can provide an additional safeguard by limiting the payments to a party or candidate from a single source (although it does not stop payments being made to people other than the party or candidate). The donation cap also has a role in preventing corruption in a broader sense. Even where there is no evidence of a direct deal, donations may be seen to impose a pressure on the politician. If a politician depends on a particular donor for substantial funds, there is a danger that the official will be influenced by the views or interests of that donor (especially if he wishes to receive donations in the future), even if the donation has not come with any strings attached. In such circumstances, there is no exchange between the donor and politician, but the presence of the donation can taint the politician's decision-making and present a conflict of interest. A cap on donations seeks to take this pressure off the politician. If donations are capped at a low enough level, politicians cannot become so dependent on a single source of funding. Under this view, institutional donations may threaten to corrupt the political process, especially if the institution is associated with a particular set of interests or causes. For example, the political interests of a pressure group or company may be more obvious to the politician, and donations from such sources may be viewed as a deliberate attempt to further a political agenda. The politician may therefore feel greater pressure to meet the demands of that institution to secure funds, and these concerns provide a case for capping the institutional donations.

The case for restricting institutional donation is not, however, so clear cut. While it is clear that political decisions should not be bought, it is less clear when the presence of a donation taints the process in the way described above. When making some decisions, politicians are expected to take into account the views of the public and sometimes to respond to the levels of support for a particular policy. Donations can be used in this process to send a message to or apply pressure on a politician. When advocating a cap on donations, the point is often made that seeking a broad base of small donations is healthy for a democracy and helps politicians engage with the public.[7] By connecting small political contributions with a channel of accountability, this argument implicitly accepts that the politician can be influenced by donations. However, it does depart from any ideal standard of politics because the politician is responding to a large group of citizens, each contributing smaller sums. Along these lines, some large institutional donations may be seen to have less of a 'corrupting' effect. For example, a donation from a political organisation to which members subscribe may be seen as part of a democratic effort of a group of citizens to collectively influence politics. While this view takes a particular approach to the role of groups in politics and to the definition of corruption, it points to a line of argument in which the influence of institutions is not 'undue' where it reflects a pooling of resources among lots of people, rather than one wealthy source buying influence.[8] This line of argument blurs with the second goal of reform, which is promoting political equality, and suggests that the need for a cap may be less pressing in relation to some institutions.

Under the goal of political equality, each individual should have an equal chance to influence political decisions.[9] This means that there is nothing objectionable with giving money in itself and that donations to political parties are a legitimate form of political participation. By giving money, citizens can express their support for a particular party and have some input in deciding which parties should have the resources to contest an election.[10] Unlike the corruption argument, the concern about political equality is not that donations may be influential, but that the chance to influence is unequally distributed. To pursue this goal, a cap on donations, while not giving everyone equal amounts of money to donate to a political party, at least limits the extent to which some individuals can out-donate others.

When thinking about political equality, whether an institutional donation should be subject to such a cap depends on the institution in question. Like the corruption argument, donations from membership organisations that aggregate funds from a large number of individuals may be seen as less problematic under this view. Institutions can serve political equality by allowing people to organise, pool resources and use the donations as a collective channel of political accountability. The group can provide a means for those normally excluded or with little political influence to be heard. When an individual makes a very small donation, his voice is just one in a sea of small contributions. However, when people organise into an institution, its leadership can articulate to the politician why the donation is being made and will be more likely to hold the politician's attention. The institution may also encourage the use of this channel of participation by showing how a single small donation can make a difference. For example, an individual may see how his or her £50 donation can have an impact when it contributes to a collective effort. In these circumstances, capping an institutional donation and treating it like that from an individual can undermine political equality by closing off certain channels for participation.

This is not true of all institutional donors. Where the institution is bankrolled by a small number of wealthy individuals, it raises the same problem as a large donation by a wealthy individual. Furthermore, institutional donations can also exacerbate political inequalities, as those institutions that are already established and have administrative machinery will face fewer hurdles in organising people into pooling their resources. For example, a large company or well-known pressure group will have the offices and staff necessary to communicate with individuals and fulfil any legal requirements. By contrast, groups that lack resources or that are dispersed throughout the community may face greater barriers to organisation and be excluded from this channel of participation. Again, the institutional donation can, in some circumstances, fit with the goal of political equality, but that depends on the particular institution and the way it is organised.

The above discussion suggests that institutional donations can fit within a reformed system of party funding by providing a vehicle for participation. The capacity to perform this function depends, however, on the relationship between the institution and the participants. In some cases, where there is little connection between the two, large institutional donations may give too much power to those controlling the institution's resources, such as a company director or trade union leader. Where the decision to give money is made by one person or a small number of people, then the donation may appear much like a large donation from an individual. In some ways, it is worse than a large individual donation, because the person secures influence not by using his own resources, but those of the institution. This would arise, for example, where members of the institution pay monthly subscriptions and the leader of that organisation uses the institution's funds to give money to a party without some form of approval from the subscribers.

If the leadership of an institution did behave in such a way, the members or subscribers at least have the option of leaving the organisation or withdrawing their support from it.[11] This blunt channel of accountability is most clear where the institution exists for the purpose of political campaigning. In those circumstances, the choice to join or give money to the institution can be taken as implicitly approving its political activities. By contrast, where the institution has mixed purposes, then membership or support of the institution may not be taken to support its political expenditures. In these circumstances, leaving the institution as a way of protesting against political spending can come with high costs as the individual loses the benefits of the other activities of the insitution. To address this problem, a number of safeguards can be introduced, which will be discussed later with a particular focus on trade unions and companies. These will include requirements that donations be made from a separate political fund, which members are not forced to pay into. That way, individuals retain the option of exiting in relation to the political activities of the institution, while remaining associated with its other activities. Alternatively, citizens could have a direct say in deciding who the institution will give money to, for example, through a vote. There are other, less direct, methods for control such as holding the leaders of the institution accountable through elections. The point here is simply to show that the institution can provide a channel for participation in a number of ways, for example, through allowing people to participate within the institution as members, by joining less formal networks of supporters, by giving money to the institution, and by having some level of say in deciding the institution's political activities.

Even if a donation does reflect the collective efforts of citizens, there remains an objection that the political influence of a group should be achieved through persuasion, information and arguments, rather than through the provision of money to parties. In other words, there are deliberative goals in designing a system of party funding. Along these lines, deliberative democrats may be suspicious of institutional donations that advance the interests of a group and threaten to turn the political process into a system of bargaining among competing factions. Measures could be taken to make the process more deliberative, for example, by insulating political parties from all sources of private funding (both individual and institutional) through the public funding of parties.[12] Such a measure would not exclude institutions from the political process. However, their role would not be 'to act as representatives of citizens, advancing their aims by means of financing campaigns' but to 'serve the citizenry by contributing to the understanding of issues'.[13] Under this view, the role of institutions in the electoral process would be through independent information campaigns rather than party funding.

The difficulty with this view is that in the current political climate there is no prospect of an outright ban of all private sources of funding, meaning complete reliance on state funds. Furthermore, the deliberative potential of institutional donations should not be written off. In some cases, the decision of an institution to donate money may be taken collectively. If an institution consults its members before deciding to make a donation, it may provoke internal debate and discussion on the merits of such an action through an opinion-forming process.[14] Once the group has made its commitment, this in turn may encourage further participation in the political process. Under the right conditions, the donation may promote the exchange of reasons within the institution.

In addition to these goals, a reformed system of party funding will seek to provide a stable source of funds to support a diverse range of parties.[15] In the UK, some institutions have developed an ongoing relationship with a party and provided an income at times when individual donations have dropped. The point can be seen most obviously in relation to trade unions and the Labour Party. Trade unions have consistently supplied funds even as support for and membership of the party has changed. The Liberal Democrats have also relied on the Joseph Rowntree Foundation to provide a regular source of income. The point should not be overstated and some wealthy individuals provide a regular source of income to parties too. Furthermore, a reformed system should not aim merely to preserve the status quo and ensure the existing leading parties remain well funded. It is, however, important to recognise that restrictions on institutional donations could leave some parties in a less secure financial position.

A final issue in a reformed system is that institutional donations can potentially be used to avoid controls on individual donations. Under the current law, donations can be made only by a 'permissible donor', which includes people on the electoral roll and companies carrying out business in the UK.[16] Consequently, if an individual is forbidden from making a direct donation to a political party by virtue of being a foreign national, that person can still make a donation through a private company which carries on business in the UK. This will fall foul of the law if the company acts as an agent for the impermissible donor, but otherwise such devices are permitted.[17] For example, while Michael Brown was not a permissible donor, the Electoral Commission found that a donation of £2.4 million by his company 5th Avenue Partners to the Liberal Democrats was permissible as the company carried on business in the UK and there was no express agency agreement.[18] The donation can be made by the institution even though the person most closely associated with that institution is not a permissible donor.

Similar problems arise in relation to transparency requirements. Under the current law, donations of £7,500 or more in any year have to be disclosed to the Electoral Commission, stating the identity of the donor. Until recently, if there was no agency agreement, then only the identity of the institution had to be disclosed and not the sources of the institution's income.[19] For this reason, controversy surrounded donations made to the Conservative Party by the Midlands Industrial Council, an unincorporated association funded by a number of wealthy donors, whose identities did not have to be disclosed to the Electoral Commission.[20] This concern was addressed in 2009 by new laws requiring unincorporated associations that donate £25,000 to a political party in any year to disclose the gifts received by the association of more than £7,500.[21] Even with this provision in place, there is still the potential for 'front' companies to mask the sources of funds that are eventually used to make a political donation.

These examples highlight that if donations by individuals are to be capped, allowing donations by institutions is likely to provide a route for evasion through similar techniques.[22] Institutional donations may also lead to the duplication of representation. Even with a limit on political donations, a number of associations funded by the same wealthy individual could make the maximum possible donation under the limit. In those circumstances, the wealthy individual does not make a large direct donation, but spreads a range of smaller donations across a range of institutions, which amounts to a significant sum in total.

To conclude, institutional donations can serve or undermine the goals of a reformed system of party funding. The effect will depend on the institution in question. The discussion so far has suggested that institutional donations are more likely to fit within a reformed system if the body is representative of citizens and where citizens have some say in the decision to make a donation. Where the institution fulfils these requirements, there are arguments that larger donations from such sources may be less problematic. It has already been noted that this rests on a particular view of politics and the role of groups. This view is open to the criticism that it places too much weight on an account of institutions in politics as mass membership organisations. Instead, the role of groups may be characterised by other types of organisations, such as research or lobbying groups.[23] However, the influence of such non-representative institutions should arguably be pursued through other means, such as persuading the public or politicians on particular issues, rather than through giving money to parties. The view taken here assumes that electoral politics should be responsive to citizens and the role of institutions in funding parties lies in promoting that responsiveness. There are, of course, other functions for groups which are not excluded by this view, but those functions should be pursued through means other than political donations.

Legal categories and controls

Having considered the role of institutional donations in relation to certain goals of a reformed system of party funding, this section will look at the extent to which those goals are promoted by the existing legal regulation of political donations in Britain. The Political Parties, Elections and Referendums Act 2000 provides that donations to political parties can be made by 'permissible donors' such as:

- individuals on the electoral register;
- companies;
- registered parties;
- trade unions;
- unincorporated associations;
- building societies; and
- limited liability partnerships.

The different categories are subject to slightly different regulations in relation to political donations, which will be discussed below. It will be argued that in relation to companies and unincorporated associations, the existing regulations do little to ensure that institutional donations promote responsiveness and participation in the political process.

Companies

Companies that are registered and incorporated into the European Union (EU), which carries out business in the UK, can donate money to a political party.[24] The term 'company' refers to the legal form rather than an entity's function, so this category includes incorporated pressure groups and think tanks, as well as for-profit companies. As a legal person, the company owns its property and economic resources.[25] Directors have a number of duties to the company when making decisions about the use of company property or funds, such as donating money. For example, directors must act in good faith, in a way that promotes the company's success for the benefit of its members as a whole.[26] While the directors act for the benefit of shareholders, those shareholders do not own the company property. Company donations are therefore made from the company's general treasuries as 'an expense in earning the return to shareholders'.[27]

It is often thought that some safeguards are necessary to protect 'dissenting shareholders' that oppose the party receiving the company donation.[28] Under this view, the shareholders should not be compelled to support or finance political views against their wishes. This objection applies when thinking about protecting rights within a political association, but seems at odds with the view of the company as a distinct legal person. Donations are not made using the shareholders' money, but come from a company's funds and are used to pursue its own goals. Where the company is formed to maximise profits, the shareholder's opposition to the donation may be beside the point. For example, a for-profit company may donate money to a party that the director believes will implement policies most favourable to the company's economic fortunes. That donation can form part of a good faith attempt to promote the success of the company, notwithstanding the political objections of shareholders. This may also explain why some companies with economic or other non-political purposes make donations to more than one political party.[29] Such a pattern of donations may promote the success of the company, but it is likely that many shareholders will oppose one of the parties receiving the funds. However, in such a case, it is not the shareholders' money being used and the purposes of the company are not being betrayed. If the donation is treated like any other corporate expenditure, shareholders do not have a right to dissent (other than through the usual channels of accountability). The case for protecting dissenting shareholders therefore rests on a view that political expenditures or donations are unlike a company's other uses of funds. The special considerations that apply to political expenditures may require a distinct decision-making procedure to provide additional protection for shareholders.[30] That argument takes a step away from the view of the company as having its own legal personality and instead sees the company as an association, in which members' political views should be respected.

The main concern with political donations addressed by the existing company law framework is not that shareholders may oppose the party, but rather that company funds may be misused by directors. Donations by companies should be made to further the purposes of the company and not to promote the directors' own personal political views. Directors are therefore constrained by a number of legal duties. It has already been noted that directors must act to promote the success of the company, and other duties include a requirement that directors act in accordance with the company's constitution and use powers for the purposes for which they are conferred.[31] A donation to promote a director's personal political beliefs would therefore constitute an 'improper purpose' and thereby amount to a breach of the director's duties. However, directors are given considerable leeway by the courts when interpreting what uses of funds are in accordance with their duties.[32] As a result, these legal controls provide a fairly limited safeguard, which has led to demands for further controls.

The Companies Act 2006 provides a further legal safeguard by requiring that political donations or expenditures be authorised 'by a resolution of the members of the company'.[33] The resolution can authorise donations for up to four years and must set a maximum amount of money that can be used for such contributions. The resolution does not authorise donations to a particular party, but must be cast in general terms to authorise any political donations in the four-year period.[34] The resolution therefore does not record support for a party or decide which party should receive the funds. The regulation has little impact on private companies with a majority shareholder, who controls a majority of votes and can thereby pass a resolution. In those circumstances, a donation from such a company may be seen, in the public and the politician's eyes, to be from the individual or body with the controlling shares, even though the legal donor is the company. The provision has greater impact on public limited companies that have a larger number of shareholders. While the rationale of the authorisation requirements was to make the regulation of company donations broadly comparable to those applied to trade union donations,[35] the regulations on companies are less onerous. The difference in regulatory regime is unsurprising given that most companies are not membership organisations. The regulations requiring a vote are therefore a limited safeguard which do not approve the political choices made by the company, but aim to prevent misuse of company funds. It does not protect a dissenting shareholder, and any shareholder who opposes a particular donation has 'no real remedy other than the sale of his or her shares'.[36]

If a company does not represent its shareholders (or anyone else) and has its own legal identity, then it may be questioned why companies are legally permissible donors at all. It might be argued that company donations provide a way of furthering certain interests, for example, by allowing the representation of commercial interests in the political process. This could be pursued in ways other than the funding of political parties, such as making representations to politicians or providing information to the public. In any event, people associated with commercial interests can still make donations on an individual basis.

Company donations can also threaten to undermine several of the goals of the reformed system of party funding. First, given the directors' duty to further the company's success, there may a greater danger that such a donation could have a corrupting effect, insofar as it seeks to pursue a specific policy goal that will benefit the company. Second, company donations may lack transparency. The source of the company's funds from which it makes donations may be unknown. A person could make a transfer into the company's general treasuries, which would not have to be disclosed to the Electoral Commission unless there was an agency agreement. Third, some company donations may exacerbate political inequalities. Given the limited controls discussed above, company directors have considerable leeway when deciding which party to give money to, which may give the director greater opportunity to influence the political process. Those resources may also have been acquired through state assistance, for example, some companies benefit from certain tax breaks, which help them to remain profitable. Furthermore, company donations can duplicate representation. For example, if a cap is imposed on individuals and that cap is also applied to companies, then a person who has control of a company would effectively be able to give double the sum specified in the cap (with one donation made individually and one by the company). Given the sheer number of companies, there are also dangers of imbalance. For example, a number of health organisations seeking stricter controls on alcohol sales would find it difficult to compete with every company giving money on behalf of the drinks industry. As a separate legal 'person', each company would be able to make the maximum donation within the limit.

The above concerns may apply to for-profit companies. However, the status as a company is merely a matter of legal form. Some interest groups and other organisations with political purposes are incorporated. For example, in the UK,

Greenpeace is a limited company that receives donations from supporters and engages in lobbying and other political activities.[37] Companies that are organised in this way may perform valuable functions and provide a vehicle for political participation. A donation from such a company is less likely to be an abuse if a political goal is part of that company's purpose, which has also been approved by the group's subscribers. In relation to such organisations, the above concerns have less force and donations from such companies may fit with the goals of a reformed system of party funding. Consequently, the status as a company says little about whether donations should be permissible or capped. In some cases the larger company donation may amplify inequalities in wealth, while in other cases, such as the incorporated interest group, donations may promote equality insofar as they enable people to act collectively. The matter depends on how the company is organised and its relationship with individual participants in the political process. Further regulation beyond the existing resolution procedure would be required to distinguish these types of company and reconcile the contributions with democratic goals.

Trade unions

Trade unions have a unique place in UK political funding. Unions are not just the largest source of funds for the Labour Party, but have a much deeper connection with the Party. The Labour Party was founded in 1900 by trade unions in order to field their own candidates. The Party was initially organised as a 'federation' of affiliated unions, rather than as an organisation of individual members. Individuals could not join the Party as members until 1918.[38] The connection has continued and a number of trade unions pay to be affiliated with the Labour Party and are consequently represented on the Party's decision-making bodies.[39] The issue of institutional donations therefore goes to the heart of the Labour Party's history and curtailing such contributions could potentially break that link.

History alone does not provide a strong reason for continuing a particular practice. The point is that people should have freedom to associate and combine in different ways.[40] The model of political parties engaging with the public directly through membership or soliciting individual donations is just one way of doing politics. The trade union intermediary model, in which people join the institution and that institution affiliates with the party, provides an alternative approach. To set a low cap on the amount that a union can give to a party might close off that form of association and prescribe a specific organisational structure on all parties. The system of party funding should aim to permit flexibility in the ways that people organise and associate, as long as those methods do not run counter to the democratic goals of that system.

Trade unions are also distinct for being the most heavily regulated political donors. Under the current law, if a trade union wishes to spend money on 'political objects', it is required by statute to ballot its members to establish a political fund separate from its general treasuries.[41] If the membership approves, a political fund from which political expenditures can be made is established for ten years. After ten years, the union must hold another ballot of its members to decide if they wish to continue making political expenditures. The political fund can be used to make donations to political parties and to finance independent political campaigns.[42] Individual union members can opt out of paying into the political fund, a provision which ensures that no member is forced to fund political messages.[43]

While the political fund ballot imposes an administrative cost on the union, it does little to give members control over political expenditures. Union members do not have a statutory right to demand that the political fund be used to support a particular party. Some union members may support the establishment of a political fund in order to fund an independent campaign on a political issue, without supporting the political party that receives donations.[44] Consequently, while union members are balloted on the establishment of a political fund, the normal decision-making procedures of the union will decide how that money is spent. This may lead some critics to portray union leaders as 'barons' that have disproportionate political power with potentially corrupting effects. This can, however, be countered by the union's internal democracy. For example, some union conferences have debated whether the political fund should be used to support any political party and, if so, which party should receive any money.[45] Union conferences may also provide direction by developing policies on how political funds should be used. Furthermore, union leadership is more generally accountable to members, providing a channel for members to register their disapproval of any uses of the political fund.[46] The internal democratic procedures are, however, separate from the specific rules requiring a ballot on establishing a political fund. Given that the political fund ballot provides little control over how the fund is used and dissenting members are protected by the opt-out provision, it may be questioned what purpose the requirement serves, other than authorising the union to engage in political activities in general.

The statutory right for members to opt out of the political fund is a stronger control. The provision allows the individual to retain the benefits of union membership while separating him or herself from the organisation's political activities. Like the ballot provision, the decision not to opt out does not mean the member approves of all the payments made from the political fund. Some members may not opt out because they support independent campaigns financed by the fund, but not the political donations. Furthermore, an opt out provision sets paying into the fund as the default rule, which is likely to increase the number of members paying into it.[47] Critics of the arrangement therefore argue that decisions not to opt out are more likely to be a sign of members' inertia rather than approval of any political expenditure.[48] They may regard an opt in provision as a better way to ensure that payment into the political fund is voluntary. The position taken in the opt in/opt out debate may appear to revolve around strategic concerns: Labour supporters prefer the opt out rule to maximise its income, while opponents of Labour support an opt in provision to minimise the flow of money.

The choice of the default rule for paying into the fund partly depends on what view is taken of a trade union. On a narrow view, unions may be seen as an organisation offering a set of services to individuals, such as representation in the workplace and legal representation where necessary, with its political activities merely being an extra, rather than a core, function. In these circumstances, joining the union may say little about a person's view of its political activities and the decision to join a union does not implicitly mean there is an agreement to support such uses of funds. Such a view would therefore point to an opt in rule. By contrast, if one views the union as a political organisation, which not only represents its members in the workplace but also campaigns on broader political issues, then an opt out provision will be thought more appropriate. Under this view, the decision to join a union can be taken to consent to its political activities, just as it consents to the union representing the member in other contexts. There is some support for the view of the union as a political organisation in the decision of the European Court of Human Rights, which upheld an organisation's right to expel a member of the British National Party from the union on ideological grounds (just as other political organisations can).[49] If this view is taken to an extreme, it may question whether an opt out provision is really necessary, as dissenting members are free to leave the union.

The position of trade unions is therefore different from the other categories of institutional donor, as it refers to a specific type of organisation performing a particular type of function. Trade unions are also regulated more heavily than other types of institution. This, however, leaves open the question of whether the status quo is acceptable. The arguments given above suggest that the objections to union donations are not based on political equality, because the union pools the resources of many individuals (assuming the channels of accountability are working correctly). If the source of the union donations is its members (and not wealthy individuals) then there is less scope for union funds duplicating representation. However, the main concern is more pragmatic and flows from the asymmetries in the sources of party funding in the UK. If the other sources of political donation are to be subject to stricter limitations and capped, then to leave union donations unregulated would give the Labour Party a strong strategic advantage in resources. If unions are to keep their status as large institutional donors, then the door must be left open for other representative organisations, which may support other parties, to donate in a similar way.

Unincorporated associations

An unincorporated association is a permissible donor, as long as it 'carries on business or other activities wholly or mainly in the United Kingdom' and its 'main office is there'.[50] While the statutes do not define an unincorporated association, the term has been taken to mean

> two or more persons bound together for one or more common purposes, not being business purposes, by mutual undertakings, each having mutual duties

> and obligations, in an organisation which has rules which identify in whom control of it and its funds rests and on what terms and which can be joined or left at will.[51]

Unlike registered companies or partnerships (or registered voters), there is no register or list to verify whether a donor constitutes an unincorporated association. Whether a political organisation fulfils the definition of an unincorporated association is not always straightforward.[52] The parties should, however, check whether a donation comes from a permissible source and where there is uncertainty consult the Electoral Commission. The extent to which parties apply the test for an unincorporated association given above, for example, by requesting evidence of the rules of the organisation, before accepting a donation is unclear and raises questions about the level of compliance with the law.

A number of different types of organisation can fall within this legal category. Many of the unincorporated associations that give money to parties are political groups, such as a local Labour Club, Conservative club, or council groups. Some other associations are not membership organisations with subscriptions, but political organisations that engage in activities to generate funds that can be given to a political party. In 2009, the National Conservative Draws Society, an unincorporated association which raises funds for the Conservative Party through lotteries, gave £824,000. Unlike companies, an unincorporated association does not own property, and its funds are owned by its members or held on trust for them.[53] Unincorporated associations are under no legal requirements to ballot members before making a donation, let alone establish a segregated political fund.[54] Since 2010, unincorporated associations that donate £25,000 or more to political parties in a year have to disclose all contributions of £7,500 or more received by the association. As stated earlier, the provision was introduced to address concerns that such associations were being used to mask the identity of those funding political parties.[55] Aside from that provision, the principal controls on unincorporated associations arise in the law of trusts or contract, and the constraints on the use of the funds will depend on the rules and purposes of the association in question. Whether an association fits with or undermines the goals of a reformed system of party funding depends on that association, how it is constituted and the terms of association. The law does not, however, attempt to steer the institution towards more democratic internal procedures.

Charities

Charities, the final type of institution to be discussed, are prohibited from making donations to political parties.[56] Such bodies must be established for a charitable purpose only, for the 'public benefit'.[57] That requirement rules out charities pursuing primarily political objectives, such as a change of government policy, because it is not clear whether such activities are for the public benefit[58] and that is something to be decided by the democratic process.[59] This does not rule out all political activity by a charity, provided such activities are merely incidental to the purposes of the charity, rather than the main purpose itself. Consequently, while a charity may support a policy of a political party, a donation to a party would amount to an expression of support of all that party's policies, including those which have no connection to the charitable purposes.[60] Furthermore, as charities receive a number of benefits, such as tax advantages, the rule also prevents such state resources being used to indirectly bankroll the political parties. As a result of the prohibition, some organisations set up both charitable and non-charitable arms. The latter can give money to a political party, but does not benefit from tax advantages and other benefits.

To summarise, the legal categories of institution are subject to varying degrees of regulation. At one end of the spectrum are trade unions, which are subject to more detailed provisions on political spending, while unincorporated associations are subject to a much looser level of control. The controls form a patchwork of different requirements depending on the legal forms of the institution. As a result, the distinctions between the existing categories do not reflect the capacity of institutions to serve the goals of the reformed system of party funding. For example, there are some companies and unincorporated associations that provide ways for people to associate and participate, while there are others in those categories that amplify inequalities and evade the spirit of the law. There is, however, scope for further legal regulation to make the power to donate conditional on the democratic credentials of the institution, in particular, showing how its activities provide a channel for citizen participation. This might help to develop an approach to institutional contributions, which can be applied universally, regardless of the legal form of the institution. The next section will consider this along with other possible paths for the future of institutional donations.

Options for reform

In this section, four main options for the future of donations will be surveyed. The first option is an outright ban on all institutional donations. The second is a uniform cap on all individual and institutional donations. The third option is to allow some institutions to make larger donations, but subject only to certain regulations of the institutions' internal affairs. The final possibility will be to maintain the status quo.

The first option is an outright ban on donations from any institution, allowing only individuals to give money. If the goal of a reformed system is to promote equality among citizens, it may be thought that only citizens should be able to give money. Along these lines, the rationale for the current ban on foreign donations is that parties should be funded by those with a 'genuine stake in the country'.[61] An extreme version of this approach would be to allow only those with the right to vote to donate to parties, as holding the vote demonstrates a 'genuine stake' in the governing of the country.[62] Taking that approach, the right to donate would not be granted to institutions, such as companies, trade unions and pressure groups, as such bodies do not have a vote in an election. Such a stance is reflected in a Conservative Party document published in 2006, which argued that a donation cap should apply to institutional donations in the short term, but eventually such institutional donations should be phased out, on the grounds that: 'Electoral politics should primarily be a matter for individuals, not well-heeled pressure groups, trade unions or corporations.'[63] The proposal has the benefit of simplicity, and avoids the dangers of institutions being used to evade restrictions on individual donations. This may, however, cut off some of the major benefits of associative action in facilitating participation.

This approach need not exclude the role of the institution in party funding. Since 2007, Canadian election laws have prohibited donations from trade unions, companies and other associations.[64] While trade unions can no longer contribute to a political party in Canada, such bodies can still affiliate to a party when union members are full individual members of a party. The role of the union is then in encouraging its members to join a party, rather than to hand over any money directly. In facilitating individual membership, the role of the group is not passive, but takes a lead in promoting party membership among its members. This approach would, however, be a dramatic change from the existing position in the UK and would require the parties to make changes to their fundraising strategies. It is also open to the objection that it prescribes a particular way for parties to organise. In any event, it may even fail to address concerns about the influence of institutions such as trade unions that, like 'bundlers' of individual donations in the US, may use their status as aggregators to make demands of politicians.[65]

A second option is to allow institutions to make donations, but to subject them to the same cap as individuals. While this might lead to a simple approach, it fails to take into account the differences between institutions, with a mass membership organisation having the same status as a small lobbying group. Under this approach, the organisation representing hundreds of thousands of people would be subject to the same limit as a single individual. At the same time, those institutions with arguably little business participating in electoral politics, such as a company owned and controlled by a single non-resident of the UK, would be able to contribute the same amount. It would also impact on some political parties more than others. The Labour Party receives the bulk of its funding from a handful of trade unions and would be severely affected by this approach. As more and more trade unions amalgamate as a response to declining membership, the Party is likely to be dependent on a smaller number of sources (even though each amalgamated union now represents a larger number of people). By contrast, the Conservatives would be less affected insofar as it can rely on moderate-sized donations from a wide range of companies. There is also scope for duplication if this approach allows individuals to make large contributions in total that are spread across a range of different company donations.

A third alternative is to allow institutions to make donations, maybe greater than those allowed by individuals, but subject to certain conditions which attempt to promote the institution's democratic credentials. The first type of condition would require the institution to set up its own political fund from which to make donations. This approach would extend the model of regulation applied to trade unions to pressure groups or other organisations that rely on subscriptions. This could be taken a stage further and impose a cap on the amount any person can pay into the political fund, to ensure that the fund cannot be used as a vehicle for large donors. This model would, however, require a major change in the approach to company donations, which make donations from general treasuries and do not receive subscriptions. It would ban donations from general funds and require the company to establish a separate fund for shareholders and employees to pay into, but not taking any of the company's money. The donation would then have a stronger claim to represent the views of those people, rather than the company itself. The approach would move away from the traditional UK approach to company donations and closer to the US Political Action Committee model. The method would also allow some protection for dissenting members of the institution, by providing a right not to contribute to the funds from which the donations are made.

Another condition is to make the institution's decisions on donating more accountable to its members and subscribers. There are a number of ways this can be done, such as requiring a ballot to authorise donations to a particular party above a certain size. Under this approach, the institution is not simply an aggregation of lots of small donations, but gives money to a party that has been approved collectively. Under this view, the institution is more than just the sum of isolated decisions to give money, but provides a forum for deliberation and contributes in its own right.[66] If these conditions are fulfilled, the overall cap on political donations from that institution could be proportionate to the number of people paying into the institution's political fund. However, to prevent this being used as a source of evasion or duplication of representation, it would be necessary to cap the amount any individual can pay into the institution's political fund.

These conditions may be appropriate for some, but not all, institutional donors. For example, if an association is established with a political goal, then all of its expenditures will be political and there will be no need to establish a separate fund. Furthermore, every person giving money to that institution will be deemed to approve its political goals. The same point may apply where an institution does not seek any subscriptions but engages in fundraising activities specifically for certain political causes. To address this, the conditions requiring a separate fund and internal democracy may be applied only to particular types of organisation, such as companies or unions.[67] In any event, requiring a separate fund and capping donations into that fund may have unintended consequences. The US experience of such regulations suggests that this model creates considerable complexity and increases the costs in securing compliance. Companies, which already have the networks and administrative machinery, will be well placed to negotiate these hurdles and encourage people to pay into a political fund. It may thereby amplify the voice of those already organised, rather than create a level playing field. The requirement for a separate political fund could have other effects. A company may not know whether it wishes to make donations in the future, so as an insurance policy may set up a political fund so the resources are there in case they do want to donate. Once a political fund has been established and the money is sitting in the account, there will at some point be an incentive to use that money on some political activity rather than for the account to lie dormant. Regulation may encourage greater political spending and the experience in the US gives many reasons to doubt the effectiveness in promoting equality or reducing the influence of 'special interests'.

The final option would be to maintain the status quo and allow institutions to continue making donations, subject to existing regulations. This would limit the effectiveness of a cap on individual donations, and allow donations to be made by wealthy individuals via their institutions. There are several reasons why this option may be appealing. The first is that it avoids the complexity, costs and administrative burdens associated with a cap on donations. The second is that it avoids the difficult political questions in finding an option for reform that the main political parties are likely to agree on. The third reason is that it would help (but by no means guarantees) the parties to receive a stable source of funding. Without the support from institutions, political parties will argue for the need for state funds to help meet the costs.

From this summary, all of the main options are problematic, either prescribing a particular model of party organisation that is too restrictive, generating complexity in the regulation, or leaving the regulations so loose that evasion is easily achieved. While the third approach does generate new administrative burdens, it is an appealing route insofar as it maintains a role for the institution while seeking to promote the goals of a democratic system of party funding.

Conclusion

Political parties in the UK have long depended on institutions as a major source of funds. The place of institutional donations is of great importance when reforming party funding, as to curtail the amounts institutions could give would create a significant shortfall in the major party's finances. More importantly, the giving of money through an institution can provide an important avenue for citizens to participate and to ensure that the system of party funding is responsive. Institutional donations have played an important role in making contributions from those groups that represent those on lower or average wages. Donations from representative groups arguably help to counterbalance some of the advantages secured by those making individual donations. While institutions have played an important role in serving these goals, the continuation of the status is also problematic. Despite the benefits mentioned above, some institutions have played a role in amplifying inequalities in the system of party funding, where the institution is not supported by a wide range of people, but is bankrolled by certain wealthy individuals or interests. The existing regulation of institutional donations is also asymmetric, applying very different conditions depending on the legal category of donor. A continuation of the status quo would also sit uneasily with a limit on donations from individuals, providing a potential route for evasion. The approach suggested here is neither to forbid nor uniformly restrict institutional donations. Instead, the approach suggested here is to impose certain conditions before an institution can give sums of money to a party. This raises difficult questions about what the criteria should be and what level of donations should be permitted. Difficult as these questions may be, it is worth attempting to devise a regulatory approach that permits institutional donations, where the institution conforms to certain democratic goals. An approach that takes institutional donations out of the equation would not only go against a tradition in British politics, but go against a tradition that has helped to provide wider participation in funding of political parties.

Notes

1 With thanks to Richard Williams and Joo-Cheong Tham for comments on an earlier draft.
2 According to data from the Electoral Commission, between 2002 and 2009, Lord David Sainsbury gave over £12.5 million to the Labour Party.
3 According to data from the Electoral Commission, between 2003 and 2009 Bearwood Corporate Services gave over £5 million to the Conservative Party. Between 2007 and 2009, Unite gave over £11 million to the Labour Party.
4 These issues are also relevant to other party funding reforms, such as extending state support. If tax relief is granted on political donations or if state funds are distributed through matching grants (in which the state matches private donations to a party), then the eligibility of institutional donations in such schemes will have to be addressed.
5 Figures 2.1–2.3 includes only the main legal categories of donor and omit categories such as limited liability partnerships and friendly societies. In each of the figures, the sums shown on the vertical axis of the graphs are different. The graphs therefore illustrate the proportion of each party's income from each source, but do not illustrate a comparison across the parties of the amounts received.
6 'Talks on new rules to restrict party funding collapse: Labour and the Tories blame each other', *Guardian*, 31 October 2007.
7 For example, see H. Phillips, *Strengthening Democracy: Fair and Sustainable Funding of Political Parties*, London: HMSO, 2007, p. 20.
8 For discussion of the role of secondary associations under democratic theories, see J. Cohen and J. Rogers, 'Secondary Associations and Democratic Governance', *Politics & Society*, 1992, vol. 20, 393. On the definition of corruption and the relation with democratic theory, see J. Rowbottom, *Democracy Distorted*, Cambridge: Cambridge University Press, 2010, pp. 81–84.
9 Rowbottom, *Democracy Distorted*, Ch. 1.
10 For an argument that money paid through membership fees represents a deeper type of engagement, see J.C. Tham, *Money and Politics*, Sydney: University of New South Wales Press, 2010, p. 80.
11 The democratic credentials also come from the way in which the institution's funds are acquired. For example, the institutional donations should themselves be funded through contributions or subscriptions from citizens, which in turn provides some level of control.
12 T. Christiano, *The Rule of the Many*, Oxford: Westview Press, 1996, p. 258.
13 Christiano, *The Rule of the Many*, p. 257.
14 See M. Warren, *Democracy and Association*, New Jersey: Princeton University Press, 2000, pp. 75–76 on the types of association most likely to provide a forum for

deliberation. On the risks and benefits of deliberation within groups, see C. Sunstein, *Designing Democracy: What Constitutions Do*, New York: Oxford University Press, 2001, pp. 45–47.

15 Ministry of Justice, *Party Finance and Expenditure in the United Kingdom: The Government's proposals*, Cm 7329, 2008, para. 4.5.

16 Political Parties, Elections and Referendums Act 2000, s. 54(2) ('PPERA').

17 PPERA, s. 54(6).

18 Electoral Commission, *Case summary: Investigation into donations to the Liberal Democrats reported as being from 5th Avenue Partners Ltd*, 20 November 2009.

19 An exception is in relation to trust funds, where the identity of those establishing and those paying into the fund must be disclosed.

20 According to data from the Electoral Commission, the Midlands Industrial Council donated over £1.5 million to the Conservative Party between April 2003 and November 2007, and made further donations to a regulated donor, the Constituency Campaigning Services Board. Those providing financial support to the Midlands Industrial Council included Conservative Party donors Anthony Bamford and Robert Edmiston. The Electoral Commission was reported to have found such donations did not violate the transparency rules: *The Guardian*, 6 October 2008.

21 PPERA, Sch. 19A.

22 *FEC* v. *Beaumont* 539 U.S. 146 (2003) at 159–160: the US Supreme Court cited the potential for evasion as a reason for upholding the ban on direct corporate donations in relation to a non-profit 'advocacy corporation'.

23 For discussion of this trend in the US, see T. Skocpol, 'Associations Without Members', *American Prospect*, 1 July 1999.

24 PPERA, s. 54(2).

25 P. Davies, *Gower and Davies Principles of Modern Company Law*, London: Sweet & Maxwell, 2008, p. 40.

26 See Companies Act 2006, s.172.

27 Department of Trade and Industry, *Political Donations by Companies – A Consultative Document*, March 1999, para. 4.17, cited in Dame Mary Arden *et al.*, *Buckley on the Companies Acts* (15th ed.), London: LexisNexis Butterworths, 2008, para. 7.3.

28 The Fifth Report of the Committee on Standards in Public Life, *The Funding of Political Parties in the United Kingdom*, Cm.4057-I, 1998, para. 6.33 ('Neill Report').

29 For example, in October 2009, Bloomberg Tradebook Europe Limited donated £28,750 to the Labour Party and £25,000 to the Liberal Democrats. In March 2009, BAA Ltd gave £3,850 to the Chelmsford Conservative Party and in April that year £3,000 to the Scottish Labour Party.

30 For discussion of these issues in relation to US law, see A. Winkler, '"Other People's Money": Corporations, Agency Costs, and Campaign Finance Law', *Georgetown Law Journal*, 2004, vol. 92, 871. On the distinction between political expenditures and ordinary business decisions in relation to US law see L. Bebchuk and R. Jackson, 'Corporate Political Speech: Who Decides?' *Harvard Law Review*, 2010, vol. 124, 83.

31 Companies Act 2006, s. 171.

32 P. Davies, *Gower and Davies Principles of Modern Company Law*, London: Sweet & Maxwell, 2008, p. 525. The extent to which donations serve the company's interest may be questioned. One study has found corporate donations tend to be motivated by the social relations of the company directors, see M. Bond, 'Elite Social Relations and Corporate Political Donations in Britain', 2007, *Political Studies*, vol. 55, 59.

33 Companies Act 2006, s. 366.

34 Ibid., s. 367(5).

35 Committee on Standards in Public Life, *The Neill Report*, para. 6.34.

36 Ibid., para. 6.35.

37 Although it has not made any political donations.
38 S. Fielding, *The Labour Party: Continuity and change in the making of 'New' Labour*, Basingstoke: Palgrave Macmillan, 2003, pp. 119–121.
39 For background see K. Ewing, *Trade Unions, the Labour Party and the Law*, Edinburgh: Edinburgh University Press, 1982.
40 K. Ewing, *The Cost of Democracy*, Oxford: Hart, 2007, p. 227.
41 Trade Union and Labour Relations (Consolidation) Act 1992, Chap. VI, esp. ss.71–73.
42 Ibid., s. 72.
43 Ibid., s. 84.
44 Leopold reports that some unions established a political fund with no intention of affiliating to the Labour Party. Instead, some unions set up a fund to act as an 'insurance policy' to retain the option of spending on political issue advocacy without falling foul of the law. J.W. Leopold, 'Trade unions and the third round of political fund review balloting', *Industrial Relations Journal*, 2006, vol. 37, 190.
45 For example, at its 2009 conference the Communication Workers Union considered whether to remain affiliated to the Labour Party.
46 For example, members of the union's executive, its president and general secretary are required by statute to be elected: Trade Union and Labour Relations (Consolidation) Act 1992, s. 46.
47 On the influence of default rules on outcomes see R. Thaler and C. Sunstein, *Nudge: improving decisions about health, wealth and happiness*, New Haven; Yale University Press, 2008, pp. 83–87.
48 V. Bogdanor, *Power and the People*, London: Gollancz, 1997, pp. 152–153.
49 *ASLEF* v. *UK* (2007) 45 EHRR 34 at para. 50.
50 PPERA, s. 54.
51 *Conservative and Unionist Central Office* v. *Burrell* [1982] 2 All ER 1 at 4.
52 *Conservative and Unionist Central Office* v. *Burrell.*
53 G. Moffat, *Trusts Law* (5th ed.), Cambridge: Cambridge University Press, 2009, pp. 887–888.
54 For those associations that have been set up to support a particular party, such requirements would be unnecessary and members of such an association can be taken to agree to this use of funds.
55 Prior to that amendment, the source of funds to an association had to be disclosed to the Electoral Commission only where association acted as the donor's agent.
56 The Charity Commission, *Charities and political donations*, April 2009.
57 Charities Act 2006, ss. 1–2.
58 Prior to the 2006 Act, this was explained in *Bowman* v. *Secular Society Ltd.* [1917] A.C. 406 at 442: 'The court has no means of judging whether a proposed change in the law will or will not be for the public benefit, and therefore cannot say that a gift to secure the change is a charitable gift.' See also *National Anti-Vivisection Society* v. *Inland Revenue Commissioners* [1948] A.C. 31.
59 *McGovern* v. *Attorney General* [1982] Ch. 321 at 337: Slade J stating that even if the court did think a change in the law were desirable, 'it must still decide the case on the principle that the law is right as it stands, since to do otherwise would usurp the functions of the legislature'.
60 Charity Commission, *Speaking Out – Guidance on Campaigning and Political Activity by Charities*, 2008, at E1.
61 Committee on Standards in Public Life, *The Neill Report*, 1998, para. 5.9.
62 Ibid., para. 5.4 citing Quebec as an example of such an 'extreme purist position'.
63 A. Tyrie, *Clean Politics*, 20 March 2006, pp. 8–9. Online. Available HTTP: www.conservatives.com/pdf/cleaninguppolitics.pdf (accessed 31 May 2010).
64 see Canada Elections Act 2000, s. 404.
65 Under US law, the identity of bundlers engaging in lobbying and sums delivered has

to be disclosed, see 2 USCS § 434. However, bundled contributions do not count towards the bundler's donation limit.

66 Along these lines, Cain criticises a proposed voucher scheme in so far as it treats groups as 'merely the sum of equal individuals'. See B. Cain, 'The Democratic Implications of Voting with Dollars', *University of Richmond Law Review*, 2003, vol. 37, 959 at p. 973.

67 For example, US law prohibits donations from the general treasuries of corporations or unions: 2 USC s. 441b. Even if the separate fund requirements are limited to such organisations, there will still be a case for capping the amount a person can contribute to a political association to fund its donations. Such a requirement may lead to such associations establishing a separate 'political donation fund' in any event, so that the contribution limit does not apply to funds that will be used for purposes other than political donations.

3 Contribution limits

A case for exempting trade union affiliation fees[1]

Joo-Cheong Tham

Graeme Orr has rightly described Australian regulation of political finance as being 'by international standards ... decidedly laissez faire'.[2] With few limits on political contributions, political parties and candidates are largely free to accept money from any source, in any amount. Spending by political parties and candidates also faces little restrictions with no election spending limits, let alone any ban on types of spending, such as political advertising. The key sources of regulation are the various federal, state and territory disclosure schemes, but even then, deficiencies abound with 'lackadaisical' disclosure obligations.[3]

There are, however, signs that Australia is about to move beyond *laissez-faire*. In late 2008, the Australian Labor Party (ALP) federal government released a Green Paper canvassing much stricter regulation of political funding. The government of New South Wales, Australia's most populous state, has committed to the next state election being conducted under 'a public funding model'.[4] Queensland's Premier, Anna Bligh, has also called for a national cap on political donations exceeding $1,000 and has signalled that Queensland will act to implement such a cap by July 2010 if there is no movement on the federal front.[5]

High on the reform agenda is the proposal to impose contribution limits, limits on the amount of private money that political parties and candidates can receive. This was a specific measure canvassed by the federal government's Green Paper,[6] the focus of the Queensland Premier's call for change and a necessary measure if New South Wales political parties and candidates are to be principally funded by the public purse. The push for contribution limits has, however, met stiff resistance from the trade union movement with the reform process at the federal level reportedly stalling because of union opposition to limits banning trade union affiliation fees.[7] This controversy throws up vexed questions of principle. At the heart of this debate is the following issue: If contribution limits are adopted in Australia, should they treat organisational membership fees (including trade union affiliation fees) in the same way as other political contributions?

This chapter argues 'no'. It begins by detailing the patterns of trade union contributions to Australian political parties. On the *assumption* that contribution limits are adopted, it argues that individual and organisational membership fees (including trade union affiliation fees) should be exempted from such limits. This exemption, it stresses, should be accompanied by a requirement that trade unions seek authorisation from their members to engage in political spending (including payment of party membership fees) on a periodic basis.

Trade union contributions to political parties

In Australia, trade union contributions to political parties fall into two categories: party affiliation fees and non-membership subscriptions. Party affiliation fees are fees paid by a union to a political party as a condition of taking out organisational membership of the party. Non-membership contributions are essentially political donations made by unions to support the cause or policies of a political party.

In Australia, the major parties – the parties that are the key contenders for government – are the ALP, a centre-left party, on one side and on the other side, the centre-right Liberal Party and the National Party (which tends to represent rural interests). The Australian Greens, a left-wing and environmentalist political party, is the most important minor party. The ALP is the principal recipient of trade union contributions, although the Australian Greens is beginning to receive modest amounts of trade union money. The ALP receives trade union money both in the form of affiliation fees and non-membership contributions, while the Greens only receives non-membership contributions.

For the ALP, trade union money is clearly of importance. Table 3.1 provides two measures of the ALP's reliance on trade union money: itemised union receipts as a percentage of the sums itemised by all branches of the ALP; and itemised union receipts as a percentage of total receipts declared by these branches (under the federal disclosure scheme, political parties are required to itemise sums exceeding $11,200 (indexed) and also declare the total amount of sums received). It can be seen from this table that the importance of trade union money to the ALP, while significant, should not be overstated. Even at its highest proportion for the financial years 2006–2007 and 2007–2008, trade union money constituted less than one-sixth of the ALP's total income.

Table 3.2 seeks to divide the amounts received by all branches of the ALP for the financial year 2006–2007 (a non-federal election year) and 2007–2008 (a year

Table 3.1 Itemised trade union contributions as proportion of ALP income, 2006–2007 to 2007–2008 (%)

	2006–2007	*2007–2008*
Itemised trade union receipts as a percentage of all itemised receipts by the ALP	13.09	10.8
Itemised trade union receipts as a percentage of total receipts by the ALP	7.52	8.18

Source: AEC Annual Returns (ALP), 2006–2007 to 2007–2008.

Table 3.2 Breakdown of ALP receipts: trade union affiliation fees and non-membership contributions, 2006–2007 to 2007–08

	2006–2007	*2007–2008*
Affiliation fees	$4,066,930.51	$4,206,835.74
Affiliation fees as a percentage of itemised trade union funding	75.44%	46.57%
Non-membership contributions	$1,323,800.00	$4,826,176.84
Non-membership contributions as a percentage of itemised trade union funding	24.56%	53.43%
Total itemised trade union funding	$5,390,730.51	$9,033,012.58

Source: AEC Annual Returns, 2006–2007 to 2007–2008.

in which a federal election was held) into affiliation fees and non-membership contributions. Sums declared by ALP branches as 'Other Receipts' and 'Subscriptions' are treated as affiliation fees while sums identified as 'Donations' are treated as non-membership contributions This breakdown provides only a rough-and-ready analysis. First, a voluntary system of self-classification exists under the federal disclosure scheme with parties themselves deciding whether a sum should be described as 'Other Receipts', 'Subscriptions' or 'Donations'. Second, the table only works on sums that are required to be itemised by the ALP and not on the total amounts received by the ALP. The disparity between the total of itemised amounts and total receipts is quite significant: for example, the amounts itemised for the 2006–2007 and 2007–2008 financial years were, respectively, 57.49 per cent and 75.78 per cent of the total funding.[8] At the same time, this disparity might not mean significant understatement of trade union political contributions to the ALP as these contributions are likely to have exceeded the threshold for itemisation.

Bearing these limitations in mind, Table 3.2 suggests that the balance between affiliation fees and non-membership contributions shifts according to whether it is a federal election year or not. In both 2006–2007 and 2007–2008, the amount received in affiliation fees was somewhat steady at slightly over $4 million. In comparison, the amount received in non-membership contributions nearly tripled from $1.3 million in 2006–2007 to $4.8 million in 2007–2008. The effect was that non-membership subscriptions amounted to more than half of trade union money to the ALP in 2007–2008.

We can now turn to the question of which unions provide affiliation fees and non-membership contributions to the ALP. With affiliation fees, it is important to appreciate that trade union affiliation occurs through the state branches of the ALP. The decision to affiliate is, therefore, made by the state branches of the various unions. As a result, for a particular union, some branches might be affiliated to the ALP while others are not.

What is striking is that an overwhelming majority of trade unions are affiliated to the ALP. Of the unions registered with various federal, state or territory industrial registrars, more than 80 per cent are affiliated to the ALP in each of these jurisdictions with the number reaching 100 per cent in Queensland, the Australian Capital Territory and the Northern Territory. In some cases, all branches of a particular union are affiliated to the ALP. The list of such unions includes

- the Shop, Distributive and Allied Employees Association (SDA);
- Liquor Hospitality and Miscellaneous Union (LHMU);
- Communications, Electrical and Plumbing Union (CEPU);
- Australian Services Union (ASU);
- Australian Manufacturing Workers Union (AMWU); and
- the Transport Workers Union (TWU).

With some other unions, all but one of their branches are affiliated to the ALP. These include

- the Construction, Forestry, Mining and Energy Union (CFMEU);
- Rail, Tram and Bus Industry Union (RTBU);
- National Union of Workers (NUW);
- Maritime Union of Australia (MUA);
- Australian Workers' Union (AWU); and
- the Australian Meat Industry Employees' Union (AMIEU).

There are, however, major unions that are not affiliated to the ALP. No branches of the National Tertiary Education Union (NTEU) or the Association of Professional Engineers, Scientists and Managers Association (APESMA) are affiliated to the ALP and only one branch of the Australian Nursing Federation (ANF) is affiliated to the ALP.[9]

Interestingly, non-membership contributions by trade unions to the ALP seem to be made either by state labour councils or affiliated trade unions. In the 2006–2007 and 2007–2008 financial years, not a single non-affiliated trade union made a non-membership contribution to the ALP.[10] Table 3.3 identifies the top five unions in terms of non-membership contributions given to the ALP by all

Table 3.3 Top five trade union contributors to the ALP in terms of non-membership contributions, 2006–2007 to 2007–2008

2006–2007		*2007–2008*	
CEPU (including ETU)	$631,800.00	CEPU (including ETU)	$1,318,122.80
CFMEU	$192,000.00	LHMU	$274,000.00
LHMU	$180,000.00	CFMEU	$230,650.00
ETU	$120,000.00	AWU	$227,000.00
ASU	$100,000.00	HSU	$176,000.00

Source: AEC Annual Returns, 2006–2007 to 2007–2008.

Table 3.4 Top five trade union contributors (all contributions) to the ALP 2006–2007 to 2007–2008

2006–2007		*2007–2008*	
CEPU (including ETU)	$1,333,397.70	CEPU (including ETU)	$1,728,621.41
LHMU	$661,022.17	SDA	$1,488,591.18
SDA	$628,245.12	CFMEU	$1,339,385.76
CFMEU	$609,799.84	LHMU	$764,906.19
AMWU	$385,277.18	AMWU	$650,934.07

Source: AEC Annual Returns, 2006–2007 to 2007–2008.

branches of the various unions (as noted earlier, trade union contributions identified as 'donations' are treated as non-membership contributions).

Table 3.4 goes beyond the amounts declared as 'donations' and lists the top five union contributors to the ALP for the financial years 2006–2007 and 2007–2008 based on the total amount of itemised contributions given to the ALP by all branches of the various unions. In other words, the figures in Table 3.4 include items declared as 'donations', 'subscriptions' and 'other receipts', and so now also include membership fees.

It remains to discuss trade union funding to the Greens. In the financial years 2006–2007 and 2007–2008, three unions gave money to the Greens: AMWU, CFMEU and ETU. The biggest giver was the ETU which contributed $219,506 during this period. The CFMEU and the AMWU donated much smaller amounts respectively giving $60,000 and $30,000. Trade union funding does not form a significant part of the Greens' budget. Of the disclosed amounts that have been itemised, trade union funding of the Greens was respectively 6.4 per cent and 3.3 per cent for 2006–2007 and 2007–2008 financial years.[11]

An exemption for membership fees (including union affiliation fees)

Greater restrictions on political contributions have support across the political spectrum. In a response to the Wollongong City Council scandal, former New South Wales Premier Morris Iemma advanced the radical proposal of completely banning political contributions in favour of a system of complete public funding.[12] Following not too far behind, his predecessor Bob Carr has advocated banning political contributions from organisations like trade unions and companies and only allowing those made by individuals. Former Leader of the Opposition Malcolm Turnbull[13] and the New South Wales Greens[14] have similar positions. As noted earlier, Queensland Premier Anna Bligh has also called for a national cap of political donations exceeding $1,000 and has signalled that Queensland will act to implement such a cap by July 2010 if there is no movement on the federal front.[15] In a bipartisan report, the New South Wales Legislative Council Select Committee on Electoral and Political Party Funding (NSW

Select Committee) recommended that there be a ban on all political donations except for those by individuals. Contributions by individuals are to be further limited to $1,000 for each political party per annum (and $1,000 for each independent candidate per electoral cycle).[16]

Assuming some type of contribution limits are adopted,[17] how should membership fees (including trade union affiliation fees) be treated? Whilst recommending a ban on all but small donations by individuals, the NSW Select Committee proposed that membership fees be exempted from the ban provided that they are set at a reasonable level (with that level being determined by the Auditor-General).[18] This is a position with considerable merit. As the NSW Select Committee correctly recognised, 'membership of political parties is an important means for individuals to participate in the political process'.[19] Specifically, it involves participation within political parties, thereby directly enhancing the participatory function of parties. Whilst contribution limits permit membership fees below the limits, an exemption goes beyond such permissiveness by encouraging party membership.

The remainder of this section argues that the exemption for membership fees should extend to organisational membership fees including trade union affiliation fees. As will be argued below, a ban on organisational membership fees will give rise to anomalies, is misdirected at 'trade union bosses' and constitutes an unjustified limitation on freedom of party association.

The anomalies of banning organisational membership fees

A ban on organisational membership fees will produce striking anomalies. Presumably, parties will still be allowed to have state and territory-based branches with intra-party transfers exempted from contribution limits. If so, collective affiliation based on geographical areas will still be allowed. But if collective affiliation is permitted on this basis, why limit collective affiliation based on ideological grounds (for example, environmental groups seeking to affiliate with the Greens) or those based on occupation or class (for example, farmers' groups seeking to affiliate with the National Party)?

A ban on organisational membership will also detract from the participatory function of parties. In case of the ALP, there will be the loss of membership participation provided by trade union affiliates. However attenuated, such participation is still a form of participation. If limits applying to party contributions are enacted without limits on third parties and their spending then money may very well flow on to third party activity.[20] This would express a preference for pressure group politics over party politics as it will strongly encourage political groups to engage in independent third party activity rather than become members of political parties. Such a preference may favour issue politics over broader and more inclusive forms of politics that are more likely to emerge through the interest-aggregation performed by political parties.[21]

A ban on organisational membership fees: misdirected at 'trade union bosses'

A ban on organisational membership fees (including trade union affiliation fees) will have a severe impact upon the trade union-ALP link by either prohibiting or severely limiting the amount of money that trade unions can contribute to the ALP. By banning or at least reducing significantly the flow of trade union affiliation fees to the ALP, such measures will most likely weaken the relationship that the trade union movement has with the ALP.

Indeed, this is one of key aims of some advocates of contribution limits. For example, former NSW Premier Bob Carr has endorsed his successor, Morris Iemma's call for banning organisational contributions on the basis that unions will not be able to affiliate with the ALP on a collective basis.[22] Discontented with the power wielded by 'trade union bosses' within the ALP, some would prefer that the ALP-union link be made illegal.

There are, in fact, three main complaints bundled up in the epithet, 'trade union bosses' and it is crucial to consider them separately. The first is the claim that the presence within the party of 'trade union bosses', or more kindly, the influence of trade union officials within the ALP, is making the ALP unelectable or at least preventing it from becoming 'the natural party of Federal government'.[23] The concern here is that the influence of trade unions has the effect of the ALP not being properly representative of the Australian community, thereby impairing – perhaps even severely damaging – its electoral prospects.

Such views may or may not be correct. The issue here, however, does not turn on the veracity of these views; the question is whether a ban on organisational membership fees is a legitimate way of dealing with concerns regarding the electability of the ALP (or for that matter, the electability of any party). The answer is 'surely not': these are matters for the ALP and its members to decide, not one for regulation, let alone contribution limits involving a ban on organisational membership fees. Should these concerns not be dealt with properly then the discipline of the ballot box will operate, with voters choosing not to support the ALP.

There are two other complaints implied by criticisms of 'trade union bosses': one relating to internal party democracy and the other to trade union democracy. Mark Aarons, a former union official who was also an adviser to Bob Carr when he was New South Wales Premier, has argued that the ALP is organised in 'a most undemocratic way'[24] because affiliated trade unions exercise 'a grossly out-of-proportion, even extraordinary, influence over policy formulation'.[25] This lack of proportion is said to arise because the level of power trade union delegates exercise within the ALP is not justified by the level of union density: how can it be right that trade unions have 50 per cent of delegates in ALP conferences when less than one-fifth of the workforce is unionised?[26]

This argument, however, turns on a fallacious use of the term, 'undemocratic'. It is true that parties have a representative function in that parties or the party system as a whole should represent the diversity of opinion within a society. This is, however, not the same as saying that a single party should seek to represent the entire spectrum of this opinion. Not only is this practically impossible but paradoxically, parties discharge their representative function by representing different sections of society. It is the cumulative effect of such sectional representation that stamps a party system as representative in overall terms. In this context, characterising the manner in which the ALP is organised as being undemocratic simply because its membership base is not wholly representative of the Australian public is somewhat perverse.

To say this is to emphasise that there is nothing self-evidently 'undemocratic' about such influence. It is not to imply that the extent of union influence over the ALP is justifiable or desirable. Some, for example, might argue that such influence results in a rather partial notion of the 'public interest'. Just as the relationships between the Liberal Party and its business supporters, the National Party and agricultural producers, and the Greens and the environmental groups, are relevant considerations for voters in deciding whether a political party adequately represents the 'public' or 'national' interest, such matters are clearly legitimate considerations for citizens deciding whether or not to vote for the ALP.

There is another difficulty with characterising the manner in which the ALP is organised as being undemocratic: reducing trade union influence will not necessarily revitalise the internal democracy of the ALP.[27] So much can be seen through a rough depiction of the power relations within the ALP, as given in Table 3.5. The party elite comprises the parliamentary leadership, the members of parliament and their staff,[28] the union leadership (including union delegates), and the party officials and bureaucrats. The rank and file, on the other hand, consist of the party members.

These relations can be analysed according to horizontal and vertical dimensions. Reducing the influence of union leadership does not mean that power will flow vertically to the rank and file. In the context of shrinking party membership within the ALP,[29] it is far more likely that power will be redistributed horizontally to others remaining within the party elite. Where the 'party in public office', the parliamentary leadership, is already ascendant over the 'party on the ground' as well as the 'party central office',[30] it is a fair bet that the parliamentary leadership will be a key beneficiary of this redistribution of power. A similar conclusion results when one casts an eye to power relations beyond the party. Looking at the 'material constitution'[31] of the ALP, that is, its relationship with class forces, diminishing the influence of trade unions within the ALP is likely to mean a corresponding empowerment of business interests but not of the rank and file. Moreover, the power of government bureaucracy also needs to be factored

Table 3.5 Power relations within the ALP

Party elite	Union leadership	Parliamentary leadership	Party officials and bureaucracy
Rank and file	Party members		

in, especially when the ALP is in government: its influence is likely to increase as sources of countervailing power like trade unions weaken in strength.

Underlying all this is a risk of throwing the baby out with the bath water. While it is true that the internal democracy of the ALP is undermined in some cases by trade unions because of their oligarchical tendencies (see discussion below), the answer is not to excise trade unions from the party. Collective organisations like trade unions play a necessary, though at times problematic, role in empowering citizens. The ambivalent character of such organisations is well captured by sociologist Robert Michels. As discussed further below, Michels is famous for his iron law of oligarchy: '[w]ho says organization, says oligarchy'.[32] He is perhaps less well known for his observation that '[o]rganization ... is the weapon of the weak in their struggle with the strong'.[33] Within the ALP, collective organisations like trade unions allow individual members to band together to secure a voice that they would not otherwise have. While they do give rise to the risk of oligarchy within the organisations themselves, functioning well they provide 'effective internal polyarchal controls'[34] that counter the oligarchical tendencies of the party. By severely diminishing the role of trade unions within the ALP, undifferentiated contribution limits will likely increase the oligarchical tendencies within the party.

The other complaint in relation to 'trade union bosses' concerns trade union democracy. Aarons has argued that because

> 'individual unionists have no practical say in whether they are affiliated to the ALP and whether a proportion of their membership fees pay for this [and] ... in how their union's votes will be cast, [there is] not a democratic expression of the union membership's wishes'.[35]

This criticism, however, is doubly misconceived. First, under any system of representative governance, most decisions are made by representatives without the direct say of their constituencies. It is this feature that contrasts representative systems from those based on direct democracy and, indeed, this is how the Australian system of parliamentary representation is supposed to work. The key question in such contexts is not whether members have a direct say but whether the representatives are effectively accountable to their constituencies, in this case, trade union delegates to their members. The real problem here is one of 'union oligarchies'[36] that are insulated from effective membership control (discussed below). Yet, and this brings us to the second misconception, a ban on organisational membership (including trade union affiliation fees) will do little to meaningfully address this problem.[37] At best, what they would do is carve out certain decisions from the remit of trade union oligarchies while still leaving the oligarchies intact.

Unjustified limitation of freedom of political association

It is essential that political finance regulation respects freedom of political association because such freedom is crucial to the proper workings of Australian democracy. Specifically, it is necessary in order to ensure pluralism in Australian politics, pluralism that is required both to protect the integrity of representative government as well as fairness in politics. This does not, however, mean that state regulation of political associations is impermissible. There can be public interest grounds for limiting freedom of political association. Whether particular measures are justified will depend upon the weight of such rationales, the extent to which the limitation is adapted to advancing such rationale(s) and the severity of the limitation.

In evaluating a ban on organisational membership fees, it is convenient to begin with the last factor, the severity of the ban. Freedom of political association possesses several key aspects, notably:

- the individual's right to form political associations, act through such associations and to participate in the activities of these associations; and
- the association's ability to determine its membership, the rules and manner of its governance and the methods it will use to promote its common objectives.[38]

Here we focus on freedom of party association and, in particular, the ability of political parties to determine their membership. Some parties, such as the Liberal Party[39] and the National Party,[40] for instance, may restrict themselves to individual memberships and are, in this way, *direct parties.* Others like the ALP[41] and the New South Wales Greens[42] allow both individual membership and membership by groups and are therefore *mixed parties.* The Constitution of the federal National Party also allows it to be a mixed party as organisations can become associations of the Party where there is no state branch.[43] Some parties, such as the New South Wales Shooters Party fall somewhere in the middle: membership is formally restricted to individuals,[44] while close links are maintained with various groups.[45] In these situations such groups, while not members of the party, act as *ancillary organisations.*[46] Such diversity of party structures should be respected because it is one of the main ways in which the pluralism of Australian politics is sustained.[47]

When viewed from this perspective, the impact of a ban on organisational membership fees on the freedom of party association is quite severe: it will mandate a particular party structure, direct parties and, while not directly banning parties that allow for organisational membership, generally make them unviable unless such parties are able to secure sufficient public funding.[48]

The specific impact on the trade union-ALP relationship can be illustrated through the typology developed by industrial relations experts Matthew Bodah, Steve Coates and David Ludlam. According to these authors, there are two dimensions to union-party linkages, formal organisational integration and a level of policy-making influence, which give rise to four types of linkages:

- external lobbying type – that is, no formal organisational integration between unions and parties, with unions having no or little influence in party policy-making;

- internal lobbying type – that is, no formal organisation integration between unions and parties, but unions are regularly consulted in policy-making;
- union/party bonding type – that is, unions occupy important party positions but do not enjoy domination of party policy-making; and
- union dominance model – that is, unions occupy important party positions and dominate party policy-making.[49]

According to this typology, the trade union-ALP link fits either the union/party bonding type or the union dominance model because of the organisational integration of trade union affiliates into the ALP. As members of state and territory branches of the ALP, affiliated trade unions are guaranteed 50 per cent representation at state and territory conferences.[50] These conferences determine state and territory branch policies and elect state party officials and delegates to National Conference.[51] The latter functions as 'the supreme governing authority of the Party'[52] and elects members of the National Executive, 'the chief administrative authority' of the party.[53] A ban on organisational membership fees will, however, make organisational integration between the ALP and unions much less viable; the menu of options is effectively restricted to the external/internal lobbying types.

Is there a compelling justification for such a severe incursion into the freedom of the ALP to organise itself as it sees fit? It is exceedingly difficult to see one. There is, first, the *prima facie* legitimacy of membership fees. Further, as the previous discussion has argued, the 'trade union bosses' objections are misdirected: amongst others, a ban on organisational membership fees will neither enhance internal party democracy nor invigorate trade union democracy. Absent an adequate rationale for limiting freedom of party association, it is hard to escape the conclusion that such a ban represents an unjustified limitation on freedom of party association.

It was such a concern with freedom of party association that led the NSW Select Committee to include trade union affiliation fees in their exemption for membership fees.[54] The key reasons given by the six-member committee, which had only two ALP members, are worth reproducing:

> The Committee considers that membership fees should not be encompassed by the Committee's proposed ban on all but small individual donations … *Similarly, the Committee believes that trade union affiliation fees should be permissible, despite the proposed ban on union donations. To ban union affiliation fees would be to place unreasonable restrictions on party structures.*[55]

Re-emphasising the scope of the argument

There are many critics of the trade union-ALP relationship: a considerable number of voters believe that this relationship casts doubt on the ability of the ALP to govern for all; within the union movement there are union members –

even union leaders[56] – who strongly take the view that this relationship fails to serve their best interests; and, even within the ALP this relationship does not enjoy unqualified support with some rank-and-file members feeling disenfranchised by the influence enjoyed by union affiliates and more than a few key party officials expressing concern that the relationship undermines the party's ability to win public office.

For the most part, this chapter says very little, often nothing, on these questions. It has focussed on whether there should be a ban on organisational membership fees (including trade union affiliation fees) under a regime of contribution limits. In concluding that there should be an exemption for such fees, the chapter does not amount to a general defence of the trade union-ALP relationship. The central point is that this relationship should not be prohibited as a matter of law. The broader question as to whether this relationship is desirable or justified raises a complex range of issues, most of which fall outside the scope of this chapter.

The imperative of internal accountability

The argument for exempting membership fees (including organisational membership fees) from contribution limits essentially derives from the value of participation *within* political parties, participation that can occur directly through individual membership or indirectly through organisational membership. For the latter to be meaningful, there needs to be effective internal accountability in relation to political spending (including decisions on whether or not to take out organisational membership) – only by members having a meaningful say over such decisions can we then conclude there is some form of participation.

For trade unions, this is a question of democratic accountability.[57] At present, federal industrial legislation requires federally registered trade unions to set out rules in relation to the spending of monies,[58] and to spend sums of more than $1,000 only when authorised by the union committee of management, which must be satisfied that such spending is in accordance with the rules of the union.[59] There is *no* requirement that such unions adopt specific rules in relation to political spending.

In some cases, unions have of their own volition adopted specific rules in relation to political spending. The rules of the AMWU, for example, require that any spending to further political objectives shall only be made from a Political Fund. The Political Fund is financed by members making a specific contribution and is segregated from other union monies. Under the AMWU rules, members also have a right to be exempted from making this contribution.[60] In most cases, however, it seems that the rules of unions do not make specific provision for political spending. The rules of the CEPU (General),[61] LHMU[62] and CFMEU,[63] for example, essentially reproduce the statutory requirements and generally authorise their committees of management to make decisions in relation to spending.

These arrangements in the context of formally democratic elections[64] provide a notional guarantee of internal accountability. Such a guarantee is, however, liable to be subverted by the reality of power relations. Here, we confront the problem of oligarchy in relation to large organisations identified by Robert Michels more than four decades ago. Michels famously argued that there was a tendency towards oligarchy in large organisations, that is, the ruling elite holding effective control, because of the general passivity of rank-and-file members and the elite's superior political skills and its control over finances and the means of communications. This, according to Michels, was the iron law of oligarchy.[65] Studies of trade union internal democracy, whilst identifying particular circumstances where such democracy can flourish (most importantly, the institutionalisation of organised opposition), have been similarly pessimistic.[66] These various studies underscore the persistent and complex challenge of installing internal democracy in large organisations including unions.

Promoting internal union democracy in relation to political expenditure is not exempt from this challenge. Indeed, decisions relating to political expenditure may involve particularly serious threats to internal union democracy. The processes of making such decisions are often hidden from the gaze of ordinary union members. With decisions on strictly industrial issues, for instance, wage rises to be claimed, union members ordinarily need to be consulted not least to enlist their support for the industrial claims to be made by the union. This is, however, not the case with decisions to engage in political expenditure whether through contributions to political parties or independent political spending, that is, third party spending. For unions that affiliate to the ALP, the influence their representatives wield by virtue of their membership of the ALP, for instance in the pre-selection of candidates, is also typically shrouded in secrecy. For example, in 2009, unions affiliated to the Victorian ALP were involved in a 'secret peace deal' that decided who should be pre-selected as ALP candidates in the upcoming federal and state elections.[67]

Also, there is a long list of union officials who have moved on to become ALP parliamentarians, with recent additions including Greg Combet, former Secretary of the Australian Council of Trade Unions, now a Minister in the Rudd Labor Government, and Bill Shorten, former National Secretary of the Australian Workers' Union, currently a parliamentary secretary. There is, of course, nothing wrong in itself with these transitions. These established pathways do, however, throw up a risk that the prospect of a parliamentary career will tempt some union officials, whether consciously or not, to either prefer their interests or the interests of the ALP over that of their members when making decisions on political spending.

Some may also infer oligarchical decision-making in relation to these decisions from the voting record of union members. This record clearly shows that not all union members support the ALP. For example, only 63 per cent of union members from 1966 to 2004 voted for the ALP.[68] This figure, however, does not necessarily provide any further evidence of oligarchical decision-making in relation to trade union political spending. Several key unions have neither affiliated nor contributed to the ALP (see above). While further examination is required, it may be the case that the number of members in unions that are supportive of the ALP corresponds to the number who voted for it. Moreover, it is quite rational for union members to endorse their union's decision to support the ALP in order to promote the importance of the union agenda, while deciding in overall terms that the Coalition is better suited for government.

That being said, there are clearly significant challenges to internal accountability in relation to trade union political contribution including trade union affiliation fees to the ALP. To meet these challenges, there should be a requirement that trade unions seek specific authorisation from their members before making political contributions. An authorisation requirement in relation to trade union political expenditure has Australian precedent: for a few years, Western Australian trade unions were required to set up a separate fund for political spending.[69] Similarly, former Democrats Senator Andrew Murray has recommended that businesses and trade unions, respectively seek authorisation from their shareholders and members at annual general meetings or at least every three years.[70]

Another possible model is the UK controls on donations made by trade unions and companies. British trade unions are required to ballot their members every ten years for authority to promote their political agendas. Once authorised, political expenditure by a trade union must be made from a separate political fund to which individual members have a right to refrain from contributing (UK companies, on the other hand, are required to seek authorisation from their shareholders every four years to make political donations and/or political expenditure).[71]

Concluding thoughts

The argument so far has paid little attention to the question of designing the exemption for party membership fees – it has focussed on making an in-principle argument for such an exemption. This is not, however, to deprecate the importance of these questions; indeed, they are crucial. While space does not permit a full examination of these questions, several key issues of design warrant mention: How should membership fees be distinguished from ordinary political contributions? What requirements should there be in place to ensure that membership fees are genuine? How should the level of the exemption be set (a flat-rate, amount per member)?

Another set of issues that does not fall within the scope of this chapter is the unfairness that is likely to result from an exemption for party membership fees. This exemption, which includes trade union affiliation fees, is likely to worsen the inequality between the ALP and the Coalition parties. Such unfairness should be addressed but not through contribution limits (or removing the exemption for membership fees). Rather, the burden of this task falls on election spending limits.[72]

Notes

1 This chapter draws on material in Chapters 3–4 of J-C. Tham, *Money and Politics: The democracy we can't afford*, Sydney: University of New South Wales Press, 2010.
2 G. Orr, 'Political Finance Law in Australia', in K.D. Ewing and S. Issacharoff (eds) *Party Funding and Campaign Financing in International Perspective*, Portland: Hart Publishing, 2006, pp. 99, 100.
3 G. Orr, 'Political Disclosure Regulation in Australia: Lackadaisical Law', *Election Law Journal* 6(1), 2007, 5. See also S. Young and J-C. Tham (eds), *Political Finance in Australia: A Skewed and Secret System*, Canberra: Democratic Audit of Australia, 2006, Ch. 2.
4 This was a commitment initially made by former Premier Nathan Rees: L. McKenny and L. Carty, 'Rees sets own agenda', *Sydney Morning Herald*, 15 November, 2009. His successor, Kristina Kenneally has, however, promised to honour this commitment: B. Robins, 'Election campaign funding hits hurdle', *Sydney Morning Herald, 2* January, 2009; ABC Television, Interview with Kristina Keneally, *Stateline* (transcript) 4 December, 2009. Online. Available HTTP: www.abc.net.au/news/video/2009/12/04/2762677.htm (accessed 27 January 2010).
5 Queensland Premier A. Bligh, 'Sweeping reforms deliver Queensland strong integrity and accountability', media release, 10 November, 2009. Online. Available HTTP: http://statements.cabinet.qld.gov.au/MMS/StatementDisplaySingle.aspx?id=67319 (accessed 27 November 2009).
6 Australian Government, *Electoral Reform Green Paper: Donations, Funding and Expenditure*, Australian Government, 2008, ch. 7.
7 See Editors, 'Voters betrayed by failure to clean up party funding', *The Age*, 14 February, 2010. Online. Available HTTP: www.theage.com.au/opinion/editorial/voters-betrayed-by-failure-to-clean-up-party-funding-20100113-m6uj.html (Accessed 3 February 2010).
8 Calculated from Annual Returns to the Australian Electoral Commission 2006–2007 to 2007–2008.
9 The information contained in this paragraph was collected from two types of sources: information published on the websites of the various ALP state branches and correspondence with these branches and some unions (copies of correspondence on file with author).
10 Annual Returns to the AEC, 2006–2007 to 2007–2008.
11 Ibid.
12 See K. Bitar, NSW ALP Secretary, *Submission to NSW Inquiry into Electoral and Political Party Funding*, March 2008. Online. Available HTTP: www.parliament.nsw.gov.au/prod/parlment/committee.nsf/0/5e44ee94d5799e04ca25741d00031357/$FILE/Submission%20107a.pdf (accessed 22 May 2009).
13 M. Turnbull, *Submission to the Joint Standing Committee on Electoral Matters Inquiry into the 2004 Federal Election*, 2005.
14 See Report of Proceedings Before the Select Committee on Electoral and Political Party Funding: Inquiry into Electoral and Political Party Funding, 3 March, 2008. Online. Available HTTP: www.parliament.nsw.gov.au/prod/parlment/committee.nsf/0/dfc9200362cf2c4aca257402000e38aa/$FILE/080303%20corrected%20hearing%20transcript.pdf (accessed 22 January 2010).
15 Queensland Premier A. Bligh, 'Sweeping reforms deliver Queensland strong integrity and accountability', media release, 10 November, 2009. Online. Available HTTP: http://statements.cabinet.qld.gov.au/MMS/StatementDisplaySingle.aspx?id=67319 (accessed 27 November 2009).
16 New South Wales Select Committee on Electoral and Political Party Funding (NSW Select Committee), *Electoral and Political Party Funding in New South Wales*, 2008, p. 105 (Recommendation 7).

17 For opposition to such limits, see K.D. Ewing, *The Cost of Democracy: Party Funding in Modern British Politics*, Oxford: Hart Publishing, 2007, pp. 227–230.
18 New South Wales Select Committee, *Electoral and Political Party Funding in New South Wales*, p. 113 (Recommendation 9).
19 Ibid.
20 See S. Issacharoff and P. Karlan, 'The Hydraulics of Campaign Finance Reform', *Texas Law Review* 77, 1999, 1705, pp. 1714–1715.
21 See also K. Ewing, *Trade Unions, the Labour Party and Political Funding*, London: Catalyst Press, 2002, paras. 4.6–4.7. This is not to deny that the Australian Labor Party is already influenced by pressure group politics. For a case-study, see P. Mendes, 'Labourists and the Welfare Lobby: The Relationship Between the Federal Labor Party and the Australian Council of Social Service (ACOSS)', *Australian Journal of Political Science* 39(1), 2004, 145.
22 Editors, 'Limit political donations: Carr', *The Australian*, 4 May, 2008. Online. Available HTTP: www.theaustralian.news.com.au/story/0,25197,23643124-2702,00.html (accessed 21 May 2008).
23 M. Aarons, 'The Unions and Labor', in R. Manne (ed.) *Dear Mr Rudd: Ideas for A Better Australia*, Melbourne: Black Inc. Agenda, 2008, pp. 86, 91.
24 Aarons, 'The Unions and Labor', p. 88.
25 Ibid.
26 In 2007, union density stood at 19 per cent of the Australian workforce: Australian Bureau of Statistics, *Employee Earnings, Benefits and Trade Union Membership, Australia, August 2007*, 2007, (cat. no. 6310.0
27 This point is made well by Bolton: J.R. Bolton, 'Constitutional Limitations on Restricting Corporate and Union Political Speech', *Arizona Law Review* 22, 1980, 373, p. 417.
28 This would include political advisers, some of which have been criticised as exercising 'power without responsibility': A. Tiernan, *Power Without Responsibility: Ministerial Staffers in Australian Governments from Whitlam to Howard*, Sydney: University of New South Wales Press, 2007. Tiernan's study was focussed on ministerial advisers.
29 For figures, see G. Johns, 'Party Organisation and Resources: Membership, Funding and Staffing', in I. Marsh, (ed.) *Political Parties in Transition?*, Sydney: Federation Press, 2006, pp. 46, 47; I. Ward, 'Cartel Parties and Election Campaigns', in Marsh (ed.) *Political Parties in Transition?*, pp. 70, 73–75.
30 Ward, 'Cartel Parties and Election Campaigns', pp. 70, 72, 85–88. On the power of trade unions within the ALP, see K. Cole, 'Unions and the Labor Party', in K. Cole (ed.), *Power, Conflict and Control in Australian Trade Unions*, Ringwood: Pelican Books, 1982, p. 100, where it was concluded that 'the power of unions within the ALP is far more circumscribed than is commonly believed and the process which each of the party's two sections (i.e. industrial and political wings) accommodates to the demands and needs of the other is complex and tortuous'.
31 T. Bramble and R. Kuhn, 'The Transformation of the Australian Labor Party', Joint Social Sciences Public Lecture, ANU, 8 June, 2007. Online. Available HTTP: http://dspace.anu.edu.au/handle/1885/45410 (accessed 6 May 2008).
32 R. Michels, *Political Parties: A Sociological Study of the Oligarchical Tendencies of Modern Democracy*, New York: Collier Books, 1962, p. 365. Michels' iron law is better understood as pointing to the 'oligarchical tendencies' of organisations. The title of the last part of Michels' book is, in fact, 'Synthesis: The Oligarchical Tendencies of Organizations': Michels, *Political Parties: A Sociological Study of the Oligarchical Tendencies of Modern Democracy*.
33 Michels, *Political Parties*, p. 61. Schattscheider has similarly observed that '[p]eople do not usually become formidable to governments until they are organised': E.E. Schattscheider, *Party Government*, New York: Holt, Rinehart and Winston, 1942, p. 28.

34 C. Lindblom, *Politics and Markets: the World's Political and Economic Systems*, New York: Basic Books, 1977, p. 141.
35 Aarons, 'The Unions and Labor', pp. 86, 89.
36 Andrew Parkin, 'Party Organisation and Machine Politics: the ALP in Perspective', in A. Parkin and J. Warhurst (eds), *Machine Politics in the Australian Labor Party*, Sydney: George Allen & Unwin, 1983, pp. 15, 22.
37 Aarons has argued that problems with 'trade union bosses' requires review of the funding provided by trade unions to the ALP: M. Aarons, 'Rein in union strongmen's ALP power', *The Australian*, 18 March, 2008. Online. Available HTTP: www.theaustralian.news.com.au/story/0,25197,23391595-7583,00.html (accessed 19 May 2008).
38 Affidavit of K. Ewing to IDSA litigation. See also H. Davis, *Political Freedom: Associations, Political Purpose and the Law*, London: Continuum, 2000, p. 46.
39 See, for example, Constitution and Regulations of the Liberal Party of Australia (NSW), cl. 2.1.
40 See, for example, Constitution and Rules of the National Party of Australia (NSW), cl. 2.
41 See, for example, Rules of the Australian Labor Party (NSW) 2005–2006, cl. A.2–A.3.
42 Constitution of the Greens (NSW), cl. 2.1.
43 Constitution of the National Party of Australia (Cth), cl. 71. Before 1945, various farmers' organisations had formal relationships with the Country Party, the predecessor of the National Party: K.O. Campbell, 'Australian Farm Organizations and Agricultural Policy', in C. Hughes (ed.), *Readings in Australian Government*, Brisbane: University of Queensland Press, 1968, p. 438.
44 Constitution of The Shooters Party (NSW), By-law (2).
45 In the case of the Shooters Party, this is made clear by its Constitution, which states that one of its aims is

> *[t]o exert a discipline through shooting organizations and clubs and within the non-affiliated shooting community*, to curb the lawless and dangerous element; and to help shooters understand that they hold the future of their sport in their own hands by their standards of conduct.

Constitution of The Shooters Party (NSW), cl. 2(g) (emphasis added). In relation to the 2003 State Election, The Shooters Party received thousands of dollars in contributions from various hunting and pistol clubs including the Federation of Hunting Clubs Inc, Singleton Hunting Club, St Ives Pistol Club, Illawarra Pistol Club and the NSW Amateur Pistol Association: Election Funding Authority (NSW), *Details of Political Contributions of More than $1,500 Received by Parties that Endorsed a Group and by Independent Group at the Legislative Council 2003*, 2003. Online. Available HTTP: www.efa.nsw.gov.au/__data/assets/pdf_file/0008/30140/2003PartyContributions.pdf (accessed 5 February 2008).
46 For fuller explanations of direct and indirect party structures, see M. Duverger, *Political Parties: Their Organization and Activity in the Modern State*, London: Methuen, 1959, 2nd revised edition, pp. 6–17.
47 For fuller discussion, see Ewing, *The Cost of Democracy*, pp. 35–38.
48 This seems to be the position in relation to the Canadian New Democratic Party that still allows trade unions to affiliate on a collective basis: see H. Jansen and L. Young, 'Solidarity Forever? The NDP, Organised Labour, and the Changing Face of Party Finance in Canada', paper presented to the Annual Meeting of the Canadian Political Science Association, London, Ontario, 2–4 June, 2005. Online. Available HTTP: www.partyfinance.ca/publications/OrganizedLabour.pdf (accessed 21 May 2008). See also the discussion in Ewing, *The Cost of Democracy*, pp. 220–221.
49 M. Bodah, S. Ludlam and D. Coates, 'The Development of an Anglo-American Model of Trade Union and Political Party Relations', *Labor Studies Journal* 28(2),

2003, starting page, pp. 45, 46; see also S. Ludlam, M. Bodah and D. Coates, 'Trajectories of Solidarity: Changing Union-Party Linkages in the UK and the USA', *British Journal of Politics and International Relations* 4(2), 2002, 222, pp. 233–241. For an application of the typology to the Australian context, see G. Griffin, C. Nyland and A. O'Rourke, 'Trade Unions, the Australian Labor Party and the Trade-Labour Rights Debate', *Australian Journal of Political Science* 39(1), 2004, 89.

50 See, for example, Rules of Australian Labor Party (NSW Branch) cl. B.25(a), B.26; Rules of Australian Labor Party Victorian Branch, cl. 6.3.2.

51 See, for example, Rules of Australian Labor Party (NSW Branch), cl. B.2; Rules of Australian Labor Party Victorian Branch, cl. 6.2.

52 National Constitution of the ALP, cl. 5(b).

53 Ibid. cl. 7(a).

54 NSW Select Committee, *Electoral and Political Party Funding in New South Wales*, pp. 107–108, 113 (Recommendation 9).

55 Ibid. p. 113 (emphasis added).

56 See, for example, D. Mighell, 'Unions must leave Labor', *The Age*, 11 February, 2010. Online. Available HTTP: www.theage.com.au/opinion/politics/unions-must-leave-labor-20100210-nsat.html (accessed 8 March 2010).

57 See, for example, s. 5(3)(d) of Fair Work (Registered Organisations) Act 2009 (Cth).

58 Ibid. ss. 141(1)(b)(ix)–(xi).

59 Ibid. s. 149.

60 Rules of the Automotive, Food, Metals, Engineering, Printing and Kindred Industries Union (current as at 7 October 2008), cl. 21.

61 Rules of the Communication, Electrical, Electronic, Energy, Information, Postal, Plumbing and Allied Services Union of Australia (current as at 3 March 2009), cl. 19.

62 Rules of the Liquor, Hospitality and Miscellaneous Union (current as at 7 July 2008), cl. 31.

63 Rules of the Construction, Forestry, Mining and Energy Union (current as at 29 August 2008), cl. 49.

64 See, for example, Fair Work (Registered Organisations) Act 2009 (Cth), ss. 143–144.

65 R. Michels, *Political Parties: A Sociological Study of the Oligarchical Tendencies of Modern Democracy*, New York: Collier Books, 1962.

66 See, for example, the study by S.M. Lipset, M. Trow and J. Coleman of the International Typographical Union where the authors concluded:

> [w]e have shown that there is much more variation in the internal organization of associations than the notion of an iron law of oligarchy would imply, but nevertheless, the implications of our analysis for democratic organizational politics are almost as pessimistic as those postulated by Robert Michels.

Union Democracy: The Internal Politics of the International Typographical Union, Glencoe: Free Press, 1956, p. 405. For discussion of the Australian situation, see Deery and Plowman, *Australian Industrial Relations*, pp. 247–253; P. Fairbrother, 'Union Democracy in Australia: Accommodation and Resistance', in L. Savery and N. Dufty (eds), *Readings in Australian Industrial Relations*, Sydney: Harcourt Brace Jovanovich, 1991, p. 297; C. Fox, W. Howard and M. Pittard, *Industrial Relations in Australia: Development, Law and Operation*, Melbourne: Longman Australia, 1995, pp. 209–215.

67 M. Dunckley, 'ALP peace deal falls foul of unions', *Australian Financial Review*, 19 January, 2009; P. Austin with M. Moncrief, '"Peace" deal has ALP in turmoil', *The Age*, 20 January, 2009.

68 A. Leigh, 'How Do Unionists Vote? Estimating the Causal Impact of Union Membership on Voting Behaviour from 1966 to 2004', *Australian Journal of Political Science* 41(4), 2006, 537.

69 Former section 97P of the Industrial Relations Act 1979 (WA). This requirement was in force from 1997 to 2002.

70 See Democrats Senator A. Murray, 'Dissenting Report' in Joint Standing Committee on Electoral Matters', *Funding and Disclosure: Inquiry into Disclosure of Donations to Parties and Candidates*, 2006, para. 2.2 (trade unions) and para. 5.5 (corporations). Online. Available HTTP: www.aph.gov.au/house/committee/em/donations/report/dissent_murray.pdf (accessed 3 June 2008).

71 For the requirements applying to trade union political expenditure, see discussion in Ewing, *The Cost of Democracy*, ch. 3; and K. Ewing, *Trade Unions, the Labour Party and the Law: A Study of the Trade Union Act 1913*, Edinburgh: Edinburgh University Press, 1982.

72 For further elaboration, see Tham, *Money and Politics*, ch. 7.

4 The trade union question in British political funding

*Keith D. Ewing**

Introduction

On 16 November 2010, Andrew Tyrie MP gave evidence to the Committee on Standards in Public Life (CSPL) about trade union funding of the Labour Party.[1] Mr Tyrie is a Tory (conservative) MP and Chair of the Treasury Select Committee, as well as the author of the Conservative Party's proposals for the funding of political parties.[2] His evidence to the CSPL appears nevertheless to have been based on ignorance of the law and an exaggerated account of the facts. According to Tyrie 'we have appalling abuse where there is not really a genuine opt-out, let alone an opt-in'.[3] Wrong. 'The vast majority of trade union members do not get a genuine choice'.[4] Wrong. 'Also, there is no regulation'.[5] Wrong. Yet so mesmerising was the evidence that no one on the Committee thought to question any of this, or any of Mr Tyrie's other fantasies. Why, for example, should the right to opt out be 'marked on the application form to join the trade union',[6] when the legislation passed by a Conservative government imposed many obligations in relation to political funds, but not this one? Why should the Certification Officer be attacked for 'not even bother[ing] to look at [trade union] application forms to check if there was an opt-out',[7] when he has neither the responsibility nor, perhaps, the power to do so? And why did no one on the Committee see fit to put to Mr Tyrie that every trade union with a political fund is regulated by statute like no other participant in the political process, that trade union members have unparalleled rights in relation to political objects, and that trade union members have a cheap and efficient way of enforcing these rights in the quasi-judicial forum he saw fit to attack? Moreover, why did no one think to confront Mr Tyrie with the views of the Better Regulation Task Force – made almost ten years ago – that trade union political funding was over-regulated (as could be said about much the rest of trade union activity)?[8]

It is not only the regulation of trade unions in British political funding that is imperfectly understood. So too is their role, trade unions being seen by many as simply an obstacle to funding reform rather than something that should be celebrated and encouraged. This is an activity that has been challenged over the years on legal, constitutional, and political grounds (from within and outside the Labour Party), the challenges being mounted in the courts, in Parliament and in the media. But trade union political activity continues to thrive, despite the rapid fall in the number of trade unionists since 1980, which has seen trade union membership decline from a peak of 13 million in 1980 to around 7 million today.[9] There are nevertheless fewer issues that more clearly illustrate the partisan nature of the debate about political funding than the demand to control trade union political activity, and fewer issues that expose the failure of political funding scholarship to look at the issue of political funding as a small piece in a bigger constitutional and political jigsaw puzzle. In the latter context, trade union political funding (because of its nature and significance) raises important questions about freedom of association and freedom of expression on the one hand, and representative and accountable parties (and governments) on the other. It is true that trade union political funding sometimes challenges the liberal principles underpinning constitutional government,[10] and it is also true that the practice of trade union political funding is at times very untidy, disarming for those of an obsessive disposition. It does, nevertheless, perform a valuable public function in the context of UK representative democracy (I make no claims for other systems), as well as providing a legitimate vehicle for the carriage of labour interests in the political process. In other systems that interest may be carried by different relationships with political parties, by a focus on electoral campaigning to secure desired outcomes, and/or by the deployment of lobbying techniques of various kinds. However, Britain is by no means alone in having a trade union-based Labour Party, with similar organisations existing in Australia, Ireland and New Zealand.

The legal framework

It is well known that trade unions were primarily responsible for the formation of the Labour Representation Committee (LRC), a parliamentary pressure group established principally to secure the reversal of a judicial decision.[11] Infamous in the folklore of the Labour movement generally, the decision in question – *Taff Vale Railway Co Ltd* v. *Amalgamated Society of Railway Servants* – threatened the very existence of trade unionism by exposing trade unions to the risk of unlimited damages and costs when they took industrial action on behalf of their members.[12] Although legislation was secured in 1906 to address this particular problem,[13] the 1906 settlement proved to be rather fragile, and in 2007 an equally serious threat of a similar nature was created in the form of a decision of the European Court of Justice,[14] against which political action is again a necessary response (though one much more difficult to engineer). As founders of the Labour Party (as the LRC became in 1906), trade unions did not simply donate money, but were part and parcel of its organisation and structure. Indeed, when the party was first created, there was no individual membership, with the only members under the constitution of the party being the organisations affiliated to it. Affiliated organisations sustained the party by the introduction of what was normally referred to as a parliamentary levy of their members, which all members had to pay even though their political loyalties might lie elsewhere.

Although the composition and structure of the Labour Party has greatly changed since 1900 when the LRC was formed, the Labour Party constitution still bears the hallmark of the party's origins despite several revisions.

Predictably, the emergence of the Labour Party did not escape the attention of the courts, enraged by the party's success in securing the reversal by statute of earlier decisions. In the equally infamous Osborne judgment in 1909,[15] the House of Lords held that trade unions could not impose a levy on their members for the purposes of parliamentary representation. Not only did the court contrive to find that there was no legal authority for trade union parliamentary levies, but two of the judges were deeply concerned by the conditions attaching to trade union candidates which bound them (at a time when there was no State payment of MPs) to follow the union line in their parliamentary activities. At least one of the members of the House of Lords (Lord Shaw of Dunfermline) drew heavily on Burke and Locke to criticise the arrangements, and to find them unlawful on the additional ground that they were contrary to public policy. The decision was, however, reversed in 1913 by legislation introduced by the then Liberal government, a prominent part in the reform being played by Winston Churchill who was – of course – to become Prime Minister in a Conservative government.[16] Under the Act trade unions were again empowered to raise money for political purposes, provided they had the authority of their members, voting in a ballot for the adoption of political objects. Once this approval had been secured, there was no requirement that it should be renewed, although it was always open to the members of a trade union to decide through their policy making bodies that they no longer wanted the union to be politically active.

The other requirement of the 1913 Act was that trade unions could fund political objects only from a separate political fund, to which members had a right not to contribute. That is to say, they could opt out – or 'contract out' in the vernacular – of the collective obligation to pay the levy. The statute did not, however, direct how the money was to be spent from the fund, any more than legislation proscribes how trade unions must spend their general funds. All it said was that if trade unions wished to spend money in support of certain defined political objects, they must do so only from the political fund, which was to be used for a range of political purposes, including affiliation to the Labour Party. If the trade union was affiliated to the Labour Party, the Act did not seek to dictate or determine the nature of that affiliation. To have done so would have been an impertinent violation of the right to freedom of association. It appears to have been the practice for most trade unions to affiliate with the Labour Party on the basis of the number of people paying the political levy. But that has never been the invariable practice, with trade unions occasionally over-affiliating and others occasionally under-affiliating.[17] This is much less significant an issue today than it was in the past, when trade unions had a much bigger share of the votes at Labour Party conferences, and when the Labour Party conference was a much more significant body in determining the policy of the party. The position is now much more fluid in terms of affiliation levels, as will be discussed more fully below.

The settlement reached in 1913 as a compromise between the then Labour and Liberal Parties is the one that remains largely in place today. Significant changes were made in 1984, though these did not affect the overall design of the scheme.[18] The first major change was to expand the definition of political objects, that is to say the range of activity that trade unions could support only with a political fund. This was designed to deal with the problem, encountered by the then Conservative government, of political campaigns against them at election time by trade unions that were not affiliated to the Labour Party and did not have political funds. But rather than discourage these unions from engaging in such activity, the statutory changes had the unintended effect of simply persuading a number of unions who had regarded themselves as being politically non-aligned to establish political funds to engage in activity they may or may not have undertaken in the past.[19] A potentially more damaging change was the requirement that trade unions with political objects should ballot their members every ten years for authority to continue to promote such objects. At a time when the political fortunes of the Labour Party were at a low ebb (after the 1983 general election), this was seen to be a very serious threat to trade union funding of the Party, a measure apparently inspired by the belief that trade union members disillusioned with Labour would vote to discontinue political objects. In practice this is not what happened, with three cycles of political fund renewal ballots now having been successfully conducted under the regulatory framework introduced in 1984.

Trade union political objects

The furtherance of trade union political objects is now governed by the Trade Union and Labour Relations (Consolidation) Act 1992, which bears the hallmark of this legacy and reflects its core principles that trade union political action should be (i) based on the collective consent of the membership, with (ii) individual members always having the right to disengage. The Act defines political objects as the expenditure of money

- on any contribution to the funds of, or on the payment of expenses incurred directly or indirectly by, a political party;
- on the provision of any service or property for use by or on behalf of any political party;
- in connection with the registration of electors, the candidature of any person, the selection of any candidate or the holding of any ballot by the union in connection with any election to a political office;
- on the maintenance of any holder of a political office;
- on the holding of any conference or meeting by or on behalf of a political party or of any other meeting the main purpose of which is the transaction of business in connection with a political party; and
- on the production, publication or distribution of any literature, document, film, sound recording or advertisement the main purpose of which is to

> persuade people to vote for a political party or candidate or to persuade them not to vote for a political party or candidate.[20]

For these purposes, a 'contribution' in relation to the funds of a political party is defined to include 'any fee payable for affiliation to, or membership of, the party and any loan made to the party'.[21]

The 1992 Act provides that if a trade union wishes to engage in such activity, it must first have the approval of its members in a ballot for the adoption of political objects (approval which still has to be approved every ten years).[22] These ballots are subject to external supervision in the sense that the ballot rules must be approved by the government-appointed Certification Officer for Trade Unions and Employers' Associations.[23] The rules must comply with a number of statutory requirements, relating to the appointment of an independent scrutineer, entitlement to vote, the counting of the votes by an independent person and the need for a scrutineer's report. So far as entitlement to vote is concerned, this should be accorded equally to all members of the union, while there is detailed regulation of the ballot paper and the method of voting.[24] So far as the latter is concerned, the procedure should be fully postal, at the expense of the union, and the process should be conducted in such a way as to ensure that the ballot is secret and that the votes are fairly and accurately counted.[25] Where a union is alleged to have held a ballot in accordance with rules which have not been approved by the Certification Officer (or in breach of such rules), a complaint may be made by a member to the Certification Officer, who may issue a declaration if the complaint is upheld and if necessary require a fresh ballot to take place.[26] So far as I am aware these powers have never been used, and it is remarkable to record that only one trade union has been required to discontinue political objects as a result of the ballots, and in that case – civil servants – the union was not affiliated to the Labour Party.

Once a union has the approval of its members, it must then adopt political fund rules. These rules must also be approved by the Certification Officer for Trade Unions and Employers' Associations, to ensure that they meet certain standards as to content prescribed by the 1992 Act.[27] Political fund rules of all trade unions will make clear that payments in furtherance of the political objects must be made only from the political fund, which is to be financed by a separate political levy of the members.[28] Here, the amount of the levy varies from union to union, but is typically a very small sum, usually less than 25 pence per week (see Table 4.1). The political fund rules will also provide that contracted out members must not be excluded from any benefits of the union, or 'be placed in any respect either directly or indirectly under a disability or at a disadvantage as compared with other members of the union (except in relation to the control or management of the political fund)'.[29] Any member who complains that the political fund rules have been breached may make a complaint to the Certification Officer, who may make such order to remedy the breach as he or she thinks just in the circumstances.[30] All this information is contained in the trade union political fund rules, to which *every member* of a trade union with a political fund is

Table 4.1 Trade union political fund contributions

Union	*Annual contribution*
ASLEF	£4.08 (average)
BECTU	£1.56
BFAWU	£3.98
Community	£10.40
CWU	£5.20
GMB	£7.62
Musicians' Union	£3.20
NUM	£14.04
TSSA	£6.75
UCATT	£6.24
UNISON	£7 (average)
UNITE	£7.32
UNITY	£4.00
USDAW	£5.20

Source: Trade Union Labour Party Liaison Organisation (TULO).

entitled to receive a copy; and they are also included in trade union rule books, to which *anyone* is entitled to receive a copy.[31] Nevertheless, the number of complaints by trade union members alleging a breach of the rules has been tiny (averaging only a few a year), and in modern times successful complaints have been extremely rare (notwithstanding the spotlight on trade union political funding).

The 1992 Act and the political fund rules go further still to ensure that trade union members are fully aware of their right to claim exemption from paying the political levy. Thus, a trade union with political objects must notify its members of (a) the right to contract out, and (b) that an exemption form can be obtained from any branch office of the union, from the head office of the union, or from the Certification Officer.[32] This notice to members is to be given in accordance with rules of the union approved for the purpose by the Certification Officer, who shall have regard in each case to the existing practice and character of the union.[33] This means in practice that the information about the contracting out procedure will be contained in the rules and constitution of the union. On giving notice within four weeks of the adoption of political objects by the union (or in some cases within four weeks of joining the union), the member will be exempt with immediate effect; otherwise, notice may be given to the union at any time, and will take effect from 1 January thereafter.[34] Once given, an exemption notice does not need to be renewed, and is valid until revoked.[35] All of these steps are clearly set out in trade union rule books, with the rules of Unite, UNISON, the GMB and the Communication Worker's Union (CWU) providing good examples of very clear guidance to members about their right to claim exemption and how to exercise that right, the rules also including a model exemption form that may be used for the purpose.[36] Although claims that it is difficult for trade union members to exercise this right are made from time to time by enemies of the trade union movement and the Labour Party, it is notable that little evidence has ever been produced to sustain these claims or to establish that the remedial structure is inadequate to deal with any problems that may arise.

In the 1960s, Mr Robert Carr (later a minister in a Conservative government), complained to the Royal Commission on Trade Unions and Employers' Associations under the chairmanship of Lord Donovan, a Lord of Appeal in Ordinary, that the contracting out procedure was indefensible and created pressure and inequities that should be removed. Mr Carr was then asked to provide details of abuses under the procedure, the Royal Commission noting in its report that

> he thought that he might be able to supply details of specific cases if given the time – an expectation apparently not fulfilled.
>
> (Royal Commission on Trade Unions and Employers' Associations 1965–1968, Report, Cmnd 3623, 1968, para. 9.23)

In 1983 the House of Commons Employment Committee examined the government's proposals for further restrictions on trade union political funding. Evidence was taken from the Engineering Employers' Federation which had made claims about trade union members paying the political levy against their will. In the course of oral evidence the following exchange took place between Frank White MP and Dr James McFarlane, Director General of the EEF:

> FRANK WHITE: ...have you any evidence at all to put before this Committee that people are paying a political levy unwillingly?
>
> DR MCFARLANE: Not anything that I think you would recognize as evidence, no.
>
> (HC 243-i. 1983–1984)

> We have received no evidence to suggest that the legislation is not working satisfactorily, and no case has been made out for any reform, We do not propose any change in the law in this respect.
>
> (Committee on Standards in Public Life, *The Funding of Political Parties in the United Kingdom*, Cm 4057-I, 1998, para. 6.23)

Trade union political funds

The rights of trade union members to approve political objects and to be exempt from the obligation to support them are complemented by the supervision of trade unions by the State. Under the comprehensive and wide-ranging Trade Union and Labour Relations (Consolidation) Act 1992, trade unions are required to file an annual return to the ubiquitous Certification Officer, which should contain the revenue accounts indicating the income and expenditure of the union for the year in question, and a balance sheet, along with any other accounts that the Certification Officer may require.[37] The accounts – which are subject to public inspection – should be accompanied by an auditor's report.[38] In addition, the Certification Officer is required to publish an annual report,[39] which includes a detailed summary of the financial position of Britain's trade unions, the Certification Officer most recently reporting that there are currently 163 trade unions with over 7.3 million members in total, making trade unions by some way one of the largest voluntary organisations in the country.[40] Most of the 7.3 million trade unionists are congregated in 15 trade unions with a membership in excess of 100,000, this group reporting some 6.2 million members. Within this group two unions boast a membership in excess of 1 million, namely Unite with 1.6 million, and UNISON with 1.3 million members respectively, these two unions thus accounting for *c.*31 per cent of all trade union members, and their joint income of £151 million and £176 million, respectively accounting for about the same proportion of total trade union income.[41] The total income of all 163 trade unions now exceeds £1 billion.

Although there are 163 listed trade unions, only 28 have political funds (of which 14 are affiliated to the Labour Party). According to the Certification Officer, these 28 trade union political funds raised a total of £20.15 million in the year ending 31 March 2009, and spent £17.8 million, with combined reserves of £12 million at the end of the year.[42] The total trade union political fund income of £20.15 million reported in 2009–2010 represents an increase in such income in recent years, with political fund income having risen from £15.8 million in 2000–2001. Nevertheless, political fund income is only 2% of total trade union income. As shown in Table 4.2, the total political fund income reported in the 10 years from 2000–2001 to 2009–2010 was in excess of £174 million, though this includes all trade unions with political funds and not only those affiliated to the Labour Party; the political fund income of the affiliated trade unions would obviously be less. Table 4.2 also shows that expenditure in the same period closely tracked income, with total expenditure for the same ten-year period being in excess of £175 million, though it does not provide a breakdown of the different purposes for which the money was spent. One explanation for the close correlation between income from the political levy on the one hand and political expenditures on the other is that trade unions are prohibited by law (i) from transferring general fund revenues into the political fund, and (ii) unlike political parties, from borrowing (either from other union funds or from other sources) to support their political activities.[43] Any excess of expenditure over income in a particular year (such as an election year) would have to be met from reserves.

Returning to the Certification Officer's most recent report, the vast bulk of the reported £20.15 million political fund income (to the tune of £17.6 million) was accounted for by five trade unions, namely CWU (communication workers) (£1 million), GMB (general workers) (£2.9 million), UNISON (public sector workers) (£5.6 million), Unite (£6.2 million), and Usdaw (shop workers) (£1.8 million), all of which are affiliated to the Labour Party. The income of 14 non-affiliated unions was generally much less, though the position in UNISON is complicated by its two funds, one of which is non-affiliated and is used for a range of political purposes other than affiliations or donations to the Labour Party. So far as the non-affiliated unions are concerned, the largest are the Public and Commercial Services Union (PCS) (civil servants) (£333,725), the Fire Brigades Union (FBU) (fire-fighters) (£278,449), RMT (transport workers) (£216,000), and the Educational Institute of Scotland (EIS) (Scottish schoolteachers) (£152,421). But it is also the case that more than half of non-affiliated unions have a political fund income of under £100,000 annually, this being true of the prison officers and tax inspectors (POA and the Association of Revenue and Customs), and the unions of professional workers of various kinds (Aspect and Connect).[44] According to the Certification Officer, this £20.15 million was raised from 4.2 million trade unionists, with 1.8 million trade unionists (in unions with political funds) being exempt from the obligation to pay the political levy of their union, either because they have contracted out or because they belong to a section of their union which is not eligible to make the payment.[45] The political levy is thus paid by only 57% of all 7.3 million trade unionists; of that 57%, many belong to unions that are not affiliated to the Labour Party.

In 2008–2009, 537,301 trade unionists contracted out of paying the political levy. This represents about 12% of trade unionists in trade unions with political funds who are eligible to pay the political levy. In the words of Professor Grunfeld written many years ago 'it is most ingenious to allege that other individuals are not perfectly free to do the same when so large a company stands as an example before them'.[46]

As has been already pointed out, the information provided by the Certification Officer does not give a breakdown of trade union political expenditure. For

Table 4.2 Trade union political fund

Year	*Income and expenditure*	
	Income (£)	*Expenditure (£)*
1999–2000	15,833,149	17,045,947
2000–2001	15,973,927	16,403,347
2001–2002	16,075,971	20,518,696
2002–2003	15,853,184	14,048,216
2003–2004	16,573,329	14,763,525
2004–2005	17,221,228	18,627,336
2005–2006	18,848,114	21,063,184
2006–2007	19,484,881	16,740,113
2007–2008	18,112,409	18,756,333
2008–2009	20,147,954	17,800,650
Total	174,124,146	175,767,347

Source: Annual Reports of the Certification Officer.

that purpose it is necessary to consult the Electoral Commission's database,[47] though this too has a number of limitations. First, the Electoral Commission treats all money transfers as donations and does not distinguish between affiliation (or membership) fees and donations – they are all considered donations. Second, it is sometimes difficult to track the activity of individual unions because there is not always consistency in the name used by the union for the purposes of recording the donation. What the Electoral Commission does reveal, however, is that from the first quarter of 2001 until the end of the first quarter of 2009,[48] trade unions made cash 'donations' of £78.2 million to the Labour Party, this accounting for 63 per cent of the reported donations of £124.4 million to Labour in that period, and about 30 per cent of the reported donations of £258.8 million to all parties in that period. This does not provide the complete picture, as it excludes donations in kind, and it excludes the few small donations made by trade unions to other parties (such as the Liberal Democrats and the Scottish Socialist party). But it does include small donations to Labour from non-affiliated unions. Most importantly, what it reveals is that reported trade union donations to the Labour Party account for 52% of trade union political fund income and 52% of political fund expenditure overall, and an inevitably higher proportion of the political fund income and expenditure were this exercise to be confined to affiliated unions only.

Trade unions and the Labour Party

Contributions to the Labour Party thus form the largest item of trade union political fund expenditure. Here it is important to recall that the definition of contributions in the 1992 Act applies specifically to both affiliation or membership fees on the one hand, and other contributions on the other hand. This reflects the fact that trade unions are not just donors to the Labour Party, but are also members of the Party. The Labour Party constitution recognises various forms of members, individual and collective, with the latter being members in their organisational capacity. So in the case of an affiliated trade union, it is the union – and not the member of the union – that as a matter of law is the member of the Labour Party.[49] As such, trade unions have voting rights at the annual conference of the Labour Party, though this has been greatly down-graded as the policy-making body of the party.[50] Nevertheless, trade unions also have seats on the National Policy Forum,[51] the National Executive Committee, and they form part of the electoral college for the election of the Party leader and deputy leader whenever there is a vacancy.[52] At constituency level, trade unions may also support local parties through constituency development plan agreements, and may have a presence on local management committees. Although the relationship between the trade union and the party is a collective one, there have been attempts in recent years more directly to involve trade union members in crucial decisions, most notably in the election of leader and deputy leader, with most recent elections being conducted on an one member one vote (OMOV) basis, though this is by no means straightforward, partly because unions ballot all their political levy paying members, though not all levy payers are affiliated to the party. It also means that trade union members who are not individual members of the Labour Party may take part, and indeed that trade union members who are members of other political parties may also take part, while controversially a Labour Party member may have several votes in the election (for example, as an individual member, trade unionist, member of an affiliated socialist society (such as the Fabian Society), and an MP).[53]

As members of the Labour Party, trade unions have a legal relationship with it, based principally on contract, which can be enforced by either side in legal proceedings. Although there is no known case of a trade union formally taking steps against the Labour Party, there are cases where trade union members have unsuccessfully brought proceedings against the Party, claiming that the contractual rights of the union have been violated. In one such case,[54] a much-admired and widely respected former general secretary of the party brought proceedings as a member of MSF, all of whose members had been excluded from the party ballot to select the party candidate for the London mayoral election in 2000, on the ground that the union had failed to pay its regional affiliation fees on time. Apart from any question of the merits of such claims, the application failed because – as indicated – the contract is between the party and the union in its organisational capacity, not with its members individually (or indeed, collectively). A recent example of the contract being enforced by the Party against a trade union relates to the expulsion of the RMT on 7 February 2004 for supporting the candidates of another party.[55] Trade unions which are affiliated to the Labour Party are expected not to support candidates standing for other parties, though this is not expressly set down in the constitution of the Party, as it is in the case of individual members who may be (and are) expelled for supporting members of other parties (as in the case of Lord Haskins who made a donation of £2,500 to the campaign of a Liberal Democrat candidate at the general election in 2005).[56] Nevertheless, the RMT continued to make payments to Constitutency Labour Parties (CLPs), with a number of payments being made to ten CLPs before and after the general election in 2005. A small payment was also made to the Labour Party nationally, and a donation of £5,000 was made to John McDonnell MP who stood unsuccessfully as a candidate for the Labour Party leadership in 2007.[57]

But although trade unions thus have a legal and constitutional relationship with the Labour Party as members of the Party, the nature of that relationship may vary from union to union. Moreover, the nature of that relationship has evolved over time, and may bear little similarity today to the nature of that relationship when the party was formed and the union (or one of its constituent parts) was first affiliated. In the past, it was likely that many unions would affiliate on the basis of the number of members paying the political levy. But this was never an invariable practice, for a variety of reasons, including, historically, a desire on the part of large unions not to play too dominant a role in the affairs of the party.[58] Contemporary practice is perhaps even more diverse than at any time in the past, with a move away from a strict 'one for one' – as it is sometimes called – being strongly criticised by the Labour Party's opponents, though it is not clear why it should be. What it represents is simply the evolving and dynamic organisational relationship between the Labour Party and its trade union members. There are thus those unions that have what might be referred to as an individual relationship with Labour, in the sense that they affiliate to the party strictly on the basis of all levy-paying members. But there are also those unions that have what might be referred to as a collective relationship, in the sense that the union decides annually what its affiliation level should be. Although it makes provision for affiliation by trade unions, the Labour Party constitution does not specify any particular model of affiliation, which is a matter within the exclusive domain of each union, though no doubt the Party has an interest in persuading affiliates not to drop their levels of affiliation.

There are several reasons why a union might choose a relationship closer to the collective rather than the individual end of the spectrum.

- First is cost, in the sense that the affiliation fee rose sharply in recent years, and at £3 per affiliated member annually exceeded the amount of the political levy in some unions. It was thus impossible for some unions to affiliate on the basis of one for one (even if it wished to do so), until such time as it was able to raise the amount of the political levy to match the affiliation fee.
- Second, some unions deliberately under-affiliate in order to spend money on other trade union activities, on other political activities, or on other Labour Party activities. Apart from funding the Labour Party nationally, most unions also have strong commitments to CLPs and to other parts of the Labour Party's organisation.
- Third, some trade unions under-affiliate in recognition of the fact that they have a body of members who are willing to pay the political levy but are not willing to have any of their political levy to go to support the Labour Party. This was true of the FBU before it dis-affiliated from the party in 2004.

As already indicated, one union (UNISON), the union has two political funds (the affiliated political fund and the general political fund), with new members being given an opportunity to contribute to either unless they have contracted out. This, however, is an arrangement which exists because of a merger of three unions, two of which were affiliated to the Labour Party while the other was not. The operation of two funds was a compromise designed to ensure that two traditions could continue to operate in the one union. No other union operates a political fund on this basis, there being no organisational reason why it should.

Trade unions and election expenditure

The other major item of expenditure from trade union political funds relates to election campaign expenditures, particularly at election time. This may be by affiliated trade unions campaigning on behalf of Labour or Labour candidates, or independent expenditure by non-affiliated unions or funds in relation to key issues in the election. As we have seen, the political objects are defined to include

> the production, publication or distribution of any literature, document, film, sound recording or advertisement the main purpose of which is to persuade people to vote for a political party or candidate or to persuade them not to vote for a political party or candidate.[59]

This was considered in *Paul* v. *NALGO*,[60] where the union did not have a political fund but nevertheless engaged in campaigning activity during the 1987 general election on a platform to promote public services, in what was seen by some as designed to persuade voters not to support the incumbent Conservative government. It was held that the expenditure was unlawful, as falling within the new definition of political objects. This meant that it could not be incurred by a union such as the National Association of Local Government Officers (NALGO) at the time which did not have political objects or a political fund. It was following that decision that NALGO balloted to establish a political fund so that it could engage in electoral activity without ever affiliating to the Labour Party. It is that fund which is now the UNISON general political fund, following the merger of public service unions NALGO, the National Union of Public Employees (NUPE) and the Confederation of Health Service Employees (COHSE) in 1993.

Trade unions wishing to engage in independent electoral activity are thus required to have a political fund and to finance election campaigning only from that fund. However, trade unions are also caught by the requirements of electoral law, which imposes additional burdens on their capacity to engage in activity of this kind, though so far these additional burdens have probably had only a limited regulatory impact. Like everyone else, trade unions are restrained in the sense that they can spend up to *c.*£1 million in national campaigns supporting or opposing a political party in the election,[61] provided they comply with a number of regulatory requirements, which involve what is in effect registration as a 'recognised third party'.[62] There are then reporting and disclosure obligations after the election[63] and, as we shall see, few organisations, trade union or otherwise, take part in national election campaigns at this level of expenditure. Unions (and others) which do not comply with the registration requirement to become recognised third parties are restricted as to their national spending to a maximum of £10,000 in England (and another £5,000 in each of Scotland, Wales and Northern Ireland) in support of, or in opposition to, a political party.[64] At local level, the rules were revised largely as a result of the decision in *Bowman* v. *United Kingdom*,[65] where it was held that the then third party limit of £5 on expenditure in support or opposition to a parliamentary candidate was a breach of article ten of the European Convention on Human Rights (ECHR).[66] Under the current rules, trade unions and other third parties can spend up to £500 supporting or opposing a candidate in the period between the dissolution of one Parliament and the election day for the next Parliament.[67]

Trade unions are also caught (for the time being) by the statutory ban on political advertising on television and radio, which applies both during and outside of election periods,[68] though the spending limits applicable during election campaigns would in any event prevent unions being able to purchase a significant amount of such advertising. But although most trade unions do not at the moment spend heavily as third parties, some trade unions nevertheless tend to spend more than anyone else (with the exception of the press to whom the restrictions do not apply).[69] At the 2001 general election, for example, there were only nine recognised third parties, of which three were trade unions. By far the largest spender was UNISON which spent £774,796, compared to Charter 88 which spent £180,868. Only three other organisations in fact spent more than the threshold £10,000, raising questions about why the others went to the trouble of registering as recognised third parties. At the general election in 2005, third party activity increased, though not to a hugely significant extent, there now being 25 recognised third parties. Again, UNISON was by some way the biggest spender, with controlled expenditure of £682,115. On this occasion it was run close by the Conservative Rural Action Group, which spent £550,370. The next biggest spenders were GMB, which spent £53,154, and USDAW, which spent £71,810. But, again, as many as eight third parties (almost a third of the total) spent less than the threshold £10,000.[70] Full details for the 2010 general election were not available at the time of writing, though one interesting feature of the information posted on the Electoral Commission website is the unusually high expenditure of two non-affiliated unions – the National Union of Teachers (NUT) (£121,935) and PCS (£84,793).

Apart from the newspaper proprietors, so far UNISON has emerged as the biggest third party spender in British elections. If anything, these figures may underestimate UNISON activity, in the sense that it does not include the cost of communications between the union and its members, while it is also the case that UNISON has made donations (duly reported) to other recognised third parties (notably Searchlight – an anti-racism group – which reports donations of £70,000 and £80,000 from UNISON in 2010 and 2009, respectively). In addition, UNISON has been the main third party at the Scottish and Welsh elections. At the Scottish Parliament election in 2003, UNISON was one of only two recognised third parties (spending £55,973), the other being Usdaw (another trade union) (spending £2,478). Similarly, at the Welsh Assembly election in the same year, UNISON was one of only three recognised third parties, spending £24,263, compared to £1,457 spent by Usdaw and £233 spent by the Society for the Protection of Unborn Children (SPUC) (an anti-abortion group). At the European parliamentary elections in 2004, we saw the same pattern of three recognised third parties, with UNISON outstripping the others with spending of £167,704, compared to £78,774 and £62,923 spent by two anti-fascist groups (Searchlight and Unite Against Fascism). UNISON was the only recognised third party at the Northern Ireland Assembly elections in 2007 (£8,884), and although it continued to be a dominant player at the Scottish and Welsh elections in 2007 it is now beginning to have competition as other players arrive on the scene. It was one of six recognised third parties at the Scottish Parliament elections in 2007, spending £55,084, compared to £38,755 spent by the EIS and £25,543 by a leisure company. UNISON's £7,008 in Wales in 2007 was eclipsed for the first time by Unite Against Fascism, which spent £7,051. Total third party expenditure in the first eight elections governed by the 2000 Act is thus £3.4 million, of which £1.7 million was incurred by UNISON.[71]

Proposals for further regulation

The most recent proposals for the reform of the party funding regime are those to be found in the draft agreement between the parties proposed by Sir Hayden Phillips, who was appointed during the cash for honours affair, which led to a police investigation, and also to a decision by the Crown Prosecution Service (CPS) that there was insufficient evidence to charge anyone for breach of either the Honours (Prevention of Abuses) Act 1925 or the Political Parties, Elections and Referendums Act 2000 (PPERA).[72] Operating under very skewed terms of reference that required him to consider both a cap on contributions and State funding, Sir Hayden made a number of recommendations, which were designed to address current problems, including better transparency, the introduction of a contribution cap of £50,000, the introduction of various forms of State funding for the political parties, the tightening up of spending limits on political parties (including a curious proposal for 'whole Parliament' limits), and changes to the Electoral Commission.[73] On the contribution cap, it was recognised that trade unions were in a special position for a number of reasons, and that it would not be possible to have a flat-rate cap that applied to all individuals and organisations, regardless of the nature and size of the latter.[74] It was proposed at one stage that –

> A6 Affiliation fees paid by trade unions will be treated for the purposes of the cap as individual donations of the members, provided the conditions at A7–A10 are all met.
>
> A7 The amounts paid by individuals into a union's political fund as their contribution to the union's affiliation fee, and the money paid by that union to a political party as its affiliation fee will be the same. This one-for-one link will be transparent and auditable.
>
> A8 The following information will be provided on all union membership application forms:
>
> - an explanation of what the political fund is and the union's affiliation to a political party;
> - an explanation of how much individual members contribute to the political fund and towards the union's affiliation fee;

- an explanation of the trade union member's right at any time to stop contributing to the political fund and the union's affiliation fee and clear information about how they can do this; and
- an explanation of the fact that if a member stops contributing, their membership subscription will be reduced accordingly.

A9 Trade union members will be reminded annually of the amount they are contributing to the union's affiliation fee and of their right to opt out of contributing to the political fund, including how they may do so.

A10 The requirements of transparency and choice set out here will be overseen by the Certification Officer acting in concert with the Electoral Commission, which will have the power to order affiliation fees to be repaid if they are not compliant with the requirements.

A11 Due to the increased transparency and choice for trade union members the ten-year review ballot on the existence of the political fund is no longer necessary and should be removed.[75]

There are essentially three proposals here, dealing with both the private and the public interest in the regulation of trade union political funding. The first is largely unexceptional, at least if the current regime of contracting out is to remain in force. Trade union members are already entitled to receive a copy of the political fund rules on joining the union, and trade unions have no reason to avoid making more transparent that which is already highly visible. This proposal does, however, raise questions about the visibility of other rights, such as the right of the employee to be a member of a trade union in the first place.[76] Should employers be required to notify prospective employees of this and other rights? The second is more questionable, this being the requirement that there should be a strict 'one for one' link between the payment of the levy and the level of affiliation. There are two objections to this, one being an issue of principle, to the extent that what is being proposed is that the State should dictate a particular form of affiliation which the relationship between trade unions and the Labour Party must take. It is not clear what is the State's interest in imposing a uniform model of affiliation and denying the active membership of a trade union the opportunity to make their own decision about the nature of the relationship (if any) they have with the Labour Party. There are also practical problems in the sense that in the past the affiliation fee has been more than the political levy of some unions, and it is still the case that one affiliated union has a political levy which is about half of the annual affiliation fee. It cannot be right that the affiliation fees of all unions would have to be set at the level of the weakest link in the chain; nor can it be right that a union should have to dis-affiliate because its members are not prepared to raise the amount of the levy, or to raise it quickly enough.[77]

The third proposal, that there should be a £50,000 cap on trade union political donations beyond affiliation fees is also strongly contestable, for a number of reasons. In the first place, it would mean that the largest union would be able to give only as much as the smallest. It would be absurd if a union representing over 1 million members (as in the case of UNISON and Unite) were to be placed in the same position as a union of only several thousand members (as in the case of Unity). Second, and closely related to the first concern is that trade unions support the Labour Party in multiple ways beyond affiliation, with support being directed to

- CLPs in the form of constituency development plan agreements;
- other parts of the party organisation; and
- election grants at election time, as well as one-off grants to help with particular events or activities.

In the case of the larger unions in particular, the £50,000 annual donation would have to be stretched to support all these activities, which in some cases far exceed the amount that could be spent. Indeed, some unions already spend more than £50,000 on constituency development work alone, with the result that this and other activity would be seriously constrained. It is true that there is an obvious loophole here in the sense that there would be no limit on the amount of the affiliation fee so that unions could transfer what is currently handed over in donations or local support under the guise of an enhanced affiliation fee, which could be as much as £50,000 per member. Although it might be considered unethical to seek to get round any statutory limit in this way, how could it be prevented without the State dictating to political parties what their membership fees should be? Does there come a point at which the intrusion of the State into the affairs of voluntary organisations becomes too intrusive?

It should be pointed out that these are not the only proposals for 'reform' that are now in circulation. In the recent past both of the main opposition parties appeared to accept the current relationship between trade unions and the Labour Party. This is no longer the case, with both now making demands that go beyond Hayden Phillips. In the case of the Conservatives, their campaign against trade union political funding led to the then Shadow Solicitor General making an ill-conceived complaint to the Office of Fair Trading alleging that trade unions breach consumer protection legislation. This allegation is based on the ground that the trade unions mis-sold membership by failing to give full details of political activities.[78] The application was (predictably) rejected. Both of the opposition parties would like to go further than Hayden Phillips, though quite how far is not clear. But one proposal that unites them both is that trade unions should be required to allow their members to decide which political party should receive their political fund contribution, an idea with a long pedigree. The reason why this is as silly today as when it was first raised by the Social Democratic Party (SDP) in the 1980s is that trade unions are voluntary bodies that are not charged with the function of raising money for political parties, and through the exclusive medium of which it is not necessary for individuals to proceed if they want to make a political donation. Although not an inevitable consequence of an individual rather than a collective relationship, this, nevertheless, is the kind of proposal that flows logically from an individualisation of a collective process. There would, however, be serious freedom of association issues if trade unions were to be required to raise funds for political parties which were contrary to their interests. If after *ASLEF* v. *United Kingdom*,[79] trade unions cannot be required by the State to admit or retain workers who are members of political parties such as the British National Party (BNP), it is difficult to see how they could be required to raise money for these same parties consistently with their rights under the European Convention on Human Rights.

Conclusion

Returning to Hayden Phillips, there is an even more important reason why his proposals are flawed and why they should be rejected. This brings me back to the point I made at the start about the narrow vision of party funding scholarship and policy development. One of the main problems of UK government is the centralisation of political power, which the last administration suggested was in reverse with its proposals for 'constitutional renewal'. What has happened within the Labour Party is visible evidence to the contrary and is a symptom of a wider problem that was perhaps more pronounced under Blair than Brown because of the relative weakness of the latter for a host of reasons that do not need to be examined here. But within the context of an insatiable demand by party leaderships for control over party machines, trade union support at local level and throughout the Party is important in ensuring the financial and organisational independence and autonomy of the grass-roots party (or what is left of it) from control by that central party machine. It allows that autonomy to be reinforced by enabling trade unions to decide how they wish to deploy their resources, which candidates they wish to support for nomination, and which candidates they wish to promote at election time. This in turn is important for ensuring an independent voice within the Parliamentary Labour Party, especially if the Party when in government is to be held to account. The Trade Union Group of Labour MPs has been an invaluable voice within the Parliamentary Labour Party (PLP) in communicating issues of concern to Labour Party members and supporters to the leadership. It is also a source of countervailing power and pressure, which helps to ensure that contentious political issues are properly addressed, seen, for example, in the support given to a carefully co-ordinated campaign for the Temporary and Agency Workers' Bill in 2008 designed to give equal rights to temporary and agency workers. Are these largely inchoate, incomplete and untidy channels of democratic accountability irregular because they are underpinned by financial support on a very modest scale? My sense is that they are not, and indeed my overwhelming sense is that there would be no public interest to be served in undermining this activity if the result would be to diminish, rather than enhance the accountability of power within the Labour Party.

In the meantime, trade union political activity remains very heavily regulated, and trade union money more heavily regulated than any other source of political money in the UK system of government. The legislation currently in force was introduced at a time when closed shop arrangements were prevalent and when people in tight-knit mining, ship-building, and other communities were under strong social pressure to be and remain in membership of a trade union. It was felt – perhaps rightly – that these people should not be compelled – on pain of losing their livelihood and perhaps their home – to support financially a political party to which they were opposed.[80] But since these heady days, the closed shop has disappeared, having been effectively outlawed in the 1980s, and there is little prospect of anyone losing his or her job today because of non-membership of a trade union. Yet far from removing the restraints on trade unions (on the ground that the principal reason for these restraints has largely disappeared), regulation has been piled upon regulation, and as we have seen, there are now proposals for still more regulation. These proposals seem extraordinary, most obviously because the trade union model of party funding is one that involves millions of people of modest means making a small annual contribution to sustain the political process. This is precisely what we should be trying to encourage rather than discourage, particularly at a time when other forms of voluntary activity are in decline. Even if there are (as yet unidentified) problems with the current arrangements, are these really on such a scale as to justify the destruction of one of the most successful forms of political financing anywhere in the world? Quite apart from that, there is another concern, that in a free society underpinned by the Human Rights Act 1998, trade unions cannot be prevented from engaging in political activity or in raising money for political purposes. That being the case, what will happen to the £100 million collected by trade union political funds over the lifetime of a Parliament if the bulk of it is not to help sustain the Labour Party? The only certain thing is that it will not disappear and that it will find new outlets, creating in the process a new regulatory headache. At some point surely someone will realise that it is better that the bulk of that money should be drawn into the centre where it will be seen, rather than pushed out to the periphery where it will be invisible. Or is there another agenda?

Notes

* Thanks to Navraj Ghaleigh, Jacob Rowbottom and Joo-Cheong Tham for advice and guidance on the preparation of this chapter.

1 www.public-standards.org.uk/Library/16112010___Uncorrected_Transcript.pdf.
2 www.conservatives.com/People/Members_of_Parliament/Tyrie_Andrew.aspx.
3 www.public-standards.org.uk/Library/16112010___Uncorrected_Transcript.pdf, para. 137.
4 Ibid.
5 Ibid., para. 138.
6 Ibid.
7 Ibid.
8 See the discussion of this issue in Department of Trade and Industry, *Review of the Employment Relations Act 1999*, 2003, Annex C. See also Better Regulation Task

Force, *Regulation – Less is More: Reducing Burdens, Improving Outcomes*, 2005, p. 43.

9 For current figures, see Certification Officer, *Annual Report 2009–2010* (2010).

10 See *Amalgamated Society of Railway Servants* v. *Osborne* [1910] AC 87.

11 For the origins of the Labour Party, see H Pelling, *Origins of the Labour Party*, Oxford: Oxford University Press, 1965, and F Bealey and H Pelling, *Labour and Politics, 1900–1906*, London: Macmillam, 1958.

12 [1901] AC 426. In the High Court, Mr Justice Farwell had referred to trade unions as organisations 'with wide capacity for evil'. He was subsequently to say that the effect of the 1906 Act that 'The legislature cannot make evil good, but it can make it not actionable': *Conway* v. *Wade* [1908] 2 KB 845, at p. 855.

13 See J. Saville, 'The Trade Disputes Act of 1906', *Historical Studies in Industrial Relations*, 1996, vol. 1, 11.

14 C-438/05, *International Transport Workers' Federation and Finnish Seamen's Union* v. *Viking Line ABP and OÜ Viking Line Eesti* [2007] ECR I-10779 798.

15 *Amalgamated Society of Railway Servants* v. *Osborne*, above.

16 For a fuller account, see K.D. Ewing, *Trade Unions, the Labour Party and the Law – A Study of the Trade Union Act 1913*, Edinburgh: Edinburgh University Press, 1982.

17 See L. Minkin, *The Contentious Alliance*, Edinburgh: Edinburgh University Press, 1991.

18 See K.D. Ewing, 'Trade Union Political Funds – The 1913 Act Revised', *Industrial Law Journal*, 1984, Vol. 13, 227.

19 For the impact of the change, see *Paul* v. *NALGO* [1987] IRLR 413. See below.

20 Trade Union and Labour Relations (Consolidation) Act 1992, s. 72.

21 Ibid., s. 72(4).

22 Ibid., s. 71.

23 Ibid., s. 74(1). On the appointment of the Certification Officer, see TULRCA 1992, s. 254.

24 Ibid., s. 74(3).

25 Ibid., s. 77.

26 Ibid., ss. 79, 80. An application may alternatively be made to a court (s. 81).

27 TULRCA 1992, s. 71(1)(b).

28 Ibid., s. 82(1)(a).

29 Ibid., s. 82(1)(c). Contribution to the political fund should not be made a condition of membership of the union.

30 Ibid., s. 82(2)–(4B).

31 Ibid., s. 27. The rule-books of the largest unions are publicly available online. See note 36 below.

32 Ibid., s. 84(2).

33 Ibid., s. 84(3).

34 Ibid., s. 84(4). In some cases new members may be permitted to claim immediate exemption within four weeks of joining the union.

35 Ibid., s. 84(5).

36 See www.unitetheunion.org/pdf/054-Unite%20Rule%20book%20-%20effective%20from%201%20May%2009%20amended%204%20Ju.pdf; and www.gmb.org.uk/pdf/RulebookfollowingCongress2010.pdf.

37 TULRCA 1992, s. 32.

38 Ibid.

39 Ibid., s. 258.

40 Certification Officer, *Annual Report 2009–10* (2010).

41 Ibid., app 4.

42 Ibid., app 9.

43 TULRCA 1992, s. 84.

44 Certification Officer, *Annual Report 2009–10* (2010), App 9.

45 Ibid.
46 C. Grunfeld, *Modern Trade Union Law*, London: Sweet and Maxwell, 1966, p. 296.
47 www.electoralcommission.org.uk/party-finance/database-of-registers.
48 The period in question is covered by the last eight entries in Table 1, accounting for a total political fund income of £143,317,069 and expenditure of £142,319,053. The CO's figures are a year behind, so that the figures for 2008–2009 are contained in the Annual Report for 2009–2010.
49 Labour Party, *Rule Book*, 2008, Ch 1, cl II(3).
50 Ibid., Ch 3.
51 Ibid., Ch 4.
52 Ibid.
53 This problem would be easy to resolve, by simply saying that no one should have more than one vote and that everyone must choose in which section they wish to vote.
54 *Mortimer* v. *The Labour Party*, *The Independent*, 28 February 2000.
55 BBC News, 7 February 2004.
56 BBC News, 23 September 2005.
57 See www.electoralcommission.org.uk/party-finance/database-of-registers.
58 See Minkin, above.
59 TULRCA 1992, s. 72.
60 [1987] IRLR 413.
61 PPERA 2000, s. 94. The activity covered by this restriction is set out in ss. 85–88.
62 Ibid., s. 88.
63 Ibid., ss. 96–100.
64 Ibid., s. 94(5).
65 (1998) 26 EHRR 1.
66 The law was then set out in the Representation of the People Act 1983, s. 75.
67 1983 Act, s. 75, as amended by PPERA 2000, s. 131.
68 Communications Act 2003, s. 321(2).
69 PPERA 2000, s. 87.
70 Nor did they spend heavily in the Scottish or Welsh elections conducted under the Act. At the end of 2010, there were 29 third parties registered under PPERA, of which only five are trade unions affiliated to the Labour Party: Community, UCATT, UNISON, UNITE, and USDAW, though three other non affiliated trade unions are also recognised (EIS, NUT, and PCS) The other 21 third parties were a mixture of individuals and pressure groups covering diverse issues.
71 All the figures in this paragraph are to be found at www.electoralcommission.org.uk/party-finance/database-of-registers.
72 www.cps.gov.uk/news/press_releases/125_07. See Ghaleigh in this volume.
73 H. Phillips, *Strengthening Democracy: Fair and Sustainable Funding of Political Parties*, London: HMSO, 2007.
74 Ibid., p. 10.
75 H. Phillips, *Proposals for the Funding of Political Parties*, London, 2007. cf. H. Phillips, *Strengthening Democracy: Fair and Sustainable Funding of Political Parties*, above.
76 See TULRCA 1992, ss. 137, 146, 152. How accessible is this to most workers?
77 There is also the problem that in unions such as the GMB, there are three categories of levy payer, one of which pays only 15 pence annually.
78 See also J. Djanogly and A. Duncan, *Labour and the Trade Unions – An Analysis of a Symbiotic Relationship*, London: Centre for Policy Studies, 2007.
79 [2007] IRLR 361.
80 See Ewing, *Trade Unions, the Labour Party and the Law*, ch 3.

Part II

The role of spending limits

5 The role of spending controls

New electoral actors and new campaign techniques

Keith D. Ewing and Jacob Rowbottom

Introduction

For various reasons discussed in Chapters 2, 3 and 4, the regulation of political donations in the United Kingdom has been fraught with difficulty. Although most of the controversies about political finance in the past have been concerned with donations, the main focus of regulation has been on expenditure. Indeed, it is perhaps supremely paradoxical that the Committee on Standards in Public Life (CSPL) should respond to the controversy surrounding the £1 million donation to Labour by the motor racing tycoon Bernie Ecclestone by proposing spending caps rather than contribution caps.[1] But although paradoxical, this was a response that was at least consistent with the regulatory tradition in the United Kingdom, where the focus has been on spending and only indirectly on contributions.[2] Since the Corrupt and Illegal Practices Act 1883, spending limits have applied to candidates,[3] one of the purposes of this legislation being captured by Lord Bingham in *Attorney General* v. *Jones*,[4] when he said that there was a need to

> achieve a level financial playing field between competing candidates, so as to prevent perversion of the voters' democratic choice between competing candidates within constituencies by significant disparities of local expenditure. At the constituency level it is the voters' perception of the personality and policies of the candidates, and the parties which they represent, which is intended to be reflected in the voting, not the weight of the parties' expenditure on local electioneering.[5]

For many years, however, this principle was undermined by the fact that there were no comparable limits on the spending by political parties and others on their national campaigns. The only control was indirect (though not insignificant), in the form of a ban on the use of television for political advertising.[6] These restraints were extended by the Political Parties, Elections and Referendums Act 2000, which introduced spending limits applicable to the activities of political parties, as well as so-called third parties. In proposing the introduction of measures of this kind, however, the CSPL denied that it was moved by a desire to promote a level playing field among all political parties, though the Committee did accept that

> the results of a number of post-war elections – for example, those of 1950, 1951, 1964 and February and October 1974 – have been very close, and common sense suggests that one major party's ability to spend substantially more than the other may well have made a difference to the outcome.[7]

The Committee was moved more by a need to control the demand for money:

> We accept that it cannot be proved that high spending buys elections. It is clear, however, that campaign spending by the Conservative and the Labour parties in recent years has accelerated, particularly in 1997, bringing with it the need to raise even larger funds to pay for the spending. Even if disclosure leads to a temporary fall in donations, the pressure to raise even greater sums will remain if there is no limit on spending. We believe that it is at least probable that limits on campaign spending are necessary to prevent undue concentration on fundraising.[8]

In this chapter, we assess the operation of these latter controls, controls that have now been used in three general elections, two European elections, as well as in numerous elections to the devolved Parliament and assemblies. In assessing the operation of these controls, the purpose is to provide some indication of

- the spending patterns of political parties (how much do the parties claim to spend and on what?);
- the levels of political engagement by third parties (apart from the trade unions identified in Chapter 3, which organisations take an active part in election campaigns and on what scale?); and
- the problems (if any) which have arisen in the operation of these controls (are there new forms of political activity escaping the regulatory net?).

The last question in turn raises other questions about whether:

- the law is flexible enough to keep up with changing political practice, in light of the new forms of expenditure taking place, associated with new campaign actors or new campaign methods;
- the methods of supervision and investigation of the political parties and others is adequate to ensure that the law is being properly applied; and
- there is a need for a fresh round of legislation to expand the current rules, including the proposal from the House of Commons Constitutional Affairs Committee (CASC) that there should be a move away from a system of election spending limits to a system of global spending limits applicable to all aspects of party activity within the period of a five-year accounting cycle.[9]

National spending by political parties

The United Kingdom is not alone in trying to regulate the national campaign spending of political parties, though it is by no means a typical method of regulation: at the time of writing there are no spending limits in the United States (where they were held to be unconstitutional),[10] Germany or Australia (where attempts to control broadcasting spending were also found to be unconstitutional).[11] But although this is a method of regulation that the United Kingdom shares with Canada (where national spending limits were ambitiously pioneered in 1974),[12] the United Kingdom's legislation goes further than its Canadian counterpart in terms of the scope and timing of its application, though the level of permitted expenditure in the United Kingdom is nevertheless high, bearing in mind in particular that (unlike in Canada) there is no television or radio advertising to be incurred. The spending limit applies to what is referred to in the Political Parties, Elections and Referendums Act 2000 (PPERA) as 'campaign expenditure',[13] a term defined to mean expenses incurred by or on behalf of a party which (i) fall within Schedule 8 and (ii) are incurred 'for election purposes'.[14] So far as the first point is concerned, this applies to expenses incurred in relation to a list of 8 items, as follows.

- Party political broadcasts.
- Advertising.
- Unsolicited material sent to electors.
- Any manifesto or other document setting out the party's policies.
- Market research or canvassing conducted for the purpose of ascertaining voting intentions.
- The provision of services or facilities in connection with press conferences or other dealings with the media.
- Transport of people (such as the party leader) with a view to obtaining publicity in connection with an election campaign.
- Rallies and other events organised to obtain publicity in connection with the election.

The amount that may be spent on these items (in the 12 months before a general election) depends on the number of seats the party contests.[15] The maximum amount that may be spent by a party that contests every seat is £19.5 million.[16] This is in addition to the money that may be spent by each candidate in the election, discussed in Chapters 6 and 7.

There has been no serious problem of compliance with these provisions in the elections conducted since this regime was introduced. True, it is to be expected that the parties will all report levels of expenditure below the maximum permitted amount; but there has been no suggestion from any quarter that the reports are inaccurate, misleading or false. Indeed, in the 2010 general election, the levels of reported expenditure were significantly lower than in previous elections and well within the statutory limit. As shown in Table 5.1, the Conservative

Party reported expenditure of £16.6 million, the Labour Party £8 million, and the Liberal Democrats £4.7 million.[17] The most striking feature here was not only that the Conservatives reportedly spent significantly more than the other two main parties combined and that Labour (the party of government) reportedly spent less than half of that incurred by the Conservatives, but that the Conservatives reportedly spent only just over 87 per cent of the level of permitted expenditure, that Labour spent only just over 42 per cent of the maximum permitted, and that the Liberal Democrats spent less than 25 per cent.[18] This alone reinforces the view expressed by some that the original cap of around £20 million proposed by the Neill Committee and accepted by the government was set too high,[19] and could easily be reduced without seriously undermining the campaigns of the parties, never mind forcing some restraint on what they do. Quite why there should be such a sharp decline in levels of expenditure is harder to explain than the decline is to identify, a decline all the more pronounced for the fact that the levels of permitted expenditure have not been increased in line with inflation (in contrast with the candidate spending limits which are increased ahead of each election). Obvious possible explanations, however, include the reduced flow of income (particularly in the case of the Labour Party), the changing nature of campaigning, with greater focus on the televised leadership debates, and the decision (again by Labour) to eschew the expensive billboard campaigns which consumed significant portions of campaign budgets in previous elections. Thus, while the Conservatives spent more than £7.1 million on advertising, the Labour Party spent 'only' £785,509.[20]

Whether the legislation has been an unqualified success is, however, much harder to assess. Although campaign expenditure is subject to legal restrictions, there are no restrictions on the general expenditures of the parties. It is a striking feature of party spending patterns that, while campaign spending has been limited in election years, elections years are also associated with significant

Table 5.1 Reported political party expenditure at general election 2010

Name of registered political party	*Total reported expenditure (£)*
Conservative Party	16,682,874
Labour Party	8,009,483
Liberal Democrats	4,787,595
Scottish National Party	315,776
Plaid Cymru	144,933
UKIP	732,782
Green Party	320,425

Source: Electoral Commission.

Note: Although Labour and the Liberal Democrats were outspent by the Conservatives in 2010, all three parties each outspent the SNP and Plaid Cymru in Scotland and Wales, respectively. Thus, the Conservatives, Labour and Liberal Democrats spent £1.2 million, £967,904, and £470,619, respectively in Scotland; and £1.1 million, £525,116, and £329,941, respectively in Wales.

spikes in the level of general expenditure by political parties. The point is brought home most forcefully in the research conducted for the review of party funding by Sir Hayden Phillips, where it is suggested that unregulated party spending tends to rise in the run-up to an election.[21] These data beg many questions about the nature of political party routine expenditures on the one hand, and the scope of the definition of campaign expenditure on the other. They raise questions about the need for global spending limits as proposed by CASC,[22] an idea that could be developed in a number of different directions. One possibility is that the parties would have a level of permitted expenditure over the lifetime of a Westminster parliamentary cycle, and it would be up to the parties themselves to decide how to allocate their resources. As Sir Hayden Phillips acknowledged, however, one objection to this most extreme form of the idea is that it tends to imply that political parties are one-dimensional in their function.[23] The implication is that parties are simply election machines dedicated to contesting and winning elections. While this is clearly an essential element of what they do, not all parties are focussed as exclusively on this as are others, with political education, internal democracy and policy making all playing an important role in party activity.[24] A second possibility then would be to embrace the idea of CASC which is that there should be campaign spending limits within the general limit in order to avoid the parties becoming no more than campaign machines. This at least would be faithful to the main purpose of spending limits, which is that each election should be competitive and should not be distorted by the capacity or willingness of one party significantly to outspend its rivals. But as Sir Hayden Phillips also acknowledged, such a regime would be in danger of imposing excessive administrative burdens on the parties and would present formidable challenges of enforcement.[25]

National spending by third parties

It is of course much too early to tell whether the fall in the levels of campaign spending by the political parties is likely to endure, or whether 2010 is a one-off. Much will depend on the availability of money and the capacity to spend it: if, for example, the ban on political advertising were to be lifted, the pressure to increase expenditure would almost certainly increase.[26] Much will also depend on the development of new forms of campaign activity and its cost, with the innovation of the leaders' debates in 2010 providing a new medium and a new focus for the parties at a relatively modest cost. The other feature of the 2010 election relates to the continuing low levels of third party activity, though there are nevertheless signs of changing patterns of such activity. But before dealing with these matters, it will be useful to remind ourselves of the limits applying to third parties So far as third parties are concerned, the controls here are based on the belief that there is little point in controlling the expenditure of the political parties if other groups could spend with impunity. Money that would be spent by political parties would be redirected to third parties, which would effectively engage in surrogate campaigns.[27] There is also the risk that, although third parties might not actively support political parties, high spending campaigns could create a cacophony in which the voices of the political parties would struggle to be heard. An additional concern – which helped inspire the introduction of the third party limits at local level for the first time in 1918[28] – is that third party expenditure would require the political parties to use up some of their limited resources in dealing with attacks from other organisations, rather than promoting their own message, a matter of particular concern in the event of an orchestrated campaign by a number of third parties towards the end of an election period when budgets may already have been allocated and additional resources are scarce.

Following the recommendation of the CSPL,[29] the 2000 Act thus applies spending limits to controlled expenditure by third parties.[30] For this purpose, 'controlled expenditure' means 'expenses incurred by or on behalf of' the third party, 'in connection with the production or publication of election material which is made available to the public at large or any section of the public (in whatever form and by whatever means)'.[31] The difficulty is that the definition is itself pregnant with uncertainty, with additional definitions being required to explain what is meant by a third party on the one hand and election material on the other. So far as the former is concerned, a third party is defined as meaning any person or body other than a registered party, but exceptionally including a registered party where the party in question is promoting the election of another party or its candidates.[32] So far as the latter is concerned, election material is defined to mean material designed to promote or procure at an election the electoral success of one or more registered parties or candidates who hold (or do not hold) particular opinions or advocate (or do not advocate) particular policies.[33] There are still further definitions of what is meant by 'electoral success', 'candidates', and various other contestable words or phrases in what is becoming a legal minefield.[34] In general terms third parties can spend a maximum of £25,000 throughout the United Kingdom without regulation.[35] Those wishing to spend more must register with the Electoral Commission as recognised third parties,[36] and as such must comply with various reporting obligations after the election.[37] There is a limit on what may be spent by a third party on controlled expenditure of just under £1 million in a national campaign.[38]

Given the flexible and potentially broad definition of third party electoral activity, it is striking that not only is there little evidence of it, but that, with the exception of UNISON, there is little evidence of third party activity which is at or near the limit set by the legislation.[39] It is true that the reported data are to be treated with a great deal of caution: they are simply the reports of third parties themselves and it is not clear what or how much they conceal, or how carefully they are inspected by the Electoral Commission.[40] It is also true that there are gaps in the legislation (which, for example, does not include internal communications with members),[41] and that major third parties (such as newspaper companies) are excluded from the scope of the legislation.[42] Nevertheless, there were only 22 recorded third parties in the 2010 general election, none of which reported expenditure in excess of £555,554.[43] Although there is no sign yet that

Table 5.2 Reported third party expenditure at general election 2010

Name of recognised third party	*Total reported expenditure (£)*
A Minority Pastime Ltd	10,969
Evershed. Patrick	14,055.60
IFAW in Action	206,634
May, Brian	151,948
National Union of Teachers	121,935.77
Political Animal Lobby Limited	172,542
Public and Commercial Services Union (PCS)	84,793.52
Searchlight Information Services Ltd	319,231
The Democratic Reform Company	299,989
The League Against Cruel Sports	62,893
UCATT (construction workers' union)	10,781.42
Unite the Union	16,927.99
Unite Against Fascism	34,858
Vote Cruelty Free	15,339
Vote For A Change Ltd	555,554
Vote-OK	19,145.13
TOTAL (including six others)	1,830,624.44

Source: Electoral Commission.

Note

The six other third parties not included in the table are organisations that reported expenditure of less then £10,000. They are 38 Degrees, the Campaign to End all Animal Experiments, Uncaged Campaigns Ltd, USDAW (shop workers' union), Wales TUC, and Mr Robin Wight.

the decline in political party spending is being matched by an increase in third party spending, there are some ominous signs that such activity is increasing. It is true that the number of third parties reporting expenditure fell from 25 in 2005 to 22 in 2010.[44] But it is also true that the aggregate levels of third party spending continues to increase, from £1.7 million in 2005 to £1.8 million in 2010 (significant for the fact that there is no entry on the 2010 register from UNISON, which has been a hugely significant player in most elections to date).[45] It is also the case that there has been an increase in the number of third parties reporting spending of more than £100,000, the numbers having increased from two in 2005 to seven in 2010. All but one were concerned with anti-racism, animal welfare, or constitutional reform.[46] Although there was also one trade union, the National Union of Teachers (NUT) (and another, the Public and Commercial Services Union (PCS) reporting expenditure just shy of £100,000), there was no business organisation – yet.[47]

New actors

Given the uncertainties in defining 'election material', there are inevitably activities that fall somewhere on the borderline between the regulated electoral activity and uncontrolled non-electoral political activity. The example of think tanks illustrates this issue. Think tanks are organisations that are normally independent of political parties, but which engage in political research. They often publish reports analysing particular areas of policy and provide their own recommendations. Such independent work is clearly valuable, providing expert analysis of political issues and disseminating information and data. At the same time, such research can have electoral effects, and a report published by a think tank can bolster a party's credibility if it provides support for its policies. There is clearly potential for the work of think tanks to fall within the third party spending limits. If a think tank openly endorses a party or its policies during an election, then its spending is likely to count as 'controlled expenditure'. Other examples are not so clear cut. Thus, if in the 12 months prior to a general election, a think tank publishes a report endorsing a policy that is closely associated with a particular political party, then would it be (to use the Electoral Commission's words) 'not reasonable to argue that the item is not election material'? According to the Electoral Commission, this will depend on the context and whether the think tank is merely continuing its previous work on that policy.[48] There is also the situation where a think tank publishes a report examining a particular area of policy and analyses each party's proposals. In such circumstances, the think tank may not endorse any particular party's policy and may say that each party's proposal fails in one respect or another. Despite such an appearance of impartiality, it may be clear from the report that the position of one party is closer to the think tank's recommended stance. The difficulty in such circumstances is that the publication is not an endorsement, but can have (and may be hoped to have) beneficial effects for a political party.

Think tanks do engage in such activities in the United Kingdom, but so far have not registered as third parties with the Electoral Commission. It is not clear whether this is because the Electoral Commission has not investigated the issue, whether the activities of the think tanks are deemed not to constitute electoral material, or whether the amounts spent on election material do not meet the threshold for registration. The line between think tanks and political parties is also blurred by institutional connections. While formally independent of political parties, some think tanks have politicians and representatives from political parties sitting on their boards, often publish material written by politicians, and receive funding from the same sources that fund particular political parties. As a result of these links, the think tank is often thought to perform a 'kite flying' role, in which ideas and proposals are tested before being adopted by a political party. If the activity is commissioned and overseen by the party, then it would count as expenditure by the political party. However, the position is less clear where the think tank independently publishes material that is later utilised by a political party. In its guidance, the Electoral Commission states that a publication does not become 'election material' simply because a candidate or party adopts that position (unless the third party subsequently publicises the party's support for the policy or increases their campaigning on that issue).[49] From the guidance, the institutional connections with a party are not considered to determine if material is designed to promote a party or candidate. There are hazards if the

Commission were to scrutinise such links, as it could render the law less certain still. However, there is potential for formally independent, charitable, non-party organisations to enjoy fairly well-established connections with certain parties, while escaping the regulatory burdens imposed by PPERA.

If such activities are to fall outside the third party regulations, then it may provide an incentive for such activities to grow, especially if the controls in the electoral sphere become stricter. If a think tank's expenditures do not fall within third party spending controls, then donations to that organisation will not be subject to the transparency requirements. Consequently, a contribution to a think tank is a type of (non-party) political donation that is not subject to public scrutiny. The effect of this was highlighted in early 2010, when in a newspaper sting, a politician advised that think tank sponsorship is a route for gaining access to ministers.[50] A donation to a political party, by contrast, may attract adverse publicity. If donations to political parties are capped, then donations to think tanks could continue without a limit. Similarly, if, as discussed earlier, political parties are subject to a permanent spending limit during the life of a Parliament, then more policy work may be informally delegated to think tanks. The think tank could spend as much money as it wishes on research and gathering data, which may at a later date be used by the political party. As long as such expenditure is not coordinated with the party, it would not fall within the proposed permanent spending controls. If the think tank's activities are thought to fall within the third party limits, such trends may be curbed. However, such controls may come at the price of freedom of speech and reduce the quantity of the political information. The only way to stop avoidance is by taking an ever-expanding definition of election material. The difficulty with such a path is that, at some point, the controls will be too excessive, and too hard to monitor and enforce.[51] No one would suggest that spending limits should be applied to all political activity all of the time. Consequently, a line has to be drawn between the electoral and general political. While the way that line should be drawn is open to debate, wherever it is drawn will leave some opportunity for avoidance by framing certain messages as non-electoral.

New actors and new methods: online campaigning

If there has been relatively little overt third party campaigning in recent elections, the various channels for communication via the internet may be changing this. It is now easy for any person to comment on and disseminate their views on an election campaign via the internet. In the 2010 general election, there were various examples of this. During the televised leaders' debates, large numbers of people posted comments in realtime via Twitter and Facebook about the politician's performance. In another high-profile example, a website was set up so that people could post their own versions of the political parties' campaign posters. The activity did not just take place in designated political forums, but also on websites established for other purposes. For example, sites such as mumsnet.com and moneysavingexpert.com hosted discussions among users about the election.[52] While the advance hype about 2010 being an 'internet election' (in which the traditional media would be overshadowed by the digital media) were wide of the mark,[53] many of the online forums did provide significant opportunities for people to participate and engage in political debate. Although the content of many websites clearly constitutes electoral advocacy, little internet activity appears to be registered with the Electoral Commission. The campaign group *38 Degrees* did file a return with the Electoral Commission, but its total spending was £9,000, which is below the threshold for mandatory registration. The other major political websites are not listed in the register of third party expenditure. Why some of the websites have not been required to register with the Commission remains unclear, and several possibilities are considered below.

Some websites are clearly less concerned with discussion than advocacy. For example, Conservative Home is a site that 'aims to provide comprehensive coverage of Britain's Conservative Party' and states that it is 'independent of the Conservative Party but supportive of it'. The site was founded by a former Conservative Party aide, is co-edited by a former Conservative Party MP and since September 2009 Lord Ashcroft has had a controlling stake in the website. Some of the content produced by the site is likely to constitute 'election material'. On the other side of the political spectrum, the website Left Foot Forward provides a forum for left-of-centre bloggers. The site states that it is non-aligned, but it also publishes some content that may constitute election material. For example, on the election day in May 2010, one of its posts told voters to 'make sure that your claim on the future enables real progress, rather than a back door route for Mr Cameron to enter No. 10'.[54] This would clearly amount to direct electoral advocacy. The legal definition of 'election material' also refers to content that promotes 'one or more' political parties.[55] Consequently, even if a site were to publish material that supports the Conservatives and other content that supports the Liberal Democrats, both would constitute 'election material' for the purposes of the spending limits. The limits cannot therefore be avoided by claiming that the overall election coverage is balanced by including advocacy favouring more than one party.

One question is whether the websites fall within the terms of the PPERA. Even if material posted online constitutes 'election material', to count as controlled expenditure it must be 'made available to the public at large or any section of the public (in whatever form and by whatever means)'.[56] The Electoral Commission has published guidance on the application of this test, stating that material on websites will fall within the regulations only if it 'is advertised (or otherwise promoted) to the public in connection with your campaign'.[57] The Commission states that such advertising and promotion includes providing the website address as a source of more information, placing links on other websites, or enhancing its position in search engine results.[58] From this guidance, it is not clear whether the vast majority of websites that are accessible to the public (i.e. not internal communications) will satisfy this test or whether the guidance seeks to narrow the application of the controls. In any event, the 2000 Act itself does not prescribe any requirement that the material be promoted or advertised. Instead, the statute merely requires that the material be 'made available' to the public, which most publicly accessible websites would appear to satisfy.[59]

The absence of online activity from the register of third party expenditure may also be due to the level of expenditure incurred by such speakers. Most political websites are run with minimal expenditure and therefore will not reach the threshold required for registration. However, in the case of some of the larger and more high-profile sites, costs may go above the relevant threshold. This is most likely to be the case where the site in question employs staff or pays some of its contributors. Even where the total cost of running the site exceeds £25,000 across all of the UK, the threshold for mandatory third party registration may not be met. When a third party engages in producing the electoral and non-electoral material, then costs can be split in deciding what proportion of those expenses are dedicated to producing election material. For example, a website might cost £15,000 per year to run and in the year of a general election dedicate 50 per cent of the material to electoral advocacy and the other 50 per cent to non-regulated content. In those circumstances, only £7,500 will have been spent on 'election material' and the £10,000 threshold for registration in England will not have been met. Through cost splitting, only a marginal amount of an organisation's expenditure may be identified as dedicated to its electoral activity. Even if such a strategy is used to avoid the national spending limits, a website may still be at risk of falling foul of the candidate spending limits. Once a general election has been called, third parties are limited to spending only £500 in support of a specific candidate. While in place for a short period of time, spending on a relatively low-cost website could be curbed by the local level limits.

Conclusion

Online campaigning is set to be a growth area. While much of the activity will not raise concerns about money in politics, further research should be undertaken, to consider how such activities are financed (if at all) and to be clear why so few organisations have registered so far, and in what circumstances they may be expected to register. In the meantime, the greatest regulatory challenge may be faced by old, rather than new, actors. The application of the third party limits to online activity is not just an issue for new media entities. It raises questions about the online activities of the traditional media, for example, where a newspaper or broadcaster also disseminates content over its website. Newspapers and broadcasters are exempt from the third party spending limits. The legislation does not, however, make any reference to websites run by such media entities, so it is unclear whether the exemption applies only to the printed version of the newspaper. A parallel issue can be found in relation to value added tax (VAT). While printed newspapers are exempt from VAT, digital versions of newspapers are not. The question is then whether political commentary and advocacy found in digital versions of newspapers should be subject to the limits on third party spending. If the digital publications are not exempt, difficult questions of cost splitting would have to be addressed to decide how much of the newspaper's spending has gone on electoral material and how much on its non-electoral content. After that question has been addressed, further cost splitting could take place to determine how much of the spending on election material has been made in relation to the print edition of the newspaper (which is exempt) and the digital version (if it is subject to the third party spending limits). In those cases where the newspaper produces content only for its digital/internet edition, that latter issue will not arise.

These difficulties could be avoided if the exemption were interpreted to extend to the online activities of print newspapers and broadcasters. Under such an interpretation, the costs of running a printed newspaper's website would also be subject to the exemption (this would mean both the re-publication of the print edition only, as well as the online-only material, as found in some newspapers' comment and blog sites). This approach does raise difficulties itself, insofar as it discriminates against other speakers. If newspaper websites are exempt from the third party spending limits, then other websites that publish political content may argue that they too should benefit from the exemption. There seems to be little reason in principle to limit the exemption to those media companies that have a printed edition of a newspaper as well as a digital edition, and not to those with only a digital edition. The danger in extending the exemption to all digital media outlets is that it could blow a large hole in the third party spending limits. Such an approach would allow interests groups, companies and other organisations to avoid spending limits by simply disseminating material through their own websites. These problems could be addressed by providing a more specific definition of an online newspaper for the purpose of the exemption. For example, the exemption could be applied to a category of 'digital newspapers', which could be defined by the frequency of publication and the types of issues covered. Distinguishing 'digital newspapers' from other online publications will be a challenge, given that most websites tend to be updated frequently and cover similar topics as newspapers.

While the current law has not caused problems so far, this is partly due to the fact that so few websites appear to be affected by the third party spending limits. If the limits were applied more strictly to the digital media, then the scope and application of the media exemption would need to be addressed. It is also the case more generally that (with the exception of the newspaper companies), third party spending has not been a major issue in the United Kingdom. This may be because most electoral spending is currently channelled through the political parties, and that the high spending limit applied to the parties has not encouraged the money to go to other organisations. It may also be the case that much independent activity in elections is not that expensive, for example, if it takes place through low-cost websites. The limited amount of third party spending recorded by the electoral commission could, however, reflect a more limited application of the spending controls. It is unclear whether the statutes are being construed narrowly, whether the activities of independent organisations go largely unmonitored, whether third parties are careful to avoid producing anything that could be seen as 'election material', or whether cost splitting means that the relevant thresholds are not met. This is an area that calls for further research. It seems reasonable to speculate, however, that tighter controls on contributions to or expenditure by political parties could lead to more rather than less third party expenditure as the opportunities for electoral advocacy increase with the rapid development of new technology.

Notes

1 Committee on Standards in Public Life, *The Funding of Political Parties in the United Kingdom*, Cm 4057–1, 1998, chs 6 and 10. On the Ecclestone affair, see K.D. Ewing, *The Cost of Democracy*, Oxford: Hart Publishing, 2007, ch 1.
2 See K. Ewing, *The Funding of Political Parties in Britain*, Cambridge: Cambridge University Press, 1987.
3 See now Representation of the People Act 1983, s. 76, as heavily amended since, most recently by the Political Parties Act 2009.
4 [1999] 2 Cr App R 253.
5 Ibid., at p. 255.
6 See now Communications Act 2003, s. 321. See further J. Rowbottom, *Democracy Distorted*, Cambridge: Cambridge University Press, 2010, pp. 202–205.
7 Cm 4057–1, 1998, op. cit., para. 10.28.
8 Ibid., para. 10.29.
9 See HC 163-I, 2006–2007, para. 89. See also the consideration of this issue by Sir Hayden Phillips in H. Phillips, *Strengthening Democracy: Fair and Sustainable Funding of Political Parties*, London: HMSO, 2007, ch 4. On the Hayden Phillips inquiry into party funding in the wake of the so-called cash for honours affair, see chapter 3 above.
10 See *Buckley* v. *Valeo*, 424 US 1 (1976). Other attempts to encourage the adoption of spending limits by incentives (so called Clean Election laws) have also been the subject of challenge. On the US position generally, see chapter 13 below (R. Hasen).
11 See *Australian Capital Television* v. *Commonwealth* (1992) 177 CLR 106. For comment, see K.D. Ewing, 'The Legal Regulation of Electoral Campaign Financing in Australia: A Preliminary Study' UWA Law Review, 1992 vol. 22; also K.D. Ewing, *Public Law*, 1993, 256.
12 For background, see K.D. Ewing, *Money, Politics and Law – A Study of Electoral Campaign Finance Reform in Canada*, Oxford: Oxford University Press, 1992.
13 PPERA, Part V ('Control of Campaign Expenditure').
14 PPERA, s. 72(2). Election purposes is defined to mean for a purpose of or in connection with promoting or procuring electoral success for the party or otherwise enhancing its standing or that of its candidates in connection with future relevant elections (s. 72(4)).
15 The number of seats contested is simply used as the basis for calculating the level of permitted expenditure, which need not be incurred in the seats in question. Moreover, the national spending limit so calculated is quite separate from the limit that applies to candidate spending, which is separately regulated.
16 PPERA, Sch 9, Part II. In practice the real limit is closer to £18.9 million, because the main parties do not contest the 18 Northern Irish seats. There are also separate limits applicable to European elections, Scottish Parliament elections, and elections to the Welsh and Northern Irish assemblies (ibid.). Additional rules deal with the situation where there are overlapping elections (Part III).
17 See http://registers.electoralcommission.org.uk/regulatory-issues/gbcampaignex.cfm?ec=%7Bts%20%272010%2D12%2D29%2015%3A11%3A39%27%7D.
18 This compares with 94.9 per cent, 95.3 per cent, and 23 per cent respectively in 2005: Ewing, *The Cost of Democracy*, p. 164.
19 The Labour Party had proposed that the cap should be set at £15 million, which the Committee thought was too low: Cm 4057-I, 1998, op cit, paras 10–71–10.73.

20 The Liberal Democrats were even less at £230,482.
21 See Sir Hayden Phillips, *The Review of the Funding of Political Parties – An Interim Assessment*, London: HMSO, 2006, p. 34.
22 See note 7 above.
23 H. Phillips, *Strengthening Democracy: Fair and Sustainable Funding of Political Parties*, op. cit., p. 14. Sir Hayden Phillips was otherwise sympathetic to the CASC proposal.
24 The danger is with fixed budgets, these activities would be quickly sidelined, and that each party would take on that persona of its rivals most calculated to secure electoral success. In other words, the danger is that resources would be directed exclusively to elections at the expense of everything else.
25 H. Phillips, *Strengthening Democracy: Fair and Sustainable Funding of Political Parties*, p. 13.
26 See chapter 10 below (S. Palmer).
27 Cm 4057-I, 1998, op. cit., para. 10.72.
28 See now Representation of the People Act 1983, s. 75. This too has been revised since, most importantly to deal with the decision of the European Court of Human Rights in *Bowman* v. *United Kingdom* (1998) 26 EHRR 1 where it was held that the existing limit in the 1983 Act breached article 10 of the ECHR. As a result of amendments made by PPERA, third parties may incur expenditure locally promoting or opposing a candidate to the tune of £500, but it must not be co-ordinated with others.
29 Cm 4057-I (1998), op. cit., paras 10.72–10.85.
30 PPERA, Part V ('Controls Relating to Third Party National Election Campaigns').
31 PPERA, s. 85(2).
32 Ibid., s. 85(8).
33 Ibid., s. 85(3).
34 Ibid., ss. 85(4), (10).
35 Strictly, if they want to spend less than £10,000 in England and £5,000 in each of the other three parts of the United Kingdom. So the controls would apply if the third party spent, say, £11,000 in England alone.
36 PPERA, s. 88.
37 Ibid., ss. 96–100.
38 Ibid., s. 94; Sch 10.
39 On UNISON, see chapter 3 above (K.D. Ewing).
40 Nevertheless, the returns must be accompanied by a declaration as to their accuracy by a responsible person (a term defined); it is a criminal offence to file a false return; and the returns are available for public inspection (PPERA, ss. 99, 100).
41 Controlled expenditure is defined to mean expenses incurred in relation to election material 'made available to the public at large': PPERA 2000, s. 85(2).
42 Ibid., s. 87(2). There was no corresponding exemption in referendum campaigns. But rather than treat this as a template for general and other elections, the response of the government has been to bring the referendum rules into line with s. 87(2) of PPERA. See Parliamentary Voting System and Constituencies Act 2011, and HC 437, 2010–2011, ch 2 (House of Commons Political and Constitutional Reform Committee) where the point is considered. See also HC 437, 2010–2011, Ev 182 (Submission by G. Orr and K.D. Ewing).
43 See http://registers.electoralcommission.org.uk/regulatory-issues/thirdpartycontexp.cfm.
44 For an analysis of third party activity at the 2005 election, see Ewing, *The Cost of Democracy*, pp. 163–166.
45 See Chapter 3 above (K.D. Ewing).
46 Respectively, IFAW in Action, Brian May, Political Animal Lobby Ltd, Searchlight Information Services, The Democratic Reform Company, Vote for A Change Ltd.
47 For an account of how in the 1940s the business lobby in the USA was provoked into

third party action by the intervention of others (mainly unions), see K.D. Ewing, 'The Legal Regulation of Campaign Financing in American Federal Elections' Cambridge Law Journal, 1988. vol. 47, 370.

48 The Electoral Commission, *Overview of non-party campaign material* (2010).

49 Ibid.

50 'Hewitt claims heighten lobbying row', *The Times*, 23 March 2010.

51 See discussion in Rowbottom, *Democracy Distorted*, pp. 119–120.

52 A. Williamson, 'Inside the Digital Campaign' in R. Gibson, A. Williamson, and S. Ward, *The internet and the 2010 election putting the small 'p' back in politics?*, London: Hansard Society, 2010.

53 D. Wring and S. Ward, 'The Media and the 2010 Campaign: the Television Election?', *Parliamentary Affairs*, 2010, vol. 63, 802.

54 www.leftfootforward.org/2010/05/vote-2010-an-election-reflection/.

55 PPERA, s. 85.

56 Ibid.

57 The Electoral Commission, *Overview of non-party campaign material*, 2010.

58 Ibid.

59 The words 'made available' suggest that the third party does not need actively to push the content to an audience. Most publicly accessible websites would appear to satisfy the words in s. 85.

6 Local parties, local money and local campaigns

Regulation issues

Ron Johnston and Charles Pattie

The regulation of British political party finance introduced in the Political Parties, Elections and Referendums Act, 2000 was both novel and partial.[1] It was novel because there had previously been virtually no regulation of how British political parties raised money, how much they obtained, and what they spent it on – even during election campaigns. The only regulation was of spending by candidates in the period immediately prior to a general election. It was partial, because its main focus, particularly with regard to election campaigns, paid little attention to local political parties, most of which serve individual Parliamentary constituencies. Transparent reporting of their income and expenditure was required by the new legislation (if either exceeded £25,000), including a separate register of every donation above a set threshold, but no limits were imposed on how much could be spent, or when, by those local parties.

The 2000 Act did, however, place a limit on the total amount that a national party could spend on campaigning during the 365 days immediately preceding an election. This total incorporated expenditure by a party's associated accounting units (most of which are local constituency parties) within the parent national party's campaign spending if it was promoting the party's cause generally, but excluded spending on their own candidates' campaigns.[2] The long-established limits on the amount that candidates could spend during election campaigns remained in place, unaltered.

The 2000 legislation – which included the creation of an Electoral Commission to oversee its implementation – was introduced as a consequence of an Inquiry undertaken by the Committee on Standards in Public Life following concerns about party finances.[3] Although the regulation it introduced marked a major innovation in political funding, it was soon deemed insufficient in its extent – not least with regard to the activities of local as opposed to national parties and also to whether spending should be capped for the entire inter-election period, rather than just for the year preceding a contest. Attempts were made to extend its scope, which it was hoped could be achieved through all-party agreement, but the efforts led by Sir Hayden Phillips foundered.[4] Subsequent legislation – the Political Parties and Elections Act 2009 – failed to address all of the issues that his report and many commentators considered important. Thus debates continue, and further legislation might ensue. The issue of local party finances and spending is part of those debates, the background to which is the subject of this chapter.

The regulation of local spending pre-2000

Until the 2009 legislation, at the sub-national level, the only limit on candidates' campaign expenditure referred to the period immediately before a general election – whose extent was not always certain but was generally taken to be from the date at which the local party formally adopted its candidate for the forthcoming election, which occurred after Parliament was dissolved.[5] (There have been separate provisions for expenditure at by-elections since 2000.) Furthermore, that regulation – which is still in force – referred not to political parties but to individual candidates (who may not be affiliated to a registered party: registration was introduced in the Registration of Political Parties Act 1998). Their agents are required to make a return of income received and expenditure incurred within 40 days of the election. Most candidates of the main political parties obtain the bulk of their income from their local party organisation, however, either as a direct grant or from a separate fund set up to raise money for the campaign.[6] Nevertheless, since the legislation refers only to expenditure undertaken to promote the candidate's election, this does not preclude other activity designed to promote a party's electoral prospects more generally.

The legislation that restricts candidates' expenditure dates back to the series of nineteenth-century acts designed to 'clean up' local campaigns, during which the 'treating' of voters by candidates involved large items of expenditure to 'buy' support in some constituencies.[7] The Corrupt and Illegal Practices Act 1883 inter alia imposed maximum campaign spending limits for each candidate, according to the constituency's size (number of electors) and nature (borough or county – i.e. urban or rural). All payments had to be authorised by the candidate's agent, and in addition the candidate could commit a further sum (to a maximum then of £100) on 'personal expenses'.

The system established in 1883 has remained largely unchanged since, apart from alterations to the amounts that could be spent. The regulation process was incorporated into the Representation of the People Act 1918 and has remained part of that core element in British electoral legislation ever since. During the following three decades, the general tenor of discussions regarding its operation involved reduction in the real-terms amount that could be spent, and at a 1944 Speaker's Conference a unanimous recommendation – enacted in the Representation of the People Act, 1949 – halved the maximum each candidate could spend.[8] That legislation introduced a formula to determine the spending maximum for each candidate.

- In a borough constituency: £450 + 1.5d (0.62p) per registered voter.
- In a county constituency: £450 + 2.0d (0.83p) per registered voter.

Constituencies are designated as borough or county according to their nature – basically their population density – by the Parliamentary Boundary Commissions during their regular reviews of all constituencies and this is very rarely controversial.[9]

This formula remained in place until 1970, when the baseline figure was increased to £750. For the October 1974 election it was increased again to £1,075, with the per voter multipliers set at 0.75p and 1.0p for borough and county constituencies, respectively. Substantial changes were made again in 1979 and 1983 during a period of rapid inflation (the baseline to £1,750 and £2,700, respectively, the borough multiplier to 1.5p and then 2.3p, and the county multiplier to 2.0p and 3.1p). Since then, increases have been introduced by Order in Council: the baseline for the 2005 and 2010 general elections was £7,150 and the two multipliers were 5p and 7p.

The 1949 Representation of the People Act specified the categories of expenditure for which reporting is necessary, and these (payments to agents and sub-agents; payments to clerks and messengers; payments for printing, advertising and stationery; payments to speakers for expenses; payments for rooms for meetings and for committee rooms; payments for postage and telegrams; and payments for miscellaneous matters – to be specified) remain the basic categories, alongside the candidate's personal expenditure, although expenditure on telephones has now been separated out. The majority of the reported expenditure has always been on printing, advertising and stationery, increasing from 67 per cent of the total in 1951 to 80 per cent by 1974.[10] In 1997 it comprised on average 71, 79, and 87 per cent of all Conservative, Labour and Liberal Democrat candidates' spending, respectively.[11] Candidates' reported personal expenditure averaged just £37 in 1951 and £65 in 1983.

Local spending and election outcomes

The money that UK Parliamentary candidates spend during their general election campaigns have thus largely gone on literature to promote their cause – basically, on posters and leaflets. Some of the latter were distributed to electors through the postal system – each candidate is allowed to send one item to each registered elector for free – and others by volunteers (mainly party members). Such promotional activity – raising the candidate's profile with the electorate and ensuring their awareness of the election – went alongside canvassing, traditionally carried out by the candidates and their supporters through face-to-face encounters (usually on the voters' doorsteps) aimed at identifying electors likely to vote for them. Their commitment could be followed up by further contact later in the campaign, especially on election day itself, when the list of believed supporters could be compared against a tally of those who had already visited the designated polling station. Apparent recalcitrant supporters could then be contacted and encouraged to get out and vote. Increasingly, the initial canvassing activity is undertaken by telephone, often from centres outwith the constituency and before the campaign starts, providing the dwindling band of local activists with a database to deploy as they plan their contacts before and on election day, focused on mobilising their party's known support in the locality.

But does such expenditure work: does local campaigning matter? From the 1950s on, as the mass media – especially TV – came to dominate many aspects of national political life it was argued (and not only in the UK: see Shin and Agnew)[12] that local campaigning was an increasingly fruitless exercise: voters were influenced by the national campaign and who they supported was not affected by contact with the local candidate's campaign. Thus, for example, Butler and Kavanagh dismissed such campaigning as 'little more than a ritual', as an irrelevant exercise providing party activists with something to do.[13] Kavanagh claimed that local campaigns could improve party morale, assist in the recruitment of new members and so create 'the conditions in which the party may more effectively pursue the goal of electoral success' but, nevertheless, he portrayed such campaigns as 'something of a confidence trick for candidates … if the local campaign could be terminated and replaced by a national constituency … the reality of British politics would not be changed much'.[14]

This view of the irrelevance of local campaigns has been challenged in recent decades by a series of studies using a range of indicators of local activity to show that 'Where we work, we win'.[15] One group, for example, has focused on constituency agents and the resources they deploy during the campaign;[16] a second has looked at the campaigning activity of political activists;[17] and a third has used the candidates' reported expenditure in each constituency.[18] All show the same pattern; the more intensive a party's campaign in a constituency, the better its performance there. Furthermore, the three indicators of activity are both related and complementary:[19] where parties campaign hard they get more votes – although challenger parties tend to get a greater return from their activity than does the incumbent party of government.[20]

All of these studies have been aggregate in nature, regressing one set of variables for British constituencies – party performance say – against another – such as party spending. Thus, the evidence for the impact of campaigning is circumstantial only – though strongly so. Other investigations have sustained those conclusions using data on individual voters gained from election surveys, however. Studies using British Election Study survey data, for example, have shown that individuals contacted by party *x* during the election campaign were more likely to vote for it than were those not contacted – although some, basically those interested in the election but not firmly committed to one of the parties before the campaign started, were more likely to be influenced by party *x*'s contact with them than were others.[21] In sum, the evidence is overwhelming: campaigning, especially well-targeted campaigning, matters.

Not surprisingly, the political parties are (increasingly) aware of this, and act accordingly. Under the UK electoral system, whether or not a large majority of the voters turn out on election day is of little immediate relevance to the parties because the outcome in the constituencies where they live is often a foregone conclusion: many seats are safe for one of them and a hopeless cause for the others. Thus the parties' campaigns focus on the marginal seats, where either victory or defeat is not almost certain and the successful mobilisation of a small number of additional supporters may make the difference as to which party's candidate prevails. In those constituencies not only are the local activists more involved and more money spent but increasingly the nature and intensity of the local campaign is strongly influenced, if not directed, by the parties' central offices.[22]

Campaigning methods have changed too, in part reflecting technological innovations and in part the lack of sufficient local party workers to undertake extensive canvassing; party membership is declining.[23] Increasing use is made of telephones to contact voters, from commercially operated centres that are not local, rather than traditional face-to-face contact. At first, it seemed that such contact had less impact on voters than the traditional mode[24] but recent evidence suggests that at the 2005 election it was more effective than face-to-face contact at mobilising support for Labour and the Liberal Democrats, though not for the Conservatives.[25]

The parties have also realised that just campaigning during the official period immediately prior to the election – of perhaps no more than six weeks – and, in effect, ignoring the voters, even their own supporters, for the rest of the time when a Parliament was sitting was not good public relations. If they wanted to mobilise support, especially in the marginal constituencies, then regular contact should surely pay off. This was clearly demonstrated in a case study of the Liberal Democrats in one constituency.[26] A wide range of activities is being undertaken in a large number of seats, and not only by new challengers making themselves known to their potential constituents. Long before the 2001 general election, for example, Labour encouraged its MPs with relatively small majorities to defend to spend more time in their constituencies and less in the House of Commons, where the government's large majority meant that their votes were not needed – and it worked; those who did so got a return when the votes were next counted.[27]

Assessing a local campaign's impact

Local campaigning is effective, therefore, and money – directly or indirectly – is important to that effort. Hence, should the amount spent be regulated? Three related reasons can be adduced for doing so. The first is that its impact is sufficient to make a difference; the second is that unless it is regulated, one party may get an unreasonable advantage over others; and the third is that if individual donors can give large sums to assist a candidate's election, this could be seen as them potentially buying influence if that individual becomes an MP (such influence being achieved either directly through the MP or indirectly from the party, as a reward for supporting her/his election). The last of these cannot be addressed here, but data can be assembled to indicate the validity of the first two arguments.

As already indicated, the more a party spends campaigning in a constituency, the more votes – on average – its candidate will accrue. But how many more? In 1997, for example, the Conservatives got 3.1 extra votes for every pound spent on constituency campaigns, whereas Labour got 5.2.[28] If both candidates spent

£9,000 in an average constituency where the incumbent was not standing for re-election (the maximum for a county constituency with 70,000 electors then was £12,050), this would mean a difference between the two of some 9,000 votes favouring Labour. These estimates assume that all voters are equally susceptible to the candidates' blandishments. Many are not, however, and will vote for the same party they supported at the previous contest regardless of the campaign. Thus, of more interest is the marginal benefit from each additional pound spent, taking into account the result of the 1992 general election: this was 0.7 extra votes per pound spent by the Conservatives and 2.1 for Labour.

The sums spent are sufficient to influence the result in a number of seats, therefore, as simulations have shown.[29] The benefits to be gained from an intensive local campaign were clearly demonstrated in several constituencies at the 2005 general election. A small number of major donors – notably Bearwood Corporate Services (owned by former Conservative Party national treasurer and later Deputy Chairman, Lord Ashcroft), the Midlands Industrial Council, and Lord Leonard Steinberg – gave some £1.25 million to selected local parties in marginal constituencies in the years leading up to the election. This additional money was used to boost the amount spent on the candidates' local campaigns there: if it increased Conservative spending by 20 per cent compared to the average of all constituencies in similar situations, then this would have yielded some 1,890 extra votes – sufficient for the party to win a number of seats (such as The Wrekin) that otherwise Labour might well have retained.[30] Because most of this 'extra' money was spent before the commencement of the official campaign, it was not subject to the legal limits on local candidates' expenditure discussed above; any such donations thus exploited a loophole in the then-current legislation to the benefit of candidates with access to such resources.

The financial health of local parties

Money matters, therefore, and increasingly large sums are involved. During the inter-electoral period 2001–2005, for example, the total sum donated to local parties in England and Wales and reported to the Electoral Commission was £5.940 million for the Conservatives, £3.679 million for Labour and £2.918 million for the Liberal Democrats. (All donations to national political parties of £5,000 or more – £7,500 after 1 January 2010 – must be separately reported, as must those from the same donor which sum to £5,000 – now £7,500 – or more during any quarterly period; for accounting units within those parties the reporting threshold was £1,000 before 2010 and £1,500 thereafter.) Much of this money – 55 per cent in the Conservative's case – was donated in the final 12 months before the 2005 election. The Conservatives' main sources were individuals and corporate bodies; Labour's were the trades unions and local party organisations; and the Liberal Democrats got most of their donations from individuals (including their own local government councillors) and local party organisations many of which – as with the other two parties – undertook a wide range of fundraising activities, among both their membership and the wider population.

The apparent efficacy of activity during what has been termed the 'long campaign' has been followed up during the 2005–2010 Parliament by the Conservative Party. Since the 2005 election, rather than make grants to individual constituency parties, Lord Ashcroft has been working through the central party organisation, which established a separate department under his direction that, among other activities, made grants to local parties to fund campaigning activities: in 2007–2008 his company, Bearwood Corporate Services Limited made cash donations totalling £575,000 and non-cash donations to the value of £2,723,379.[31] Scrutiny of those local parties' annual accounts – all 'accounting units' affiliated to a political party must lodge a copy of their audited accounts with the Electoral Commission if either their income or their expenditure exceeds £25,000 in the calendar year – indicates the extent of this activity.[32]

As far as can be identified from the copies of those accounts available on the Electoral Commission website, 60 such grants were made during 2007, totalling £680,620 and ranging in size from £1,629 to £48,549: the median grant was £9,506 and the inter-quartile range £3,175–£17,232.[33] Of those grants, 55 were to individual constituency parties, with a median of £8,201. The other five were to local parties covering more than one constituency: four covered two each, and the other covered three. In 2008, 72 such grants were identified in the local party accounts, totalling £803,301: the median grant was £9,564, the minimum and maximum were £1,500 and £42,497, and the inter-quartile range £5,536–£16,221. Of those grants, 62 were to individual constituency parties; among the other ten, as well as five to parties covering two constituencies, others went to larger organisations, including the West Midlands regional party, which obtained a grant of £26,849.

These monies were spent by the local parties on campaigning: some reported very substantial increases compared to previous years in their expenditure on stationery, printing and postage; others just reported spending large sums – in many cases more than the grant received – on 'campaigning', without any further details. In some cases, the annual report attached to the accounts indicated that part of the money had been spent on surveys and in others the description of the year's work reported activities designed to increase a new candidate's visibility to the electorate.

Most of that Conservative money has, not surprisingly, been focused on marginal seats where the next election would be won or lost. A few were very marginal seats that the Conservatives won in 2005 and were estimated to remain so after the redistribution of constituencies implemented in 2007. Most, however, were seats that the Conservatives need to win from other parties in order to form a government after the 2010 general election – and preliminary analyses suggest that the Conservatives gained more seats from Labour (though not the Liberal Democrats) in constituencies where Conservative local parties received target grants than in those where they did not.[34]

Campaigning grants to local Liberal Democrat parties were also reported in their accounts for 2007 and 2008. Some were from the party's central office; others were from the Association of Liberal Democrat Councillors, which are specifically for local election campaigns, although these are often closely linked to the national situation. Only 54 separate Liberal Democrat local parties made returns of their accounts to the Electoral Commission in 2007 (along with 32 other, multi-constituency parties), compared to 352 for the Conservatives; of the 54, 35 reported receiving one or both of the grant types, averaging £10,738 – the smallest was only £492 and the largest £31,977. In 2008, 85 local parties made a return to the Electoral Commission (the comparable figure for the Conservatives was 334), with 71 including a campaigning grant among their income. Those grants averaged £13,132 and most of the money was spent on materials – such as regular newsletters – designed to keep the party and its activities (especially in places where it was in control of the local government) in the public eye.

Whereas the Conservatives and the Liberal Democrats have clearly been targeting money on marginal constituencies through grants to their local parties, there is little evidence that this has also been the case with Labour. Indeed, the financial situation of its local parties looks very weak. In 2005 – the year of the last general election – only 42 reported income and/or expenditure greater than £25,000 to the Electoral Commission (compared to 252 Conservative and 63 Liberal Democrat local parties: Johnston and Pattie, 2008b), and in 2007 and 2008 the figures for Labour were just 29 and 42. None of these reported grants from the central party for campaigning purposes, so if the party was centrally funding local campaigns it was not doing so through the local party infrastructure. A September 2009 press report indicated that 'Labour is withholding campaign money from lazy MPs and candidates in marginal seats who are not showing an appetite to fight the [next] election'.[35] There is no evidence that any such money was being transferred to local parties in either 2007 or 2008; indeed, a later article suggested that the central party would be raiding the local parties' coffers to fund the national campaign.[36]

Few local parties are wealthy, therefore, and most have only very small reserves that could be drawn upon to sustain an expensive local campaign, let alone contribute substantially to the national effort. Almost all indicate the size and nature of their reserves in their annual accounts. Among the 320 local Conservative parties that provided such data in 2008, the median level of reserves was £57,206; the range was from only £19 to £1,540,575, with an inter-quartile range of £23,868–£131,730. Almost all of those with assets exceeding £100,000 had major fixed assets – in most cases buildings from which they obtained (substantial in some cases) rental income. This enabled most of them to employ a full- or part-time agent and to engage in substantial amounts of electioneering and other campaigning that other local parties had to raise money for – through donations and fundraising events[37] – supplemented in many marginal seats by grants from the central party.

Of the 84 local Liberal Democrat parties in 2008, the average level of reserves was just £16,132; for almost all of those with substantial sums in reserve these are largely fixed assets, buildings on which they obtain rental income. The same situation also applied to the small number of local Labour Parties with substantial reserves.

There are substantial differences in the financial status of local accounting units across the three main parties, therefore, with many more Conservative Parties turning over £25,000 or more each year. Even so, most local Conservative Parties have insufficient funding to spend more than a few thousand pounds on the 'long campaign' each year and central party grants are necessary to ensure substantial activity. This is even more the case with the Liberal Democrats, and the overall picture for local Labour Parties suggests that few are financially able to sustain continuous campaigning: as with the other two parties, the ones that are able to – without central party grants – are those that, largely through historical accident, have substantial investments (in most cases commercial buildings) from which rents provide substantial supplementary income.[38] There is also considerable variation in the volume and value of donations received by local accounting units. Between 2007 and 2009, for example, 420 Labour accounting units received a total of £3.2 million in registered donations (i.e. of £1,000 or more), compared to 249 Liberal Democrat accounting units, whose total income was £3.4 million, and 314 Conservative units, whose total income from such sources was £6.5 million. In the first quarter of 2010 – in the build-up to the general election – the numbers of accounting units receiving recorded donations and their total value, was: Labour, 249 and £940,000; Liberal Democrats, 103 and £448,000; and Conservatives, 202 and £1.5 million.[39]

There has been considerable debate over the growing Conservative practice of funding 'long campaign' activities in selected constituencies, not least during the negotiations conducted by Sir Hayden Phillips. Labour, in particular, argued that this should be regulated because their opponents were gaining an advantage. The Conservative response was that opposition parties were disadvantaged in constituencies held by their opponents because MPs are not only better able to get local visibility through their activities there but also because they can use their Parliamentary resources to promote themselves to their constituents. These have long included a 'House stationery and postage' allowance, some of which may have been used to communicate with constituents; although members couldn't use it for general postal shots, responding to individual contacts helped visibility with the electorate.[40] However, in 2007 MPs voted to create another allowance for 'Communications Expenditure' of up to £10,000 per annum which could be deployed, inter alia, for 'regular reports and constituency newsletters; questionnaires, surveys and petitions' as well as distribution costs and establishing/maintaining websites – although such expenditure should be solely for informing 'constituents about your work as a Member' and neither 'material which could be construed as campaign expenditure' nor 'party political material'.[41] In the first year of the availability of this allowance, the median expenditure by an MP was £8,144, with a range from £0 to £21,587 (members can vire up to ten per cent of the staffing allowance – a maximum of £103,812 in 2009 – to the communications allowance). All of the receipts for this expenditure are available online,[42] and illustrate its use for mail shots, newspaper advertisements, surveys and other activities. Analyses of MPs' expenditure in 2004–2005 (i.e. immediately prior to the general election but before introduction of the communications allowance) showed that those seeking re-election spent more on stationery and postage than those who were not, and that the more that Conservative candidates (but not those of the other two parties) spent, the better their performance at the 2005 election. With more to spend in the three years prior to the 2010 contest, this could have a significant impact on re-election chances.[43]

Regulating local expenditure?

The growing importance of the 'long campaign', especially to the Conservatives and Liberal Democrats, and the amounts spent on contacting voters in the years, let alone months, prior to a general election was one of the issues that divided the parties during the discussions that led to Sir Hayden Phillips' failure to obtain all-party agreement on the regulation of party finances and funding.[44] Some wanted a limit on parties' spending – including their local accounting units[45] – at all times, with either an annual maximum or a maximum for a full inter-election period.[46]

Given the lack of agreement, no resolution of the issue regarding regulation of 'long campaign' expenditure was achieved. Instead, limits to what is termed 'pre-candidacy' spending have been added to the Representation of the People Act 1983, applying only to the period after a Parliament has been sitting for more than 55 months (i.e. they apply to the last five months only of a Parliament that lasts for its full five years).[47] These regulations (section 21 of the Political Parties and Elections Act 2009) limit the amount of spending between the end of the 55th month after a Parliament first sat and the date at which the candidate is formally adopted for the election to be held after the Parliament's dissolution, as follows:

> The maximum sum that a candidate can spend is
>
> > In a county constituency, £25,000 plus 7p for every entry in the register of electors
> > In a borough constituency, £25,000 plus 5p for every entry in the register of electors
>
> This maximum only applies if Parliament is dissolved in the final (60th) month of its term. If the dissolution comes earlier, then the maximum is reduced to the following percentage:

Table A

Dissolution month	*Percentage*
56th	60
57th	70
58th	80
59th	90

Thus, in a county constituency with 70,000 electors, the maximum a candidate could spend would be £29,900 if Parliament runs for its full term, reducing to £17,940 if the general election is called in the 57th month. This is additional to the amount that candidates can spend once they are formally adopted, when the limits set by the Representation of the People Act 1983 apply – which in 2005 and 2010 was £7,150 plus 7p for every elector on the roll (£12,050 in an average county constituency with 70,000 electors).[48]

That introduction of limits to candidate spending in the final months of a Parliament that runs for its full term is almost certainly an interim measure only. The revival of local campaigning and the increasing focus given by central party organisations to marginal constituencies have brought the issue of regulating such expenditure firmly onto the political agenda – especially since several Labour MPs claimed that they lost their seats at the 2005 contest as a result of the grants to Conservative constituency parties made by Bearwood Corporate Services and other interested groups and individuals. The extension of that practice since 2007 with central parties (especially the Conservatives) making large grants to local accounting units to promote their candidate's cause at the next election has further focused attention on the issue. Arguments have been made that expenditure by accounting units should be regulated either on an annual or a 'whole Parliament' basis – as indeed, it is also argued, should expenditure by national parties. (Under the Political Parties, Elections and Referendums Act, Schedule 9, Part II, 2, only campaign expenditure by national parties – including that spent by local accounting units that is relevant to the national campaign – in the year prior to an election is regulated, to a maximum of £30,000 multiplied by the number of constituencies contested. In the UK, which had 632 constituencies at the 2010 general election, the maximum that a party could spend was just under £19 million.[49])

Several problems would arise if regulation were to be introduced for sub-national accounting units for either the full inter-election period or some longer period than currently included in the relevant legislation – the Representation of the People Act 1983 and the Political Parties and Elections Act 2009. The first is the distinction between spending by a candidate and spending by an accounting unit – such as a local party. Both items of current legislation refer to the candidate only and not also to the local party, reflecting that the original late-nineteenth century legislation identified no role for local parties – if they existed; all campaigning was done by the candidate, and virtually all of it in the few weeks immediately preceding a contest. That is no longer the case. Some local parties – especially, it has been shown here, some local Conservative and Liberal Democrat parties in marginal constituencies – were involved in substantial campaigning preparing for the 2010 general election as much as three years before it need be called (as was the Labour Party until recently, notably prior to the 1997 general election). Although much of that campaigning and related activity was, directly or indirectly, promoting a candidate's cause, not all of it was – such as canvasses intended to identify likely supporters irrespective of candidacy. Even during the defined campaign period – either after the candidate has been adopted under the Representation of the People Act 1983 regulations, or in the pre-candidacy period defined in the regulations included in the Political Parties and Elections Act 2009 – a local unit may continue campaigning activity on behalf of the party generally rather than of its candidate. (Guidance issued by the Electoral Commission in 2007 notes that distinguishing whether expenditure should be returned against a candidate's total is not straightforward, but concludes that 'parties should consider whether the material promotes or refers to a specific/local candidate. Where an item promotes a candidate or candidates, it is likely that the expenditure should be treated as candidates' expenses'.[50] The guidance document for the 2010 general election – referred to in note 48 – states in section 5.12 that 'You may have to split expenses between your own campaign and other local campaigns, or with your party's regional or national campaign', with subsequent paragraphs illustrating the issues involved.)

It may be that, given the contemporary situation, expenditure by candidates and their local parties should be combined, within a maximum that can be spent on any campaigning during a specified period. Such legislation would have to ensure that it did not disadvantage independent candidates not associated with any of the registered parties, however. There would also be problems because local accounting units are also involved with campaigns for other elections that vary both geographically and temporally. All could be involved in European Parliament elections for example, but only some in the campaigns for elections to the National Assembly of Wales, the Northern Ireland Assembly, and the Scottish Parliament. And although all could be involved in local government election campaigns, the frequency of these varies; in some parts of England, for example, elections are held in three years out of four whereas in others they are held only quadrennially. Regulating for such variation would be complex.

An associated problem comes with the definition of a local accounting unit. As noted above, the existing legislation applies to parties with some form of hierarchical structure of accounting units operating under/within the national organisation: among the three main UK political parties almost all of these are local and many if not most of them are constituency-based local branch organisations but there are others, such as a party's youth wing. There may, however, be other organisations committed to a party's cause but not formally affiliated with it. Some can be identified through the local party annual accounts discussed earlier. In several parts of England (Gloucestershire, Oxfordshire and Hampshire, for example) local parties undertake little or no campaigning and other activity themselves according to their annual accounts and reports: they raise money in the usual ways (through subscriptions and various fundraising events and activities) and transfer much of it to another, usually multi-constituency, organisation. As those organisations do not make returns to the Electoral Commission – although their income and expenditure certainly exceeds £25,000 in each calendar year – they are clearly not formally affiliated to the party concerned, but it is assumed that they undertake campaigning and other activities on behalf of the party's candidates there.[51]

Such organisations ought to be regulated under the legislation that covers the activities of 'third parties' – bodies not affiliated with individual parties but which undertake activities aimed at either promoting or attacking political causes associated with a particular party. This comes under the category of 'controlled expenditure' in Part VI, Section 85 (2) of the *Political Parties, Elections and Referendums Act*, which covers election material 'made available to the public at large or any section of the public' designed to promote the standing or procure electoral success for one or more of the registered political parties. Under Schedule 10 of that Act, such controlled expenditure by a registered 'third party' should not exceed £793,500 in England, £108,000 in Scotland, £60,000 in Wales and £27,000 in Northern Ireland during the 365-day period immediately prior to a general election. None of the bodies identified in the local party accounts can be found in the Electoral Commission's register of third parties, however.[52] Many other bodies campaign in a variety of ways that implicitly, if indirectly, promotes the cause of one party (or even candidate) over another[53] – explicit campaigning against a candidate is covered by the regulations, however.

Expenditure by third parties promoting a particular candidate has long been regulated under various versions of the Representation of the People Act. This was replaced in the Political Parties, Elections and Referendums Act (Section 131; with an ambiguity removed by Section 25 of the Electoral Administration Act 2006) by a regulation that limited spending which either promotes or disparages a particular candidate in a general election to £500 – although there was no requirement for returns to the Electoral Commission of such expenditure (unless it was undertaken on behalf of the candidate's agent).

Finally, there is the potential problem of double-counting. If both the national party and its local accounting units are to be capped in the amounts that they can spend, either during a specified period prior to an election (as with the pre-candidacy allowances) or throughout a Parliament's lifetime, then intra-party transfers could count against both. This might be circumvented by having a single maximum that could be spent by the party and its accounting units together.

Conclusions

Relatively little attention has been paid in recent debates about party funding in the UK to constituency and other local units within the national parties. These are key to the organisation of a significant component of general election campaigns in the Parliamentary constituencies – the 'marginal or target seat strategies' – as well as campaigns for local government elections. Indeed, their significant role in general election campaigning has been extended during the last three decades as the national parties have realised the importance of mobilising support in those marginal constituencies where an election overall can be won or lost. During the 1950s–1960s, when turnout was high and the competition for seats dominated by just two parties – Conservative and Labour – local campaigning declined in apparent importance: the national campaign, fought through the mass media, was considered sufficient to mobilise a party's support. But as abstention rates and competition from other parties increased, it was realised that this was insufficient. The Liberal Democrats (and their predecessor Liberals) built their electoral renaissance on strong local campaigning in particular constituencies, sustained by success in local government elections there and/or Parliamentary by-elections; the Labour Party built on that experience from the 1990s on but is having difficulty sustaining the effort in many localities as membership has dwindled; and the Conservatives – which until recently had been more able to rely on high levels of turnout from their supporters without much effort from the party – are now building a very strong, centrally directed local campaigning component into their overall strategy.

This growing importance of local campaigning – whose intensity is clearly linked to the success of parties undertaking it – raises issues of regulation paralleling those that have been partially addressed during the last decade with regard to national party organisations. Some regulation has been introduced but at its core is a fundamental problem – virtually all of it applies to candidates only and not also to parties: the amount that the latter can raise and spend within their defined territory (in most cases, a Parliamentary constituency) is unconstrained, provided that they file annual accounts if their turnover exceeds a certain threshold and all large external donations are separately declared – as long as they do not promote a defined candidate's cause either in the last few weeks or, if a Parliament runs for its full five-year course, the last five months before a general election. Instead of creating a total new regulation regime with the 2000 Political Parties, Elections and Referendums Act and its successors, Parliament instead legislated for a new set of regulations relating to parties and their local accounting units which were superimposed upon, rather than integrated with, the Victorian legislation regulating candidates' expenditure, which is obsolescent in the context of modern campaigning strategies and methods.

Such money expended on local campaigns – either by the party organisation or its candidates – has an impact on election outcomes. This research finding strengthens some claims that party finances should be more tightly regulated than is currently the case – especially, it is claimed, because some parties are better able to raise money for such campaigns than others. Although it is unlikely that the amounts donated to local parties and spent promoting their candidates would generate the sort of abuse that some associate with very heavily funded campaigns (as in the United States),[54] nevertheless – as has been recognised by a range of commentators and also within some of the political parties – greater regulation appears desirable, associated with greater powers and resources for the Electoral Commission to monitor such financial activity. As we have shown here, this will involve greater clarity about means and ends than that which characterises the current legislative framework.

Notes

1 On the Act's origins, see K.D. Ewing, *The Cost of Democracy: Party Funding and Modern British Politics*, Oxford: Hart Publishing, 2007.

2 This clause thus prevents parties from making large grants to their local units to spend

on the national campaigns that would otherwise fall outwith the national cap on expenditure during the prescribed period.

3 Committee on Standards in Public Life, *The Funding of Political Parties*, London: HMSO, Cm 4057–1, 1997.

4 H. Phillips, *The Review of the Funding of Political Parties: an Interim Assessment*, London: HMSO, 2006; H. Phillips, *Strengthening Democracy: Fair and Sustainable Funding of Political Parties*, London: HMSO, 2007.

5 The situation is clarified in the Election Administration Act 2006, which (para. 27) defines election expenses as 'any expenses incurred at any time … which is used for the purposes of the candidate's election after the date when he becomes a candidate at the election'.

6 R. Johnston, I. MacAllister and C. Pattie, 'The funding of constituency party general election campaigns in Great Britain', *Environment and Planning C: Government and Policy*, 1999, vol. 17, 391–409; R. Johnston and C. Pattie, 'The financial health of political parties in English constituencies, 2004–2005', *Journal of Legislative Studies*, 2008, vol. 14, 500–516.

7 C. O'Leary, *The Elimination of Corrupt Practices in British Elections 1868–1911*, Oxford: Oxford University Press, 1962; C. Seymour, *Electoral Reform in England and Wales*, Newton Abbot: David and Charles, 1950 (first published, 1913). Some seats – especially 'rotten boroughs' with very few electors – were 'bought' by people wishing either to become MPs themselves or to control who did: Lord Caledon, for example, is reported to have 'bought' the Old Sarum seat in 1804 for £66,000 (£2.4 million today) and his relatives represented it until the 1832 Great Reform Act. In contests for the two Wiltshire seats, one candidate was reported to have spent £32,000 (£1.3 million today) in 1818 and another £43,000 (£2.4 million).

8 (On the history of this legislation see R. Johnston, *Money and Votes: Constituency Campaign Spending and Election Results*, London: Croom Helm, 1987; M. Pinto-Duschinsky, *British Political Finance 1830–1980*, Washington DC: American Enterprise Institute, 1981; M. Pinto-Duschinsky, 'Trends in British political funding', *Parliamentary Affairs*, 1985, vol. 38, 328–347.

9 See D. Rossiter, R. Johnston and C. Pattie, *The Boundary Commissions: Redrawing the UK's map of Parliamentary Constituencies*. Manchester: Manchester University Press, 1999. The *House of Commons (Redistribution of Seats) Act 1949* (subsequently amended, though not with respect to this issue) requires each Commission to recommend whether 'each constituency … should be a county constituency or a borough constituency'. Such designations are including in the names for each constituency in the Commissions' provisional and final recommendations.

10 Johnston, *Money and Votes.*

11 Johnston, MacAllister and Pattie, 'The funding of constituency party general election campaigns in Great Britain'.

12 M. Shin and J. Agnew, *Berlusconi's Italy: Mapping Contemporary Italian Politics*, Philadelphia: Temple University Press, 2008.

13 D. Butler and D. Kavanagh, *The British General Election of 1987*, London: Macmillan, 1988. See also D. Butler and D. Kavanagh, *The British General Election of 1992*, London: Macmillan, 1992.

14 D. Kavanagh, *Constituency Electioneering in Britain*, London: Longman, 1970, p. 80 and p. 111.

15 D. Cutts, '"Where we work we win": a case study of local Liberal Democrat campaigning', *Journal of Elections, Public Opinion and Parties*, 2006, vol. 16, 221–242.

16 D. Denver, and G. Hands, *Modern Constituency Electioneering: Local Campaigning in the 1992 General Election*, London: Frank Cass, 1997; J. Fisher and D. Denver, 'From foot-slogging to call centres and direct mail: a framework for analysing the development of district-level campaigning', *European Journal of Political Research*, 2008, vol. 47, 794–826; J. Fisher and D. Denver 'Evaluating the electoral effects of

traditional and modern modes of constituency campaigning in Britain 1992–2005', *Parliamentary Affairs*, 2009, vol. 62, 196–210; Fisher, Chapter 7 in this volume.

17 P. Seyd and P. Whiteley, *Labour's Grassroots: the Politics of Party Membership*, Oxford: The Clarendon Press, 1992; P. Whiteley, P. Seyd, and J. Richardson, *True Blues: the Politics of the Conservative Party*, Oxford: The Clarendon Press, 1994; P. Whiteley, and P. Seyd, 'Party election campaigning in Britain: the Labour Party', *Party Politics*, 2003, vol. 9, 637–652.

18 Johnston, *Money and Votes*; R. Johnston and C. Pattie, *Putting Voters in their Place: Geography and Elections in Great Britain*, Oxford: Oxford University Press, 2006.

19 Johnston and Pattie, *Putting Voters in their Place*; C. Pattie, P. Whiteley, R. Johnston and P. Seyd, 'Measuring local campaign effects: Labour Party constituency campaigning at the 1987 British general election', *Political Studies*, 1994, vol. 42, 469–479.

20 R. Johnston and C. Pattie, 'How much does a vote cost? Incumbency and the impact of campaign spending at English general elections', *Journal of Elections, Parties and Public Opinion*, 2008, vol. 18, 129–152; C. Pattie and R. Johnston, 'Still talking but is anybody listening? The changing face of constituency campaigning in Britain, 1997–2005', *Party Politics*, 2009, vol. 15, 411–434.

21 C. Pattie and R. Johnston 'Talking to the converted or reaching out to the uncommitted. Who do political campaigns influence?', *Journal of Political Marketing*, 2011, vol. 10.

22 D. Denver and G. Hands, 'Labour's targeted constituency campaigning: nationally directed or locally produced?', *Electoral Studies*, 2004, vol. 23, 709–726; J. Fisher, D. Denver, E. Fieldhouse, D. Cutts and A. Russell, 'Constituency campaigning in 2005: ever more centralization?', in D. Wring, J. Green, R. Mortimore and S. Atkinson (eds), *Political Communications: the General Election Campaign of 2005*, Basingstoke: Palgrave Macmillan, 2007.

23 Johnston and Pattie, 'The financial health of political parties in English constituencies, 2004–2005'; Fisher, Chapter 7 in this volume.

24 C. Pattie and R. Johnston, 'Hanging on the telephone? Doorstep and telephone canvassing at the British general election of 1997', *British Journal of Political Science*, 2003, vol. 33, 303–322.

25 Pattie and Johnston, 'Talking to the converted or reaching out to the uncommitted'.

26 D. Cutts, 'Continuous campaigning and election outcomes: the Liberal Democrats in Bath', *Political Geography*, 2006, vol. 25, 72–88.

27 R. Johnston, P. Cowley, C. Pattie and M. Stuart, 'Voting in the House or wooing the voters at home: Labour MPs and the 2001 general election campaign', *Journal of Legislative Studies*, 2002, vol. 8, 9–22.

28 All of the material presented here is taken from R. Johnston and C. Pattie, 'How much does a vote cost? Incumbency and the impact of campaign spending at English general elections', *Journal of Elections, Parties and Public Opinion*, 2008, vol. 18, 129–152.

29 R. Johnston and C. Pattie, 'The effectiveness of constituency campaign spending at recent general elections', in House of Commons Session 1992–1993 Home Affairs Committee *Funding of Political Parties: Minutes of Evidence and Memoranda of Evidence*, London: HMSO, Cm. 726, 1995, pp. 177–187.

30 R. Johnston and C. Pattie, 'Funding local parties in England and Wales: donations and constituency campaigns', *British Journal of Politics and International Relations*, 2007, vol. 9, 365–395.

31 These data are taken from the Electoral Commission's website register of donations. The description of the nature of all of the non-cash donations is 'Consultancy focus groups opinion research printing and related costs'. A further £156,971 of non-cash donations had been recorded in the months January–October 2009. In addition, the party received £268,000 in cash donations and £125,120 in non-cash during the same period from Ms Susan Anstey – who is Lord Ashcroft's wife.

32 The Labour MP for one marginal seat claimed in a letter to *The Guardian* (29 May 2009) that 'a tsunami of Ashcroft money … has engulfed my Pendle constituency … the Conservatives are on course to spend £250,000 here'. See also his website where he claims that 'Transfer of money from the central Party organisation to a constituency are secret and do not have to be disclosed' (www.gordonprenticemp.com/index.php/reportingto-you/campaigns/buying-the-election). The accounts of the Pendle Conservative Party returned to the Electoral Commission show grants from Conservative Central Office of just under £20,000 in each of 2007 and 2008. Such grants are not disclosed – either separately or in aggregate – in the central party's accounts deposited with the Electoral Commission available at www.electoralcommission.org.uk/__data/assets/pdf_file/0010/62299/SoA-Index.pdf.

33 Because of the substantial changes to constituency boundaries in many parts of the country, which required the re-constitution of constituency parties, data for 2006 and earlier are not readily compared for any of the parties. It is, however, very unlikely that many grants aimed at preparing for the next election were made before 2007.

34 R. Johnston and C. Pattie, 'The local campaigns and the outcome' in J. Bartle and N. Allen (eds), *Britain at the Polls 2010*, London: SAGE Publications, 2010.

35 www.timesonline.co.uk/tol/news/politics/article6854512.ece.

36 www.timesonline.co.uk/tol/news/politics/article6857706.ece.

37 see Johnston and Pattie, 'How much does a vote cost? Incumbency and the impact of campaign spending at English general elections'.

38 Some record substantial income from the MP representing the constituency, in the form of rent for premises and payment for secretarial and other services.

39 All of the data reported here are taken from the registers on the Electoral Commission's website: www.electoralcommission.org.uk/party-finance.

40 R. Johnston and C. Pattie, 'MPs expenditure and general election campaigns: do incumbents benefit from contacting their constituents?', *Political Studies*, 2009, vol. 57, 580–591.

41 Details can be found in the House of Commons *The Green Book: a Guide to Members' Allowances* (July 2009), available at www.parliament.uk/documents/upload/GreenBook.pdf.

42 At http://mpsallowances.parliament.uk/mpslordsandoffices/hocallowances/allowances-by-mp/.

43 The Committee on Standards in Public Life (2009) recommended in November 2009 that this allowance be discontinued, but because legislation is required for that to be achieved, it did not take place before the 2010 general election.

44 see Phillips, *Strengthening Democracy: Fair and Sustainable Funding of Political Parties*, p. 14.

45 Accounting units are defined in the *Political Parties, Elections and Referendums Act 2000* – section 26, 2(b) – as 'constituent or affiliated organisations each of which is to be responsible for its own financial affairs and transactions'.

46 In the past the latter has been difficult to define because many British Parliaments do not run for their full five-year term. The decision of the Cameron administration elected in 2010 to have fixed-term Parliaments of five years, unless the House of Commons votes by a 55 per cent or more majority to request a dissolution from the monarch, will remove the uncertainties for party treasurers associated with the Prime Minister's former ability to request a dissolution at any time.)

47 Such an extension of the regulation of candidates' expenditure to the four months preceding an election was proposed by the Electoral Commission, but not included in the *Electoral Administration Act 2006* because – according to Phillips (*The Review of the Funding of Political Parties: an Interim Assessment*, p. 41) – 'of practical concerns over finding election agents for the four-month period and uncertainty as to when the four-month period would start'.

48 The full requirements were set out for candidates and their agents at the 2010 general

election in the Electoral Commission's December 2009 document *Guidance for Candidates and Agents*, www.electoralcommission.org.uk/__data/assets/pdf_file/0006/83337/UKPGE-C-and-A-Final-web.pdf.

49 Phillips, *Strengthening Democracy: Fair and Sustainable Funding of Political Parties* argued that this limit should be extended to the full inter-election period, as also did the House of Commons Constitutional Affairs Committee, *Party Funding*, London: HMSO,2006.

50 We could not locate this document on the Commission's website. It is referred to in notes on election expenses prepared by the House of Commons Library available at www.parliament.uk/topics/Election-expenditure.htm.

51 In 2008, the six Conservative constituency parties in Gloucestershire, according to their accounts filed with the Electoral Commission, transferred £319,670 to 'Gloucestershire Conservatives': the sums ranged from £23,700 (from Gloucester constituency) to £134,500 (from The Cotswolds). Gloucestershire Conservatives has an uninformative website at www.gloucestershireconservatives.co.uk/.

52 This register can be found at http://registers.electoralcommission.org.uk/regulatory-issues/regthirdparties.cfm?ec=%7Bts%20%272009%2D10%2D07%20 16%3A53%3A54%27%7D.

53 As an example of such expenditure, *The Times* carried on 3 May 2010 a full-page advertisement claiming that 'A Hung Parliament means a weak Government' placed by the Young Britons' Foundation. This is not affiliated to any political party, but the message of its advertisement was consistent with a major theme of the Conservative campaign. The Foundation (see www.ybf.org.uk/) presents itself as a 'non-partisan, not-for-profit research and training organisation'; its President has been a Conservative MEP since 1999, its Vice-President is a Conservative local councillor, and many of its other staff members are linked to the Conservative Party.

54 R. Briffault, 'Soft money, Congress and the Supreme Court', in K.D. Ewing and S. Isacharoff, (ed.s), *Party Funding and Campaign Financing in International Perspective*, Oxford and Portland OR: Hart Publishing, 2006, pp. 191–211; N. Persily, 'The law of American party finance', in Ewing and Isacharoff, pp. 213–239.

7 Legal regulation and political activity at the local level in Britain

Justin Fisher

Introduction

Underlying much work on the impact of party and candidate spending are two broad assumptions. The first is that expenditure may be regarded as a useful surrogate for campaign intensity. In short, what many scholars have sought to test is whether higher spending (and therefore stronger campaigning) yields electoral payoffs – if it does, the case is stronger, it is argued, to regulate party and candidate spending so that the electoral process is not distorted by disparities in candidate or party wealth. The second assumption is that money is a constant sum. In one sense, this is obviously the case – the monetary value of £1 is the same for all candidates. But there is another argument, which suggests that this assumption is potentially flawed because it assumes that money is used with equal degrees of skill.[1] This may be the case, of course, but the assumption of money being a constant sum is certainly open to challenge. In this chapter, therefore, I seek to evaluate the impact of expenditure-based campaigning at constituency level over the course of four general elections (1992, 1997, 2001 and 2005). Importantly however, the chapter relies not on raw expenditure data, but on surveys of electoral agents, the data from which indicate the degree to which their campaigns relied on techniques that incur expenditure (costed campaigning) and those that are supplied through volunteer effort alone (free campaigning).[2] By evaluating the issue in this way, a fuller assessment can be made (alongside work that uses expenditure data) of the extent to which costed campaigning is electorally significant, but also the extent to which free campaigning – not captured by expenditure data – is itself significant.

Trends in constituency campaigning

Over the last four elections a number of trends have emerged in the ways in which political parties campaign at constituency level.[3] These can be summarised as follows: an increasing focus on target seats, increasing central oversight and direction of campaign organisation, declining levels of 'traditional' campaign activities, and an increase in more 'modern' forms of campaigning, which make strong use of technology. In terms of targeting, whilst central parties never fully subscribed to the view that constituency campaigning was effectively a ritual with no discernible impact on the result, as suggested by some studies,[4] it is the case that parties have taken an increasingly strong interest in constituency campaigns over the last four elections. This has manifested itself in a number of ways, such as centrally determined target lists and allocation of central resources (particularly staff) to key seats. The empirical test for these developments is the extent to which target seats have run stronger campaigns than other seats – a rational party will seek, where possible, to redistribute its finite resources where they are needed most in electoral terms. In the case of Labour and the Liberal Democrats, this is broadly what has occurred – the strongest campaigns have, by some margin, occurred in target seats.[5] Of course, not all party resources can be moved to target seats with equal ease – human resources, for example, are notoriously difficult to re-deploy to neighbouring target constituencies, let alone elsewhere. But by and large, Labour and the Liberal Democrats have been successful in focussing campaigns where they are needed most. Evidence for the Conservatives in this respect has been more mixed. Fuelled to an extent by a tradition of local autonomy in the party, the Conservatives have found it more difficult to focus resources on target seats, though significant progress has been made in recent years.[6]

Linked to this is the second trend: a growth in central party oversight and direction of constituency campaigns. This takes its form in a number of ways, such as more regular contact with central and regional staff, the use of special organisers (paid for by the central party), as well as the standardised design of printed materials and the provision of central facilities (such as software) for the running of campaigns. Again, this has been most prevalent in target seats.[7] The third trend is the decline in 'traditional' forms of campaigning, such as public meetings, doorstep canvassing, and other labour-intensive forms of campaigning. This has been largely a function of two related phenomena. First, party membership has been in broad decline.[8] As a result, there are lower levels of volunteer labour available (upon which much traditional campaigning relies). The second reason has been the falling relative cost of technology (especially computers), which has enabled parties to replace some tasks traditionally undertaken by volunteers (such as addressing envelopes) with technological solutions. Linked to this is the fourth trend: the growth in the use of more modern campaigning techniques that utilise computers, telephones and techniques such as direct mail. This has arisen not only because of the falling relative cost of the relevant technology, but also because, as in other countries, parties have increasingly turned to technology in the face of falling levels of volunteer labour.[9] In addition, technology has offered a number of efficiency gains in terms of reaching voters – particularly in the case of canvassing – making it especially attractive because more voters can be contacted (for example, by telephone) using fewer people and in a shorter period of time, though as Fisher and Denver show, the electoral impact of these efficiency gains have been mixed.[10]

All of these factors have, of course, influenced the degree to which party campaigns at the constituency level have relied on free or costed campaigning. Table

7.1 illustrates the decline in forms of activity that incur no cost; being based on the efforts of volunteer labour. As is clear across almost all indicators, there has been a steady decline. The proportions of the constituency canvassed on the doorstep, the proportion of the electorate covered by number-takers on polling day, and public meetings (one of the forms of 'in-kind' state funding) have all fallen. Perhaps most striking, however, has been the decline in the mean number of campaign workers and polling day workers – the latter having declined by over 50 per cent over the four elections. For only two indicators – manual 'knocking-up' on polling day and the mean number of volunteers coming in from other constituencies – has this downward trend been resisted. The first has 'flat-lined', yet the second suggests that parties are becoming (albeit in a rather modest way) a little better at targeting their human resources.

In order to better illustrate the overall trend in free campaigning, it is preferable to create a scale which includes all of these items. The results are shown in Table 7.2 (for numbers of cases, see Appendix). The scale is constructed using Principal Components Analysis with the scores then standardised around a mean of 100, allowing comparisons between parties and over time.[11] As is clear, there has been a broad decline, despite a small rally in respect of the Liberal Democrats in 2005. Table 7.2 also suggests a rather bigger rally for the Conservatives in 2005. However, data on the Conservatives in 2005 should be treated with some caution due to a low response rate to our survey of agents in that year. This figure, therefore, is almost certainly an exaggeration.

By way of contrast, the use of campaign techniques that incur cost has been growing (see Tables 7.3a and 7.3b – for numbers of cases, see Table 7.1). As with free campaigning, the trends are not uniform – poster production and the number of leaflets produced locally (until 2005) has fallen. Similarly, the proportion of constituencies producing a traditional election address has fallen very slightly. Nevertheless, the use of leaflets produced outside the constituency, telephones, direct mail and websites have all increased. It is also very clear that computers and their relevant software are now a core component of constituency campaigns.

Again, to get a better overall picture of trends in costed campaigning, it is preferable to create a scale of all of these items. The approach is the same as for

Table 7.1 Trends in free campaigning by technique

Mean	*1992*	*1997*	*2001*	*2005*
Per cent canvassed on doorstep	28	22	17	19
No. of campaign workers	54	49	35	33
No. of public meetings	3	1	1	1
No. of polling day workers	138	109	70	61
Prop. covered by no. takers	44	40	30	31
Volunteers used to 'knock up' (Y/N) (%)	55	62	59	63
Volunteers came from other constituencies (Y/N) (%)	17	15	10	19
N	1,004	1,300	1,329	614

Table 7.2 Trends in overall free campaigning

	1992	*1997*	*2001*	*2005*
Conservative	134	111	106	125
Labour	114	111	97	95
Lib Dems	86	84	78	86

Table 7.2 and the results are illustrated in Table 7.4. As expected, costed campaigning is broadly increasing, although Labour has effectively 'flat-lined' since 1997. If we disaggregate costed campaigning by seat seats status, we observe expected patterns (see Table 7.5). Here, seats are divided into three categories – Targets (seats where a party is either seeking victory or defending narrow majorities), Held Not Targets (safe seats), and Not Held Not Targets (seats where the party has almost no chance of winning). As expected, costed campaigning is most prevalent in target seats – generally by some margin. As we would expect, parties tend to allocate the mobile resource of expenditure where it is most needed. And in general, it is Labour and the Liberal Democrats who have been most successful in maximising this differentiation.

Overall, the trend is clear. Forms of campaigning that incur expenditure are increasing in importance. This becomes even more apparent when a net score is produced comparing costed and free campaigning. This is calculated simply by subtracting the costed campaigning score from that of free campaigning. Thus, a positive score indicates more free campaigning relative to costed, and *vice versa.*

Table 7.3a Trends in costed campaigning by item (means)

Mean	*1992*	*1997*	*2001*	*2005*
No. of posters	1,864	1,801	1,249	1,216
No. of reg./nat. produced leaflets	17,000	24,525	32,188	30,282
No. of locally produced leaflets	46,000	37,971	27,634	43,687
Per cent locally telephone canvassed	n/a	8	7	8

Table 7.3b Trends in costed campaigning by item (%)

	1992	*1997*	*2001*	*2005*
Election address	100	96	97	97
Used computers	74	85	89	93
Used party software	34	56	61	70
Website	n/a	n/a	43	63
'Good Morning' leaflet	43	49	49	59
Phone 'knocking up'	n/a	38	45	52
Direct mail	n/a	49	48	62
Telephone canvassing	32	52	50	60

Table 7.4 Trends in overall costed campaigning

	1992	*1997*	*2001*	*2005*
Conservative	99	105	107	129
Labour	100	114	111	111
Liberal Democrats	74	85	87	103

Table 7.5 Costed campaigning by seat status

	1992	*1997*	*2001*	*2005*
Conservative				
Held not target	104	114	116	124
Target	120	126	128	139
Not held not target	80	91	85	129
Labour				
Held not target	115	106	111	117
Target	144	148	138	137
Not held not target	95	110	94	92
Liberal Democrats				
Held not target	*	*	122	133
Target	102	132	137	149
Not held not target	72	81	82	92

* Too few cases for analysis.

Table 7.6 Net scores in free and costed campaigning

	1992	*1997*	*2001*	*2005*
Conservative	35	6	–1	–4
Labour	14	–3	–14	–16
Liberal Democrats	12	–1	–8	–18

The results are shown in Table 7.6. Both Labour and the Liberal Democrats have relied progressively on more costed campaigning since 1997, while for all three parties, 2001 represents the 'tipping point'.

The electoral impact

As is clear from the above discussion, constituency level campaigning is changing in a number of ways. Moreover, money is becoming more significant as parties increasingly focus on forms of campaigning that incur expenditure. This may present a case for the regulation of candidate expenditure in itself – limiting the scale of campaigns. After all, the 1883 Corrupt and Illegal Practices (Prevention) Act limited candidate spending for just that reason – concerns about excessive spending. The principle of that Act has remained in force ever since – the only significant amendments being redefinitions of the commencement of the candidates' campaigns for the purpose of regulation (which, as Johnston and Pattie show in this volume, the provisions introduced in 2009 are somewhat complex) (Political Parties, Elections and Referendums Act, 2000; Political Parties and Elections Act, 2009). However, if candidate spending is to be regulated further in any substantive way – such as a significant extension to the regulated spending period – it needs to be demonstrated that campaigning which incurs expenditure has a significant and growing impact on electoral outcomes.

In order to test this, a number of calculations are required. First, the electoral impact of the use of costed campaigning techniques needs to be evaluated. Second, an evaluation needs to be made of the impact of costed campaigning relative to the impact of free campaigning. In other words, costed campaigning may be electorally significant in isolation. But, as is clear from the discussion above, campaigning does not just consist of techniques that incur expenditure – they also include techniques for which there are no costs. Thus, showing that costed campaigning is electorally significant only tells part of the story. It is possible, for example, that costed campaigning could be electorally significant, but of far less relevance than other forms of campaigning. Since the question is not to limit the level of campaigning per se, but rather the financial aspect of campaigning, it is essential to assess the relative impact of expenditure on electoral success.

The approach to testing this is relatively straightforward – in the first instance, the levels of costed campaigning are regressed against the parties' constituency vote shares, whilst controlling for vote share at the previous election. The use of this lagged endogenous variable introduces a dynamic effect which effectively controls for the demographic factors which may influence election results. Moreover, it also recognises the fact that election results are themselves influenced by previous results. The use of the lagged endogenous variable means that demonstrating any electoral impact of costed campaigning is a stiff test, but is one that will produce robust results.[12]

To test the relative electoral effects of costed campaigning, the analyses are then re-run, adding the level of free campaigning as a further independent variable in the model. As we might expect, there is a relationship between levels of free and costed campaigning – we would expect constituencies that had high levels of free campaigning to also have significant levels of costed campaigning – largely because they will be running stronger campaigns overall. And indeed, over the four elections the two scales are positively correlated with a coefficient of 0.589. But this relationship is far from absolute (explaining 35 per cent of the variance) and running the models independently, and then with costed and free campaigning together in the same model reveal no significant problems with collinearity.

Table 7.7 illustrates a summary of the impact of costed campaigning alone (i.e. with no other forms of campaigning included in the model). What is clear is that costed campaigning generally yields positive electoral benefits for Labour and the Liberal Democrats. That said, while Labour's costed campaigning produced a statistically significant impact on vote share in 2005, the effect was

Table 7.7 Regression coefficients for costed campaigning 1992–2005

Year	*Conservative*	*Labour*	*Liberal Democrats*
1992	n/s	0.054**	0.063**
1997	n/s	0.062**	0.041**
2001	n/s	0.013*	0.040**
2005	n/s	–0.016*	0.058**

Note: Table contains b values for costed campaigning when regressed against party vote share, while controlling for party vote share at the previous election. ** $p<0.01$, * $p<0.05$. n/s = not statistically significant.

actually *negative* in terms of the impact on Labour vote share. However, in none of the cases does Conservative costed campaigning yield electoral payoffs.

The second point of note is that there is no particular trend in terms of the impact of costed campaigning – indeed, since 1997, the impact of Labour's costed campaigning has declined. However, it should be noted that the impact of constituency campaigning by incumbents is likely to be lessened over time, as they are principally defending seats.[13] Moreover, comparative evidence shows that parties experience the 'costs of governing' – a decline in popularity the longer the party is in power.[14] And, so it is with Labour. Nevertheless, there is no particular trend for the Liberal Democrats either, suggesting that effects of costed campaigning are becoming no more significant over time.

Table 7.8 introduces the additional independent variable of free campaigning, thus allowing us to test the relative importance of costed campaigning. Key patterns emerge. First, 1997 represents the high point of Labour's costed campaigning. While both free and costed campaigning had an impact, the impact of costed campaigning was greater to a statistically significant degree. Thereafter, Labour's costed campaigning had no statistically significant impact in 2001 and a negative impact in 2005. Second, it is clear that for the Liberal Democrats, the relative impact of free campaigning has declined – as the party has become more successful in terms of seats won (and, therefore, more targets to both defend and attack), the impact of free campaigning has declined – probably due to the party's relatively small party membership. As a consequence, costed campaigning has become progressively more significant for the party.

A key question that arises, however, is why the Conservatives' efforts have not been rewarded in the same way as Labour's, and particularly those of the Liberal Democrats. The answer is almost certainly the impact of effective targeting. While the Conservatives have improved in this respect, as Table 7.5 shows, the differentiation in effort between target and safe seats is not nearly as pronounced as it is for Labour, or indeed for the Liberal Democrats. Thus, the overall effects for the Conservatives are not electorally significant, because the impact of intense campaigning in safe or hopeless seats is likely to be of marginal significance. In addition, the data for Labour and the Liberal Democrats suggest that campaigning may be most effective when the party is the challenger at national level. In the case of Labour, it is very clear that the impact of their campaign efforts has lessened as they have needed to defend their gains (and experienced the 'costs of governing').

Moreover, what is evident from these results and indeed other work on the ways in which campaigns have changed and developed is that the amount spent by a party or candidate tells only part of the story.[15] Perhaps more important is how and where the money is spent. Fisher and Denver show, for example, that the level of Liberal Democrat campaign development is almost the same as for the Conservatives, despite the significant disparities in wealth.[16] That broad pattern is repeated here – the Liberal Democrats do not have large sums to spend, but they spend money effectively. This clarification is important, because it moves us away from the erroneous assumption that higher expenditure will always yield higher electoral payoffs.

Of course, the data analysed here do not adequately capture long-term spending (that is, constituency spending outside the regulated campaign period). It is that spending that has proved to be so controversial in discussions about further reform of constituency campaign expenditure.[17] Arguments for further reform are given more weight by Johnston and Pattie's findings that there were electoral payoffs in seats where considerable pre-campaign spending occurred.[18] What the results do illustrate, however, is that the level of raw expenditure does not tell the whole story. In other words, the data here would suggest that pre-campaign activity which did not incur expenditure could be as, if not more effective in delivering electoral payoffs. Of course, money is more susceptible to regulation as it is 'mobile' in a way that other campaign resources are not. The state would presumably have no strategic interest in limiting campaigning that did not incur cost, despite the fact that disparities in electoral outcomes could still arise from variations in available campaign resources – in this case, human resources. However, the question is one of degree – to be sure, spending can impact upon

Table 7.8 Regression coefficients for costed and free campaigning 1992–2005

Year	*Type*	*Conservative*	*Labour*	*Liberal Democrat*
1992	Free	n/s	0.038**	0.095**
	Costed	n/s	0.028**	0.026*
1997	Free	0.025**	0.027**	0.084**
	Costed	n/s	0.049**	n/s
2001	Free	n/s	0.037**	0.045**
	Costed	n/s	n/s	0.025**
2005	Free	n/s	n/s	n/s
	Costed	n/s	–0.016*	0.058**

Note: Table contains b values for costed and free campaigning when regressed against party vote share, while controlling for party vote share at the previous election. ** $p<0.01$, *$p<0.05$. n/s = not statistically significant electoral outcomes at constituency level. But the evidence presented here suggests that disparities in spending power can, up to a point, be counteracted by disparities in campaigning skills. Thus, finding that money can influence electoral results is not the same as saying that it is the only campaign factor that matters, or that it is the most important factor – the evidence here suggests that neither of those two claims are supported.

Regulation and realism

Of course, none of what is analysed above suggests that expenditure in constituency campaigning should not be regulated. As argued, money has a greater potential to distort the electoral process in favour of wealthier parties because it is portable and can be more easily utilised in seats that will deliver the most electoral payoffs than other campaigning resources. Moreover, the empirical evidence presented here and by Johnston and Pattie in Chapter 6 indicates that increased expenditure can influence election results. So the regulation of constituency spending at some level is necessary. In addition, the evidence from Johnston and Pattie's work is that there has been a growth in pre-campaign spending – especially by the Conservatives. Coupled with broader evidence of longer-term pre-campaign activity, which includes items that incur expenditure (especially in target seats),[19] there is a good case to be made that the regulated campaign period (effectively standardised by the Political Parties, Elections and Referendums Act as from the point of dissolution) was not capturing significant activity which could influence the electoral result.

As a consequence, the then Labour government originally proposed a return to 'triggering' – the system that had been in place prior to the Political Parties, Elections and Referendums Act – to better capture such activity.[20] 'Triggering' was a system whereby the beginning of a candidate's regulated campaign spending was triggered by his or her promotion as the prospective parliamentary candidate. However, 'triggering' barely worked prior to its reform following the Political Parties, Elections and Referendums Act. Parties were easily able to circumvent the law by simply not naming the candidate, or referring to him or her in terms other than as the official candidate. The lack of legal clarity was such that there had been only one case in recent times that had come to court (in the constituency of Newark following the 1997 election), which was ultimately thrown out on appeal.

The failings in the pre-2001 position were widely recognised. The Fifth Report of the Committee on Standards in Public Life noted that 'the absence of a specified time period [for candidate election expenses] undoubtedly caused uncertainty and there is no doubt that some candidates evade the Act'.[21] Moreover, in the Standing Committee reviewing the Political Parties, Elections and Referendums Bill, Labour MP Martin Linton noted that '...candidates can have a real problem in not knowing when their candidacy starts and perhaps inadvertently forgetting to use the word "prospective"'.[22]

Enforcement of the regulations pertaining to candidate expenses was also minimal, then being the responsibility of the Home Office. The result overall was that the means of effectively regulating candidate expenses were no longer fit for purpose. In addition, the nature of 'triggering' meant that there could be as many campaign start points as there are candidates. At the 2005 election, for example, there were 3,354 candidates.[23] Even if we examine just the three largest Westminster parties, who could have fielded up to 632 candidates each at the 2010 election in the UK, there would still potentially have been 1,896 different start points for candidates' campaigns. The result would be that a return to 'triggering' would have been almost impossible to police and regulate effectively.

The idea was subsequently dropped. Instead, a new and rather complex method was introduced in the Political Parties and Elections Act 2009, which effectively only applies in the case of a five-year parliamentary term and may well prove problematic to enforce due to its complexity. The method is outlined in Chapter 6, and as the authors indicate, given that most Parliaments run for four years, there are likely to be further changes to the regulations on constituency campaign expenditure. Even if fixed-term parliaments were introduced, changes would be required. For example, a fixed five-year term would make the gradations on long campaign spending redundant. Equally, the sudden fall of a government would require different legislation given that there would be no long campaign period.

Key questions associated with any further regulations are proportionality and enforcement. Proportionality refers here to the degree of regulation required, in particular, the period of time subject to regulation. In this case, there is a good argument to extend the period that captures candidate spending from the period following dissolution in four- (or fewer) year terms (the new regulations apply only to five-year terms). The key debate is how long the period of regulation should be – or to consider the proportionality of the response to the apparent problem. Some have argued that the period of regulation should be extended such that it matches that of national spending (at present, 365 days from polling day).[24] Based on the empirical evidence analysed above, however, there is a case for restraint. Costed campaigning does not always yield electoral payoffs, nor does it generate consistently stronger effects than free campaigning. Thus, it is possible to argue that reactions to the impact of costed campaigning may be overstated, given that parties can counteract the effects with free campaigning.

Linked to the proportionality argument is one about enforceability. Central parties are staffed by professionals whose campaign work it is reasonable to regulate for longer periods of time. The vast majority of constituency agents (who are legally responsible for the conduct and expenditure incurred in campaigns), however, are volunteers. At the 2005 election, for example, around 75 per cent of agents from the five principal parties (Conservatives, Labour, Liberal Democrats, Scottish National Party and Plaid Cymru) were volunteers.[25] Excessive regulation could, therefore, create at least two potential problems. First, it would create a barrier to participation. As volunteers, agents already subject themselves to liability. However, under the rules created by the Political Parties, Elections and Referendums Act, the period of liability was effectively limited to around a month (the normal period between dissolution and polling day). Were the period of liability to be extended to a year, it is highly unlikely that volunteers would be as willing to expose themselves to that degree of risk. Second, by virtue of being volunteers, it is far less likely that agents can devote their full attention to the task of an extended period such as 12 months. Nearly 70 per cent of volunteer agents at the 2005 election were occupied in significant other activities (such as employment, running their own businesses, studying, or caring for others). As a consequence, there is a stronger likelihood that there would be a growth in unintended breaches of the law. Such a growth would make compliance and enforceability more difficult to achieve.

An associated problem is the provision of appropriate training for agents to cope with long regulatory periods. For example, fully 42 per cent of agents at the 2005 election from the five principal parties were appointed within six months of the election date and 17 per cent just before the campaign. Thus, were the regulatory period to be extended to anything like a year, it is clear that a significant minority would require training to cope with a significantly longer campaign period – especially as nearly 60 per cent of agents had either run only one or no campaigns prior to 2005. A further issue is that there is an asymmetric distribution of non-volunteer agents. Although a large majority in all parties are voluntary agents, the Conservatives are much more likely to have paid agents than Labour or the Liberal Democrats. Thus, the impact of increased regulation of constituency-level regulation on parties would differ by party.

For all these reasons, there is arguably a balance to be struck between regulation that eliminates any financial advantages and minimising the detrimental impact on those that the move would seek to regulate. In other words, extending regulation at constituency level to that commensurate with national campaigning would arguably represent a disproportionate one as it is reasonable to argue that the level of impact of campaign spending does not warrant it, that it has significant potential to act as a barrier to participation, that it would create significant issues in terms of compliance and enforcement, and that the impact would be asymmetric. Put bluntly, there needs to be a greater sense of realism in discussions about the regulation of party and candidate spending at constituency level.

Conclusions

The positive impact of increased expenditure on party and candidate electoral performance has long been assumed. Indeed, the work of Johnston and Pattie at constituency level has suggested that there is an empirical basis to these assumptions; though Fisher's analysis at national level has not suggested the same degree of electoral gains.[26] Moreover, given the growing importance of campaigning methods at constituency level that incur expenditure, there is a logic that suggests that far greater regulation of constituency-level spending is required in order to ensure that contests are not distorted by differential party wealth.

However, this chapter has shown first that expenditure is also about how money is spent – it is not only how much you spend, but where you spend it and what you spend it on. Examined in this way, it is clear that the positive impacts of expenditure that incur cost (costed campaigning) are not uniform. Second, it is clear that campaigning is not just about costed campaigning, but also campaigning that relies on volunteer labour and requires no cost (free campaigning). And, the positive effects of free campaigning can equal those of costed campaigning, if not outscore them. Thus, the argument advanced here is that the electoral impact of costed campaigning may not be as strong as has been commonly thought – especially because its effects can be counteracted by free campaigning. As a consequence, any further regulation of expenditure at constituency level needs to be proportionate to the degree of impact of differential spending, as well as balance the needs of effective regulation against the enforceability and desirability of further regulation amongst a group that submits itself to liability on a voluntary basis. This chapter suggests, therefore, that some extension (and simplification) of regulated periods is sensible, but that any attempt to put constituency spending on the same footing as national spending would be disproportionate as things presently stand.

However, that is not to rule out that in future, more extensive regulation could be necessary and desirable. As this chapter has shown, costed campaigning constitutes an increasingly important aspect of constituency campaigning. Moreover, the decline in party membership means that free campaigning is unlikely to increase in intensity in the longer term, meaning that the portable resource of money may well require more regulation as its importance grows. That time, however, has not yet arrived, and before any decisions are made, the positive and ongoing electoral effects of differential party wealth need to demonstrated rather than assumed.

Appendix

The numbers of cases involved in Tables 7.2, 7.4, 7.5, 7.6, 7.7 and 7.8 are as follows:

	1992	*1997*	*2001*	*2005*
Conservative				
Held non-target	136	166	122	39
Target	45	64	103	23
Not held not target	84	204	150	6
Total	265	434	375	68
Labour				
Held non-target	98	168	183	162
Target	94	65	96	51
Not held not target	163	222	164	121
Total	355	455	443	334
Liberal Democrat				
Held non-target	–	1	10	23
Target	33	29	33	24
Not held not target	350	381	389	165
Total	383	411	432	212

Notes

1 J. Fisher, 'Party Expenditure and Electoral Prospects: A National Level Analysis of Britain', *Electoral Studies*, 1999, vol. 18, 519–532.
2 The data used in this chapter are derived from surveys completed by election agents of all five major parties in the UK (Conservative, Labour, Liberal Democrats, Plaid Cymru and the Scottish National Party) immediately after the respective general elections. These surveys were funded by the ESRC in 1992, 997 and 2001 (grant reference numbers Y304253004, R000222027, R000239396) and by the Electoral Commission in 2005.
3 J. Fisher and D. Denver, 'From Foot-Slogging to Call Centres and Direct Mail: A Framework for Analysing the Development of District-Level Campaigning', *European Journal of Political Research*, 2008, vol. 47, 794–826; J. Fisher and D. Denver, 'Evaluating the Electoral Effects of Traditional and Modern Modes of Constituency Campaigning in Britain 1992–2005', *Parliamentary Affairs*, 2009, vol. 62, pp. 196–210.
4 See, for example: D. Kavanagh, *Constituency Electioneering in Britain*, London: Longman, 1970; D. Butler and D. Kavanagh, *The British General Election of 2001*, Basingstoke: Palgrave Macmillan, 2002.
5 D. Denver, G. Hands, J. Fisher, and I. MacAllister, 'Constituency Campaigning in Britain 1992–2001: Centralisation and Modernisation', 2003, *Party Politics*, vol. 9, 541–559.
6 Fisher and Denver 'From Foot-Slogging to Call Centres and Direct Mail'.
7 Ibid.
8 Fisher and Denver, 'Evaluating the Electoral Effects of Traditional and Modern Modes of Constituency Campaigning in Britain 1992–2005'.
9 Ibid., and Fisher and Denver 'From Foot-Slogging to Call Centres and Direct Mail'.
10 Fisher and Denver, 'Evaluating the Electoral Effects of Traditional and Modern Modes of Constituency Campaigning in Britain 1992–2005'.
11 The technique used to create these scales of this kind was first developed by Denver and Hands, see D. Denver and G. Hands, *Modern Constituency Electioneering*, London: Frank Cass, 1997. See pages 246–255 for details of the technique employed.
12 It would be preferable to use share of the electorate rather than share of the vote as the dependent and lagged endogenous variables. However, significant boundary changes prior to the 1997 election make this impossible for all elections. As a consequence, share of the vote is used throughout to enable comparisons of the relative impact of free and costed campaigning over time.
13 D. Denver, G. Hands, J. Fisher, J. and I. MacAllister, 'The Impact of Constituency Campaigning in the 2001 General Election', 2002, *British Elections and Parties Review*, vol. 12, 80–94.
14 D. Sanders, 'Popularity Function Forecasts for the 2005 UK General Election', *British Journal of Politics and International Relations*, (2005) vol. 7, 174–190.
15 See Fisher and Denver 'From Foot-Slogging to Call Centres and Direct Mail'.
16 Ibid.
17 J. Fisher, 'Party Funding: Back to square one (and a half) or every cloud has a silver lining?', *Political Quarterly*, 2008, vol. 79, 119–125.
18 R. Johnston and C. Pattie, 'Funding Local Political Parties in England and Wales: Donations and Constituency Campaigns', *British Journal of Politics & International Relations*, 2007, vol. 9, 365–395.
19 Fisher and Denver 'From Foot-Slogging to Call Centres and Direct Mail'.
20 Ministry of Justice, *Party finance and expenditure in the United Kingdom*, London: HMSO, 2008; J. Fisher, 'Hayden Phillips and Jack Straw: The Continuation of British Exceptionalism in Party Finance?' *Parliamentary Affairs*, 2009, vol. 62, 298–317.
21 Committee on Standards in Public Life, *The Funding of Political Parties in the United Kingdom*, London: HMSO, 1998, para. 10.44.

22 S.C. Deb., 10 February 2000, c365.
23 J. Fisher, E. Fieldhouse, D. Denver, A. Russell and D. Cutts, *The General Election 2005: Campaign Analysis*, 2005, Report produced for the Electoral Commission.
24 Fisher, 'Party Funding: Back to square one (and a half) or every cloud has a silver lining?'.
25 Data on agents' occupations and experience are derived from the post-election survey of agents.
26 J. Fisher, 'Party Expenditure and Electoral Prospects: A National Level Analysis of Britain' *Electoral Studies*, 1999, vol. 18, 519–532.

Part III

The role of other actors

8 The press

The media and the 'Rupert Murdoch problem'

Andrew Geddis

What is the 'Rupert Murdoch problem' (and what to do about it)?

Insofar as the electronic broadcast media (and television in particular) are especially effective in shaping or conditioning the voting public's choices at election time, there are reasons to regulate it by law.[1] Central to these reasons is the fact that private ownership of television broadcasters by individuals or corporate interests gives those owners extensive communicative power within society. In the Anglo-American context, Rupert Murdoch provides the obvious exemplar of this issue, due to the combination of his owning extensive broadcast and other media outlets and his reputation as an interventionist proprietor who is prepared to set the editorial line of his companies.[2] Casting a broader net, Silvio Berlusconi's political career provides an even more emphatic illustration of this power and the problems it may cause.[3]

Communicative power necessarily flows from the general property rights conferred by private ownership of broadcasting assets; namely, the basic privilege to use (or not use) the proprietor's property in the way that he or she wants. The concern with regard to private ownership of television stations is that such use rights may be exercised in ways that are detrimental to the overall health of a properly democratic electoral process, such as:

- using the medium to promote directly the personal political ambitions of its owner;
- granting preferential access to the medium to candidates, parties or political viewpoints that the owner sympathises with;
- giving preferential coverage (in terms of editorial comment or general presentation) to candidates, parties or political viewpoints that the owner sympathises with;
- denying access to the medium to candidates, parties or political viewpoints that the owner disapproves of; and
- giving detrimental coverage (in terms of editorial comment or general presentation) to candidates, parties or political viewpoints that the owner disapproves of.

Of course, such communicative power and the potential for its misuse are not limited to privately owned television broadcasters. Publicly owned (or state-run) television stations are vulnerable to similar forms of manipulation for partisan political ends – as the contemporary examples of Russia and Venezuela attest. However, while recognising this fact, this chapter focuses on the issue of privately owned broadcasters for three reasons.

1. In those Anglo-American countries with a strong history of publicly owned broadcast networks, there is strong public and intra-institutional resistance to such manipulation. Therefore, at least in the context of this chapter, public broadcasters have not been regarded historically as presenting as great a risk of abusing communicative power as private broadcasters.
2. Should an issue or controversy undermine the public's belief in the impartiality of publicly owned broadcasters, the primary response of these institutions is to seek to regain that trust. There is thus a general commitment to a set of 'Public Service Broadcast' ethics, or a kind of internalised role morality, that causes such broadcasters to 'self-correct' in the face of allegations of partisanship.[4]
3. There is less ideological resistance to imposing legal controls on such publicly owned broadcasting institutions to prevent potential abuses of communicative power, or to correct such abuses if they should occur. Regulating publicly owned broadcasters does not raise the same level of concern about state interference with property rights (as well as free speech rights) as are involved with privately owned broadcasters.

Therefore, this chapter will proceed on the dual assumption that the communicative power of privately owned broadcasters provides the primary cause for concern in a liberal democracy; but that insofar as any regulatory constraints legitimately may be placed on privately owned broadcasters, they also will be imposed on any publicly owned broadcaster. That is to say, what is good for the privately owned goose is, at a minimum, good for the publicly owned gander. There may then be further forms of regulation that are relevant to publicly owned broadcasters but do not necessarily apply to privately owned ones: controls on the appointment of management; statutory guarantees of editorial independence; financial accounting mandates; and requirements to screen 'quality' programming are four examples that spring to mind.

Wherever the potential abuse of the communicative power held by privately owned broadcasters is considered a problem, there are (at least) three approaches to trying to prevent it from taking place.

Restrictions on media monopolies

A first regulatory response is to reduce the threat posed by privately owned communicative power by preventing any single individual or corporate group from securing a dominant position in the broadcast media market. One method of doing so is to diffuse the private ownership of television broadcasters amongst multiple private interests. Thus, limits may be imposed on the overall shareholding that any one person or corporation can own in a particular broadcaster, with the goal of preventing effective control of the broadcaster from residing in the hands of any one set of private interests. A second regulatory method is to permit individuals or corporations to gain full control of a broadcast network, but then limit the number of stations they may own in a particular media market. This latter approach has the aim of ensuring a diversity of communicative outlets, thereby preserving an effective 'speech market' that no one broadcaster can dominate.

These sorts of controls on media ownership are ubiquitous, whether specifically adopted to guard against the potential concentration of communicative power or simply to prevent monopolistic inflation of advertising rates and barriers to entry into the media market. However, such controls are always contentious in nature. The question of what level of ownership constitutes a 'controlling' stake in any given entity is a somewhat vexed question. Furthermore, any ownership limits inevitably create an economic cost in terms of foregone potential efficiency gains. That is to say, regulatory authorities must attempt to reconcile an inescapable tension between the goals of protecting diversity of ownership and maximising the value of the private enterprise. Finally, even a guaranteed 'speech market' of diverse private broadcasters may not be a sufficient guarantee of democratic health. Cass Sunstein warns of the risk of group polarisation, or 'niche-ification', created by multifarious media sources that present information in partisan, ideologically slanted forms.[5] Such an information environment, Sunstein warns, resembles a giant echo chamber, in which like-minded participants drive each other to ever more extreme positions, to the detriment of the dialogue and compromise required to make democracy work.

Fairness of access provisions

A second regulatory response is to require private owners of television stations to provide guaranteed direct access to all electoral competitors on a non-partisan basis. Such regulation may demand the provision of 'free time' to qualifying candidates or parties, or require that stations sell access to all qualifying candidates or parties at the same price and on the same terms. The aim of such regulation is to prevent private owners from exercising their property right to admit or exclude others in a manner that discriminates amongst electoral contestants. Instead, they must operate (at least in part) as neutral conduits of the electoral contestants' messages to the voter.

Given the fact that elected politicians (in the final analysis) set the rules governing the terms of access to the broadcast media, perhaps it is not surprising that fair access rules are commonplace. However, such rules carry costs. In the case of 'free time' mandates, the cost is obvious – these effectively expropriate the private broadcasters' right to screen paid advertising during that period.

Although 'same price and terms' limits do not carry the same immediate financial cost, they do involve administrative difficulties in determining what might constitute 'the same' treatment in different time slots or media markets. Furthermore, such regulation may have unintended consequences in terms of discouraging broadcasters from accepting any electoral advertising rather than have to accept all contestants' adverts.[6]

Finally, while fair access rules may create a formal equality amongst the electoral contestants' right to access the broadcast medium, they do not necessarily lead to any real equality between them. If contestants are required to pay for access to private broadcasters' facilities, contestants with greater financial resources will be able to gain more airtime. Hence, even scrupulous adherence to fair access rules by private (and public) broadcasters may still lead to an 'unfair' final distribution of communicative power, derived from the unequal distribution of resources in society as a whole. For this reason, in order to ensure a measure of genuine electoral fairness, it may be considered necessary to impose additional, overall controls on how much direct access to the broadcasting medium any electoral contestant may have.

This last form of regulation obviously goes beyond concerns about the consequences of private ownership of the broadcast media. It instead responds to more generic fears about the effect that unequally distributed financial resources might have on a process for choosing society's rule-makers that assumes a basic equality of all participants.[7] As such, concerns about the communicative power of private owners of broadcasting assets shade into broader concerns about how wealth may buy communicative power at election time. In this sense, fairness of access provisions form a subset of broader campaign finance regulations and must be viewed in light of the wider measures adopted to control the use of money in electoral campaigns.

Mandating impartiality in programme content

A third regulatory response is to impose notions of impartiality upon the programme content of privately owned broadcasters. One means of doing so is to require broadcasters to provide right of reply access to individuals or parties who are the subject of negative commentary or editorialising.[8] More invasively, the private owner of a broadcaster may be prohibited entirely from using the airwaves as a vehicle to promote his or her own preferred political perspective. Broadcasters instead may be required to adopt a non-partisan or balanced position in their coverage of the various political claims advanced within society. This state-mandated separation of ownership from editorial control takes the form of general statutory duties imposed as a condition of receiving a licence to broadcast, backed up with detailed codes of conduct and enforced by a regulatory agency. Where a complainant believes that a broadcaster has failed to abide by the requirements of fairness and balance, the regulatory agency may adjudicate on that complaint and (if necessary) impose penalties upon the broadcaster for its breach.

Clearly, such regulatory intrusions on the programming choices of broadcasters raise important free speech issues. Beyond a threshold question of whether it is justifiable to try to enforce 'impartiality' on private broadcasters looms the question of who will do the enforcing, and how it will be done. Can a regulatory body be trusted to deliver fair and balanced outcomes? Does it amount to unacceptable second-guessing of the editorial decisions of various media outlets? Does it reduce all current affairs coverage to a bland homogeneity? These are all challenges posed to the idea that impartiality in editorial approach is the most desirable default position for the broadcast media.

Addressing the Rupert Murdoch problem in the United Kingdom and New Zealand

Since the broadcast media's inception, both the United Kingdom (UK) and New Zealand (NZ) have regulated heavily its use for electoral (as well as more general political) purposes. Broadcasting in both countries began as a quasi-nationalised public service, raising obvious concerns about its susceptibility to governmental interference for partisan ends. However, strict controls have survived the introduction of commercial advertising and subsequent granting of licences for privately owned television and radio stations. This diffusion of ownership of, and access to, the broadcast media means that the main justification for the ongoing regulation of politically related content now revolves around equality of access concerns. The fear that private owners may use their control of the airwaves to promote political parties or viewpoints that they support, or that political parties or viewpoints supported by wealthy backers may purchase an undue amount of access to the airwaves, has resulted in significant forms of legal intervention.

Some context is necessary before reviewing the precise form that this regulation takes. The UK and NZ have quite different broadcasting landscapes. The most watched broadcaster in the UK is the publicly owned British Broadcasting Corporation (BBC),[9] which is funded by an annual licence fee paid by owners of television sets and so does not carry any commercial advertising on its two channels. Channel 4 also is publicly owned, but is funded through commercial activities (e.g. the screening of paid advertising).[10] The main privately owned broadcasters are the various regional stations commonly referred to as Independent Television (or ITV), but legally termed Channel 3. There are 15 such stations, most of which are owned by a single company (ITV plc).[11] An additional privately owned broadcaster, Five, has a far smaller share of the viewing audience.[12] In total, these 'terrestrial' broadcasters account for more than half the total hours spent watching television,[13] with the remainder distributed amongst a very wide range of satellite and cable providers. As a condition of their broadcast licence, terrestrial broadcasters are required to meet 'public service broadcasting' obligations – screening a certain level of local news coverage, as well as current affairs, arts and religious programming. However, the future of these obligations is the subject of ongoing debate in light of the transition from analogue to digital television,[14] which is expected to increase vastly the number of freely available channels.

The television market in NZ largely was deregulated in 1989. Although the country's largest broadcaster, Television New Zealand (TVNZ), remains publicly owned, it is required to operate as a commercial entity and accepts paid advertising on both its main channels.[15] The country's main privately owned broadcaster is TV3, which ultimately is owned by a private equity group, HT Media Ltd.[16] A second free-to-air channel, Prime, is owned by Sky TV and has a much lower share of the viewing audience. Sky TV also provides satellite-based broadcasting services to subscribing customers. A publicly owned, Maori language channel, Maori Television, began screening in 2005. Numerous small, local television stations exist alongside these nationwide free-to-air terrestrial broadcasters.

In recent years, two developments have somewhat roiled New Zealand's broadcasting waters. The first is the government's decision in 2003 to reimpose a number of public service broadcasting obligations on TVNZ, requiring through the 'TVNZ Charter' that it screen substantially more locally made current affairs, documentary, drama, arts, youth and children's programmes. The second development is the impending move from analogue to digital television, dramatically expanding the potential number of channels that all households will be able to receive. As has occurred in the UK, this impending greater diversity in freely available content raises questions about current forms of broadcast media regulation, which the government is currently reviewing.[17]

The upcoming transition to a digital broadcast platform in both the UK and NZ means that the issues considered in this chapter are in a state of some flux. Whether current forms of regulation will continue into this new digital age, or whether the diversification of content (as well as increasing integration between the internet and 'traditional' forms of broadcasting) will lead to wholesale change, is not entirely clear. Consequently, it is quite possible that this chapter describes a regulatory environment that will become as obsolete as the nineteenth-century rules governing the use of canals to move coal. With that caveat in place, I turn to examine how these two countries deploy each of the three regulatory strategies to combat the 'Rupert Murdoch' threat to their politics.

Restrictions on media monopolies

The first means of addressing fairness concerns with respect to broadcasting is to ensure that no one private owner gains an 'unhealthy' or 'undue' control over the broadcasting marketplace.[18] Such diversity of ownership requirements may be considered sufficient in themselves to guard against the threat of private domination of the airwaves. Certainly, it has become the primary means of regulatory control applied to the United States broadcast market, following the slow demise of other forms of content control.[19] However, there are two separate justifications for imposing this sort of marketplace restriction, which may lead to quite different regulatory approaches in practice. The first is concern about how the existence of monopoly (or near monopoly) power can be abused to generate artificially high returns or depress competition by locking new entrants out of the market. This approach treats the broadcast media as fundamentally no different from any other utility service provider requiring substantial capital outlay (i.e. akin to electricity or gas companies). The second approach recognises that the broadcast media provides an important role in servicing the democratic needs of society as a whole. Therefore, decisions on appropriate levels of ownership must take into account the need to ensure diverse content is provided and potential political power is diluted. While both approaches target the same matter – private ownership stakes in broadcast stations or companies – the conclusions that they suggest may be markedly different.

The United Kingdom

The Enterprise Act 2002 generally regulates 'relevant merger situations' between large companies.[20] Under this legislation, the decision on whether such mergers should occur generally is delegated to independent, expert competition authorities: the Office of Fair Trading and the Competition Commission. If the Office of Fair Trading considers, after an initial review, that the merger risks creating a 'substantial lessening of competition' in the marketplace, it refers the matter to the Competition Commission for an in-depth investigation under the Competition Act 1998. Where the Competition Commission concurs with the Office of Fair Trading's view that a 'substantial lessening of competition' will take place, it has substantial remedial powers (including prohibiting the merger altogether).

In addition to these general restraints on any large-scale merger that threatens to undermine competition in the marketplace, certain specific types of mergers will raise potential 'public interest considerations'. In the context of this chapter, it is relevant that public interest considerations are raised by:[21]

- newspaper mergers;
- mergers involving broadcast media; and
- cross-media mergers involving both broadcast media and newspaper enterprises.

The Enterprise Act 2002 specifies exactly what public interest considerations apply to such media mergers. Regarding mergers involving broadcasting entities, the public interest considerations are the need for

- there to be a sufficient plurality of persons with control of the media enterprises serving every different audience in the UK, or in a particular area or locality of the UK;[22]
- the availability throughout the UK of a wide range of broadcasting that (taken as a whole) is both of high quality and calculated to appeal to a wide variety of tastes and interests;[23] and

- persons carrying on media enterprises, and for those with control of such enterprises, to have a genuine commitment to the attainment in relation to broadcasting of the standards and objectives set out in the Communications Act 2003.[24]

Where the Secretary of State considers that any media merger that meets the 'relevant merger situation' test also raises one of these public interest considerations, she or he may issue an intervention notice. The effect of such a notice is to set up a dual-track scrutiny of the merger, with the Office of Fair Trading advising the Secretary of State on the competition grounds and the Office of Communications (OFCOM) reporting to the Secretary of State on the relevance of the public interest considerations to the merger. If, after receiving this advice, the Secretary of State considers the merger raises either competition or public interest concerns, he or she must refer the matter to the Competition Commission for an inquiry and report. The Secretary of State is then bound to accept the Commission's findings on competition matters, but may exercise independent judgment on whether public interest grounds should prevent the merger from taking place irrespective of its effect on competition.

There is then an additional process by which the Secretary of State may issue a 'special intervention notice' on public interest grounds for *any* merger involving an entity with 25 per cent or more share of supply of newspapers or broadcasting in the UK (or a substantial part thereof). If such a notice is issued, the merger is only reviewed on public interest grounds and not general competition grounds. OFCOM advises the Secretary of State on these public interest matters, with the Secretary of State then deciding whether to refer the matter to the Competition Commission for further inquiry. Following the Commission's report, the Secretary of State decides whether or not the merger should proceed, or what conditions should attach to it.

The effect of this regulatory system is that large-scale mergers between broadcasters, or mergers that give large newspaper owners control over a part of the broadcast market,[25] may be prohibited if they fail to meet the 'public interest' in having diverse ownership of such enterprises, as well as having them screen diverse, quality programming. The decision on whether to invoke these public interest considerations, or whether a given merger is consistent with them, lies in the hands of an elected politician, albeit subject to advice from independent bodies. What is important, therefore, is when and how these public interest considerations will be applied in practice.[26] At the time of writing, the Secretary of State has invoked them only once, in relation to BSkyB's purchase in 2006 of 17.9 per cent of the shares in ITV plc. This purchase was blocked by the Competition Commission on the ground that it constituted a 'relevant merger situation' that would result in a 'substantial lessening of competition',[27] with BSkyB subsequently ordered to sell down its holding to 7.5 per cent. On appeal, the Competition Appeals Tribunal upheld the Commission's finding on this point, but also found that the purchase conflicted with the public interest in 'there [being] a sufficient plurality of persons with control of the media enterprises serving every different audience in the UK'.[28] These conclusions presently are the subject of an appeal to the Court of Appeal, so whether they will provide precedent for future media mergers remains somewhat uncertain.

New Zealand

The situation in NZ is comparatively straightforward. Following the enactment of the Commerce Act 1986,[29] no special regulatory controls apply to ownership of the broadcast media beyond the general competition law rules that seek to prevent the opportunity for monopolistic or anti-competitive behaviour.[30] Consequently, the distribution of media ownership only becomes a matter of concern to the Commerce Commission if it threatens to create a 'substantial lessening of competition' in the relevant market.[31] In practice, quite intensive concentration of ownership of NZ's media sources has been permitted under this test.[32] Ownership of all but one of the country's major daily newspapers, for example, is in the hands of just two companies. The situation with respect to television is somewhat more diluted, given the continued state ownership of the nation's most-watched channels. Nevertheless, the present rules allow one company to own both satellite and terrestrial television stations,[33] while substantial cross-ownership of television and radio stations also is permitted.[34] It therefore appears unlikely that the 'substantial lessening of competition' test would prevent a newspaper owner from gaining control of a television broadcaster, should one wish to do so at any time.

What this means in practice is that the control of New Zealand's private broadcast stations has regularly passed from owner to owner without attracting the ire of the Commerce Commission. Furthermore, should a future government wish to privatise either or both of the currently publicly owned channels, the only restriction on a current media owner increasing their communicative power by purchasing them is whether doing so would lead to 'a real lessening of competition [for advertising revenue] that is not minimal'.[35] Questions regarding the overall suitability of a potential owner, or the owner's likely editorial approach or commitment to providing 'quality' broadcasting, simply do not figure in the decision.

Fairness of access provisions

A 'prohibited unless authorised' regulatory model governs the electoral contestants' direct access to the broadcast media in both the UK and NZ. This model prevents broadcasters from screening (at least some types of) political advertising, unless the law positively permits that advertising. The rationale for such draconian restrictions on accessing the broadcast media lies 'in the greater immediacy and impact of television and radio advertising',[36] as compared with other forms of communication. Not only does this regulatory approach effectively preclude private owners from giving favourable (or unfavourable) direct access to particular electoral contestants, it also permits rationing of that access in an effort to achieve 'fair' electioneering outcomes. In pursuit of this aim, both the UK and NZ have adopted mechanisms that allocate access to the broadcast media amongst qualifying political parties. It should be noted that in both countries, these allocation mechanisms exist alongside more general restrictions on the overall 'election expenses' that political parties may incur in respect of election campaigns. Therefore, they constitute a second level of rationing; limiting not just how much the parties may spend, but also what they may spend on.

The United Kingdom

The BBC's agreement with the Secretary of State for National Heritage prohibits it from carrying any form of paid advertising.[37] The Communications Act 2003 governs privately owned broadcasters (as well as Channel 4). Under this Act, OFCOM is tasked with ensuring that no broadcaster, at any time, includes any 'political advertising' in its television or radio services.[38] 'Political advertising' is defined broadly to encompass far more than overtly election-related material:[39]

> [any] advertisement contravenes the prohibition on political advertising if it is –
>
> (a) an advertisement which is inserted by or on behalf of a body whose objects are wholly or mainly of a political nature;
> (b) an advertisement which is directed towards a political end; or
> (c) an advertisement which has a connection with an industrial dispute.

The phrases 'objects of a political nature' and 'political ends' are further defined to include aims as general as 'influencing public opinion on a matter which, in the UK, is a matter of public controversy'; or 'promoting the interests of a party or other group of persons organised, in the UK or elsewhere, for political ends'.[40]

This ban's extreme reach was underscored by the House of Lords' decision in the *Animal Defenders International* case.[41] An animal rights group brought the case after the broadcasters refused to screen its proposed advertisement calling for equal rights for Great Apes, on the ground that the group's general objects meant the message was a 'political advertisement'. The group sought a judicial declaration under the Human Rights Act 1998, s.4 that even if this refusal was lawful under the Communications Act 2003, it nevertheless was inconsistent with the group's right to freedom of expression under Article 10 of the European Convention on Human Rights. However, the House of Lords unanimously rejected the claim. It ruled that the UK's virtually complete ban on political advertising is justified because the broadcast media represents a uniquely powerful communicative tool,[42] while any more liberal means of restricting or rationing access would be ineffective, difficult to apply, and already had been rejected by Parliament.[43] Therefore, in order to avoid 'the grosser distortions which unrestricted access to the broadcast media will bring',[44] completely prohibiting the use of the airwaves for overtly political purposes constitutes a justifiable limit on the expressive rights of individuals and groups.

Because this general ban on broadcasting political messages only applies to advertising activities, it does not affect the broadcasters' news gathering and reporting activities. It does mean, however, that the only avenue for anyone wishing to directly access the broadcast media for electoral or other political purposes is the free airtime made available by the broadcasters on specific occasions. The BBC has provided such airtime since the 1950s as a part of its obligation to provide a 'public service for disseminating information, education and entertainment'.[45] Donating airtime for this purpose is a required condition for any broadcast licence granted by OFCOM to an independent terrestrial broadcaster.[46] OFCOM sets rules that establish the minimum conditions under which such free airtime is provided.[47] These specify which independent broadcaster must offer free time in which situation.[48] They also state that 'major parties will normally be offered a series of broadcasts before each election',[49] while 'registered parties may qualify for a broadcast on the basis of contesting one sixth or more of the seats up for election, modified as appropriate for proportional representation systems.'[50] OFCOM's rules further restrict the format that the free airtime may take, stating that political parties 'may choose a length of 2'40", 3′40″ or 4′40″ on TV'.[51] The broadcasters also must screen the party's messages between specified hours.[52]

While independent broadcasters are under a general duty to abide by these rules, the final decision on when to schedule the free airtime (as well as how much to offer and who to offer it to) lies with them. In practice, airtime is made available in four circumstances:

- for Party Election Broadcasts (PEBs), offered in pre-election periods to qualifying political parties that are registered with the Electoral Commission;
- for Party Political Broadcasts (PPBs), usually offered twice yearly to the major political parties;
- for Budget Broadcasts, which are offered to the major political parties at the time of the Chancellor of the Exchequer's Budget statement; and
- for Ministerial Broadcasts, offered in exceptional circumstances to the government and followed by a response from the main opposition parties.

To help coordinate decisions on these matters and ensure some consistency in approach, the Broadcasters' Liaison Group was formed in 1997.[53] This body consists of representatives of each broadcaster offering free time, with representatives from OFCOM and the Electoral Commission attending as observers. It has no formal power to bind its members, instead acting as a forum for reaching consensus amongst the various broadcasters.

Consequently, a mix of government regulation and autonomous broadcaster discretion governs the distribution of free access to the airwaves to political parties. In practice, this approach radically restricts the use of the broadcast media for political purposes, even during general election campaigns. For example, on the second-to-last evening of the 2005 election campaign, the *sole* political party message broadcast was a single PEB for the Labour Party (which did not even screen in Scotland or Wales). The UK's method of distribution also favours larger, established political parties over smaller or emerging ones.[54] To qualify for a single PEB across the entire UK, a party must run candidates in at least 108 constituencies (requiring the payment of £54,000 in potentially non-refundable deposits). Furthermore, during the 2005 election campaign, the Labour and the Conservative parties were each entitled to five PEB's covering the entire UK, the Liberal Democrats four, while the Green Party received but one.

Nevertheless, in spite of these flaws, there appears to be a high level of support for retaining this overall regulatory approach. The Electoral Commission concluded in 2003 that;[55]

> The case for retaining the ban on paid advertising is persuasive. The ban is in the interests of the electorate and therefore the public interest. It is also in the interests of political parties and broadcasters.

The voting public also appears broadly supportive of limits on political advertising. OFCOM's polling of public attitudes toward television coverage of the 2005 election reveal that 54 per cent of respondents believed political parties should not be permitted to pay for television advertising,[56] while 55 per cent believed that the right number of PEBs had been shown during the campaign.[57] There does not, therefore, appear to be any great pressure for change from either institutional sources or the public generally.

New Zealand

NZ's overall regulatory approach is similar to the UK model, although it is comparatively much more liberal in application. All broadcast media in NZ, whether privately owned or state run, operate under the Broadcasting Act 1989. This legislation prohibits any broadcaster, at any time, from broadcasting an 'election programme'.[58] An election programme is defined as:[59]

> a programme that –
>
> (a) Encourages or persuades or appears to encourage or persuade voters to vote for a political party or the election of any person at an election; or
> (b) Encourages or persuades or appears to encourage or persuade voters not to vote for a political party or the election of any person at an election; or
> (c) Advocates support for a candidate or for a political party; or
> (d) Opposes a candidate or a political party; or
> (e) Notifies meetings held or to be held in connection with an election.

Only a few specific exceptions apply to this blanket ban on using the broadcast media for partisan political ends,[60] of which the most important for the purpose of this chapter are those allowing registered political parties some limited access to the broadcast media during an election campaign.[61] This access is provided in the period immediately before an election in two forms. First, the State allocates money to qualifying political parties to enable the purchase of broadcasting time direct from the broadcasters.[62] The present amount of this 'broadcasting allocation' is NZ$3.2 million. In addition to this money, the nation's publicly owned broadcasters are required to provide time for the broadcasting of political parties' opening and closing statements. The Electoral Commission is responsible for apportioning this money and time between all of the qualifying political parties that request a share.[63] In order to qualify for this distribution, a party simply needs to have requested a share by the due date, and then be registered as a party with the Electoral Commission at the time Parliament is dissolved for a general election.[64]

Criteria set out in the Broadcasting Act 1989 then govern the Commission's allocation decision.[65] These require the Commission to reward parties for their popularity (based on evidence such as the vote received at the last election and 'any other indications of public support for that political party such as the results of public opinion polls and the number of persons who are members of that political party'), while also recognising 'the need to provide a fair opportunity for each political party … to convey its policies to the public by the broadcasting of election programmes on television'. Obviously, these factors demand quite different things of the Commission. Furthermore, the section gives no indication as to how much weight to attach to each factor, nor does it require the Commission to apply each factor in the same way at each election contest.[66] Therefore, it is hardly surprising that following every allocation decision there have been complaints by some political parties that they have been unfairly treated.[67] The High Court has, however, upheld the Commission's broad discretion to choose how to apply the various factors when allocating time and money, on the ground that:

> The weight to be given to particular considerations which are, as a matter of law, relevant, is for the Commission. The intensely political content of the allocation process makes it important that the supervisory role of this Court by way of judicial review should be strictly confined within appropriate administrative law boundaries.[68]

Once made, the Commission's allocation decision provides the political parties with their sole means of directly accessing the broadcast media.[69] A political party may only broadcast an election programme within the time allocated to it for opening and closing statements, or purchased directly from a broadcaster using money allocated to it for that purpose. Additionally, any money provided to a political party as a part of the broadcasting allocation may be used only for the purpose of making and screening an election programme.[70] However, while the costs of producing an election programme can be paid for from the broadcasting allocation, they do not have to be. Therefore, a political party may spend its own funds on the production costs of any broadcast advertising, although this expenditure will then qualify as an 'election expense' to be counted towards the total that party may spend on its general election advertising.[71]

In addition to the statutory prohibition on broadcasters transmitting an election programme outside of the circumstances canvassed above, they are prohibited from offering access in a manner that favours one political participant over another. It is an offence for a broadcaster to sell or give any political party or candidate time for broadcasting on terms more advantageous than those offered to any other party or candidate wishing to buy comparable time from that broadcaster.[72] Therefore, broadcasters must either allow all parties and candidates access under the same general terms or refuse to carry any campaign advertising at all. Broadcasters must also provide the Electoral Commission with a post-election return, specifying all the election programmes that the broadcaster aired in the three months before the election.[73]

The overall effect of NZ's election broadcasting regime is to tightly restrict the political parties' direct access to the broadcast media. They can directly access the airwaves for election-related advertising only to the extent allowed by the time and money allocated to it by the Electoral Commission. Aside from the general issue of whether electoral participants' access to the broadcast media should – as a matter of principle – be restricted, the particular outcomes generated by this allocation process have been a perennial target of allegations of unfairness. Claims that the distribution is inequitable have been voiced ever since the present allocation system was introduced in 1989, and have been sharpened by the move from a two-party, first-past-the-post voting system to a more diverse electoral climate following the advent of the Mixed Member Proportional (MMP) voting system in 1996. The net result is that the present election broadcasting regime is the subject of near universal condemnation by those electoral participants who are most affected by it. In addition, the Electoral Commission has stated that it 'considers the current system of allocating time and funds to the political parties for election broadcasting is unfair and unsatisfactory, and that the procedures required by the [Broadcasting] Act are very time-consuming, cumbersome, and expensive'.[74]

Quite what ought to be done about the regime is, of course, a different matter, on which there is much less agreement. The roots of this difference in opinion partly lie in self-interest – clearly, each electoral participant has reason to support a broadcasting regulation regime that they feel will best advance their own partisan political interests. However, issues of principle also arise. The question of how far electoral participants' access to the broadcast media for political purposes should be restricted requires a judgment about the extent to which the State ought to be permitted to safeguard some purported social good by imposing limits on the right of an individual or group to communicate with the voting public.[75]

Mandating 'impartiality' in programme content

Both the UK and NZ significantly limit how all broadcasters, including the privately owned, can present political information or analysis to the viewing public. These restraints take the form of legislatively imposed duties on broadcasters to demonstrate 'due impartiality' or 'balanced coverage' with regard to matters of public importance. Independent regulatory bodies oversee these duties, with the power to impose sanctions on broadcasters who operate in breach of them. Obviously, such restraints stand in some tension with the broadcasters' right to freedom of expression, guaranteed in both UK and NZ law.[76] This right does accord the broadcaster some editorial leeway in the manner it chooses to address matters, as well as which matters it chooses to address. Nevertheless, both the UK and NZ consider it justifiable to impose overarching content restrictions on the broadcasters' right to speak.[77] Jacob Rowbottom summarises the rationale for these limits on broadcasters' expressive rights as reflecting[78]

> the danger that media freedom will be asserted simply to protect the economic interests of the media company or other property owner, rather than to serve democratic goals or the public interest. The mass media, with the high costs of access and control in the hands of an elite, requires some oversight to prevent its important social and democratic functions being skewed in the interests of a small number of speakers or gatekeepers.

Although these concepts of 'due impartiality' or 'balanced coverage' apply to the broadcasters' at all times, they have special relevance during an election campaign. The tight restrictions on the primary participants' direct access to the broadcast media, as detailed in the previous section, mean that 'free' media coverage of their campaigns is the primary way that they can communicate to the public. Therefore, policy announcements, as well as the activities and schedules of political party leaders, are aimed at gaining prominence on the daily television and radio news bulletins, while party spokespeople seek public exposure through press conferences and media interviews. Any decision to cover one party's campaign more intensively or favourably than another's can thus confer a significant electoral advantage on that party.

The United Kingdom

OFCOM is responsible for overseeing the objectives of the Communications Act 2003, most pertinently the 'impartiality of television and radio services'.[79] Under the 'OFCOM Broadcasting Code', broadcasters are required: 'To ensure that news, in whatever form, is reported with due accuracy and presented with due impartiality.'[80] The code then further specifies what this duty of 'due impartiality' entails:

> 'Due' is an important qualification to the concept of impartiality. Impartiality itself means not favouring one side over another. 'Due' means adequate

> or appropriate to the subject and nature of the programme. So 'due impartiality' does not mean an equal division of time has to be given to every view, or that every argument and every facet of every argument has to be represented. The approach to due impartiality may vary according to the nature of the subject, the type of programme and channel, the likely expectation of the audience as to content, and the extent to which the content and approach is signalled to the audience.[81]

Additional rules regarding the preservation of due impartiality apply to 'political or industrial issues on which politicians, industry and/or the media are in debate'. The Code requires that programmes 'must exclude all expressions of the views and opinions' of the broadcaster on such matters,[82] while 'due impartiality on matters of political or industrial controversy and matters relating to current public policy must be preserved [by the broadcaster]'.[83] Furthermore:

> In dealing with matters of major political and industrial controversy and major matters relating to public policy an appropriately wide range of significant views must be included and given due weight in each program or in clearly linked and timely programmes.[84]

The Code also contains a separate section covering the broadcasters' specific duties during the election period, which requires discussion and analysis of election issues to cease once the poll opens, restricts the appearance of candidates in programmes, and sets out obligations to cover the campaigns of individual candidates with due impartiality.[85]

Members of the public can complain to OFCOM if they believe a broadcaster has acted in breach of the Broadcasting Code. After reviewing the broadcast, a copy of which the broadcaster must supply on OFCOM's request, and considering any submissions made by the broadcaster, OFCOM may decide to uphold or not uphold the complaint. Alternatively, it may declare the complaint 'resolved' as the result of action taken by the broadcaster in the interim (i.e. issuing an apology or taking steps to ensure no repetition will occur). Where OFCOM upholds a complaint, its Broadcasting Sanctions Committee ('the Committee') may then decide to impose a sanction upon the broadcaster. The Committee possesses powers delegated from the OFCOM Board and consists of five members, three from OFCOM's Content Board and two from the OFCOM Board.[86] It can apply a range of potential sanctions under the Communications Act 2003.

- It can direct a broadcaster not to repeat a programme or advertisement;
- direct a broadcaster to publish a correction or adjudication;
- fine a broadcaster; or shorten or revoke a licence.[87]

However, the imposition of such sanctions is comparatively rare, taking place only 'if [the Committee] considers that a broadcaster has seriously, deliberately, repeatedly, or recklessly breached the terms of its licence conditions.... This includes any breach of any relevant OFCOM codes from time to time in force.'[88] In most cases where OFCOM upholds a complaint, therefore, the mere finding that a breach of the Broadcasting Code has occurred (along with any warning against repeating the breach) is considered a sufficient remedy.

Nevertheless, OFCOM's complaints and sanctions regime does cast a considerable shadow over the broadcasters' coverage of political and electoral matters, by imposing a heavy potential cost for breaching the Broadcasting Code. The extent of that cost became apparent in May 2008, when OFCOM levied a total £5.675 million fine on ITV stations for misleading viewers over phone-in competitions.[89] While nothing approaching that level of sanction has ever been applied to a broadcaster for breaching the 'due impartiality' standards, the case of the Islam Channel demonstrates what can happen where these are ignored.[90] The Committee fined this broadcaster £30,000 for permitting two candidates in the upcoming local body elections to continue to present programmes,[91] while also allowing one of these candidates to actively promote his campaign for Mayor of London while presenting.[92] It regarded these breaches of the Broadcasting Code as significantly serious as to deserve a fine because:

> The potential harm caused by a disregard of democratic processes such as these is considerable. These rules are in place to ensure that elections are conducted fairly and that no unfair advantage is given to candidates through promotion in the broadcast media, irrespective of whether the candidate can be shown to have actually benefited in practice.[93]

The OFCOM complaints and sanctions regime may also involve it adjudicating on matters of current political dispute. A good example is the complaints laid against ITV's reporting of an interview with Tony Blair, in which he may have indicated that his belief in God played a part in the decision to invade Iraq. OFCOM concluded that as ITV's news coverage

> reported as fact its interpretation of the interview ... when the interview was, at the very least ambiguous, and open to a number of differing interpretations, ITV was in breach of the requirement for reporting news with due accuracy (Rule 5.1).[94]

While OFCOM considered referring this case to the Committee for possible sanction, it decided not to do so after ITV voluntarily screened a summation of OFCOM's finding.[95] Nevertheless, the mere finding that ITV had 'been rapped by the broadcasting watchdog',[96] or that 'media watchdogs [had] rebuked ITV News',[97] for misreporting the story inserts OFCOM into what was (and remains) a highly controversial political matter.

The existence of broadcast standards also has implications for the role of the broadcasters as the 'gatekeepers' or 'vetters' of the content of PEBs or PPBs.

Broadcasters have the ultimate responsibility for ensuring that these do not contain material that breaches OFCOM's Broadcasting Code,[98] meaning that the broadcasters may on occasion act as censors of political parties' messages by refusing to screen advertisements they believe breach the Code's requirements. The House of Lords has endorsed such action,[99] ruling that the broadcasters acted correctly when refusing to screen graphic abortion footage as part of a PEB, as this would breach their legal obligation not to broadcast material that 'offends against good taste or decency'.[100] Similarly, in 2004, Channel 5 required the far-right British National Party to heavily edit their PEB for the European elections, on the ground that it was 'likely to stir up racial hatred, as prohibited by the existing Programme Code'.[101]

New Zealand

The NZ broadcast media's general treatment of political and electoral matters also is subject to regulatory control to ensure 'balanced coverage'. The Broadcasting Act 1989 requires broadcasters to respect the principle that:[102]

> when controversial issues of public importance are discussed, reasonable efforts are made, or reasonable opportunities are given, to present significant points of view either in the same programme or in other programmes within the period of current interest.

The Broadcasting Standards Authority (BSA) oversees the broadcasters' statutory duties, and adjudicates on any complaints that these have been breached.[103] A lawyer chairs this body, with its four members appointed after consultation with broadcasters.[104] It has the power to punish breaches of a broadcaster's statutory duties by ordering the broadcast of a statement acknowledging the breach, effectively fining broadcasters by forbidding them from screening advertising for a period of up to 24 hours, while in serious cases it can order a broadcaster to cease broadcasting altogether for up to 24 hours.[105]

The BSA has explained the rationale of the 'balanced coverage' principle in the following terms: 'The balance requirement means that competing arguments must be advanced with sufficient purpose to enable a viewer to arrive at an informed and reasoned opinion.'[106] It has further fleshed out the broadcasters' duty to provide 'balanced coverage' by specifying more extensive standards of 'balance', 'accuracy' and 'fairness' in the 'Free-to-air Television Code'.[107] The BSA then clarified the application of this Code in the context of an election campaign through its decision on Prime Minister Helen Clark's complaint about her treatment during a televised interview preceding the 2002 election.[108] It found this interview to be unbalanced, inaccurate, lacking impartiality and objectivity, and unfair because the broadcaster did not tell the Prime Minister in advance either the nature or the source of the accusations put to her during it. Furthermore, the broadcaster's subsequent coverage of the affair lacked balance because:[109]

> significant viewpoints were not advanced during the period of current interest to the extent necessary to counter the high impact of the strong allegations which called into question the accountability and trustworthiness of the Labour Government.

Consequently, a broadcaster cannot satisfy its statutory duty to display 'balanced coverage' simply by putting a politician on the air, or mentioning the existence of other points of view on an issue. Instead;[110]

> The standard is interpreted taking into account the impact and timing of the programme, and the seriousness of the allegations it contains. The higher the impact and the more serious the allegations, the greater the onus to provide balance. Programmes said to provide balance in the period of current interest are first assessed individually and then cumulatively to determine overall effect. Sheer numbers of broadcasts dealing with the topic will not automatically determine the matter since their content is all-important.

Furthermore, although this regulatory approach does not expressly forbid broadcasters from engaging in editorialising, it allows it only where the 'material [is] presented in such as way as to allow the viewer to concur with or dispute the editorial stance adopted'.[111]

Political parties and individual candidates also face restrictions on the content of their election advertisements. The Broadcasting Act 1989 mandates that all programmes (including election campaign advertisements) must observe basic standards of good taste and decency, the maintenance of law and order and the privacy of the individual.[112] It also authorises the BSA to create further codes of broadcasting practice.[113] Consequently, the BSA has issued the Elections Programmes Code containing five standards to govern the content of election programmes.[114] While these recognise that 'robust debate, advocacy and expression of political opinion are a desirable and essential part of a democratic society',[115] they also require that

- 'factual information should be clearly distinguishable from opinion or advocacy';[116]
- election programmes 'may not include material which denigrates a political party or candidate';[117] and
- election programmes 'may not imitate an existing programme, format or identifiable personality in a manner which is likely to mislead'.[118]

A broadcaster may refuse to screen an election programme that it considers to be in breach of any of these standards.[119] Furthermore, a viewer who considers that the broadcast of a particular election programme breaches any of these standards may complain to the broadcaster concerned. The broadcaster is then required to respond to this complaint in writing within 48 hours, stating its decision on the complaint or what action it will take because of the complaint.[120] If the complainant is dissatisfied with this response, or the broadcaster fails to respond within 48 hours, the complainant may lodge a formal complaint with the BSA.[121] The authority will then endeavour to issue its decision on that complaint within 48 hours, and if it upholds the complaint, can order the broadcaster to undertake a range of remedial actions.

Conclusion

Television stations in the UK and NZ operate in a highly regulated environment, subject to forms of legal control that would be considered unacceptable if applied to other forms of media (such as newspapers or the internet). Any explanation for why television has been singled out for such intensive oversight must combine history — the original assumption that the airwaves are a 'public resource' to which private owners have only a limited right of access — and a fear of the societal consequences of unbridled private control of an especially potent form of communication. Whether these justifications still apply in an era of fragmenting audiences and emerging 'new media' is open to question. Certainly, both the UK and NZ are going through a period of reflection upon their existing rules, which may lead to wholesale changes in the future. But until any such changes take place, the laws of each country are firmly committed to stopping any Rupert Murdoch figure from dominating national politics by virtue of his control over the broadcasting media.

Notes

1 See, e.g. J. Rowbottom, 'Access to the Airwaves and Equality: The Case Against Political Advertising on the Broadcast Media' in K. Ewing and S. Issacharroff (eds), *Party Funding and Campaign Financing in International Perspective*, Portland, Oregan: Hart Publishing, 2005, pp. 77–96; J. Rowbottom, 'Media Freedom and Political Debate in the Digital Era', *Modern Law Review*, 2006, vol. 69, 489.

2 A reputation he apparently accepts; see House of Lords Select Committee on Communications, 'Minute of the visit to New York and Washington DC, 16–21 September 2007', 17 September 2007, p. 10 ('Mr Murdoch did not disguise the fact that he is hands on both economically and editorially.').

3 G. Doyle, *Media Ownership: The Economics and Politics of Convergence and Concentration in the UK and European Media*, London: Sage Publishing, 2002, p. 20.

4 See, e.g. BBC Trust, *From Seesaw to Wagon Wheel: Safeguarding Impartiality in the 21st Century*, 2007 at p. 6 ('The BBC has the mechanisms to improve its delivery of impartiality, in the form of Editorial Policy (its editorial advisory department) and its new College of Journalism. Both need an extended role').

5 C. Sunstein, *Republic.com 2.0*, Princeton: Princeton University Press, 2007.

6 As has happened in Canada; see *Canada (A.G.)* v. *Reform Party of Canada* [1995] 123 D.L.R. (4th) 366; A. Geddis, 'Reforming New Zealand's Election Broadcasting Regime', *Public L. Rev.*, 2003, vol. 14, 164, 172–174. New Zealand has experienced a similar phenomenon, albeit on a far smaller scale; see J. Stokes, 'Iwi stations silence Labour ad', *NZ Herald*, 2 September, 2005.

7 K. Ewing, *The Cost of Democracy: Party Funding in Modern British Politics*, Oxford: Hart Publishing, 2007, pp. 27–29.

8 As applied in the United States under the (now defunct) 'Fairness Doctrine' see *Red Lion Broadcasting Co* v. *FCC* 395 U.S. 367 (1969).

9 In June, 2009, BBC1 and BBC2 accounted for 28.9 per cent of total viewing; see Broadcasters' Audience Research Board, 'Monthly Total Viewing Summary'. Online. Available HTTP: www.barb.co.uk/report/monthlyViewingSummaryOverview?_s=3 (accessed 19 May, 2010).

10 In June, 2009, Channel 4 accounted for 6.9 per cent of total viewing: Broadcasters' Audience Research Board, 'Monthly Total Viewing Summary'.

11 In June, 2009, ITV channels accounted for 16.2 per cent of total viewing: Broadcasters' Audience Research Board, 'Monthly Total Viewing Summary'.

12 In June, 2009, Five accounted for 5.1 per cent of total viewing: Broadcasters' Audience Research Board, 'Monthly Total Viewing Summary'.

13 In June, 2009, they accounted for 57.1 per cent of total viewing: Broadcasters' Audience Research Board, 'Monthly Total Viewing Summary'.

14 See, e.g., OFCOM, *Ofcom's Second Public Service Broadcasting Review: Putting Viewers First*, 2009. Online. Available HTTP: www.ofcom.org.uk/consult/condocs/psb2_phase2/statement/psb2statement.pdf (accessed 19 May, 2010); House of Lords Select Committee on Communications, *Public Service Broadcasting: Short-Term Crisis, Long-Term Future?*, HL Paper 61, 2009.

15 TVNZ is a State-Owned Enterprise under the State-Owned Enterprises Act 1986 (NZ). Under s. 4(1) of this Act, 'The principal objective of every State enterprise shall be to operate as a successful business and, to this end, to be—(a) As profitable and efficient as comparable businesses that are not owned by the Crown'.

16 TV3's parent company also owns a music and youth-oriented television channel, C4, as well as numerous commercial radio stations.

17 Ministry for Culture and Heritage, *Digital Broadcasting: Review of Regulation* (2008). Online. Available HTTP: www.mch.govt.nz/publications/digital-tv/DigitalBroadcastingReviewofRegulationVolumeOne.pdf (accessed 19 May, 2010).

18 For why it matters who owns the broadcast media, see C. Edwin Baker, *Media Concentration and Democracy: Why Ownership Matters*, Cambridge: Cambridge University Press, 2007. See also House of Lords Select Committee on Communications, *The Ownership of the News Volume I: Report* (HL Paper 122–I, 2008) pp. 32–40.

19 C.H. Tillinghast, *American Broadcast Regulation and the First Amendment: Another Look*, Iowa: Iowa State University Press, 2000.

20 The criteria for whether such competitive concerns exist are set out in the Enterprise Act 2002 (UK) s. 23. In brief, a 'relevant merger situation' requires either that a takeover target have a turnover of more than £70 million, or that the merger will create or enhance control of at least 25 per cent of the relevant market. See also *Merger Assessment Guidelines: A joint publication of the Competition Commission and the Office of Fair Trading*, 2009, at pp. 9–15. Online. Available HTTP: www.oft.gov.uk/shared_oft/consultations/OFT1078con.pdf (accessed 19 May, 2010).

21 These 'public interest provisions' were inserted into the Enterprise Act 2002 (UK) by the Communications Act 2003 (UK). For a detailed overview of how they apply, see Department of Trade and Industry, *Enterprise Act 2002: Public Interest Intervention in Media Mergers*, May 2004. Online. Available HTTP: www.berr.gov.uk/files/file14331.pdf (accessed 19 May, 2010).

22 Communications Act 2003 (UK) s. 58(2C)(a).

23 Ibid., s. 58(2C)(b).

24 Ibid., s. 58(2C)(c). See below at note 79–85 and accompanying text.

25 In addition to the merger regime discussed above, the Communications Act 2003 (UK) imposes additional specific limits on the ownership of ITV stations, so that a company holding a national ITV licence cannot merge with a company owning 20 per cent of the national newspaper market, nor can it merge with a company owning more than 20 per cent of the newspapers of that region.

26 See the discussion of this in House of Lords Select Committee on Communications, *The Ownership of the News Volume I: Report*, HL Paper 122–I, 2008, pp. 68–78.
27 A conclusion the Secretary of State is required to accept under the Enterprise Act 2002 (UK).
28 *British Sky Broadcasting Group Plc* v. *(1) The Competition Commission (2) The Secretary of State for Business, Enterprise and Regulatory Reform supported by Virgin Media, Inc; Virgin Media, Inc* v. *(1) The Competition Commission (2) The Secretary of State for Business, Enterprise and Regulatory Reform supported by British Sky Broadcasting Group Plc* [2008] CAT 25. For commentary on this decision, see Howard Cartlidge and Dervla Broderick, 'BSkyB/ITV: Competition Appeal Tribunal Dismisses BSkyB's Appeal', *Utilities Law Review*, 2009, vol. 17, 47.
29 The Broadcasting Act 1989 (NZ) originally contained provisions restricting the ownership of private broadcasters by overseas persons, but these were repealed in 1991.
30 See R. Ahdar, 'Freedom of the Press and Newspaper Mergers under the Commerce Act 1986', *Canterbury Law Review*, 1986, vol. 3, 42.
31 Commerce Act 1986 (NZ) s. 47. See generally, Commerce Commission, *Mergers and Acquisitions Guidelines*, 2004, pp. 11–13. Online. Available HTTP: www.comcom.govt.nz/Publications/ContentFiles/Documents/MergersandAcquisitions-Guidelines.PDF (accessed 19 May, 2010).
32 B. Rosenburg, *News Media Ownership in New Zealand*, 2007. Online. Available HTTP: www.pmc.aut.ac.nz/docs/papers/rosenberg_mediaown07.pdf (accessed 19 May, 2010).
33 *Sky Network Television Limited and Prime Televison New Zealand Limited*, Commerce Commission Dec. No. 573, 8 Feb 2006.
34 The parent company of TV3 and TV4 also owns MediaWorks Radio, which operates out of 23 markets in New Zealand.
35 Commerce Commission, *Mergers and Acquisitions Guidelines*, 2004, pp. 12. Online. Available HTTP: www.comcom.govt.nz/Publications/ContentFiles/Documents/MergersandAcquisitionsGuidelines.PDF (accessed 19 May, 2010).
36 *R (on the application of Animal Defenders International)* v. *Secretary of State for Culture, Media and Sport* [2008] UKHL 15, at para. 30.
37 See *Agreement with the Secretary of State for National Heritage*, Cm 3152, 25 January 1996, para. 10.10. This agreement puts into effect the BBC's obligations under its governing *Royal Charter for the Continuance of The British Broadcasting Corporation*, Cm 3248, 1996.
38 Communications Act 2003 (UK) s. 319(2)(g).
39 Ibid., s. 221(2).
40 Ibid., s. 221(3).
41 *R (on the application of Animal Defenders International)* v. *Secretary of State for Culture, Media and Sport* [2008] UKHL 15; [2008] 2 W.L.R. 781. *See also R* v. *Radio Authority, Ex p Bull* [1998] QB 294 (CA) (upholding a refusal to broadcast advertisements by Amnesty International calling attention to the unfolding genocide in Rwanda). For a discussion of the *Animal Defenders International* decision, see T. Lewis and P. Cumper, 'Balancing Freedom of Political Expression against Equality of Political Opportunity: the Courts and the UK Broadcasting Ban on Political Advertising', *Public Law*, 2009, 89.
42 *Animal Defenders* [2008] UKHL 15 at para. 30.
43 Ibid., at para. 31.
44 Ibid., 48.
45 *BBC Agreement* at para. 3(2)(a).
46 Communications Act 2003, s. 333(1)(a). Private broadcasters are also required to follow OFCOM's decision on how much time is to be allocated to each particular party: Communications Act 2003 (UK) s. 333(1)(b).

47 OFCOM, *OFCOM Rules on Party Political and Referendum Broadcasts*, 14 October 2004. Online. Available HTTP: www.ofcom.org.uk/tv/ifi/guidance/ppbrules/ppbrules.pdf (accessed 19 May, 2010). See especially para. 2 ('These rules reflect minimum requirements. They are not intended to fetter broadcasters' discretion to make additional allocations.') OFCOM currently is consulting on proposed new rules to govern the allocation of free airtime; see OFCOM, *A review of the Rules on Party Political and Referendum Broadcasts*, 16 September 2009. Online. Available HTTP: www.ofcom.org.uk/consult/condocs/pprb/pprb.pdf (accessed 19 May, 2010).

48 OFCOM, *OFCOM Rules*, Rules 5–9.

49 Ibid., Rule 10. 'Major parties' include 'Labour, Conservative, Liberal Democrats and, in Scotland and Wales respectively, the SNP and Plaid Cymru. Major parties in Northern Ireland are defined as Democratic Unionist, SDLP, Sinn Fein and Ulster Unionist.'

50 Ibid., Rule 11.

51 Ibid., Rule 14.

52 Ibid., Rule 15.

53 See *Broadcasters Liason Group* at www.broadcastersliaisongroup.org.uk/index.html (accessed 19 May, 2010).

54 The High Court rejected a challenge to the distribution of PEBs on this ground in *R.* v. *The British Broadcasting Corporation and the Independent Television Commission, ex parte The Referendum Party* [1997] EMLR 605.

55 The Electoral Commission, *Party political broadcasting: report and recommendations*, 2003, p. 16; see also the range of respondents who agreed with this conclusion at p. 42, fn. 41. The Commission's conclusion echoed that earlier reached by the Committee on Standards in Public Life, *The Funding of Political Parties in the United Kingdom*, 1998, p. 176.

56 OFCOM, *Viewers and Votes: Attitudes to Television Coverage of the 2005 Election*, 2005, p. 30.

57 Ibid., p. 28. What is more, some 36 per cent believed *too many* PEBs were screened.

58 Broadcasting Act 1989 (NZ) s. 70(1).

59 Ibid., s. 69(1).

60 The ban does not apply to 'the broadcasting, in relation to an election, of news or comment or of current affairs programmes', Broadcasting Act 1989 (NZ) s. 70(3). The official bodies charged with overseeing New Zealand's electoral process may place an election programme 'for the purposes of the Electoral Act 1993', and broadcasters may carry 'non-partisan advertisements' as a community service: Broadcasting Act 1989 (NZ) s. 70(2)(b).

61 Individual candidates also enjoy a limited exception to the blanket ban on using the broadcast media for political advertising. A candidate may purchase time to broadcast an election programme, so long as it solely relates to the promotion of his or her candidacy, and is broadcast in the three months prior to the election occurring: Broadcasting Act 1989 (NZ) s. 70(2)(c). However, any such spending by a candidate constitutes an 'election expense', and must therefore be counted towards the maximum of $20,000 that each candidate may spend on advertising his or her campaign: see Electoral Act 1993 (NZ) s. 205B.

62 Broadcasting Act 1989 (NZ) s. 74.

63 Broadcasting Act 1989 (NZ) ss. 73, 74A. The Electoral Commission is an independent Crown entity, which 'must act independently in performing its statutory functions and duties, and exercising its statutory powers': Electoral Act 1993 (NZ) s. 7. It has a current or retired High Court judge as its chair, and three additional independent, non-partisan members.

64 The main impediment to a party registering is the requirement it have at least 500 current financial members: Electoral Act 1993 (NZ) ss. 63(2)(c)(v11), 66(1)(b). At

the 2008 election, there were 21 registered parties, of which 14 requested and received a share of the broadcasting allocation.

65 Broadcasting Act 1989 (NZ) s. 75(2).

66 The way in which the Commission chose to apply the statutory criteria at the most recent general election is explained at Elections New Zealand, 'Broadcasting allocation 2008 – revised final allocation decision'. Online. Available HTPP: www.elections.org.nz/rules/advertising/ broadcasting-allocation-2008-initial-allocation-decision.html (accessed 19 May, 2010).

67 See S. Corban, 'Funding Political Party Broadcasting' *Auckland University Law Review*, 1997, 265 at pp. 272–282. See also 'Campaign broadcasting grants attract flak', *New Zealand Herald*, 20 June, 2002, p. 5; 'Labour pleased with $1.2m for election but Act says it's a rort', *New Zealand Herald*, 19 April, 2005, p. 10.

68 *The Alliance* v. *Electoral Commission* (unreported, NZ High Ct, CIV 2008–409–1253, 18 September 2008), para. 22.

69 Broadcasting Act 1989 (NZ) s. 70(2)(a).

70 Ibid., s. 74(1)(a).

71 A registered political party's allowable 'election expenses' are limited to a total of $1 million, plus $20,000 per constituency contested (equating to a current maximum of $2.4 million): Electoral Finance Act 2007 (NZ) s. 98. In relation to a political party, an 'election expense' is defined as spending on advertising, or the production of advertising materials, which takes place during an election year: Electoral Finance Act 2007 (NZ) s. 94. However, the value of any time or money allocated to a party under the Broadcasting Act 1989 does not count towards that party's maximum election expenses: Electoral Finance Act 2007 (NZ) ss. 94(2)(f).

72 Broadcasting Act 1989 (NZ) s. 79B(1) and (2). The offence carries a tariff of a fine of up to $100,000: s. 80(a)

73 Ibid., s. 79C. A failure to supply this return constitutes an offence punishable by a fine of up to $100,000: s. 80(a).

74 See also Electoral Commission, *Annual Report of the Electoral Commission, 2002–2003*, 2003, at p. 26 ('The Commission has been urging fundamental review of the election broadcasting regime since 1996, when it was given responsibilities relating to election broadcasting.')

75 My own views are set out in A. Geddis, 'Reforming New Zealand's Election Broadcasting Regime', *Pubic Law Review*, 2003, vol. 14, 164, pp. 180–182. The Government currently is reviewing the rules on broadcasting election programmes as a part of a general reform of the law on election financing: see Ministry of Justice, *Electoral Finance Reform: Proposal Document*, 28 September, 2009. Online. Available HTTP: www.justice.govt.nz/policy-and-consultation/electoral/electoral-finance-reform/consultation-papers/proposal-document (accessed 19 May, 2010).

76 See the Human Rights Act 1998 (UK) (incorporating the ECHR, Article 10(1) right to freedom of expression); New Zealand Bill of Rights Act 1990 (NZ), s. 14 (affirming the right to seek or impart information and opinion).

77 See ECHR, Article 10(2); New Zealand Bill of Rights Act 1990 (NZ), s. 5.

78 J. Rowbottom, 'Media Freedom and Political Debate in the Digital Era', *Modern Law Review*, 2006, vol. 69, 489, p. 493 (internal citations omitted).

79 Communications Act 2003 (UK) ss. 319(2)(c)&(d), 319(8), 320. In matters of impartiality and accuracy, the BBC is responsible for regulating itself.

> Due impartiality ... requires us to be fair and open minded when examining the evidence and weighing all the material facts, as well as being objective and even handed in our approach to a subject. It does not require the representation of every argument on every occasion or an equal division of time for each view.

The BBC describes this commitment to impartiality as seeking: 'To provide a properly balanced service consisting of a wide range of subject matter and views broadcast over an appropriate time scale across all our output. We take particular care when dealing with political or industrial controversy or major matters relating to current public policy.' See www.bbc.co.uk/guidelines/editorialguidelines/edguide/impariality/ (accessed 19 May, 2010).

80 OFCOM, *The OFCOM Broadcasting Code* (2008), p. 21. Online. Available HTTP: www.ofcom.org.uk/tv/ifi/codes/bcode/bcode.pdf (accessed 19 May, 2010).
81 Ibid.
82 Ibid., p. 22. See also Communications Act 2003 (UK) s. 320.
83 Ibid., pp. 22–23.
84 Ibid., p. 24.
85 Ibid., s. 6.
86 OFCOM, 'The Broadcasting Sanctions Committee: terms of reference'. Online. Available HTTP: www.ofcom.org.uk/about/csg/obsc/ocsc_tor2/ (accessed 19 May, 2010).
87 OFCOM, 'Procedures for statutory sanctions in content and content-related cases', para. 2. Online. Available HTTP: www.ofcom.org.uk/radio/ifi/ifiguidance/sanctions/ (accessed 19 May, 2010).
88 OFCOM, 'Procedures for statutory sanctions', para. 5.
89 Under OFCOM's statutory sanctions, 'the maximum fine is normally £250,000 or 5% of the relevant broadcaster's "Qualifying Revenue", whichever is the greater': OFCOM, 'Procedures for statutory sanctions', para. 2.
90 OFCOM Sanctions Committee, 'Consideration of sanction against Islam Channel Limited in respect of its service Islam Channel', 31 July, 2007. Online. Available HTTP: www.ofcom.org.uk/tv/obb/ocsc_adjud/islamchannel.pdf (accessed 19 May, 2010).
91 In breach of OFCOM, *The OFCOM Broadcasting Code*, 2008, Rule 6.6.
92 In breach of OFCOM, *The OFCOM Broadcasting Code*, Rule 6.12.
93 OFCOM Sanctions Committee, 'Consideration of sanction against Islam Channel Limited in respect of its service Islam Channel', 31 July, 2007, para. 1.10. Online. Available HTTP: www.ofcom.org.uk/tv/obb/ocsc_adjud/islamchannel.pdf (accessed 19 May, 2010).
94 OFCOM, *Broadcast Bulletin*, 26 February, 2007, p. 10.
95 Ibid., p. 11.
96 S. Noah, 'ITV News breached rules on Blair Iraq interview', *The Independent*, 27 February, 2007. Online. Available HTTP: www.independent.co.uk/news/media/itv-news-breached-rules-on-blair-iraq-interview-438042.html (accessed 19 May, 2010).
97 O. Gibson, 'ITV News rebuked for misreporting Blair interview', *The Guardian*, 27 February, 2007. Online. Available HTTP: www.guardian.co.uk/politics/2007/feb/27/uk.media (accessed 19 May, 2010).
98 See OFCOM, *OFCOM Rules on Party Political and Referendum Broadcasts*, 2004, para. 3; OFCOM, *The OFCOM Broadcasting Code*, 2008, p. 26.
99 *R* v. *British Broadcasting Corporation, ex parte ProLife Alliance* [2004] 1 AC 185 (HL); see also A. Geddis, 'If thy right eye offend thee, pluck it out: *R* v. *BBC* (ex p Prolife Alliance)', *Modern Law Review*, 2003, vol. 66, 885.
100 Broadcasting Act 1990 (UK) s. 4(1)(a).
101 See 'BNP forced to edit election film', *BBC News*, 29 May, 2004. Online. Available HTTP: http://news.bbc.co.uk/2/hi/uk_news/politics/3757641.stm (accessed 19 May, 2010).
102 Broadcasting Act 1989 (NZ) s. 4(1)(d). However, this principle does not apply to election advertising: s. 79.
103 Ibid., s. 8. See generally S. Price, *Media Minefield: A Journalists Guide to Media Regulation in New Zealand*, Wellington: New Zealand Journalists Training Organisation, 2007, pp. 31–61; J. Sneyd, 'The balancing act: what the BSA has said.

Analysis of 10 years of decisions', in Broadcasting Standards Authority, *Significant Viewpoints: Broadcasters Discuss Balance*, 2006, at p. 107.

104 Broadcasting Act 1989 (NZ) s. 26.

105 Ibid., s. 13(1).

106 *The Prime Minister (Rt Hon Helen Clark)* v. *TV3* (BSA2003–055/061), at para. 358.

107 Broadcasting Standards Authority, 'Free-to-air Television Code' (2006). Online. Available HTTP: www.bsa.govt.nz/codesstandards-freetv.php (accessed 19 May, 2010).

108 *The Prime Minister (Rt Hon Helen Clark)* v. *TV3* (BSA2003–055/061); *Owen* v. *TV3* (BSA2004–064). See also *TV3 Network Services Ltd* v. *Prime Minister (Rt Hon Helen Clark)* [2004] BCL 294.

109 *The Prime Minister (Rt Hon Helen Clark)* v. *TV3* (BSA2003–055/061), at para. 358.

110 John Burrows and Ursula Cheer, *Media Law in New Zealand*, 5th ed., 2005, p. 595.

111 *MAF* v. *TVNZ* (BSA 1995–025) at para. 29.

112 Broadcasting Act 1989 (NZ) ss. 4(1)(a)–(c) and 79. However, election campaign advertisements are exempt from any requirement to respect the 'balance' principle.

113 Ibid., s. 21(1)(e)–(f).

114 Broadcasting Standards Authority, 'Election Programmes Code', 2005. Online. Available HTTP: www.bsa.govt.nz/election.htm (accessed 19 May, 2010).

115 Broadcasting Standards Authority, 'Election Programmes Code', Standard E1.

116 Ibid., Standard E2.

117 Ibid., Standard E3.

118 Ibid., Standard E4.

119 But see *Raukawa FM and the Māori Party* (BSA2005–103, 13 September 2005).

120 Broadcasting Act 1989 (NZ) s. 8(1)(ba).

121 Ibid., s. 8(1).

9 The regulator

The first decade of the Electoral Commission

Navraj Singh Ghaleigh

As with many democratic devices, party finance supervisory bodies (PFSBs)[1] come in a long array of shapes and sizes, something that can easily be lost on those who study only one or very similar such bodies. For example, a UK scholar with some knowledge of the US Federal Election Commission might be forgiven for assuming that all PFSBs are unified entities overseeing the range of party and campaign finance laws and practices, their supervision, monitoring and enforcement.

In many jurisdictions, however, these tasks are shared between two or more institutions, owing to constitutional or other institutional arrangements. In Lithuania the functional roles of PFSBs are shared between the Central Election Commission and State Tax inspectorate, in Croatia between the State Audit Office and tax administration, and in Albania the electoral commission, tax authorities and State Supreme Audit are all involved. *In abstracto* the unified model – as in France, Germany, Belgium and Poland – may be thought preferable in affording the supervisory body with an overall view of the finances of candidates and parties, better information and avoidance of the coordination and cooperation difficulties that may afflict inter-agency relations.[2]

Similarly, in terms of institutional affiliation, supervision may be undertaken by a unit of the public administration (the Ministry of Finance or tax authorities or national audit offices), or of the legislature (an assembly leader, speaker or cross-party committee of elected officials), or of the judiciary (the constitutional court, court of audit or dedicated electoral court) or by a permanent independent bodies (the electoral commission or anti-corruption body). In each case strengths and weaknesses present themselves. Are supervisory bodies populated by ordinary civil servants reliably independent from their political masters? Can the impartiality of legislators be taken for granted, with the risks of conflict of interest negated? Do general courts have sufficient expertise and resources? Are dedicated commissions too divorced from the practice of politics to understand properly the community they seek to regulate?

It is in this context that the present chapter addresses the role of the UK's Electoral Commission as regards party funding monitoring and enforcement during the historical phenomenon of New Labour.[3] If plotted against the axes of non-unitary/unitary and independent/affiliated identified above, the Electoral

Commission would be located firmly in the top right quadrant – it is a designedly unitary body with a series of mechanisms that preserve its independence from other institutional actors. This would suggest that the Commission, benefiting from a 'last movers advantage', and substantially immune from inter-institutional pressures as well as being expert and well informed, would be an exemplar in comparative terms. The experience of recent years suggests something different, or that there are other parts of the party finance system that require attention. Since 2005 party funding scandals have emerged with troubling regularity. Of the scandals discussed, all involve the then governing Labour Party. However, it should not be inferred from this case selection that only that party was so implicated – serious funding questions arose in respect of all the major parties in this period – but those discussed herein were certainly the most damaging to the body politic, not least because they concerned the governing regime.

This chapter proceeds by first exploring the extent to which there are international legal standards for party finance monitoring. Whilst the relevant instruments are few in number and perhaps not fully mature or articulated, they do provide a yardstick by which to consider the Electoral Commission. The Commission itself is then analysed, its legal duties and powers considered as well as the external scrutiny to which it has recently been subjected. This gives way in turn to an examination of the four most prominent party finance scandals of recent years, the shortcomings of the system that they reveal and the remedial action taken to date.

International legal standards

Public international law has to date had little to say about PFSBs and their legal functions. While relatively rudimentary aspects of civil and political rights such as discrimination against women remain highly contested at this level, it is not surprising that more nuanced issues remain largely unaddressed. The UN Convention Against Corruption 2004[4] (UNCAC) contains several provisions of relevance for present purposes, namely Article 7.3,[5] Article 6[6] and Article 36,[7] which when read together establish a legal framework not only for the conduct of free and fair elections but also for PFSBs to combat corruption through legal means, operating in an independent fashion. Admittedly, the obligations are not addressed exclusively to PFSBs nor to party finance, but the framework certainly accommodates them. Nonetheless, there is considerable vagueness surrounding precise legal obligations at this level of the law, perhaps foreseeable given the focus of this particular instrument – whilst action against corruption captures a significant degree of regulatory activity pertaining to party funding, it is clearly not its entirety.

A shift to the regional level reveals instruments of greater conceptual focus and legal clarity. A prominent example of a regional regime giving detailed attention to party finance matters is the Council of Europe Committee of Ministers' Recommendation Rec (2003)4 on Common Rules Against Corruption in the Funding of Political Parties and Electoral Campaigns.[8] The Committee's role is to consider action required to further the Council's aim, including the conclusion of agreements or the adoption by governments of a common policy with regard to particular matters, in response to findings of violations. Such recommendations are non-binding but indicate to member states the steps they should take at the national level to facilitate execution.[9] This is obviously a more focused tool than the UNCAC, containing common rules on the sources of support to parties (Art 1), expenditure limits (Art 9), and transparency rules (Arts 11–13). Article 13 in particular requires that parties' accounts be maintained in addition to the Article 14[10] requirement for public monitoring, supported by personnel specialisation as per Article 15.[11]

Here we have something approaching a workable set of international standards for PFSB. Indeed, the Recommendations form the basis for the three key themes – transparency, supervision and sanctions – upon which the Group of States Against Corruption's (GRECO's) Third Evaluation Round of its 47 member states focus.[12] Recognizing the necessity for political parties, who aspire to control the levers of the state, to be publicly accountable for their income and expenditure, the Recommendations impose a duty for detailed reports to be regularly reported to an independent PFSB. Precisely what 'independent monitoring' entails is left unstated. Does it include the inspection and auditing of parties? Do PFSBs have a legislative aspect that enables them to issue regulations to their regulated community? What is the relationship between the PFSB and the 'specialised personnel'? Given the large and transnational composition of the Council of Europe, many of these issues must be left necessarily under-articulated in the Recommendations, but the core principles of close control of sources, income and expenditure, transparency and the necessity of independent supervision form the basis for a comprehensive international legal standard for party finance regulation. The elaboration of these Recommendations by the GRECO evaluation process is of scholarly interest and not without practical impact.

The Electoral Commission – 'incompetent, dysfunctional and politically unworldly'?[13]

The Political Parties, Elections and Referendums Act 2000 (PPERA) creates a substantially novel ecosystem for the conduct of elections and referendums in the UK so far as matters of party funding are concerned.[14] Whilst matters of electoral administration[15] have benefitted from detailed regulation in the UK since the nineteenth century, party funding had fallen into a rather arid regulatory zone.[16] With the enactment of PPERA, nearly every aspect of political finance came under regulatory scrutiny and control. For example, permissibility requirements on donations to political parties, candidates and cognate entities were introduced, as were sophisticated mechanisms to ensure transparency on the income and expenditure of all those entities, additional public funding was made available to parties, and so on. As the heading to this section indicates, the operation of this ambitious new regime has not been without controversy.

Functions

As noted by Ewing, the Electoral Commission plays a pivotal role in the architecture of PPERA and its various constituent parts – 'the whole package is held together by the provisions for the creation of a new Electoral Commission'.[17] Its wide-ranging duties include the obligation to prepare and publish reports on the administration of elections or referendums (PPERA, s. 5); to keep under review and submit reports pertaining to *inter alia* the redistribution of seats, the registration of parties and their income and expenditure and political advertising; and to attend election proceedings and observe the working practices of electoral officials (ss. 6, 6A, 6B).

Further to such administrative functions, the Commission enjoys the entitlement to be consulted on changes to electoral law (s. 7); for broadcasters to have regard to their views on party political broadcasts (ss. 11, 144) to participate in changes to electoral procedures (s. 9), to set and report on performance standards for electoral administrators (ss. 9A, 9B); to give advice to specified bodies 'as respects any matter in which the Commission have skill and experience' (s. 10); to keep under review and make recommendations to the Secretary of State on the operation of the policy development grant scheme (s. 12); and to promote public awareness of electoral and democratic systems.[18]

In addition, at each of the key stages of electoral and party finance administration, the Commission plays an important role. The entry point into the regulatory regime for political parties is the requirement that they 'register' (PPERA, Part II). The Commission maintains the register of political parties (PPERA, ss. 23, 31, 32, 34, 36), approves the financial scheme of political parties (a prerequisite for their registration) (s. 26) and administers the process of registration (ss. 28, 28A, 28B, 29, 30). The scope of the fundamental duty of political parties to account for their income and expenditure is substantially determined by the Commission (ss. 41, 48), as are the regulations pertaining to parties' statements of accounts (s. 42(2)(a)). The Commission may require such accounts to be audited (ss. 43, 44), and it is the conduit by which party accounts are made available for public inspection (ss. 46, 149). The failure to submit to the Commission proper accounts is a criminal offence (s. 47), as is the act of making false statements to it (s. 39).

The system of donation reporting by parties is a key transparency safeguard of the regime, and here, too, the Commission is involved, as the body to whom donation reports must be delivered (s. 65(1)), with the failure so to do being a criminal offence (s. 65(4)). The register of recordable donations is maintained by the Commission (s. 69). As with donations, so with returns of campaign expenditure which must be delivered to the Commission (s. 82(1)), whereupon they are made available for public inspection (ss. 84(1), 149). This applies to campaign spending both by political parties and by third parties (such as interest groups and trade unions).

Moving from elections – now a near annual event with general, European, local, mayoral and devolved contests falling hard on one another – to referendums, there are statutory duties to discharge here too. The UK is notorious in direct democracy studies for deploying the referendum device sparingly.[19] Nonetheless, when the referendum is deployed, the Commission considers the intelligibility of the question (s. 104), determines the status of participants for the purposes of public funds and assistance and reporting requirements (ss. 105, 106, 108), as well as prescribing the form of expenditure returns and making the same publicly available (ss. 120(5), 121, 124). Further, and unlike the procedure for elections, the Chief Counting Officer for the referendum is either the chairman of the Commission, or his or her appointee (s. 128(2)).

As to the crucial issue of enforcement, 'the Commission shall have the *general function* of monitoring compliance with … the restrictions and other requirements imposed by or by virtue of [PPERA and other enactments]' (s. 145),[20] to which end the Commission is granted broad supervisory powers. These include the ability to require supervised organisations to produce or furnish the Commission with '*any* such books, documents or other records relating to the income and expenditure of the organisation or individual as [it] may reasonably require for the purposes of the carrying out by them of their functions' (s. 146(1)(a)).[21] Attendant powers of copying such records (s. 146(2)), and even 'enter[ing] at any reasonable time premises occupied by a supervised organisation' (s. 246(3)), are granted. The failure to deliver up such documents incurs civil penalties (s. 147), which attach to a far greater range of non-compliance activities with the amendments brought by Political Parties and Elections Act 2009, s. 3.[22]

Owing to the Commission's duty being to monitor compliance without also being a prosecuting authority (s. 145), it is the police, not the Commission who have the responsibility for initiating enforcement actions for criminal offences committed under the Act.[23] This had often left the Commission in an invidious position. Where it detected wrongdoing it could either issue a reprimand – essentially, do nothing – or refer the matter to the criminal prosecution authorities, a 'nuclear option' often not appropriate to party finance infractions. This lack of proportionate sanctioning was felt by the Commission to undermine the capacity for its sanctions to be effective and dissuasive. The cases of Watt and Hain (discussed below) would likely have been dealt with differently had more proportionate sanctions been available to the Commission.

Whilst certain functions originally allocated to the Commission by PPERA have subsequently been removed, such as its wide-ranging electoral boundary[24] and educational[25] functions, this is self-evidently an extensive range of powers, duties and responsibilities. Arguably, it is over-extensive. Although the Commission is far from the only public body engaged in party funding – *inter alia* it reports directly to Parliament, receives submissions from the Parliamentary Parties Panel[26] and the police and prosecuting authorities investigate criminal wrongdoing and take final decisions on prosecution – it is at the heart of almost every non-legislative aspect of party funding (although it has legislative functions too).[27]

The vesting of power on such a scale would be presumptively dubious were it not for the splendid isolation of the Commission (though not so splendid as it was until recently – see below). Like the National Audit Office, the Commission is a corporate body independent of any government department. Similar to the National Audit Office (NAO), the Commission is not regarded as a servant or agent of the Crown nor is its property regarded as the Crown's (Sch 1, para. 1). Its financing is not in the gift of the government or a simple parliamentary majority but is safeguarded by a complex procedure, outlined in PPERA, Schedule 1(14). It was the case until 2009 that Election Commissioners were radically apolitical in that individuals were barred from holding office as a Commissioner if they were members of political parties (s. 3(4)(a)), had held a political office in the previous ten years (s. 3(4)(d)), or had donated to a political party (s. 3(4)(d)).

Other employees of the Commission were subject to cognate (though lesser) political restrictions. In the face of very significant opposition from academic opinion and the Commission itself, the principle and effect of strictly apolitical Commissioners was undermined by s. 5 of the Political Parties and Elections Act 2009 which makes provision for four of the nine Commissioners to be the nominees of the parties. The provision was supported by all major political parties, who had long felt that the Commission was insufficiently attentive to or knowledgeable of, the practical workings of political parties. Whether the innovation will make a positive difference to this issue or indeed any other aspect of the Commission's work is very much open to question.

Travails and reform

This necessarily brief account of the Electoral Commission's functions reveals the impressive range of responsibilities, duties, consultation roles, functions, and review powers that are vested within it. There is some attraction in having a single unified body undertaking what are after all, a range of tasks – electoral administration, the conduct of elections and referendums, and the monitoring and investigating standards of propriety in the financing of political parties – that shares obvious family resemblances. But although there is an intellectual coherence to the scheme, it has been increasingly argued that this was not matched by operational excellence. In addition to the episodes of dubious party finance discussed below, the UK democratic processes have been disfigured in recent years by concerns about the process of voter registration, and postal voting on demand, along with attendant allegations of significant electoral fraud.

Of the various reports and inquiries into the Electoral Commission, the most influential was that undertaken by the Committee on Standards in Public Life (CSPL). Their report[28] was motivated by concerns about electoral administration as well as party finance, two roles which, opined the CSPL 'should have been core tasks and priorities of the Electoral Commission [but] this has not been the case to date'.[29] So far as they pertain to party funding, the CSPL's criticisms addressed three issues – the Commission's regulatory strategies, the need to strengthen its governance by the inclusion of 'political' commissioners and other staff, and the shearing off of various ancillary functions to tighten its regulatory focus. The CSPL strongly argued for the Commission to adopt a more nuanced mode of regulation, from mere information collection, collation and verification to one that identifies 'high risk' actors and activities and enables greater communication between regulator and the regulated.

In other words, less monitoring and more regulating.[30] The distinction might be conceptualised as one between regulatory strategies that are 'deterrence-based' and those that are more 'responsive'. Such models can run the risk of casting too crudely, what are invariably complex processes. The former characterises the Electoral Commission as a dumb data repository, with action being mechanically taken where breaches occur. The contrast is with the latter's 'smart' approach of risk identification, negotiatory contacts with and approaches to parties, and so on. However, given the Electoral Commission's subsequent adoption of the Report's findings in this area (in particular, the creation of an 'enforcement unit' separate from the 'guidance and policy unit') and subsequent statutory bolstering by the Political Parties and Elections Act 2009,[31] this recommendation appears to have been well taken.

A more controversial criticism from the CSPL, that was amplified by the Hayden Phillips Review in 2006, relating to the political valency of Commissioners and in particular the need for party representatives among the Commissioners.[32] The claim was that the disqualification rules for Commissioners deprived the body of adequate political intelligence, an argument made particularly forcefully by Peter Hain MP, who 'found [the Commission] to be incompetent, dysfunctional and politically unworldly', and to have 'very little idea of the political world that it was regulating'[33] In the teeth of strong opposition from academics and the Commission itself, political commissioners were introduced to the 2009 Act, s. 5.

Finally, the scope of the Commission's remit was considered over-broad by the CSPL, which argued for the Commission to focus on its core regulatory role. Other tasks, such as the obligation to promote understanding and awareness of systems of government from local to European, were considered 'non-core', a view reflected in the 2009 Act which, at section 8, removes the Commission's duty to provide education about systems of local and national government and institutions of the EU. Whilst it is certainly the case that the Commission was perhaps not the body best placed to undertake this work, it is worrying that the functional void has not been filled by other public bodies being tasked to undertake such public education. More broadly, the issue of the proper scope for PFSB is not a simple one, as noted in several studies by GRECO[34] which have highlighted difficulties in this respect that have been faced by Estonia, Albania and Croatia.[35]

Having been present at the birth,[36] there is a pleasing symmetry in the CSPL having had such a decisive hand in the re-ordering of the Electoral Commission.

Its central message that the Commission's range of responsibilities was too broad is intuitively correct, and appears to have met little resistance from the Commission itself. Indeed, some of latest statements of the latter very much chime with the approach urged by the CSPL. In reviewing and investigating possible breaches of the law, the Commission's enforcement unit adopts a multi-threaded approach, monitoring returns, responding to complaints and acting on its own initiative where necessary.[37] Similarly, in comparison to its much criticised and inflexible approach to providing guidance in the 'loans for honours' affair – see below – the current approach is

> to secure compliance by helping those we regulate to understand the law and get things right, rather than by taking enforcement action after things go wrong. [We] provide informal advice and can also provide formal written opinions on difficult issues if needed.[38]

Party funding scandals and the responses of the Commission

For a party finance regime to operate effectively, certain basic regulatory elements must be in place. Parties must register with a PFSB so that their activities can be supervised, and that body must be supplied with adequate resources, powers of inquiry and control and so on. In addition, sound statutory definitions of the building blocks of party finance – what constitutes a 'permissible donor' (s. 54). or 'campaign expenditure' (s. 72), or a 'donation' (s. 50) – are necessary. It was a loophole in the last of these definitions that ignited the most damaging party funding scandal in recent British history.

'Cash for honours'

The episode that came to be known as 'cash for honours' was coloured by a toxic relationship between the Labour Party and the Electoral Commission, and brought into sharper focus by the Party's parlous financial position. Of the former, the key official recalls a 'virtually permanent state of conflict', in a period when the Party

> had been very blasé about [its] financial and administrative arrangements, and did not take sufficient care to ensure that everything we did was legal ... Often we forgot that the measures the government passed [PPERA] actually applied to us as well.[39]

Simultaneously, the Labour Party found itself in straitened circumstances, with debts of approximately £35 million[40] throughout the post-2005 period, and with a very real threat of insolvency – a remarkable state of affairs for the party of government.[41]

Immediately prior to, and after, the 2005 General Election, the Party's chief fundraiser, Lord Levy began to solicit and receive very large loans from wealthy individuals,[42] totalling £13 million.[43] Why did the Party seek loans instead of donations? The apparently irrational preference for loans is explicable only by reference to PPERA, section 50. In the words of Watt, 'There was nothing illegal about this. If the loans were *below* market rates, they would have to be declared to the EC, but *commercial loans did not*.'[44] Watt's analysis is correct. Section 50 requires only that loans 'otherwise than on commercial terms' count as donations for the purposes of the Act's reporting requirements. By contracting with sympathetic lenders that the loans be on commercial terms, the reporting obligation was side-stepped.[45]

These arrangements came under severe strain and public scrutiny for the first time as newspapers began to note that all those that had donated over £1 million to the Labour Party had been awarded an honour or peerage,[46] and that several of the Prime Minister's nominations for peerages had been 'high value' donors to the Labour Party. Appointments to the House of Lords are made via number of avenues, though for present purposes the House of Lords Appointments Commission (HoLAC) is most relevant.[47] The Commission – three representatives of the major political parties and three 'independents' – recommends individuals to the Queen for elevation, including those nominated by political parties as working peers. Deference is accorded to the parties in this process such that nominees are only scrutinised to ensure there are no issues as to propriety of potential appointees – suitability is outwith the Committee's ambit. In December 2005, HoLAC blocked several of the Prime Minister's nominations,[48] on account of its duty to 'satisfy itself that the person would be a credible nominee irrespective of payments made to a political party'.[49]

The tipping point in the affair was the March 2006 reference of the matter to the Crown Prosecution Service by Mr Angus MacNeil, a Scottish National Party MP, for a potential breach of the hitherto obscure Honours (Prevention of Abuses) Act 1925. That Act was the response to a once thriving piece of political commerce, the sale of honours and peerages,[50] which it criminalised. Only one person has ever been prosecuted under the Act, the person for whom the legislation was specifically enacted, though the prosecution of Mr Maundy Gregory took place several years after enactment and long after his influence had waned.[51]

The 1925 is a short Act, its key provisions being:

1 If any person accepts or obtains or agrees to accept or attempts to obtain from any person, for himself or for any other person, or for any purpose, any gift, money or valuable consideration as an inducement or reward for procuring or assisting or endeavouring to procure the grant of a dignity or title of honour to any person, or otherwise in connection with such a grant, he shall be guilty of a misdemeanour.

2 If any person gives, or agrees or proposes to give, or offers to any person any gift, money or valuable consideration as an inducement or reward for procuring or assisting or endeavouring to procure the grant

> of a dignity or title of honour to any person, or otherwise in connection with such a grant, he shall be guilty of a misdemeanour.

For the purposes of section 1, a loan comes within the definition of 'any gift, money or valuable consideration', but for an offence to be committed it is necessary to show an offer of a loan in exchange for an honour, or an agreement for a loan in exchange for an honour. In other words, there must be an agreement between the parties. Mere hopes or expectations are insufficient. Similarly, the decision to award an honour, having taken a loan into consideration, is insufficient. There must be a developed and definite relationship between the offer of the loan and the award of the honour.[52]

The evidential burden that the obscure language of the 1925 Act creates for the prosecution is thus high. In the absence of a written agreement (rather improbable), it requires the prosecutor to produce very strong circumstantial evidence that would trump any innocent explanation offered in defence. Further, and this was a consideration common to the scandals discussed herein, the Crown Prosecution Service was required to consider its own 'Code for Crown Prosecutors', administrative guidelines that set out the general principles Crown Prosecutors should follow when they make prosecution decisions on individual cases. Of particular importance here is not only whether there is enough evidence against the defendant, but also whether it is in the public interest for the CPS to bring the case to court?[53]

In pursuit of the evidence presented to it, the Metropolitan Police undertook an intensive inquiry that involved the arrest and questioning of key government advisers, donors and most prominently, the Labour Party's chief funder, Lord Levy. The arrest of a figure so intimately connected to the Prime Minister caused a political storm of rare ferocity, matched only by the subsequent police questioning of the Prime Minister himself – a first in such circumstances in the UK. After a politically[54] and personally[55] damaging investigation of 16 months, the Crown Prosecution Service eventually decided not to prosecute.[56]

Of the various aspects of this episode, the Electoral Commission's absence from the scene is noteworthy. Although it is an offence under PPERA to fail to report the receipt of a loan made other than on commercial terms, as the loans in question were made on commercial terms, the reporting requirement was obviated. This loophole neatly sidestepped the Commission, almost entirely. To the extent that it was involved, the Commission was criticised for failing to provide guidance to parties on the precise definition of a 'commercial loan' for the purposes of the Act.[57] It is not clear whether the provision of such clarifications would have enabled donors and recipients to act in a less suspect manner, but the example has been used to highlight the Commission's 'unresponsive' approach to regulation.

The shortcomings of the 1925 Act, its tortuous language and impossibly high standard of proof are perhaps besides the point. An antiquated statute cannot be expected to regulate a world of political finance which it could not have imagined. Criticisms are better directed to the UK's legal arrangements directed against corruption. As noted by the Public Administration Select Committee's report into the affair, there are no less than 11 statutes and more common law offences purportedly addressing aspects of corruption.[58] Although that broader regime remains unaddressed, the PPERA 'loophole' of section 50(e) has since been repealed by the Electoral Administration Act 2006,[59] with a new regime for regulating loans also added.

The Prime Minister's response was to invite the former civil servant Sir Hayden Phillips to 'examine the case for state funding of political parties, including whether it should be enhanced in return for a cap on the size of donations and to consider the transparency of political parties' funding'. These terms of reference indicate that state funding as a trade-off for limiting the vast donations that have become the staple of British party funding, is at the heart of the matter. Such an arrangement would be problematic for the Labour Party's relationship with the union movement, a consideration that led to the ultimate failure of the 'Hayden Phillips' process.[60]

The thoughtless think-tank and Mr Peter Hain MP

The mid-2007 Prime Ministerial transition from Tony Blair to Gordon Brown took place without a campaign for the job of Leader of the Labour Party,[61] with the former Chancellor being the only candidate for the job. The position of Deputy Leader, vacated by John Prescott was, however, contested by six candidates, one of whom was Mr Peter Hain MP. He was placed fifth in the contest despite having spent more than double that of the eventual winner and having outspent all other rivals.[62]

The House of Commons' 'Register of Members' Interests',[63] indicated that a number of donations were made to the Hain campaign ('Hain4Labour') from January to November 2007, with those received after the conclusion of the campaign being necessary to clear its debts. Consistent with the rules of the Register, the ten donations received prior to May were registered within four weeks of receipt (totaling £77,000). However, in late 2007 and early 2008 it emerged that 19 further donations to *Hain4Labour*, totalling £103,156.75, were received but not reported. Approximately £50,000 of these unreported donations were donated to Hain4Labour by a previously unknown think tank, a members' association called the Progressive Policies Forum, which since its inception in December 2006 had never published any thoughts, nor employed anyone to think, nor filed any accounts.

This matter assumed very significant proportions,[64] and generated a new round of public outcry and media attention, leading to Mr Hain's resignation on 24 January 2008 as a Cabinet Minister. As a matter of law, the failure to disclose was serious in two respects. First, as regards the law of parliament, it contravened the parliamentary rules governing the disclosure of Members' Interests. After complaints to him, the Parliamentary Commissioner for Standards inquired into matter finding that the

> failure to register donations on this scale [to be] both serious and substantial … Because of the seriousness and scale of this breach and noting the considerable, justified public concern that it has created, we would ordinarily have been minded to propose a heavier penalty.[65]

However, on this occasion the Commissioner accepted an apology on the floor of the House from Mr Hain as he had evinced no intention to deceive and had already paid a high political price for his failings.[66]

The ordinary law was less readily able to arrive at such a clear cut answer. PPERA requires the reporting of 'controlled donations' (Sch 7(1)(3))to 'regulated donees' (Sch 7(1)(7)) (donations to MPs or members' associations rather than the party), to be reported within 30 days of receipt. Failure to do is a criminal offence.[67] After two months of reviewing the circumstances of the disclosure failure, the Electoral Commission 'referred matters to the Metropolitan Police for them to consider whether [a criminal] investigation should commence'.[68] For his part, Mr Hain accounted for the non-disclosure by way of poor office management: 'I should have given higher personal priority to the day to day administration and organisation of my campaign.'[69] This rather homely excuse was fine as far as it went but it failed to account for the fact that large sums were channeled through a 'think tank' that seemed to have come into existence only for the purpose of acting as a conduit for the purposes of supporting Mr Hain's campaign.

Nor could Mr Hain claim to have been unaware of his reporting obligations to the Commission. With more than a nod to the mode of 'compliance' procedures, the Commission wrote to all the Deputy Leader candidates at the beginning of the campaign, outlining their obligations and duties relating to the declaration of donations. The letter explained to them that they were legally responsible for their campaigns, and that it was their responsibility to ensure that all donations were declared within 30 days of receipt. Forms were provided for candidates or their teams to do just that and these forms had to be signed personally by the candidates. Indeed, it was on these forms that some donations were properly and timeously declared. The dismal failure of their persuasive approach of compliance-seeking no doubt contributed to Electoral Commission's determination for the police to investigate the matter.

As with Levy, the police investigation was not swift, a matter of understandable anguish to those directly affected. Almost 11 months after the Electoral Commission's referral, the Crown Prosecution Service (CPS) decided that there was insufficient evidence to charge Mr Hain.[70] The principal difficulty, in the CPS's judgment, arose from a combination of fact and ambiguous law. Schedule 7 (12)(1) criminalised the act of non-delivery of a donation report by the 'regulated donee' or, if a members association, the 'responsible person'. The difficulty for the CPS was in identifying Mr Hain as either. Although Hain4Labour was constituted of Labour Party members, and although the campaign was run through it and cheques donated through its account, Mr Hain was not a signatory and did not in the CPS view, direct where the funds should be spent. Nor was it possible to prove from the evidence available that any one was the responsible person.

Accordingly, no prosecution was forthcoming. The Electoral Commission's disappointment with this decision was plainly put:

> The Electoral Commission [...] referred the matter to the police because there was evidence that an offence may have been committed ... The decision on whether or not to bring a prosecution is a matter for the CPS [who] have said that Mr Hain was not the person responsible for reporting the donations, and that it is not possible to prove that anyone else involved with his campaign was responsible ...We will [...] be reviewing the implication of the CPS's decision carefully and considering what steps will be needed to achieve this certainty, including possible changes to the law.[71]

As with loans for honours, the hope for 'possible changes to the law' was acted upon swiftly. PPERA, Schedule 7(1) was amended by Political Parties and Elections Act 2009, s14(3) which requires members' associations with no treasurer to appoint one within 30 days of receiving a controlled donation, it being an offence to fail to do so. Should this precise combination of circumstances occur again the law is forearmed, belatedly. Section 15 of the same Act also permits holders of elected office to appoint a 'compliance officer' to assist them with discharging their donation reporting obligations.

Proxy donations and Mr David Abrahams

A scandal that further sapped the dim perception of the governing party broke almost simultaneously with that concerning Mr Hain. It was revealed in November 2007 that a major donor had used intermediaries to channel over £630,000 (in 19 donations between 2003 and 2007) to the Labour Party. In this way the donor, Mr David Abrahams, was able to conceal his true identity as the Electoral Commission's register showed only the details of his associates who acted as his proxies. That these 'associates' were of perfectly ordinary means – a 'jobbing builder', a secretary and a lollipop lady – was devoured by the press.[72] The arrangement was known to senior Labour officials who believed it to be lawful,[73] whilst the donor himself justified his actions thus: 'I donated money to the Labour Party through intermediaries because of a desire for anonymity, not secrecy'.[74]

For the purposes of PPERA, the issue revolved around the requirement in section 56, read together with Schedule 6, that a series of steps had to be undertaken by a registered party before a recordable donation (that is, at £5,000 or more, at the time) could be accepted. Amongst these steps was the obligation to take all reasonable measures to verify or ascertain the identity of the donor. The registered treasurer of a party is in turn obliged to make an annual return to the Electoral Commission containing the names and addresses of those who have donated more than £5,000 in a calendar year. Inaccuracies in that report as to the identity of the donor may be an offence, subject to the statutory defence of the treasurer having taken all reasonable steps and exercised due diligence to ensure that the report complied with the Act's requirements. This put the General Secretary of the Labour Party in the firing line, and he promptly resigned.

The subsequent referral of the matter by the Electoral Commission to the police triggered one more lengthy investigation which, after 18 months, once more resulted in the CPS declaring that there was 'insufficient evidence to charge anyone with any offences in relation to the incorrect declaration of donations to the Labour Party'.[75] Although the various treasurers' donation reports formed the basis of the offence, incorrectly identifying the conduits as the donor, the CPS took the view that the 'further enquiries by police highlighted inconsistencies in the evidence which meant that the prosecution would not be able to present a reliable account [of whom knew what and when] concerning the identity of the donor'. It was decided that the evidential test would not be met and that there was 'not a realistic prospect of securing a conviction'[76] The legislative response to this affair was the introduction of an obligation for donations to registered parties in excess of £7,500, to be accompanied by a written declaration that it is in fact from that person and not from some other third party, with the true donor's name and address. Donations without such a declaration must be returned and the making of a false statement is a criminal offence.[77] Yet more efficient sweeping up by the legislator.

Conclusion

Whether the 'scandals' are properly so-called also requires some attention. Fisher seems to regard them as mere episodes, either because there were no convictions, or because the alleged offences did not involve 'any desire to seek personal material gain'. The former argument is overly formalistic. To say that no wrong has occurred because legal processes determined this to be so is to place the institutions of law in a position of infallibility. The unsustainable nature of this position is shown by the amendment of the law, at the first opportunity, pertaining to 'proxy donations', members' associations and loans after PPERA's inadequacies were revealed. The absence of an effective legal scheme does not cause to vanish 'a grossly discreditable circumstance, event, or condition of things'.[78]

As to the question of material gain, this too is dubious. Lawyers are familiar with the distinction between *mala in se* and *mala prohibita* – conduct which is wrong in itself, and conduct which is wrong because the law determines this to be the case.[79] Fisher argues that because the events surrounding Watt, Abrahams, Levy and Hain 'represented first and foremost, reporting irregularities', they are properly viewed as *mala prohibita*, 'technical' breaches perhaps, and therefore not 'real crimes'. This again is an odd argument for a couple of reasons, first because the act of non-disclosure goes to very real issues of morality including the duty to obey the law and to provide citizens in a democracy with the full information to make value judgments about those that would seek to wield power for and over them. Even if one were to conclude that there is nothing at all wrong 'in itself' with political actors not disclosing their funding sources properly, to argue that a different (and lesser) standard of opprobrium attaches to them can 'lead to massive under-deterrence and to inefficiency in regulatory regimes'.[80]

It is often said of sporting contests that they are won on the field of play, not on paper: no matter how impressive a team sheet or record, only the performance matters. On one view, applying that test to PPERA's performance in the Abrahams affair reveals a dismal mismatch between the law as written and its ability to direct the conduct of those it seeks to regulate, much less punish them when that conduct falls short. The statute as now amended appears to rule out a repeat performance but as with the two earlier episodes, there seems to be an ongoing contest between the regulator (broadly defined) and the regulated community, with the latter tirelessly probing the limits of the law. Watt has admitted as much when he wrote that 'fundraising for political parties is so difficult that those involved are frequently forced to stretch the law as far as it will go. The rule of thumb [for parties] is that as long as the law is not actually broken, it is just about acceptable.'[81]

Alternatively, the narrative of the three party finance scandals considered above could be seen as one of considerable regulatory success. Whilst there were no prosecutions in any of the cases, all resulted in the detection of the malfeasance, suggesting that the regulatory regime's transparency provisions are at least contributing to light being shone on malpractice. Although the real concern above may relate to the absence of legal sanctions, in each case the mis-stepping political actor was severely sanctioned, being forced into resignation and permanently tainted. In each case, the weaknesses of the regime were swiftly addressed by legislative responses, closing up the loophole previously exploited. And all cases related to the then governing party, ruling out the suspicion that the regime protected the politically well placed. Indeed, given the electorate's rejection of the Labour Party in May 2010, public opinion seems well able to provide a highly effective sanction of its own.

Successive rounds of amending PPERA do, however have their own cost. The complexity of the statute, whatever substantive merits it may now have, does impose a regulatory burden that risks unintended consequences. 'Everyday' provisions for local parties – those relating to the definition of a 'permissible donor',[82] or what payments may be made in respect of campaign expenditure[83] – have now been so heavily amended that is it implausible that volunteer campaigners and party officers could read them with certainty. Coupled with a very real concern as to their own liability, the risk of non-engagement in political activity is a very real. Parties have responded to such concerns by offering training to their accounting units, but this raises the related risk of authority shifting from local and constituency parties to regional and central offices. Such concerns of centralisation through juridification have existed at least since PPERA first made its appearance, and although there is legislative awareness of it,[84] the increasingly involved nature of the legislation will likely amplify, not diminish, activists' wariness and hence their propensity to engage.

Despite the criticisms of the Electoral Commission since 2005, the failings of the PPERA's regimes cannot all be laid at their door, not least because of its failings in respect of regulatory scope – an excess of duties and a shortage of powers – were not of its own making and have now been addressed. Not being obliged to undertake public awareness campaigns and the like will hopefully allow for a more focused regulator. Combined with the adoption of enforcement strategies that focus less on simple deterrence and more on responsive mechanisms for dialogue, the hope would be that the state of entrenched hostility between parties and the Commission will diminish, though it could never disappear. Similarly with affiliation, the lack of detailed knowledge about the workings of political actors and institutions has been a repeated criticism of the Commission.

Whatever the substance of that claim, once the decision had been taken to address it, a variety of approaches were available. One might have been modelled on the traditional German approach of allocating certain supervisory tasks to the speaker of the House of Commons, that is, a figure of independence, expertise and adequate resourcing.[85] The reforming zeal of the UK legislator was constrained however by considerations of path dependency with PPERA and its model of greater institutional autonomy for the Commission. By bringing the mountain of party appointees to the Mohammed of the Commission, a *via media* has been sought. One hopes it will not be a *via dolorosa.*

Notes

1 The term refers to those bodies in a given jurisdiction that have principal responsibility for the supervision, monitoring and enforcement of the legal and non-legal rules pertaining to the funding of political parties, campaigns and actors. The term is borrowed with thanks from Luís de Sousa, but the formulation is the author's.

2 Detailed country studies undertaken by GRECO, a body established by the Council of Europe in 1999 (www.coe.int/greco; last visited on 27 May 2010) in its Third Evaluation Round suggest that these intuitions are supported by considerable empirical data.

3 The focus herein is on the later stages – 2005 to 2010 – of that period. An account of the Political Parties Elections and Referendums Act 2000 introduced by the then New Labour government and its pre-history can be found in N.S. Ghaleigh 'Donations and Public Funding under the UK's Political Parties, Elections and Referendums Act 2000-And Beyond' in K.D. Ewing and S. Issacharoff (eds), *Party Funding and Campaign Financing in International Perspective*, Oxford: Hart Publishing, 2006. The early impact of that Act regarding donations is analysed in K.D. Ewing and N.S. Ghaleigh, 'The Cost of Giving and Receiving: Donations to Political Parties in the United Kingdom', *Election Law Journal*, vol. 6, 2007 and more comprehensively in K.D. Ewing, *The Cost of Democracy*, Oxford: Hart Publishing, 2007.

4 UN Doc. A/58/422., ratified by the UK on 9 February 2006.

5 'Each State Party shall also consider taking appropriate legislative and administrative measures, consistent with the objectives of this Convention and in accordance with the fundamental principles of its domestic law, to enhance transparency in the funding of candidates for elected public office and, where applicable, the funding of political parties'.

6 Each State Party shall, in accordance with the fundamental principles of its legal system, ensure the existence of a body or bodies, as appropriate, that prevent corruption … Each State Party shall grant [this] body or bodies … the necessary independence … to enable the body or bodies to carry out its or their functions effectively and free from any undue influence.

7 Article 36 substantially repeats the text of Article 6, with an additional emphasis on the investigative and prosecutorial functions of specialised authorities.
8 CM (2001)195 revised, GR-J (2003)7, adopted by the Committee of Ministers on 8 April 2003.
9 See D.J. Harris, M. O'Boyle and C. Warbrick, *Law of the European Convention on Human Rights*, 2nd ed, Oxford: Oxford University Press, 2009, pp. 872, 875.
10 Independent monitoring: *a.* States should provide for independent monitoring in respect of the funding of political parties and electoral campaigns; *b.* The independent monitoring should include supervision over the accounts of political parties and the expenses involved in election campaigns as well as their presentation and publication.
11 'Specialised personnel: States should promote the specialisation of the judiciary, police or other personnel in the fight against illegal funding of political parties and electoral campaigns'.
12 For details of GRECO's evaluation rounds, see www.coe.int/t/dghl/monitoring/greco/evaluations/index_en.asp (last visited on 27 May 2010).
13 HC Debs, 9 February 2009, col 1149. Compare Ghaleigh above, at p. 43.
14 See generally, Ghaleigh, ibid.
15 See for example, B. Watt, *UK Election Law: A Critical Examination*, London: Glasshouse Press, 2006.
16 See K.D. Ewing, 'Transparency, Accountability and Equality: The Political Parties, Elections and Referendums Act 2000' [2001] *Public Law*, 542–570, at pp. 542–543.
17 Ibid. at p. 565.
18 PPERA, s.13 – amended by PPEA 2009, s. 9 to remove references to systems of government and EU institutions.
19 For further analysis of the increasing use of referendums at various levels in the UK, see N.S. Ghaleigh, 'Sledgehammers and Nuts?: Regulating Referendums in the UK', in S. Hug and K. Gilland (eds), *Financing Referendum Campaigns*, Basingstoke: Palgrave Macmillan, 2009.
20 Emphasis added.
21 Emphasis added.
22 Not yet in force at the time of writing.
23 Protocols are in place between the Electoral Commission and all UK police forces for dealing with the criminal offences created by PPERA – see Association of Chief Police Officers/Electoral Commission, Guidance on Preventing and Detecting Electoral Malpractice (2008), Appendix H.
24 Former ss. 14–20 PPERA, now repealed by Local Democracy, Economic Development and Construction Act 2009 c. 20 Sch.7(3) para.1 (April 1, 2010 as SI 2009/3318).
25 s.13 PPERA – amended by s. 9 Political Parties and Elections Act 2009 to remove references to systems of government and EU institutions.
26 Ibid. s. 4.
27 Supra n.5 (Ewing) at 566.
28 Committee on Standards in Public Life, *Review of the Electoral Commission* (11th Report), Cm 7006, 2007.
29 Ibid. at p. i.
30 Ibid., paras 3.2–3.3.
31 In particular, at s. 1 (more proactive monitoring), s. 2 (greater investigatory powers), and s. 3 (expanded range of civil sanctions).
32 CSPL, 11th Report, above, Recommendation 29. The Hayden Phillips inquiry ran conterminously with that of the CSPL, and there was close contact between the two.
33 HC Debs, 9 February 2009, col 1149.
34 See note 2, above.
35 See the respective evaluation studies undertaken by GRECO at www.coe.int/t/dghl/monitoring/greco/evaluations/index_en.asp (last visited on 27 May 2010).
36 The CSPL's Fifth Report, *The Funding of Political Parties in the United Kingdom*,

Cm 4057, 1998, was the foundation stone upon which PPERA built. It contains 100 recommendations, 99 of which were adopted in PPERA – see N S Ghaleigh [1999] *Public Law* 43.

37 Electoral Commission, *Better Regulation of Party and Election Finance*, Consultation Paper, July 2009, para. 4.10.

38 Ibid., para. 2.6.

39 P. Watt, *Inside Out*, London, Biteback, 2010, p. 37. Watt was the Labour Party's Director of Compliance, then Director of Finance and Compliance and finally its General Secretary during the Levy and Abrahams scandals.

40 Ibid., p. 100.

41 Watt gives a detailed account of the numerous occasions on which the Party's bankers threatened to call in their loans and for its auditors not to sign the Party's accounts off as a 'going concern' capable of trading for the coming twelve months (pp. 83–113).

42 The Conservative Party also engaged in such arrangements and in fact these were first reported in *The Guardian*, 21 April 2005.

43 Watt, above, p. 40. See also, A. Rawnsley, *The End of the Party: The Rise and Fall of New Labour*, London: Viking, 2010), pp. 357–358.

44 Watt, ibid., at p. 36. Emphasis added. As the matter progressed it became apparent that a remarkably small number of people in the Labour Party were aware of these arrangements, a coterie that excluded the Treasurer of the Labour Party, Mr Jack Dromey. See Rawnsley, above, p. 359.

45 Rawnsley, ibid.

46 The two are distinct in numerous ways, not least in that the latter entitles the recipient to sit in the House of Lords, where she or he has a legislative and potentially executive function. As such, honours are awarded for past good deeds, peerages in the expectation that further good deeds will be forthcoming.

47 See generally, http://lordsappointments.independent.gov.uk/ (last visited on 27 May 2010).

48 *Daily Telegraph*, 27 December 2005.

49 Ibid.

50 See N.S. Ghaleigh, 'Corruption', in P. Cane and J. Conaghan (eds), *The New Oxford Companion to Law*, Oxford: Oxford University Press, 2008.

51 See T. Cullen, *Maundy Gregory: Purveyor of Honours*, London: The Quality Book Club, 1975.

52 See the analysis of Mr Christopher Sallon QC in 'Propriety and Privelege', House of Commons Public Administration Select Committee, HC 153 (2007–2008), p. 64ff.

53 Available at www.cps.gov.uk/publications/code_for_crown_prosecutors/ (last visited on 27 May 2010).

54 'A toxic cloud hung over Number 10 for the remainder of Blair's time in office ... The impact of the debilitating affair was not ultimately legal [,] it was political [.] Polls indicated that a majority believed peerages had been traded for cash', Rawnsley, above. at pp. 361 and 373.

55 See the accounts of Watt, above, and Lord Levy, *A Question of Honour*. London: Simon & Schuster, 2009.

56 Crown Prosecution Service, CPS Decision: 'Cash For Honours' Case, 20 July 2007 – 'there is insufficient evidence to support proceedings against any individual, for any offence under either the 1925 Act or the 2000 Act, or for any offence of perverting, or attempting or conspiring to pervert, the course of justice'.

57 'The Commission's position had been quite reasonable – it had not wanted to issue guidance where there was clear legal ambiguity. However some saw this as a failure on the Commission's part': J. Fisher, General Note on Political Parties and Elections Act 2009, *Current Law Statutes Annotated*, 12/2.

58 HC 153 (2007–2008), p. 68.

59 2006 Act, Schedule 2, paragraph 1.

60 See J. Fisher, 'Hayden Phillips and Jack Straw: The Continuation of British Exceptionalism in Party Finance?' *Parliamentary Affairs*, 2009, vol. 62, 298.
61 For background and details, see *Leadership Elections: Labour Party*, House of Commons Library: SN/PC/3938.
62 *The Guardian*, 8 January 2008.
63 The Register is maintained by the Committee Office of the House of Commons and is available for public inspection. Complaints about MP conduct are made to the Parliamentary Commissioner for Standards who in turn reports, where appropriate, to the Standards and Privileges Committee.
64 According to Fisher, disproportionately so as these events cannot:

> really be deemed [as] scandals. Whilst it is true that it appears that regulations were breached, they were not seemingly done so through any desire to seek personal material gain. Rather, although they resulted in some high-profile resignations, they nevertheless represented first and foremost, reporting irregularities.
> (J. Fisher, 'Hayden Phillips and Jack Straw, above, p. 307)

65 Mr Peter Hain, Report of the Committee on Standards and Privileges, HC 183 (2008–2009), p. 5.
66 He returned to the post of Secretary of State for Wales in June 2009.
67 PPERA, Schedule 7 (12)(1) and Schedule 20.
68 Press Statement, Electoral Commission, 24 January 2008.
69 Press Statement and Full Declaration of Donations to Hain4Labour, Mr Peter Hain, 11 January 2008.
70 Press Release – Crown Prosecution Service, *CPS decides no charges for Peter Hain MP*, 5 December 2008.
71 Press Release – Electoral Commission, *Statement on the CPS Decision on Peter Hain MP*, 5 December 2008.
72 *The Mail on Sunday*, 25 November 2007: Reporting on Labour's 'third largest donor', it was said 'He lives in a council house, drives a beat up van – and said he knows nothing about the £200,000 the party received from him'.
73 Watt, above, at p. 179: 'There was never any great secret about [these donations.] Nobody at [Labour Party] HQ ever really thought these donations were anything other than lawful'.
74 *The Guardian*, 1 December 2007.
75 CPS Press Release – *CPS Decides No Charge Over Labour Party Donations*, 7 May 2009.
76 Ibid.
77 Political Parties and Elections Act 2009, s. 9, amending PPERA, s.54.
78 *Oxford English Dictionary* (2nd ed.), 'scandal, *n*'. definition 3.a.
79 See R. Baldwin, 'Regulatory Offences', in Cane and Conaghan (eds), *The New Oxford Companion To Law*, above.
80 Ibid.
81 *Inside Out*, above, p. 199.
82 PPERA, s. 54, as amended.
83 PPERA, s. 76, as amended.
84 PPEA, s. 12 amends PPERA, s. 56 to provide a defence for party treasurers who have erroneously accepted donations where they have taken 'all reasonable steps' to verify the permissibility of the donor.
85 Practical shortcomings in the institutional capacity of the Bundestag President in respect of party finance supervision have been noted in GRECO's 'Evaluation Report on Germany on Transparency of Party Funding', of 4 December 2009, esp paras 112–114.

10 The courts

Legal challenges to political finance and election laws

Stephanie Palmer

The regulation of political broadcasting and campaign finance is a contested and paradoxical area of law. This chapter explores the following questions: is government regulation fundamentally antithetical to democracy or is it the only way to achieve political equality by providing a level playing field between powerful and less powerful groups in society? Is regulation a self-serving device that favours those holding political power? Does the enforcement of individual rights help or hinder the integrity of the democratic political process? Finally, is it appropriate for the judiciary to pay considerable deference to political institutions even though restrictions on political speech are viewed as requiring a high level of judicial scrutiny?

This chapter will examine the competing principles and tensions underlying the law in the area of political broadcasting. The focus of this chapter is on the role of the courts and the analytical frameworks adopted to justify the differing viewpoints evident in the jurisprudence. The chapter begins with the recent US Supreme Court ruling[1] that the government may not ban political spending by corporations in candidature elections. Controversial and politically divisive – the Supreme Court was split five to four – President Obama has publicly criticised the decision, calling it 'a major victory for big oil, Wall Street banks, health insurance companies and the other powerful interests that marshal their power every day in Washington to drown out the voices of everyday Americans'.[2] The judgment neatly encapsulates the differing arguments, principles and vision of democracy underlying the majority and minority opinions. Each nation has developed its own institutional mechanisms to address these issues but the underlying principles and the ideological weight attached to political values by the judiciary in this decision serve to highlight the tensions that the judiciary must navigate in the UK as well as in the US. Importantly, for the purposes of this chapter, the US Supreme Court decision also highlights the potential pitfalls for the judicial branch given the political nature of the issues at stake.

UK law is the subject of the second part of the chapter. Political advertising on television and radio is highly regulated. The UK courts to date have been reluctant to interfere with the system. Finally, the compatibility of the Strasbourg and the UK system is assessed. Recent decisions of the European Court of Human Rights (ECHR), such as *TV Vest AS and Rogaland Pensjonistparti* v.

Norway,[3] suggest that the UK approach may be vulnerable to a challenge based on Article 10, which protects freedom of expression.

A triumph for free speech rights? Campaign finance and advertising in the USA

The US Supreme Court, in *Citizens United* v. *Federal Election Commission*, struck down the limits that the McCain–Feingold campaign finance legislation placed on independent political expenditures by corporations and unions.[4] The federal legislation prohibited corporations from using general treasury funds to support candidates for federal office through direct contribution, through independent expenditures that expressly advocate the election or defeat of a candidate ('express advocacy') or through 'electioneering communication' defined as 'any broadcast, cable, or satellite communication' that 'refers to a clearly identifiable candidate' and is made in 30 days before a primary or 60 days before a general election.[5] In reaching this decision, the Court overruled two previous decisions that had upheld limits on political advertising.[6]

The facts of the case are straightforward. Citizens United is a wealthy non-profit corporation. It operates a political action committee with substantial financial assets. In January 2008, it released a film called 'Hillary: The Movie', a highly derogatory movie about then Senator Hillary Clinton who was a candidate in the 2008 Presidential primary elections. Although released in theatres and on DVD, Citizens United wished to increase distribution through a video-on-demand cable television channel and to air advertisements to promote the program within 30 days of the primary election. As the corporation feared that the broadcast would violate the 'electioneering' restriction, it applied to the courts for injunctive and declaratory relief. The decision raises myriad issues but this section focuses on only a few of them.[7]

Free speech values and the democratic process

The majority opinion was written by Justice Anthony Kennedy and joined by Chief Justice Roberts and Judges Samuel Alito, Antonin Scalia and Clarence Thomas who adopt a traditional understanding of the First Amendment: 'Congress shall make no law … abridging the freedom of speech'. According to Justice Kennedy, the First Amendment is 'premised on mistrust of governmental power'.[8] First, the majority had no hesitation in concluding that campaign expenditures are equivalent to speech. The complex rules regulating the integrity of the election process operate as the equivalent of a prior restraint and produce a chill upon speech.[9] Second, the majority found that corporations are entitled to First Amendment protection. Any restrictions based on the identity of the speaker are suspect as they may disguise a means to control the content of speech[10] and to 'restrict disfavored speakers'.[11] According to Kennedy, the First Amendment protects both 'speech and speaker and the ideas that flow from each'.[12] Finally, the majority rejected any government rationale in providing some financial equality in the influence of different groups' political expression. A healthy democracy survives on robust political competition which ensures an informed electorate. Moreover, limits on finance may help to entrench incumbents in office.

The majority and dissenting justices[13] agreed on the importance of speech to the integrity of the election process itself. But their views diverged on the principles underlying free speech. For Justice Stevens, who delivered the dissenting judgment, speech contributes to democratic deliberation by informed citizens. Speech, funded by corporations, leads to corruption or the appearance of corruption that corrodes the democratic integrity of the system. The cost of purchasing advertising time on television is enormous and is exercised by those who have more wealth and power in society.[14] Such funding and advertising to support or oppose electoral candidates may distort the political debate, by purchasing votes and influence, and give rise to political inequality.[15]

Justice Kennedy, who delivered the majority opinion, considered the important governmental issue of corruption and concluded that 'Congress has created categorical bans on speech that are asymmetrical to preventing quid pro quo corruption'.[16] Influence or access to elected officials does not imply corruption nor will it lead to the electorate losing faith in democracy.[17] The governing rule should be more speech not less to enhance civic discourse in the political market place. The First Amendment is violated when it prohibits speakers from engaging in political speech at election time, 'when it matters most'.[18] It is not the role of the court to adjust the system to make it fairer or more representative. Thus, the majority assumes that freedom of speech and democracy work together and there exists no rationale to limit it. The flaw in this argument is that it assumes that the market place will not be distorted by vast sums spent on corporate financing. Even where the source of the communication is identified, political advertisements financed by wealthy corporations aimed at affecting voter choices are more likely 'to undermine rather than improve the public's political education'.[19]

The decision has exposed an ideological schism at the heart of the US Supreme Court. The majority and minority justices disagree vehemently over the role of free speech in a democracy and the legitimacy of providing some equality in the electoral discourse. For the majority, political campaign contributions generate political speech and restrictions will not be tolerated.

A political decision

Congress has placed limits on campaign spending by corporations since the early twentieth century and the McCain–Feingold legislation represented a significant attempt to regulate the position of corporations and unions in electoral politics. The majority were not prepared to redraw the lines of the legislation to deal with the changing nature of election communication and finance. According to Justice Stevens' dissenting opinion, 'the majority throws up its hands' and refuses to deal with the fluid and slippery nature of campaign finances.[20] He concludes:

'While American democracy is imperfect, few outside the majority of this Court would have thought its flaws included a dearth of corporate money in politics.'[21]

Drawing the court into these 'political' questions poses a substantial threat to the integrity of the court, as evidenced by President Obama's unprecedented criticism. In the New York Review of Books, Dworkin comments that 'the reasoning the majority offered is ... so poor as to suggest some motive other than a desire to reach the right legal result'.[22] The majority did not consider that it was for the court to rectify inequality in the democratic system but nor would it permit Congress to draw lines in relation to political speech.

Regulation during the formal 'election period'

One novel aspect of the McCain–Feingold campaign finance legislation was the attempt to demarcate the 'election period' as one of greater regulatory control over campaign activity. In the UK, the election period is highly regulated. For example, candidates for Parliament are restricted in their campaign spending.[23] Issacharoff has commented on this difference between the British and the American systems. While '[t]he American First Amendment tradition has treated electoral speech as the vehicle for expression and citizen engagement' the British tradition is closer to 'an administrative tallying of preferences as they exist'.[24] Although the UK approach avoids some of the pitfalls of the US approach, it does have some disadvantages of its own.

The United Kingdom's regulation on broadcasting

In comparison to the US, a striking feature of British life is the absence of privately funded political representations channelled through the television and radio. In the field of broadcasting, the regulation of content on grounds of both political nature and standards of decency is a controversial but well-established feature. In 2003, the House of Lords upheld restrictions on the latter grounds in *R (On the Application of Prolife Alliance* v. *BBC*,[25] discussed below. The Communications Act 2003 is the most recent UK legislation regulating broadcasting and maintaining a ban on political advertising or 'advocacy advertising' on television and radio.[26] Political parties have considerable access to the broadcast media through news coverage, debates and direct access via party political broadcasts: time is allocated free of charge to the major political parties for party and political broadcasts.[27] In stark contrast to political parties, interest groups have no free direct access.

The grounds of due impartiality in the Communications Act 2003 casts its net widely and imposes far-reaching constraints.[28] Tessa Jowell M.P., as the then Secretary of State for Culture, Media and Sport, put forward the following instrumental rationale for maintaining the prohibition on political advertising: 'By denying powerful interests the chance to skew political debate, the current ban safeguards the public and democratic debate.'[29] Such a prohibition is potentially at odds with the robust protection of political expression in Article 10 of the ECHR and the Human Rights Act 1998. Indeed, when introducing the Communications Bill in Parliament, the government did not feel able to accompany it with a statement of compatibility with the European Convention on Human Rights. Section 19 of the Human Rights Act requires the Minister to make a written statement acknowledging that in their view a proposed Bill is compatible with Convention rights, or that, even though such a statement cannot be given, they wish the House to proceed with the Bill.[30] The Joint Committee on Human Rights acknowledged that, in the light of the Strasbourg jurisprudence, the obligation of OFCOM to prohibit political advertising could be considered incompatible with freedom of expression, as protected in Article 10.[31] They recommended, 'that the Government examine ways in which workable and Convention-compatible restrictions of this kind could be included in the Bill'.[32]

An advertisement will breach the Communications Act if it is 'by or on behalf of a body whose objects are wholly or mainly of a political nature'[33] or is 'an advertisement which is directed towards a political end'[34] or 'an advertisement that has a connection with an industrial dispute'.[35] The Act defines 'objects of a political nature' and 'political ends' broadly. It includes: 'influencing the outcome of elections or referendums'[36]; 'bringing about changes in the law ... or otherwise influencing the legislative process'[37]; 'influencing the policies or decisions of governments'[38]; 'influencing the policies or decisions or persons on whom public functions are conferred by law'[39] or 'international agreements'[40]; 'influencing public opinion on a matter which, in the UK, is a matter of public controversy'[41]; and 'promoting the interests of a party or other group of persons organised in the UK or elsewhere for political ends'.[42] The definition is non-exhaustive and the objectives mentioned are confined to the UK but also include influencing the law of a foreign country or territory.

The over-inclusiveness of the ban has been the subject of severe academic criticism on the basis that it excludes interest groups and non-mainstream views from political debate and is a violation of Article 10 of the ECHR.[43] Groups campaigning on issues such as the environment or world poverty would find it difficult to suggest that their objects were not political as their purpose is to influence government policy. As Fenwick and Phillipson point out, the Communications Act creates an important distinction between special interest groups:

> a group deemed not to be of a political nature can still advertise so long as its advertisements are not directed to a political end, whereas a group deemed "mainly or wholly" political by Ofcom cannot advertise at all, however non-political a particular advertisement is.[44]

Broadcasting regulation and the judiciary

How have the courts articulated the implications of freedom of expression in relation to the elaborate broadcasting regulations that operate in the UK? In two important decisions, the House of Lords has upheld broadcasting restrictions. These decisions, however, are unlikely to stem further challenges surrounding the regulation of political broadcasts given the developing jurisprudence of the ECHR.

The application of the broadcasting constraints relating to taste and decency in a party election broadcast (PEB) were challenged in *R (on the application of Prolife Alliance)* v. *BBC*.[45] The Prolife Alliance is a registered political party under the Political Parties, Elections and Referendums Act 2000. One of its primary campaigning aims is the prohibition of abortion. During the 2001 general election, the Alliance was fielding a sufficient number of parliamentary candidates in Wales to qualify for one PEB. In May 2001, the Alliance submitted a tape of its proposed broadcast to the BBC, ITV, Channel 4 and Channel 5. The tape contained detailed descriptions of the processes involved in different forms of abortion and included 'prolonged and graphic images of the product of suction abortion: aborted foetuses in a mangled and mutilated state, tiny limbs, a separated head, and the like'.[46] On the basis of a duty not to screen material that offends against "good taste or decency",[47] each of the broadcasters refused to show the tape either in its original or a modified form, as suggested by the Alliance. Five days before the election, a video was screened, which replaced the offending images with a blank screen bearing the word 'censored' accompanied by a soundtrack describing the images contained in the banned video. The Alliance was not prevented from commenting in any way it wished about abortion.

The Alliance argued that content-based limitations on broadcasts, restrictions on political speech, and regulations which operate via prior restraint are required to be scrutinised strictly by the courts as demanded by Article 10 of the ECHR. The distressing images, using real-life examples, were intended to shock and challenge the viewers' opinion of abortion. The broadcasters could have accepted the suggestion of the Alliance to transmit the PEB after 10pm with an appropriate warning at the beginning of the broadcast. In effect, their argument was that the BBC's refusal to broadcast the PEB was unlawful. The Alliance did not argue that the legislation setting out the taste and decency rule was itself in breach of Article 10. They did not seek a declaration of incompatibility under section 4, Human Rights Act 1998.

Discerning the court's view of political expression and its role in this decision is not straightforward. A salient aspect of the Alliance's challenge is the difference in approach to the issue adopted by the appellate courts. In the Court of Appeal, Laws LJ adopted a stance that examined closely the importance of political speech.[48] Relying on the Strasbourg decision of *Bowman* v. *UK*,[49] he concluded that state authorities have restricted discretion to interfere with political speech. On issues of taste and decency, the court would pay considerable deference to a legislature and the expertise of regulators but this is dependent on the context. However, given the nature of the speech at issue and that this decision was made during an election period, he concluded that the decision to censor the PEB was unlawful. It is worth noting that Laws LJ assumed that the Prolife tape, although disturbing and distressing, was not dishonest or sensationalist. This is a disputable fact. The vast majority of abortions carried out in the UK are within the first 12 weeks, whereas the images used by Prolife were from abortion procedures carried out many weeks later. In this sense, the video, if screened, could have fostered a misleading understanding of the reality of abortion in the UK.[50]

By a majority of four to one, the House of Lords allowed the appeal of the broadcasters. The majority pointed out that no human right to broadcast on television exists.[51] Moreover, the intrusive nature of the television justified stricter regulations for this medium: 'The citizen has a right not to be shocked or affronted by inappropriate material transmitted into the privacy of his home.'[52] Lord Hoffmann acknowledged that Article 10 is still engaged:

> Instead of being a right to be prevented from expressing one's opinion, it becomes a right to fair consideration for being afforded the opportunity to do so: a right not to have one's access to public media denied on discriminatory, arbitrary or unreasonable grounds.[53]

In his view, the Court of Appeal had elided two distinct questions: first, whether PEBs should be subject to the same standards of taste and decency as other programmes; and second, if so, whether the broadcaster had properly applied those standards in this particular case.[54] The Court of Appeal had asked whether it was consistent for the broadcaster to apply such standards at all whereas the majority of the House of Lords considered only the second question to be in issue.

Lord Hoffmann's decision was influenced by institutional considerations and the separation of powers. He addresses 'whether Parliament was entitled to require PEBs to comply with standards of taste and decency and so the relevant decision-maker is Parliament.'[55] Lord Nicholls and Hoffmann concluded that the BBC had clearly acted within the scope of its responsibility to ensure the application of the taste and decency standard to the PEB. Lord Hoffmann then concluded that the Alliance PEB failed to comply with the required standard as adjudged by the broadcaster.

Lord Scott, in dissent, framed the question as: 'was [the broadcaster's] rejection of the Alliance's desired programme necessary in a democratic society for the protection of the right of home-owners that offensive material should not be transmitted into their homes?' In his view, to restrict a PEB in a 'mature democracy', 'denigrates the voting public, treats them like children who need to be protected from the unpleasant realities of life, seriously undervalues their political maturity'.[56]

The *Alliance* decision has divided academic opinion.[57] Lord Walker noted the paradox in broadcasting cases. Although political communication is accorded great importance, there may exist good democratic reasons to impose certain restrictions.[58] The majority decision recognised the intention of Parliament, after examining policy and principle, to ensure that PEBs conform to standards, in the words of Lord Hoffmann, that are part of the traditional cultural life of the country.[59] In other words, it was for the legislature to strike the balance between freedom of expression and other competing interests. Once this was accepted, the majority of the House of Lords examined the decision-making process by the

BBC as an issue of competence. Lord Hoffmann acknowledged that public opinion is 'often diverse, sometimes unexpected and in constant flux'.[60] It would be unlikely that there would be unanimous agreement on such an emotive issue. Eric Barendt persuasively argues that no 'serious attempt was made to explain why the application of the [standards] rule to the Pro-Life Alliance broadcast should be regarded as necessary to protect viewers' rights'.[61] Given the numerous shocking and distressing pictures in news broadcasts, it is difficult to understand how the House of Lords could accept the need to restrict political speech during an election to protect viewers against offence.[62] Due to the narrowness of the legal issues addressed by their Lordships, there is a sense that important factors had not been aired in this decision.

In the US, such content-based restrictions would be protected under the First Amendment. In the UK there are administrative restrictions in place aimed at electoral equality. Nevertheless, difficult questions remain to be addressed to determine the scope of these restrictions in order to ensure robust debate and an informed electorate, especially during the election period. The *Prolife* decision makes uncomfortable reading for anyone who is committed to free speech.

The ban imposed by the Communications Act 2003, sections 319 and 321(2) on was the subject of a legal challenge before the House of Lords in *R (On the Application of Animal Defenders International)* v. *Secretary of State for Culture, Media and Sport.*[63] In contrast to the Alliance case, the compatibility of this broadcasting restriction was directly challenged as a breach of Article 10 of the ECHR and a declaration of incompatibility under s. 4 of the Human Rights Act was sought. Their Lordships upheld the blanket ban on political advertising in a decision that deferred to the institutional competence and policy choices of Parliament.

Animal Defenders International (ADI) is a nonprofit company which campaigns, by lawful means, to alleviate the suffering of animals and for the conservation and protection of animals and their environment. In order to publicise their 'My Mate's a Primate' campaign, concerning the use and abuse of primates by humans, an advertisement was submitted to the Broadcast Advertising Clearance Centre.[64] Clearance was declined on the ground that its transmission would breach s. 321(2) Broadcasting Act as ADI was considered 'a body with mainly political objectives as defined by the Act'.[65]

The decision directly confronts the tension between freedom of expression, as protected in Article 10 of the ECHR, and the need to protect the integrity of the democratic process. According to Lord Bingham, the democratic process is enhanced if the 'playing field of debate should be so far as practicable level'.[66] Political debate will be subverted if political parties can use their wealth to buy advertising in effective forums: 'elections become little more than an auction'.[67] The danger exists if individuals or organisations, which are not political parties, are able to use their wealth to promote their ideas.

> The risk is that objects which are essentially political may come to be accepted by the public not because they are shown in public debate to be

> right but because, by dint of constant repetition, the public has been conditioned to accept them.[68]

Lord Bingham concludes that it is legitimate to restrict freedom of expression in order to protect 'the rights of others' against the potential mischief of distorting advertising. He is suggesting that freedom of expression is an instrumental tool to promote a particular conception of democratic politics rather than as an end in itself: the position of the minority Supreme Court Justices in the *Citizens United* decision.

Lord Bingham's concerns are legitimate, as evident from the experience in the USA, but fears about subversion would not necessarily justify a blanket prohibition of political advertising on television and radio. Is such a widespread ban a disproportionate response to a legitimate concern? Could these concerns be addressed through less restrictive measures? Lord Bingham, without exploring the possibility in detail, concluded that 'regulating political advertising by time or frequency or expenditure or by the nature and quality of the adverts in question' would not be satisfactory.[69] It would be difficult to devise a system which could not be circumvented; broadcasters would find it even more difficult to discharge their duty 'to present a fair, balanced and reasonable comprehensive cross-section of public opinion on the issues of the day'; and the government had concluded that 'no fair and workable compromise solution could be found which would address the problem'.[70] Moreover, other means to convey speech remained open and this included the print media, direct mail shots, billboard posters, public meetings and demonstrations.[71]

As in the *Prolife Alliance* decision, the House placed considerable weight on the judgment of Parliament: in effect, it was for Parliament to decide where the line should be drawn. General rules should not be invalidated 'if judged in the round, it is beneficial'.[72] The other reasons provided by Lord Bingham for respecting Parliament's judgment raise troubling questions. First, the fact that Parliament has proceeded with the ban of political advertising on television and radio in spite of the relevant Minister alerting the House that there may be a conflict with scheduled Convention rights in the Human Rights Act is not a reason to defer to Parliament.[73] Surely the courts should make their own assessment of compatibility with Convention rights? The second reason submitted, that the approval of this ban by our democratically elected politicians who are 'peculiarly sensitive to the measures necessary to safeguard the integrity of our democracy', avoids addressing the issue that the ban may also be self-serving. Politicians in established political parties who are entitled to free PEB may have an ulterior motive to regulate political communications and limit spending in order to gain a competitive advantage.[74]

Baroness Hale's concurring judgment embodies an implicit theory of democracy. Citizens, as voters, have the right to equal participation in a healthy democracy. A right to equal participation as voters entails a corollary right to equal participation in election campaigns. Free exchange of information and ideas, an essential aspect of democracy, will be undermined if expensive paid political advertisements on televisions and radio are permitted. It will distort the public debate. Thus, the ban on advertising is justified in order to ensure a system of political equality. Can a principled distinction be drawn between, on the one hand, party politics and electoral influence and, on the other, political advertising to achieve social, policy or legal changes? She responds:

> There has to be the same rule for the same kind of advertising, whatever the cause for which it campaigns and whatever the resources of the campaigners. We must not distinguish between causes of which we approve and causes for which we disapprove.[75]

Even though the advertisement by ADI was not objectionable, it could not bypass the blanket prohibition.

Their Lordships did not find it difficult to give great weight to Parliament's decision in this context because of their acceptance of the need to protect the integrity of the democratic process. Baroness Hale specifically stated: 'we do not want our Government or its policies to be decided by the highest spenders'.[76] The instrumental view of freedom of expression allowed the judges to consider the broadcasting ban as proportionate to the legitimate aim of protecting the democratic rights of others. Nevertheless, there were some indications in the decision that the advertising ban is vulnerable at its margins and its breadth may be susceptible to a successful challenge in the future. Baroness Hale acknowledged that 'there may be room for argument' on a different factual scenario.[77] According to Lord Scott, ADI's lack of success should not be understood as 'franking sections 319 and 321 against any possible attack on Article 10 grounds'.[78] Lords Bingham and Scott acknowledged that commercial advertising on an issue of public controversy may provide an organisation with strong grounds for demanding a right to respond in order to promote their own beliefs and principles from a broadcaster. As Lord Scott commented:

> it was not suggested that the purpose of ADI's "My Mate's a Primate" campaign was to counter the broadcasting of advertisements promoting a zoo or zoos in which primates were kept in cages but if that had been the case the arguments justifying the statutory prohibition might have been difficult.[79]

The recent advertising of abortion clinics, by the charity Marie Stopes, on TV may provide the basis for a challenge along these lines.[80]

It would indeed be odd for a regulatory system to permit advertisers to broadcast commercial speech, with its accompanying subliminal messages, without ever permitting a response from an organisation with a 'political viewpoint'.

The Strasbourg jurisprudence

A response to counter the effect of commercial advertising relating to an issue of public controversy was the subject of a decision of the European Court of

Human Rights in 2001. The claimants in *ADI* had relied heavily on the conclusion of the European Court of Human Rights in *VgT Vereingegen Tierfabriken* v. *Switzerland*,[81] which concerned political advertising in the broadcast media. The *VgT* decision had led to the Ministerial statement to Parliament under s.19(1)(b) HRA. The Joint Committee on Human Rights had also expressed concern that this decision may mean that the UK advertising ban was not Convention compatible.[82]

The applicant, a Swiss organisation concerned with animal welfare, wished to broadcast a television advertisement exhorting people to eat less meat and urging protection for animals. A private entity, the Commercial Television Company, (CTC) had been placed in charge of advertising on the Swiss Radio and Television Company, which was the only television station providing 'home news' throughout Switzerland. The CTC refused to accept the applicant's advertisement in its proposed form on the basis that it was clearly 'political' in nature and by Swiss law such advertising was prohibited.[83] Moreover, CTC also suggested that it cannot be obliged to broadcast advertisements damaging to its own business interests.[84] The implication was that, in the future, meat sellers may decline to advertise, leading to loss of revenue. A challenge to the Swiss courts was unsuccessful and *VgT* petitioned the European Court of Human Rights, claiming a breach of Article 10 of the ECHR as domestic Swiss law made lawful the CTC's refusal to broadcast. Before the European Court, the Swiss government argued that refusal to broadcast was aimed at prohibiting financially strong groups in society obtaining a competitive advantage; to provide equality of opportunity; to ensure the independence of broadcasters from powerful sponsors and to support the press.[85] As this matter, in the Court's opinion, concerned a restriction of political expression, prohibiting *VgT*'s participation in a debate of general interest, the margin of appreciation accorded to a State is reduced.[86] The Court acknowledged that political equality was a legitimate aim: the State is the 'ultimate guarantor' and protecting equality of opportunity is 'especially valid in relation to the audiovisual media'.[87] The prohibition of 'political advertising' may, in some circumstances, be compatible with Article 10.[88] The European Court found that the Swiss authorities had not provided 'relevant and sufficient' reasons for the prohibition. VgT was not one of those wealthy groups who may skew political opinion. As the Court noted, 'all [VgT] intended to do with the commercial was to participate in an ongoing general debate on animal protection and the rearing of animals'.[89] Nor did the Court accept the government's claim that other adequate opportunities to broadcast existed. The Court sidestepped the issue of whether or not the right to freedom of expression entailed any right to broadcast, referred to by the Court as a 'right to an antenna'.[90]

This decision posed a problem for the House of Lords in the *ADI* case, especially the 'apparent' rejection of the argument that the special impact of the audio-visual media could have a more persuasive and potent influence on passive recipients. In Lord Bingham's view, the potential danger to the democratic process was not adequately aired and argued before the European Court. He sought to distinguish the two cases further by stressing that in *VgT*, the applicant was seeking to respond to advertisements broadcast by the meat industry.[91] Lord Bingham also contrasted the decision of *VgT* with *Murphy* v. *Ireland*,[92] where the European Court had upheld the prohibition of religious broadcasting on the grounds of guaranteeing fairness to all religious groups, irrespective of their financial position.[93] While Lord Scott and Baroness Hale stressed the sensitive nature of Strasbourg jurisprudence.[94]

The context-sensitive nature of the European Court's decision in *VgT* did not make it easy to predict the compatibility of the UK's broadcasting laws with Article 10 ECHR. A more recent decision of the European Court, *TV Vest AS and Rogaland Pensjonistparti* v. *Norway*,[95] suggests more pointedly that the extensive prohibition on advertising in the Broadcasting Act 2003 may need to be reconsidered.

The case concerned the broadcasting of three paid advertisements, in the run-up to local and regional elections, of a small political party, 'the Pensioners Party'. The short commercials aimed to portray the values of the Party and included an invitation to vote for it. Pursuant to Norwegian law, political advertising is banned and a fine was imposed on the broadcaster. After the Norwegian courts rejected their appeal, the applicants petitioned the European Court of Human Rights.

The UK government intervened as a third party and 'invited the Court to confine *VgT* to its factual circumstances or alternatively to depart from its reasoning' and it submitted the House of Lord's decision in *ADI* to the Court for its consideration.[96] In effect, the European Court declined the invitation and reiterated, in less opaque terms, its decision in *VgT*. The European Court again concluded that there was no 'reasonable relationship of proportionality between the legitimate aim pursued by the prohibition on political advertising and the means deployed to achieve that aim'.[97] The prohibition on advertising in Norway was permanent – it did not apply specifically to elections – and was absolute. It applied only to broadcasting on television. While the Court considered that measures designed to preserve the political impartiality of television broadcasting and ensuring a level playing field in elections were relevant, they could not agree that these objectives could justify the interference in this particular case. The ban failed to have 'the desired effect'.[98] Minor political parties, such as the Pensioners Party, did not fall within the category of parties that could skew the integrity of democratic processes. The ban was aimed at supporting the democratic process but, in practice, it put minor political parties at a disadvantage. Paid advertising on television was the only way the Pensioners Party could convey their message. The disadvantage was further exacerbated when compared to the major political parties who were given a substantial amount of free edited broadcast coverage. Using other, less powerful, media outlets could not compensate for this disadvantage.[99] The European Court specifically rejected two further propositions that may lead to a reconsideration of the broadcasting ban in the UK. First, the Court accepted the 'immediate and powerful effect' of the audio-visual media but this could not justify an absolute prohibition.[100] Second, the argument that there was no alternative to a blanket ban, as filtering advertisements on a case-by-case basis was not viable, was rejected.[101]

Conclusion

A strong cultural antipathy to political advertising exists in the UK, as evidenced by the strongly worded judgments of the House of Lords in the *ADI* case. Nevertheless the absolute ban on political advertising may need to be reconsidered in the light of the European Court's jurisprudence. While some access to the broadcast media by political groups may need to be considered given the recent Strasbourg decisions, wealth should not be the determining factor.

The courts in the UK have been unwilling to reassess the prohibition as a breach of Article 10 ECHR. Freedom of expression is perceived as instrumental in promoting the health of a democratic society. According to the European Court, 'free elections and freedom of expression, particularly freedom of political debate, together form the bedrock of any democratic system'.[102] In *TV Vest*, the European Court acknowledged that states enjoy a wide margin of appreciation in striking the appropriate balance between these two potentially conflicting rights.[103] It is implicitly recognised that democratic values may be subverted by individuals or organisations willing to spend large sums promoting particular views through the broadcasting system. Thus, freedom of expression must be regulated to some extent in order to promote and sustain the democratic system. Expression cannot operate if those with the greatest financial muscle dominate the marketplace of ideas. These views chime with the minority opinions in the *Citizens United* decision.

One difference between the House of Lords judgment and the European Court decisions lies in the level of scrutiny appropriate when expression is implicated in the political process and the issue of proportionality. How far should the regulation of broadcasting extend? The European Court's views in *TV Vest* shed retrospective light on the *ADI* case. Although *ADI* remains the leading domestic precedent, the pressure has intensified on the legislature to finely tune the broadcasting ban in the legislation.

The UK courts in the *ADI* and the *Alliance* decisions have displayed considerable deference to the legislature. In *TV Vest*, the European Court considered the weight that should be given to the opinion of the legislature and concluded that it was for states 'to take a stance on such issues of national constitutional law character'. The constitutional culture of the country is relevant in determining the issue of political advertising but in a system where a political majority is left to decide on the limits of such speech, judicial oversight is essential. It may be tempting for those who hold political power to prohibit advertising in an attempt to stifle opposition or criticism. Limits on political expression require objectives that can justify any interference.

The highly potent power of the broadcasting medium may be a reason to consider that the absolute ban is a breach of Article 10. The operation of the law undoubtedly works to the disadvantage of minority parties and pressure groups. The internet has made some inroads into the lack of access to broadcasting. Video campaigns on the internet and YouTube are influential in the USA and there is evidence of their growing importance in the UK. Such popularity is understandable: at a fraction of the cost of television, they provide a powerful and effective new way to reach and influence an audience. The campaign by Greenpeace concerning the popular chocolate bar, KitKat, and the loss of rain-forest is one example that springs to mind.[104]

Although the courts must retain oversight on limits of political expression, there are dangers for the judiciary. As Baroness Hale emphasised in *ADI*, the courts cannot decide where the balance should be struck on a case-by-case basis. In her view:

> There has to be the same rule for the same kind of advertising, whatever the cause for which it campaigns and whatever the resources of the campaigners. We must not distinguish between causes of which we approve and causes of which we disapprove.[105]

The need to look at each example of campaign spending, if the McCain–Feingold legislation was upheld, was one of the reasons put forward by Chief Justice Roberts in *Citizens United* for 'throwing in the towel' and refusing to draw lines.[106] The decision of the five conservative US Supreme Court justices allowing big corporations to spend unlimited funds influencing the electoral process has not enhanced the reputation of the court. Being drawn into making 'political' decisions could undermine the legitimacy of constitutional decisions.

Notes

1 *Citizens United* v. *Federal Election Committee* (2010) 558 U.S.; (2010) 130 S.Ct. 876.
2 State of the Union Address, Washington D.C. January 2010.
3 (2009) 48 EHRR 51.
4 The Bipartisan Campaign Reform Act 2002.
5 2 U.S.C. §§ 441b(a), 441b(b)(2), 431(17)(A), and 434(f)(3)(A).
6 *McConnell* v. *Federal Election Commission* 540 U.S. 93, 203–209 (2003) and *Austin* v. *Michigan Chamber of Commerce*, 494 U.S. 652 (1990). (The Supreme Court restricted political speech on finding a compelling governmental interest in preventing the corrosive and distorting effects of wealth: an anti-distortion interest.)
7 Such other important issues include, for example, the activism of the Supreme Court, the interests of shareholders in corporations and the weight the judges gave to judicial precedent. Arguably the court could have decided the issue on a narrower ground but Justice Kennedy declined to adopt an interpretation that would require a case-by–case determination. In his opinion vague law chills speech. *Citizens United* at p. 12. See R. Dworkin's criticism of this approach. 'The "Devastating" Decision' (February 25, 2010) 57 *New York Review of Books*.
8 *Citizens United*, p. 24.
9 Ibid., p. 19.
10 Ibid., p. 24.
11 Ibid., p. 25.
12 Ibid., p. 24.
13 The dissenting opinion of Justice Stevens was joined by Justice Ginsburg, Justice Breyer and Justice Sotomayor.

14 Corporations can use shareholders' or union members' money to support or oppose a candidate
15 Justice Stevens criticized the majority for failing to explain why corporate identity and individuals should receive the same treatment. *Citizens United*, p. 32.
16 *Citizens United*, p. 45.
17 Ibid., p. 44.
18 Ibid. (Roberts CJ concurring), p. 14.
19 R. Dworkin, 'The Decision that Threatens Democracy', *The New York Review of Books*, (May 13, 2010).
20 *Citizens United*, p. 8.
21 Ibid., p. 90.
22 R. Dworkin, Letter to New York Review of Books, Vol 57, Number 7 (April 29, 2010).
23 *Bowman* v. *United Kingdom* (1998) 26 EHRR 1.
24 S. Issacharoff, 'The Constitutional Logic of Campaign Finance Regulation' *Pepperdine Law Review*, 2009, vol. 26, 373, 383–384.
25 [2002] UKHL 23.
26 Note also *R* v. *Radio Authority, Ex p. Bull* [1998] QB 294 CA (Civ. Div). Ofcom's duty is to ensure that the ban is observed. See Communications Act 2003, s. 319(1) and the Ofcom Broadcasting Code which took effect on 16/12/09. Similar limits are imposed on the BBC through the BBC's Licence Agreement. The BBC does not carry paid advertisements, thus the ban is of less significance.
27 Political Parties, Elections and Referendums Act 2000, ss. 37 and 127.
28 See generally E. Barendt, *Freedom of Speech*, 2nd edition, Oxford: Oxford University Press, 2005) and H. Fenwick and G. Phillipson, *Media Freedom under the Human Rights Act*, Oxford: Oxford University Press, 2006, pp. 1018–1020.
29 Hansard, HC vol. 395, col. 788 (3 December 2002).
30 Human Rights Act 1998, s. 19(1)(b).
31 Joint Committee on Human Rights, Nineteenth Report of Session 2001–2002 (19 July 2002, HL Paper 149; HC 1102) at para. 64.
32 Ibid.
33 Communications Act 2003, s. 321 (2)(a).
34 Ibid., s. 321 (2)(b).
35 Ibid., s. 321 (2) (c).
36 Ibid., s. 321 (3)(a).
37 Ibid., s. 321 (3)(b).
38 Ibid., s. 321 (3)(c).
39 Ibid., s. 321 (3)(d).
40 Ibid., s. 321 (3)(e).
41 Ibid., s. 321 (3)(f).
42 Ibid., s. 321 (3)(g).
43 See e.g. E. Barendt, *Freedom of Speech* at p. 445 and pp. 484–486; A. Scott, 'A Monstrous and Unjustifiable Infringement?: Political Expression and the Broadcasting Ban on Advocacy Advertising', *Modern Law Review*, 2003, vol. 66, 224 and H. Fenwick and G. Phillipson, *Media Freedom under the Human Rights Act* at pp. 1012–1036.
44 Fenwick and Phillipson, ibid., at 1p. 017.
45 [2003] UKHL 23.
46 Ibid., per Lord Nicholls at [3].
47 Broadcasting Act 1990 s.6(1)(a). The BBC was subject to a non-statutory obligation.
48 [2002] 2 All ER 756. Although one critic commented that 'parts of the decision … make greater appeal to rhetoric rather than to reason'. I. Hare, 'Debating Abortion – The right to offend gratuitously', *Cambridge Law Journal*, 2003, vol. 62, 525, at 528.
49 (1998) 26 EHRR 1.

50 Fenwick and Phillipson, *Media Freedom under the Human Rights Act.*, at 581.
51 *Prolife Alliance*, [57].
52 Ibid., [123] per Lord Walker.
53 Ibid., [58].
54 Ibid., [49].
55 Ibid., [74].
56 Ibid., [99].
57 See E. Barendt, 'Free Speech and Abortion', *Public Law*, 2003, 580 and I. Hare, 'Debating Abortion – the Right to Offend Gratuitously' *Cambridge Law Journal*, 2003, vol. 62, 525 who criticize the decision of the House of Lords. But see J. Rowbottom, 'Article 10 and Election Broadcasts' *Law Quarterly Review*, 2003, vol. 119, 553.
58 *Prolife*, [130].
59 Ibid., [70].
60 Ibid., [80].
61 *Public Law*, 2003, 580 at 585.
62 Ibid., at 586.
63 [2008] UKHL 15.
64 Ibid., [4]. The BACC is the body funded by commercial broadcasters to monitor proposed advertisements for compliance with the law and codes of practice.
65 Ibid., [4].
66 Ibid., [28].
67 Ibid.
68 Ibid.
69 Ibid., [31].
70 Ibid.
71 Ibid. [32]. He compared this situation to *Bowman* v. *UK* (1998) 26 EHRR 1 where the legislation absolutely prohibited Mrs. Bowman from communicating her views.
72 Ibid., [33].
73 See s. 19(1)(b) Human Rights Act 1998.
74 See J. Rowbottom, 'Political Advertising and the Broadcast Media', *Cambridge Law Journal*, 2008, vol. 67, 450 at 452 and T. Lewis and P. Cumper, 'Balancing Freedom of Political Expression against Equality of Political Opportunity: The Court's and the UK's broadcasting ban on political advertising', *Public Law*, 2009, 89 at 101.
75 *Animal Defenders International*, [51].
76 Ibid., [48].
77 Ibid., [52].
78 Ibid., [41].
79 Ibid., [41].
80 www.guardian.co.uk/media/2010/may/24/marie-stopes-abortion-services-ad. I am grateful to J. Rowbottom for suggesting this example.
81 (2001) 34 EHRR 154. Hereafter referred to as *VgT*.
82 Nineteenth Session, supra n.
83 The applicant refused to make changes that would moderate the advertisement's message. *VgT* at [14].
84 *VgT* at [15].
85 Ibid., [61].
86 Ibid., [71].
87 Ibid., [73].
88 Ibid., [75].
89 Ibid.
90 Ibid., [78].
91 *ADI* at [29] and [34]. Note also at [31] Lord Bingham's reference to *Murphy* v. *Ireland* 38 EHRR 212 at [77]. See Lord Scott's comments at [43].

92 (2003) 38 EHRR 212.
93 Ibid. at [78].
94 *ADI* at [43] per Lord Scott and at [52] per Baroness Hale.
95 (2009) 48 EHRR 51.
96 *TV Vest*, [55] and [57].
97 Ibid., [78].
98 Ibid., [73].
99 Ibid.
100 Ibid., [76].
101 Ibid., [77] and [75].
102 *Bowman* v. *UK* [42].
103 *TV Vest* [65].
104 Kit Kat: Give the orang-utans a break: Greenpeace (March 2010).
105 *ADI* at para [51].
106 Issacharoff in *Party Funding and Campaign Financing.*

Part IV

Lessons from abroad

11 State intervention in party politics

The public funding and regulation of political parties[1]

Ingrid van Biezen

Introduction

The question of how parties are, and ought to be, financed and regulated, has assumed an increased importance in recent years. As the levels of popular disengagement, disaffection and cynicism are rising and as party leaders are increasingly perceived as incompetent, dishonest and corrupt, a growing number of voices has joined the chorus for more transparency, tighter controls and stricter regulations of the activities of political parties and politicians.

A host of national and international governmental institutions and non-governmental organisations, such as the Council of Europe, the International Institute for Democracy and Electoral Assistance (IDEA), the European Parliament, the Organisation for Economic Co-operation and Development (OECD) and Transparency International (TI), are now independently investigating the funding practices of political parties and election campaigns, and are reporting on the ways in which illicit modes of party financing might be curtailed. Even the parties themselves have begun to show an increased interest in the issue of party funding and regulation. The UK, for example, where the financing of parties had been largely unregulated and unmonitored until the adoption of the 2000 Political Parties, Elections and Referendums Act, recently carried out a major independent review of the funding of political parties. Its purpose was to evaluate, not merely the success of the new law in effectively regulating party financing but also, and perhaps more importantly, to assess the potential that changes to the law might have in addressing the high levels of popular discontent with the seemingly self-interested behaviour of the parties. Reform of the party funding system was deemed essential to restore public trust in the parties and the democratic system.[2]

Indeed, an important motivation underlying the general interest in party financing and regulation is a growing concern with the low levels of public confidence in political parties. While parties may well be seen as necessary for the effective functioning of democracy, this does not mean that they are very much liked or respected. If anything, parties are increasingly seen as being driven primarily by their material self-interest. Political parties today are regarded by the public as the institution most susceptible to corruption and, perhaps as a consequence, they are one of the least trusted democratic institutions.[3] As a result, an increasingly widely accepted view is that higher levels of external control and monitoring of party activity and behaviour are warranted in order to ensure that they perform their democratic functions more effectively.

More specifically, the general response to the perceived failings of parties has tended to involve conceding a greater responsibility to the state in managing their activities and behaviour, to the point that the state has now assumed a considerable, and increasingly legitimate, role in dealing with internal and external party affairs. Broadly speaking, this increased state intervention falls into two categories. On the one hand, there has been a significant increase of state support to political parties in the form of direct public subsidies, as access to public funding should relieve them of the need to satisfy private interests, should promote fair and equal party competition, and might even boost public engagement. On the other hand, the state has substantially increased its control over party affairs through public legislation, as external control should enhance the transparency of party activity and improve the accountability of parties more generally.

This article is concerned with a closer examination of these two trends – the increased availability of public funding to political parties, and the increased levels of public regulation of party activity and behaviour – arguing that both these dimensions constitute part of the way in which parties have strengthened their linkages with the state in recent years. It looks more closely at the extent of party regulation in European democracies from a comparative perspective, and discusses the underlying normative paradigms. Second, it examines the availability public funding, and explores the motivations for its introduction in light of particular understandings of party democracy.

Political parties and the state

The role of political parties in contemporary democracies has changed profoundly over the course of the twentieth century and into the twenty-first. Consequently, conceptions of party democracy have changed almost beyond recognition since parties first appeared and consolidated themselves with the advent of mass democracy, when they emerged to serve as the necessary linkage between citizens and the state. Political parties are typically understood as intermediary institutions located somewhere between society and the state. However, they have been analysed primarily in terms of their relationship with society, as they used to be firmly rooted within civil society and drew their legitimacy from their capacity to represent key constituencies and interests within society. Although they have always fulfilled public functions, their real justification was derived from their representative character rather than their capacity to provide government. In fact, the legitimacy of the party as a mechanism for the recruitment of public office holders was given by the fact that the party constituted a channel of expressive selection and thus provided for representative leadership.[4]

As the increased disengagement from conventional party politics demonstrates, however, the linkages between parties and society have substantially weakened in recent years, thus undermining the representative capacities of the parties. This is part of a process of organisational transformation of European political parties whereby, as Katz and Mair have argued, the erosion of the linkages between parties and society is accompanied by a concomitant intensification of their relationship with the state.[5] Parties have maintained or even increased their institutional roles, in that they have retained exclusive control over candidate recruitment, have become more office-seeking and are thus increasingly prioritising their role as governing agencies as opposed to representative organisations, and are working together in taking advantage of the resources of the state – such as public subsidies, state-regulated media access, or party patronage – to ensure their collective survival. Indeed, parties are seen to have strengthened their relationship with the state such that they have almost become absorbed by the state and have begun to act as semi-state agencies.[6] However, while the erosion of the representative linkages between parties and society in recent years has been relatively well documented and explored theoretically and empirically, the precise dimensions of the relationship between parties and the state have been analysed much less systematically, and with much less conceptual clarity.[7]

One of the reasons why relatively little scholarly attention has been paid to the linkage of parties to the state is that this relationship has traditionally been temporal, contingent and loose.[8] To the extent that parties were linked to the state, this relationship tended to be confined to government rather than the state overall: parties recruited candidates for public office, placed their representatives in government positions and sought influence in the state, without necessarily becoming part of it. Parties did not depend on the state for their resources and legitimacy, nor were they managed by the state. The two key developments in the recent processes of organisational adaptation outlined above have altered these patterns: On the one hand, parties in contemporary democracies have become more dependent on the state, especially in financial terms. On the other hand, they are also increasingly managed and regulated by the state through public law. The relevance of state subsidies to political parties has received considerable attention since the cartel party article was first published, in particular because the parties' increasing dependence on public subsidies was given a pre-eminent position as a key indicator of cartelisation by Katz and Mair.[9] The increased state regulation of party activity, organisation and behaviour, however, has scarcely been the subject of systematic and comparative scholarly consideration.[10] In the following section, we will turn to this aspect first.

The regulation of parties

In addition to an increased financial dependence on the state, to which we will return later, parties in contemporary democracies are to a growing extent managed by the state, in that their activities are, to an increasing degree, subject to regulations and state laws which govern their external activities or determine the way in which their internal organisation may function. Traditionally, given the fundamentally private and voluntary character of political parties, the state in liberal democratic societies would not intervene in the regulation of their behaviour and organisation, but in recent years the legal regulation of parties has become more and more customary, to the point that party structures have now become 'legitimate objects of state regulation to a degree far exceeding what would normally be acceptable for private associations in a liberal society'.[11] Many of these regulations were first introduced or were substantially extended in the wake of the introduction of public funding for parties, as the provision of state subventions inevitably demanded a more codified system of party registration and control. Controlling party access to the public broadcasting media has also required the introduction or extension of the system of regulation, which again has acted to codify the status of parties and their range of activities.

The evidence suggests that legislation on political parties is indeed extensive, as is illustrated by the data in Table 11.1. Naturally, the body of party law that determines the legal status of political parties and that specifies how parties may operate, must organise, or should be funded, may take a variety of forms. Party law is generally derived from a series of related bodies of law, including laws on political parties, political finance laws, electoral laws, campaign laws, and the constitution, as well as statutes, administrative rulings and court decisions.[12] Table 11.1 provides an overview of only three, albeit significant, types of party regulation, namely through the constitution (C), special party laws (PL), and the regulation of political financing (PF).

As can be inferred from the Table 11.1, the large majority of European democracies have established a regulatory framework for the financing of political parties. There are some, but only marginal, differences between the older and the more recently established democracies. For example, a system of regulation of party finances is in place in most countries that provide state support to parties, as we shall see later, although there are some exceptions to this pattern (e.g. Denmark, Norway, and Sweden). Switzerland is the only country without regulation of political parties which also lacks public funding, and where parties are thus not strongly linked to the state in the sense of being financially dependent on, or regulated by, the state.

Table 11.1 also indicates how many countries have adopted a special law on political parties. Here, the difference between old and new democracies is more pronounced. Only a handful of the established democracies – of which some in this context are probably better understood as re-established democracies – have adopted a special law on political parties (Austria, Finland, Germany and, most recently, the UK). In the younger democracies, on the other hand, including those in southern Europe and central and eastern Europe, such party laws are more common, with only one country lacking such a law (Greece). Indeed, it appears that party regulation in the newer democracies is generally much more exacting than in the older ones,[13] tending to follow a 'prescription model' of regulation, whereby it seeks to mould parties to conform to a certain ideal type.[14]

Table 11.1 Party regulation in European democracies

Established democracies	*C*	*PL*	*PF*	*New democracies*	*C*	*PL*	*PF*
Austria	✓	✓	✓	Bulgaria	✓	✓	✗
Belgium	✗	✗	✓	Czech Republic	✓	✓	✗
Denmark	✗	✗	✓	Estonia	✓	✓	✗
Finland	✓	✓	✓	Greece	✓	✗	✗
France	✓	✗	✓	Hungary	✓	✓	✓
Germany	✓	✓	✗	Latvia	✓	✓	✗
Ireland	✗	✗	✗	Lithuania	✓	✓	✓
Italy	✓	✗	✓	Poland	✓	✓	✗
Netherlands	✗	✗	✓	Portugal	✓	✓	✓
Norway	✓	✓	✓	Romania	✓	✓	✓
Sweden	✓	✗	✓	Slovakia	✓	✓	✓
Switzerland	✓	✗	✗	Spain	✓	✓	✓
UK	n/a	✓	✓				
Total N = *13*	*Yes: 8* *(66.7%)*	*Yes: 5* *(38.5%)*	*Yes: 10* *(76.9%)*	*Total* N = *12*	*Yes: 12* *(100%)*	*Yes: 11* *(91.7%)*	*Yes: 8* *(61.5%)*

Source: Adapted and updated from van Biezen and Kopecký 2007; Karvonen 2007.

Notes
C = constitution; PL = party law; PF = regulation of party finance law.

Table 11.1, furthermore, shows that a large majority of the countries now have enshrined political parties in their constitutions. Also here we see a significant difference between the old and new democracies, although slightly less pronounced than in the case of party laws. All of the recently established democracies have constitutionally codified the role of political parties, but the constitutionalisation of parties is much less common in the established democracies, where only about two-thirds of the countries with a written constitution records a positive score. This absence is probably a legacy of the past, and a particular understanding of political parties that corresponds to their historically private character.

The body of party law broadly conceived may regulate a wide variety of aspects, ranging from the legal status and definition of parties to issues about their internal organisation, mechanisms of candidate selection and party finance. Broadly speaking, party laws have been enacted for three basic purposes.[15] First, the law may determine what formally constitutes a political party, who qualifies for ballot access, who benefits from public resources such as subsidies or broadcast media, etc. Second, laws may exist to regulate the type and form of activity in which parties may engage, such as campaign activities, or the raising and spending of (private and public) funds. Finally, and probably most controversially, the law may lay down the appropriate forms of party organisation and behaviour, prescribing, for example, the mechanism for the selection of public office holders, demanding ethnic or gender parity on electoral lists, or constraining the ideological content of the party programme or electoral manifesto. It is this last aspect, by which the state intervenes in the parties' internal organisational structure or their political profile, which is most likely to infringe upon associational freedoms.

From the perspective of normative democratic theory, the legal regulation of political parties raises serious questions and concerns. The presence of laws specifically targeted at political parties often implies that, in comparison to other organisations, the law either imposes greater restrictions on political parties or, conversely, confers special privileges upon them. This raises the fundamental question of whether parties ought in fact to be regulated differently from other types of organisations, and whether the special regulation of parties can be reconciled with basic freedoms, such as freedom of speech and association, which are thought to be essential to democracy.[16] Other concerns which may arise are similar to those emerging from the diffusion of constitutional review and the expansion of opportunities for judicial activism: these processes arguably undermine fundamental principles of democracy by effectively transferring powers from representative to non-representative institutions. Although the courts might sometimes act as a powerful constraint on the possible undemocratic behaviour of political parties, the legal regulation of parties not only evokes anxieties about the state centralisation and control of political participation and public life, but also about the democratic legitimacy of transferring the ultimate decision-making authority on their behaviour and organisation from the responsible organs of the party to a non-elected body of judges.[17]

Despite the increased levels of party regulation, the empirical or normative dimensions of this phenomenon have thus far received relatively little systematic and comparative scholarly attention. This is even more so for their juridification through the formal constitution. Although the constitutional regulation of political parties has acquired an increased relevance in European democracies in recent years, constitutions are not normally considered as a source of party law. However, in the post-war period the relevance of political parties for democracy gradually has become more widely acknowledged also in constitutional terms, to the point that pluralism, political participation and competition in many contemporary democratic constitutions have come to be defined increasingly, if not almost exclusively, in terms of party. Perhaps it is because the law has been so late in recognising political parties, that scholars have taken insufficient note of the fact that parties are so central also to the institutional arrangements of contemporary democracies.[18]

According to Persily and Cain,[19] different paradigms can be distinguished that govern and inform the contents of the law and the nature of the rules that affect political parties. In the 'managerial paradigm', for example, the primary goal is the preservation of the democratic order. With the primary interest of the state lying in the preservation of the stability of the party system, the party system is largely a state instrumentality. According to this approach, the state has the authority to set the rules of party behaviour and organisation, with little importance accorded to a political party's freedom to associate. This creates the potential for governing parties to prevent competitors from effectively organising themselves and, furthermore, implies that parties lose their own organisational autonomy. This type of regulation can probably most clearly be associated with the cartelisation of the parties and the party system.

In the 'libertarian paradigm', on the other hand, far from being instruments to serve the state, parties are a particular species of private, organised interest groups, whose primary purpose is to express the opinion of their members. They should therefore be given maximal rights of association, privacy, expression, and freedom from state intervention. This not only implies that parties are not the proper subject of state regulation, but also that they should not receive any state benefits (such as direct or indirect funding). Pushed to its logical conclusion, the libertarian paradigm is best reflected in the absence of any state regulation of parties (and public funding for that matter). In empirical and normative practice, the increased relevance and legitimacy of both state funding and state regulation suggests that this paradigm is rapidly becoming irrelevant.

For the advocates of the 'political market paradigm', values to be maximised are electoral choice and party competition, and the primary purpose of political parties is to offer political alternatives to their voter-consumers. The state interest in the party system is to facilitate effective political competition, and thus to construct rules that maximise or at least provide adequate competition between parties. Hence, the laws intervening in the political market serve to correct market failures and to prevent possible monopolistic partisan practices. Some of the principles that govern the public funding of parties, in particular, those that aim to encourage fair and equal competition between parties, can serve as an example of this paradigm.

Finally, according to the 'critical approach', the primary purpose of political parties is to represent social cleavages. On this view, the state interest is to construct rules that maximise interest representation, and possibly to intervene to compensate for existing biases of the social and political system. In terms of the electoral system, the various mechanisms that enhance the proportionality of the system might serve as an example. In terms of party laws, one might think of norms that regulate gender balances on party electoral lists.

Because the regulation of parties has only recently become a focus for party and legal scholarship, it is too early to tell which, if any, of these paradigms applies to the regulation of parties by law and the constitution. However, they suggest that party law has become an important source for investigations into the character of modern democracy and the prevailing ideas about the place of political parties within it. Few, if any, institutional preferences and reforms are politically neutral, and choices and decisions about the character of regulation are themselves not above politics.[20] In fact, the position of political parties in this respect is particularly interesting because the parties themselves are of course the principal agents of their own legal regulation. The law thus reflects a particular vision of what the distribution of power actually is, as well as what it should be, as decisions on the regulation of party activity, organisation and behaviour follow from particular conceptions of party and the preferred roles and functions of parties. Different norms and conceptions thus lead to different prescriptions about the appropriate legal regulation of parties.[21] The position of political parties as defined by public law and the national constitution, therefore, sheds light on a number of the crucial questions in the legal regulation of politics, ranging from questions about how parties should be understood in terms of normative democratic theory, to how they are to be financed.

State funding of parties

Public funding for political parties is a relatively recent phenomenon in European democracies, having gained importance only in the post-war period. Historically, political parties in the liberal democracies of western Europe primarily depended on private contributions to finance their activities. Cadre parties generally relied on contributions from wealthy individuals or donations from private business; mass parties typically secured a structural flow of income from the fees paid by their members and the donations from affiliated trade unions; and catch-all parties broadened their financial support base by securing access to a wider variety of interest groups. Today, however, virtually all European democracies provide direct state subventions to political parties. The introduction of public funding for parties has encouraged the emergence of cartel parties, which depend to an important extent on the financial resources of the state for their own survival. Hence, while parties in western Europe traditionally relied on contributions that were in one way or another derived from society (membership subscriptions, contributions from individual donors, private business or affiliated associations), for most parties today the direct subsidies from the state have become a much more important, if not principal, resource.

The evidence suggests that political parties in the vast majority of the liberal democracies now have access to direct state subsidies, although the actual amounts and their relative importance may vary. For the European democracies, this is demonstrated by Table 11.2, which summarises the availability of direct public funding for political parties. As the table suggests, public subsidies have indeed become a widespread phenomenon, with little significant difference between the established and the newer democracies. It is only in three countries (Latvia, Malta and Switzerland) that the national parties do not have access to direct state support.

The growing prevalence of public subsidies can in itself be interpreted as an indication of the increasing financial dependence of parties on the state. In order to establish precisely how dependent parties are on the state, the key question, of course, is how important these public subsidies are in relation to the total party incomes. Existing studies suggest that there are significant differences between countries and between parties within one country.[22] In some central and eastern European countries such as the Czech Republic, Slovenia, Hungary, and Estonia, the relative importance of state money is very large, with the state being the key provider of party income. The same is by and large true for the southern European democracies of Spain and Portugal, where many parties are, financially, almost entirely dependent on the state. In other countries, public funding is

Table 11.2 Availability of public funding for parties in European democracies

Established democracies		*New democracies*	
Austria	✓	Bulgaria	✓
Belgium	✓	Croatia	✓
Cyprus	✓	Czech Republic	✓
Denmark	✓	Estonia	✓
Finland	✓	Greece	✓
France	✓	Hungary	✓
Germany	✓	Latvia	✗
Iceland	✓	Lithuania	✓
Ireland	✓	Poland	✓
Italy	✓	Portugal	✓
Malta	✗	Romania	✓
Netherlands	✓	Slovakia	✓
Norway	✓	Slovenia	✓
Sweden	✓	Spain	✓
Switzerland	✗		
United Kingdom	✓		
Total N = *16*	*Yes: 14* *(87.5%)*	*Total* N = *14*	*Yes: 13* *(92.9%)*

Source: Updated from van Biezen and Kopecký 2007.

merely symbolic in comparison to the resources parties obtain from private and corporate donations. Examples include Bulgaria or, amongst the non-liberal democracies, countries such as Russia and the Ukraine. Among the established democracies, parties in countries such as Germany and France benefit from significant amounts of subsidies. The UK, on the other hand, provides only token amounts of financial support to parties, although there does seem to be increasing cross-party support in favour of an increase in direct state funding. A comparative analysis of several European democracies showed that state support ranged from just over one-fifth (Denmark) to almost 85 per cent (Finland) of total party income.[23] Unfortunately, more comprehensive cross-national data to evaluate the actual financial dependence on the state are not available. What we do know, however, is that the introduction of state support for parties has encouraged a dependence on public money that is critical, in a lot of cases, and at the very least non-trivial in many others.

The introduction of direct state funding has thus made parties increasingly dependent on public money and state support. Although this has not implied that other financial resources have become entirely irrelevant, the introduction of state subsidies represents a turning point in the financing of political parties, in that it represents 'a fundamental change in the character of the party, furthering its transformation from a private association into a semi-public entity'.[24] In this sense, state subsidies have contributed to a process by which parties are increasingly seen as an essential public good for democracy and less exclusively as private voluntary associations, which are the instruments of civil society. This can be illustrated by an exploration of the most common arguments advanced in favour of state subventions to political parties, all of which underline the importance that parties are now seen to have for modern democracy and the positive contribution they (ought to) make to the public interest.

The first argument in favour of direct state subsidies relates to the desire to restrict the influence of private money and to limit its potential for distortion of the democratic political process. The concern here is that certain private interests rather than the general public interest would come to guide the conduct of parties and elected officials. Since public funding relieves parties from having to satisfy their financial supporters, it is anticipated that they have a diminishing effect on corruption. Coupled with the legislation on party financing, public funding gives the state a larger degree of control over the role of money in politics and a greater opportunity legitimately to exercise some degree of supervision over financial party activity, which should further reduce the potentially excessive influence of private contributors at the expense of the public interest.

A second motivation is concerned with the rising cost of politics, coupled with the decreasing revenues of political parties. Politics in the western liberal democracies has become progressively more expensive as the result of the increased use of the mass media and more cost-intensive campaigning techniques, and as a consequence of the internal professionalisation of parties. The overall resources of parties have increased substantially as well: Their central headquarters and parliamentary groups are better staffed than they were 20 to 30 years ago, their annual income has increased and they are spending more money on election campaigns.[25] At the same time, parties have seen their membership bases decline, which has had two important consequences. First of all, this has deprived parties of an important source of revenue, as it has implied an effective reduction in the income derived from membership subscriptions. Second, the erosion of their membership organisations has implied that parties have lost a substantial share of their reservoir of volunteers who would work for the party as unpaid employees or who would carry out labour-intensive campaigning activities. For this loss, they have compensated by recruiting larger numbers of paid professionals. The public subsidies to parties and candidates should thus in part be understood as a response to the rising cost of the democratic process in a context of decreasing in revenues to what are seen as its principal protagonists. This motivation corresponds closely with the 'managerial paradigm' and with the public interest in maintaining party democracy.

A third justification for the state to be directly involved in the financing of political parties is associated with concerns for the fairness and equality of political competition. On this view, not all parties are equally resourceful and those who cannot successfully tap into the resources of private contributors should not necessarily be at a disadvantage. This consideration is primarily relevant for smaller parties, newly established parties, parties whose political programme is unlikely to appeal to wealthy or established interests, and parties which lack any linkages with affiliated interest organisations. State subsidies should thus create a more level playing field by enabling new, small and less resourceful parties to compete on a more equitable basis with the dominant and financially more privileged ones. This concern corresponds with the 'political market paradigm' and with the state's interest in facilitating electoral choice and party competition.

All of these motivations in favour of a more prominent role of the state in the funding of political parties can be understood in light of the currently predominant discourse, which holds that parties make a positive contribution to democracy. The growing extent of state intervention in party financing, and indeed regulation, has in fact been legitimised by an ideational transformation, which has accompanied the development of modern democracy, whereby parties have developed from organisations perceived as antagonistic to democracy, to institutions that are generally seen as necessary and desirable.

This transformation can be seen as having occurred in three sequential stages, with the introduction of universal suffrage and the reconstruction of democracy in the post-war period acting as the two major watershed events. The first of these stages corresponds with the period which is demarcated by the first appearance of political parties and the introduction of universal suffrage. In this period, parties were not seen as necessary, let alone desirable, institutions for democracy. On the contrary, they were primarily perceived as a threat to the general interest or as overriding the interests of the individual. Indeed, their existence was fundamentally incompatible with both the liberal democratic tradition rooted in the political philosophy of Locke and the radical democratic tradition inspired by Rousseau. Both of these are difficult to marry with partisan institutions, which by their very nature transcend individual interests and contest the existence of a general will.

However, the advent of mass democracy brought about by the introduction of universal suffrage, and the consequent final push in the adaptation of democracy to the scale of the modern nation-state, made the direct links between the state and the individual increasingly unrealistic and effectively impossible. The introduction of universal (male) suffrage thus served to legitimise the existence of parties as intermediary institutions between individual citizens and the state. In this second period, therefore, which is demarcated roughly by the democratisation of competitive oligarchies through the extension of the franchise to all (male) adult citizens, on the one hand, and the restoration of democracy in the immediate post-war period, on the other, political parties came to be seen as necessary (or at least inevitable) institutions for democracy. From a normative perspective, however, for the same reasons as before, they were still largely seen as unwelcome and, at best, an unpleasant consequence of free government.

A more broadly shared and explicitly positive connotation came to be attached to the role of parties in representative democracy only in the immediate post-war period, nearly two centuries after Burke had come to see that parties had a positive and necessary quality for democracy and made what Mansfield subsequently described as 'the first argument in the history of political philosophy for the respectability, not merely the necessity, of parties'.[26] Beginning with the restoration of democracy in Italy and West Germany, the political parties came to be seen as valuable and indispensable, to the point that they are now generally considered as the necessary condition for the organisation of the modern democratic polity and for the expression of political pluralism and participation. The centrality of political parties for representative democracy is generally accepted both by contemporary party scholars – although arguably not by many political theorists[27] – and by policy-makers charged with fostering the development of newly emerging democracies and with improving the quality of democracy in established democratic polities.

In sum, the gradual appreciation over the course of the twentieth century of the positive contribution that parties make to democracy signals a dramatic shift in the normative conceptions of parties and democracy. Because political parties have now come to be seen as key democratic institutions, it has seemed possible, if not essential, for the state to intervene with direct financial support in order to facilitate their continued existence, to foster a level playing field, and to eradicate particularistic forms of financing. Indeed, it is only from a conception of democracy in which parties are the indispensable protagonists of representative democracy that the state should have come to play such an important and legitimate role in party financing.

The direct involvement of the state in internal party affairs has contributed to a transformation of parties from their traditional understanding as voluntary and private associations towards parties as public service agencies or, as I have argued elsewhere, public utilities.[28] The notion of parties as public utilities, which was observed earlier by Epstein for the American context,[29] implies at least four aspects. First, parties perform important functions that are necessary and indispensable for democracy. As these benefit the community as a whole, they are non-excludable and can be considered as a public good. Generally speaking, however, the delivery of public goods tends to suffer from market failures, but state intervention can be a solution in order to ensure the effective and efficient provision of the good. This can take several forms, an important one of which is government subsidies. Second, therefore, the value of the services provided by parties justifies financial support from the state. In contemporary democracies, this takes the form of indirect subventions and an increasing relevance of direct state subsidies. Third, because of their special role in representative democracy, the internal affairs and external activities of political parties should be regulated by the state, both to enforce the proper management of their finances and to ensure that they perform their unique democratic services effectively. As is true for public services more generally, which are usually subject to a degree of regulation going beyond that applying to other economic sectors, this implies that, fourth, relative to other types of organisations, political parties merit a privileged status in public law. This is evidenced by the growing importance of party regulation. Hence, the notion of parties as public utilities entails not only that parties ought to be financially supported by the state, but also that the state has a legitimate role in the regulation of their activities. It is this conception of parties and democracy that provides the core foundation of state intervention in party politics.

Conclusion

This article has shown that state intervention in contemporary European party politics has assumed significant proportions, in particular in the form of the extensive regulation of party activity and the widespread availability of public funding. The involvement of the state is legitimised by underlying normative paradigms according to which the state has an interest in maintaining the democratic party system, facilitating electoral choice and party competition, and maximising the representation of social interests. As a consequence of the growing levels of state intervention in party affairs, the relationship between parties and the state has assumed an increased importance both in terms of legitimacy and organisational resources.

The increased dependence on public money and the growing involvement of the state in internal party affairs, whereby parties become subject to a regulatory framework which grants them an official status as part of the institutions of the democratic state, has contributed to the transformation of parties from voluntary private associations to a special type of public utility. As the internal life and the external activities of parties become regulated by public law, and as party rules become constitutional or administrative rules, the parties themselves become transformed into public service agencies, with a corresponding weakening of their own internal organisational autonomy,[30] and a shift of the primary locus of accountability from the internal organs of the party towards external and non-majoritarian institutions.

Whereas parties once drew their legitimacy from their capacity to represent key constituencies within civil society, they now justify themselves by appealing to a conception of democracy which sees parties as an essential public good. In this capacity, they are both supported and supervised by the state, which contributes to the financing of their activities and monitors their behaviour through an increasingly tighter framework of regulation. Because the linkages between parties and society have become increasingly loose and contingent with time, while those with the state have progressively acquired more prominence, political parties are now perhaps best understood in terms of their permanent linkages with the state, rather than society. As the parties themselves become increasingly defined as semi-state agencies, modern party democracy effectively becomes a service provided by the government to its citizens.

Notes

1 Financial support from the ESRC (RES-061–25–0080) and the ERC (ERC_Stg07_205660) is gratefully acknowledged.
2 See *The Review of the Funding of Political Parties*. Online. Available HTTP: www.partyfundingreview.gov.uk (accessed 14 June 2010).
3 For example, R.J. Dalton and S.A. Weldon, 'Public Images of Political Parties: A Necessary Evil?', *West European Politics*, 28(5), 2005, 931.
4 G. Sartori, 'Party Types, Organisation and Functions', *West European Politics*, 28(1), 2005, 5.
5 R.S. Katz and P. Mair, 'Changing Models of Party Organization and Party Democracy: the Emergence of the Cartel Party', *Party Politics*, 1(1), 1995, 5.
6 S. Bartolini and P. Mair, 'Challenges to Contemporary Political Parties', in L. Diamond and R. Gunther (eds) *Political Parties and Democracy*, Baltimore: Johns Hopkins University Press, 2001.
7 I. van Biezen and P. Kopecký, 'The State and the Parties: Public Funding, Public Regulation and Rent-Seeking in Contemporary Democracies', *Party Politics*, 13(2), 2007, 235.
8 P. Kopecký and P. Mair, 'Political Parties and Government', in M. Salih (ed.), *African Political Parties: Evolution, Institutionalisation and Governance*, London: Pluto, 2003.
9 'Changing Models of Party Organization and Party Democracy: the Emergence of the Cartel Party', *Party Politics*, 1(1), 1995, 5.
10 D. Avnon, 'Parties Laws in Democratic Systems of Government', *Journal of Legislative Studies*, 1(2), 1995, 283.
11 R.S. Katz, 'The Internal Life of Parties', in K.R. Luther and F. Müller-Rommel (eds), *Political Challenges in the New Europe: Political and Analytical Challenges*, Oxford: Oxford University Press, 2002, p. 90.
12 K. Janda, 'Adopting Party Law', Working paper series on *Political Parties and Democracy in Theoretical and Practical Perspectives*, Washington DC: National Democratic Institute for International Affairs, 2005.
13 L. Karvonen, 'Legislation on Political Parties: A Global Comparison', *Party Politics*, 13(4), 2007, 437.
14 Janda, 'Adopting Party Law'.
15 R.S. Katz, 'Democracy and the Legal Regulation of Political Parties', Paper prepared for the USAID conference on 'Change in Political Parties, Washington DC, 1 October 2004.
16 Ibid.

17 Avnon, 'Parties Laws in Democratic Systems of Government', p. 285.
18 V. Bogdanor, 'The Constitution and the Party System in the Twentieth Century', *Parliamentary Affairs*, 57(4), 2004, 717, p. 718.
19 N. Persily and B. Cain, 'The Legal Status of Political Parties: A Reassessment of Competing Paradigms', *Columbia Law Review*, 100(3), 2000, 775.
20 Katz, 'Democracy and the Legal Regulation of Political Parties'.
21 J.A. Gardner, 'Can Party Politics be Virtuous?', *Columbia Law Review*, 100(3), 2000, 667.
22 For example, P. Kopecký, 'Political Parties and the State in Post-Communist Europe: The Nature of Symbiosis', *The Journal of Communist Studies and Transition Politics* 22(3), 2006, 251; M. Pinto-Duschinsky, 'Financing Politics: A Global View', *Journal of Democracy*, 13(4), 2002, 69.
23 J. Pierre, L. Svåsand, and A. Widfeldt, 'State Subsidies to Political Parties: Confronting Rhetoric with Reality', *West European Politics*, 23(3), 2000, 1.
24 Katz, 'The Internal Life of Parties', p. 115.
25 D. Farrell, 'Campaign Modernization and the West European Party', in K.R. Luther and F. Müller-Rommel (eds), *Political Challenges in the New Europe: Political and Analytical Challenges*, Oxford: Oxford University Press, 2002.
26 Quoted in S.E. Scarrow (ed.), *Perspectives on Political Parties: Classic Readings*, New York and Basingstoke: Palgrave Macmillan, 2002, p. 37.
27 See I. van Biezen and M. Saward, 'Democratic Theorists and Party Scholars: why they don't talk to each other, and why they should', *Perspectives on Politics*, 6(1), 2008, 21.
28 I. van Biezen, 'Political Parties as Public Utilities', *Party Politics*, 10(6), 2004, 701.
29 Epstein defined them as 'An agency performing a service in which the public has a special interest sufficient to justify governmental regulatory control, along with the extension of legal privileges, but not governmental ownership or management of all the agency's activities.' L. Epstein, *Political Parties in the American Mold*, Madison: University of Wisconsin Press, 1986, p. 157.
30 Bartolini and Mair, 'Challenges to Contemporary Political Parties', p. 340.

12 Canadian political finance regulation and jurisprudence

Colin Feasby

Introduction

Canada's contemporary political finance regime is an organic system that has grown and adapted to the changing political and legal landscape since it was established in the late nineteenth century. The adoption of the Canadian Charter of Rights and Freedoms in 1982 brought enhanced judicial scrutiny to the political finance regime.[1] The Charter allows courts to weigh the objectives of political finance regulation against infringements of individual rights including freedom of expression, equality, and the right to vote. Since 1982, changes to the political finance regime have been influenced by judicial decisions and principles espoused by the courts. Despite the constant threat of constitutional challenge, judicial review of the political finance regime under the Charter has not led to significant deregulation. Indeed, the courts have reinforced many of the core concepts of political finance regulation and left most of the mechanisms for controlling political finance undisturbed. The Courts, if anything, have pushed the political finance regime to adhere more closely to the principles that are said to justify regulation. The result is a political finance regime that is more open and less dominated by the major political parties.[2]

The second part of this chapter briefly traces the origins of political finance regulation in Canada, describes the current political finance regime, and explains the principles used to justify the regulations. Part three of this chapter reviews the main constitutional challenges to the political finance regime since the adoption of the Charter. The fourth part of this chapter describes the impact of the 2003 and 2006 changes to the political finance regime and considers the constitutionality of the political finance regime in its current form.

Political finance regulation in Canada

Origins of political finance regulation[3]

Canada's first political finance regulation, the Dominion Elections Act (DEA),[4] was adopted in 1874 and was modelled on the British Corrupt Practices Prevention Act of 1854.[5] The DEA set up an election expenditure reporting regime for candidates. Candidates were required to appoint an agent and to incur expenses only through the agent. The agent and candidate were required to prepare a financial report detailing election expenditures. The DEA did not limit the amount of expenditures, require disclosure of expenditures by political parties and third parties, or apply to expenditures by candidates outside an election period. There was also no requirement to disclose the amount of contributions or the identity of contributors. The DEA was amended in 1908 to prohibit corporate contributions to candidates.[6] A further amendment to the DEA in 1920 mandated disclosure of all contributions to candidates and extended the ban on corporate contributions to all corporations and unincorporated associations including trade unions.[7] The restrictions on corporations and unions were ineffective, easily circumvented, and were repealed in 1930.[8]

Political finance again became an issue in the mid-1960s as election campaigns became more sophisticated and expensive. The Barbeau Commission in 1966 and the Chappell Committee in 1970–1971 recommended a number of changes including spending controls on candidates and political parties.[9] Comprehensive election finance reform was adopted in 1974 in the Election Expenses Act[10] which amended the Canada Elections Act 2000 (CEA). The Election Expenses Act introduced fundamental changes to the election finance regime. For the first time, political parties were regulated, political party and candidate expenditures were limited, some contributions and contributor identities were required to be disclosed, public funding in the form of tax deductions and candidate expense reimbursement was provided, and third party expenditures were prohibited. These changes became the core of the CEA political finance regime for the next 30 years. Also as part of the 1974 reforms, rules governing political broadcasting migrated from the Broadcasting Act to the CEA.

Current framework of political finance regulation[11]

Contemporary Canadian political finance regulation is based on several key principles:

- political parties are the principal vehicles for communal political organization and expression;[12]
- fairness, i.e. competition between candidates and between political parties must be fair;[13]
- equality of opportunity;[14] and
- anti-corruption.[15]

The Supreme Court of Canada has described Canadian election regulation as being an ‘egalitarian model’.[16] The label ‘egalitarian model’ does not mean that the other objectives of the political finance regime are not relevant or important, but it distinguishes the Canadian approach to political finance regulation from the US which tends to devalue the importance of equality.[17]

Today, the core of the CEA remains election expense controls and disclosure. Political party and candidate expenses are only regulated during an election period. An 'election period' is defined by the CEA as being 'the period beginning with the issue of the writ and ending on polling day'.[18] An expense includes 'any cost incurred, or non-monetary contribution received, by a registered party or candidate ... used to directly promote or oppose a registered party, its leader, or candidate during an election'.[19] Outside an election period, political parties and candidates may spend unlimited amounts of money. Prior to the recent adoption of contribution limits, election expense limits were the only mechanism restricting the flow of money. The election expense limits for political parties and candidates are determined by a statutory formula that is adjusted annually for inflation.[20] Candidates and political parties must file financial returns with the Chief Electoral Officer following an election.[21] The returns are posted on the Elections Canada website.[22]

Since 1974, political contributions have been regulated by way of mandatory disclosure. Contributions are defined broadly to include monetary and non-monetary contributions[23] and also a candidate's own funds spent on election expenses.[24] The regulation of contributions is intended to capture money being transferred from the private to the political domain. The transfer of money amongst entities within the political domain – candidates, constituency associations, and registered political parties – is not a 'contribution'.[25] Contributions may not be made indirectly to conceal the identity of the contributor.[26] The name and address of all individuals making contributions of over CAD$200 must be disclosed by the candidate or political party receiving the contribution.[27] Elections Canada publishes all of the contributor data on its website.

The existing contribution disclosure approach was augmented by the introduction of contribution limits in amendments to the CEA in 2003.[28] Contributions by corporations and trade unions were prohibited, subject to a limited exception for contributions of up to CAD$1,000 to candidates and constituency associations.[29] Individual contributions were limited to CAD$5,000 adjusted annually for inflation to 'each registered political party and its registered associations, nomination contestants, and candidates'.[30] Further amendments to the CEA contained in the 2006 Federal Accountability Act reduced individual contribution limits to CAD$1,000 adjusted annually for inflation and extinguished the right of corporations and trade unions to contribute even CAD$1,000 to candidates and constituency associations.[31]

There are three forms of public funding in the Canadian political finance regime: tax deductions for contributors; reimbursement of election expenses for candidates and political parties; and political party allowances. Candidates who receive ten per cent of the vote are entitled to be reimbursed 60 per cent of their election expenses.[32] Political parties that receive two per cent of the national popular vote or at least five per cent of the votes in the electoral districts in which it endorsed candidates are entitled to be reimbursed 50 per cent of their election expenses.[33] Political parties that qualify for reimbursement of election expenses also qualify for a quarterly allowance determined by the number of votes cast for the political party in the last general election.[34]

The reservation and allocation of free and discounted time for political broadcasting during an election period by the CEA is akin to a form of public funding.[35] The CEA requires the major radio and television networks to reserve an amount of free time[36] for political broadcasts and 390 minutes to be sold at the lowest commercial rate.[37] The CEA provides a formula for the allocation of the free and discounted broadcast time. The formula takes into account the number of seats won in the previous general election, the share of the popular vote in the previous general election, and the number of candidates endorsed in the previous general election.[38] The actual allocation is performed by the Broadcast Arbitrator, who has residual discretion to 'modify the allocation in any manner he deems fit' if he considers the allocation produced by the statutory formula to be unfair or contrary to the public interest.[39]

Constitutional challenges to political finance regulation

The Canadian Constitution

The Canadian Constitution comprises two main statutes, a number of minor statutes, and unwritten principles.[40] The first of the main statutes is the Constitution Act, 1867 which, amongst other things, delineates the division of powers between the federal government and the provinces.[41] The second of the main statutes is the Constitution Act, 1982, which contains the Charter. The Charter is a constitutional bill of rights that sets out rights that limit the power of the state. Charter analysis begins with consideration of whether the challenged legislative provision violates a protected right. The complainant bears the burden of establishing that a right has been infringed. The Charter, unlike the US Bill of Rights, contains an explicit limiting principle. Section 1 of the Charter provides that rights guaranteed are subject 'to such reasonable limits prescribed by law as can be demonstrably justified in a free and democratic society'.[42] Once a complainant proves the violation of a right, the state bears the burden of proving that the limit on the right is reasonable and justified. The justification test comprises two main aspects. First, the Court must determine whether the legislation addresses a pressing and substantial objective. Second, the Court must determine whether legislative means are proportional to the objective. The second part of the test considers:

- whether the means and objective are rationally connected;
- whether the means minimally impair the right in question; and
- the salutary and deleterious effects of the legislation.[43]

Third party spending limits

Shortly after the adoption of the Charter, the National Citizens Coalition, a conservative interest group, challenged the CEA prohibition on third party election expenses.[44] The CEA defined 'election expenses' as being expenses incurred for the purpose of 'promoting or opposing, directly and during an election, a particular registered party, or the election of a particular candidate'.[45] The government maintained that the prohibition was required to protect the equality amongst electoral participants fostered by the election expense controls on political parties and candidates.[46] The trial court held that the restriction on third party election expenditures violated s. 2(b) of the Charter which guarantees freedom of expression and that the government's justification for limiting third party expenditures did not satisfy the requirements of s. 1 of the Charter. No appeal of the decision was taken.

Third party election spending restrictions were adopted again in amendments to the CEA in 1985. Instead of a complete prohibition, this time third parties were permitted to spend up to CAD$1,000 to promote or oppose a political party or candidate. The new limits were challenged again in *Somerville* v. *Canada (Attorney General)* before the 1993 federal election.[47] The government again defended third party limits on the grounds that the limits were necessary to protect the election expense controls on other electoral participants and that the legislative scheme as a whole promoted equality and competitive balance amongst political parties and candidates.[48] The Alberta Court of Appeal recognised that, as a practical matter, the new third party limits remained a complete prohibition on third party advocacy. The Court went on to conclude that 'the very purpose of this legislation is to ensure that third parties cannot be heard in any effective way and that political parties are entitled to preferential protection.'[49]

The turning point for third party election spending restrictions came in *Libman* v. *Quebec (Attorney General)*.[50] The legislation challenged in *Libman* was a prohibition on expenditures (subject to some narrow exceptions) on political advocacy during a referendum by individuals and groups not affiliated with the official 'Yes' or 'No' campaigns. The Supreme Court of Canada made it clear, however, that its reasons were to be understood to apply to the election context as well. The Court rejected the conclusion in *Somerville* that the purpose of the Quebec legislation was to silence third parties and noted that the objective of both the Quebec legislation and the CEA was to 'ensure a certain equality of resources' amongst the participants and that this objective was 'highly laudable'.[51] Despite endorsing the objective of third party spending limits, the Court held that the specific limits in question were unconstitutional because they were too strict. The clear signal from the Court to Parliament was that if reasonable limits were adopted, they would pass constitutional muster.

Third party spending limits were re-introduced in amendments to the CEA in 2000. The new third party limits applied to communications that 'promote or oppose the election of one or more candidates in a given electoral district, including by

- naming them;
- showing their likeness;

- identifying them by their respective political affiliations; or
- taking a position on an issue with which they are particularly associated.'[52]

The monetary limits, subject to annual adjustments for inflation, were set at CAD$3,000 per electoral district subject to an aggregate national limit of CAD$150,000. The new third party limits were more restrictive than the limits considered previously by courts because of the breadth of the definition, but were less restrictive because of the increased expenditure permitted.

Once again. Third party limits were challenged in Alberta.[53] The challenge was successful at trial and in the Court of Appeal. A reversal of fortune occurred at the Supreme Court of Canada. Justice Bastarache, writing for the majority of the Court, followed *Libman*, holding that third party restrictions were necessary to promote equality and fairness in the electoral context, particularly by preventing the circumvention of spending limits on candidates and political parties. One of the main arguments advanced by the challenger was that there was scant evidence of harm caused by third party expenditures. In other words, the legislative objective was not pressing and substantial and should not override the Charter guarantee of freedom of expression. The Court rejected this argument stating that 'a reasoned apprehension of harm' can be sufficient when there is inconclusive or conflicting social science evidence of harm.[54]

The key point of disagreement between the majority and minority in *Harper* was whether the monetary limits satisfied the minimal impairment test. Chief Justice McLachlin and Justice Major, writing for themselves and Justice Binnie, noted that the danger that the third party limits were intended to address was 'wholly hypothetical' and that the infringement on freedom of expression was 'draconian'.[55] The minority viewed the limits as being no different from those considered in *Somerville* and *Libman* in that 'the limits imposed on citizens amount to a virtual ban on their participation in political debate during the election period'.[56] The majority disagreed, concluding that the limits allowed for modest informational campaigns. This conclusion was reinforced by the two observations. First, some communications – editorials, news, debates, and interviews – are excluded from the third party limits.[57] Second, the minority 'ignores the fact that third party advertising is not restricted prior to the commencement of the election period'.[58] In other words, the majority concluded that the infringement is not as serious as the minority suggests because third parties can disseminate their message in advance of an election without monetary constraint, so long as they comply with the limits after the election writ is issued.

The lack of evidence in *Harper* is in the process of being remedied through the third party election expense disclosure regulations that were introduced in tandem with the third party election expense limits. The data on third party election spending collected by Elections Canada provides a much better picture of third party activities than existed before. The data set out below in Table 1 show that few third parties have approached the CAD$150,000 limit in the last four federal general elections. This is the opposite of what would be expected if there was an appetite amongst third parties for big money campaigns. Moreover,

Table 12.1 Third party expenditures in the 2000, 2004, 2006, and 2008 General Elections

	Number of registered third parties			
Expenditure levels	*2000*	*2004*	*2006*	*2008*
No return	0	4	7	4
$0.00	6	12	7	3
$0.01–$4,999.99	30	31	44	32
$5,000.00–$9,999.99	8	4	2	4
$10,000.00–$24,999.99	2	4	5	7
$25,000.00–$49,999.99	1	3	8	5
$50,000.00–$99,999.99	1	4	5	4
$100,000.00 and over	2	1	2	5
Total number	50	63	80	64
Total expenditures	$573,854.20	$720,227.93	$1,067,680.75	$1,430,579.14
Average expenditure	$11,477.08	$12,207.25	$14,625.76	$23,842.99

Source: All data compiled from third party returns filed with Elections Canada and available online at www.elections.ca (accessed 25/05/10). The data for 2000 is compromised by the fact that during mid-campaign an injunction was issued by the Alberta Court of Queen's Bench suspending the rules applicable to third parties and then reinstated by the Supreme Court of Canada. 'Average Expenditure' figures do not include third parties with no return filed.

third party expenditures in the aggregate in the 2008 federal general election were small compared to total political party expenditures which totalled over CAD$58 million, not including candidate expenditures. Despite the rising total of third party spending, the number of third parties – between 50 and 80 over the last four elections – and the lack of co-ordination between third parties suggests that third parties are not affecting electoral fortunes on a national level. Perhaps as further evidence accumulates, there will be a renewed challenge to third party spending limits on the grounds that, instead of being a threat of unknown danger as in *Harper*, there is, at most, a threat of modest danger.

Broadcasting

The Reform Party emerged in the late 1980s and early 1990s as a regional populist party. Prior to the 1993 federal election, the Reform Party commenced a challenge to the rules governing political broadcasting during election campaigns.[59] The Reform Party, as a political party with no electoral history and only a single member of Parliament, received only a small quota of free broadcasting time and broadcasting time for purchase. By contrast, the established political parties were allocated significant shares of the free broadcast time and time for purchase at a discount.

The Reform Party's constitutional challenge may be broken down into two elements. First, the Reform Party challenged the constitutionality of the formula used to allocate free broadcasting time and discounted time for purchase. The Reform Party argued that the statutory formula for allocating time favoured established political parties. Essentially, the formula was backward looking because its criteria included seats won in the previous election, popular vote in the last election, and the number of candidates endorsed in the last election. As a result, the formula entrenched established interests and did not account for emerging political parties. Second, the Reform Party challenged the prohibition on the purchase of broadcasting time outside the statutory scheme.

The majority of the Alberta Court of Appeal concluded that the provisions reserving and allocating time for political broadcasts did not violate freedom of expression or the right to equality. Freedom of expression was not engaged because the provisions facilitated expression rather than limited expression. The right to equality was not infringed because political parties and members of political parties are not amongst the categories of people protected by s. 15 of the Charter.[60] The majority of the Court nevertheless went on to consider the objective of the legislation and the justification for infringement offered by the government. The rationale for the election broadcasting rules offered by the government was consistent with the rationale offered for political finance controls – regulation is required to prevent wealth from distorting the political marketplace. The majority accepted the government's submission and concluded that ensuring the availability of broadcast time and controlling the cost of broadcast time were pressing and substantial objectives.[61] Although the majority of the Alberta Court of Appeal acknowledged that the allocation provisions in the CEA could be unfair to parties with increasing popularity,[62] it was held that any infringement caused by the statutory formula was negated by the Broadcast Arbitrator's discretion to deviate from the statutory allocation formula in cases of unfairness.[63]

The prohibition on the purchase of broadcast time was found by the majority of the Court to be an infringement of freedom of expression. The government justified the infringement on the grounds that it was necessary to protect the balance created amongst the political parties by the allocation provisions.[64] Further, it was submitted that the limit on purchase of additional broadcast time helped to control overall expenditures in elections.[65] This submission was effectively countered by the Reform Party pointing out that election expenses were controlled by express limits and the ban on the purchase of broadcast time could not be justified as an indirect control on expenses.[66] The Court held that the prohibition was not integral to the allocation of free time and time reserved for purchase.[67] As a result, the prohibition on the purchase of broadcast time for advertising was declared unconstitutional.

The minority of the Court took a different approach. Justice Conrad held that the very purpose of the provisions was to reserve time and distribute it disproportionately in favour of established political parties and to restrict the ability of political parties to obtain time outside the legislative scheme.[68] Such an objective, she concluded, was unconstitutional in itself and could not be justified under s. 1 of the Charter. In Justice Conrad's view, the government, fearing an inequitable allocation of broadcasting time caused by unequal distribution of wealth, had institutionalised an inequitable allocation of broadcasting time that favoured incumbent political parties. Unlike the majority, which separated the reservation and allocation provisions from the prohibition on the purchase of time, Justice Conrad dealt with the legislative scheme as a whole. To her, the allocation provisions were as much a problem as the prohibition provisions because political expression vital to public debate was controlled. She concluded that the provisions 'restrict, regulate and allocate the use of the most effective means of communication of political expression. I cannot conceive of a more gross interference with a fundamental right enshrined in the Charter.'[69]

With the Reform Party's constitutional challenge pending, the Broadcast Arbitrator solicited suggestions from the registered political parties as to how he should exercise his statutory discretion. The Broadcast Arbitrator considered the equal allocation of time amongst all registered political parties. Equal allocation was rejected on the grounds that it was contrary to the statutory formula and would result in significant amounts of time going unused through some registered political parties being unable to use the time reserved because of financial constraints. The Broadcast Arbitrator settled on an approach that distributes one-third of the available time equally amongst all registered political parties and then divides the remaining two-thirds of the available time according to the statutory formula.[70] The Broadcast Arbitrator has used this approach for every general election since 1993. While the Reform Party's constitutional challenge was unsuccessful in changing the rules for allocating time, it prompted the Broadcast Arbitrator to soften the statutory formula for allocating broadcast time, resulting in a more open and egalitarian approach.

Public funding

As with the allocation of broadcast time, public funds are allocated to political parties and candidates based on statutory criteria. The statutory criteria operate to deny funding to small political parties and candidates with limited support. For most forms of public funding, political parties and candidates must meet thresholds of voter support based on the results of the previous election. One justification for the funding criteria is that the public purse is limited and funds should be directed to electoral participants that play a significant role in public debate. Parliament, in adopting the funding criteria, appeared to be concerned about satirical political parties and commercial enterprises qualifying for funding. The most egregious example of this was the Natural Law Party, which ran candidates in the 1993, 1997, and 2000 federal elections on a platform that included 'yogic flying'.[71]

The leading case on public funding did not specifically consider the thresholds for election expense reimbursement or for qualifying for ongoing funding grants. Instead, the Supreme Court of Canada considered the rights of small parties generally in a case brought by Miguel Figueroa, leader of the Canadian Communist Party.[72] Figueroa challenged the CEA requirement that a political party must endorse 50 candidates in a general election to become a registered political party. Many benefits are associated with registration as a political party including ballot identification of party affiliation and public funding in the form of the right to issue tax receipts to contributors. Figueroa's position was that the 50-candidate threshold violated s. 3 of the Charter, which protects the right to vote.

Justice Iacobucci, writing for the majority of the Court, began by considering the meaning of s. 3. The right to vote, he held, extends beyond the mere formality of marking a ballot and extends to the 'right of each citizen to play a meaningful role in the electoral process'.[73] Justice Iacobucci rejected submissions that the electoral process was a means to an end – merely a way to choose a government – and that regulations that favour the political parties with a reasonable chance of forming the government are justified. He held that 'participation in the electoral process has an intrinsic value independent of its impact upon the actual outcome of elections'.[74] Recognising the expressive and deliberative function of the electoral process led Justice Iacobucci to conclude that the contributions of all candidates and political parties are important. He emphasized that 'The ability of a political party to make a valuable contribution to the electoral process is not dependent on its capacity to offer the electorate a genuine "government option".'[75]

Once the potential value of contributions to the electoral debate from all participants is recognised, the question of discriminatory access to funding for communications becomes problematic. Justice Iacobucci expressed concern about the 50-candidate threshold because it enhanced the ability of some political parties to raise funds by issuing tax receipts. Of course, the parties aided by the right to issue tax receipts were already the largest parties, with the greatest resources. The 50-candidate threshold exacerbated the existing disparity in resources between small and large political parties. While the freedom of expression of small political parties was not limited, the legislation allowed larger political parties to occupy a disproportionate amount of the space for public discourse. Justice Iacobucci concluded that 'legislation that bestows a benefit upon *some* political parties, but not others, requires scrutiny'.[76]

The government attempted to justify the 50-candidate threshold on the grounds that the public funding diminished public resources and that the public funding system must be 'cost efficient'. Justice Iacobucci dismissed this argument. He noted that if cost was really a concern, there would be limits on the number of citizens that could claim the tax credit or the size of the tax credit available would be reduced.[77] Moreover, the government adduced no evidence to support the argument that cost was a legitimate concern.[78] The government further tried to justify the 50-candidate threshold on the grounds that it protected the integrity of the political finance regime. In particular, the government argued that the threshold prevented third parties from constituting themselves as political parties for the sole purpose of obtaining the right to issue tax receipts.[79] The government also submitted that the 50-candidate threshold promoted the formation of majority government by conferring benefits on the major political parties and that majority government was a legitimate objective of rules governing the electoral process. Justice Iacobucci dismissed this argument holding the government had failed to show through evidence or argument that majority government was preferable to minority government, let alone that the benefits of majority government would outweigh the negative impact of the threshold on the right to vote.[80] Even though Justice Iacobucci dismissed every argument advanced by the government, he noted that his decision did not 'stand for the proposition that an infringement of s. 3 arising from the differential treatment of political parties could never be justified'.[81]

Following *Figueroa*, the Marijuana Party and a number of other minor political parties challenged the election expense reimbursement and annual allowance thresholds in *Longley* v. *Canada (Attorney General)*.[82] These political parties contended that the funding thresholds violated s. 3 of the Charter for the same reasons that the 50-candidate threshold considered in *Figueroa* violated s. 3. The application judge concluded that, since the funding thresholds exacerbated a pre-existing disparity amongst political parties, s. 3 was infringed. He went on to find that the government had not adduced sufficient evidence to justify the differential treatment of political parties.[83] He made several key points about the thresholds. First, the only real beneficiaries of the thresholds were the major political parties.[84] Second, the thresholds served no practical purpose as funding is already allocated based on the share of popular vote.[85] Third, the funding thresholds are a disincentive to small political parties that wish to run a broad slate of candidates. Indeed, it encourages small political parties to only run candidates in districts where they stand a chance of gaining five per cent of the popular vote.[86] Fourth, connecting funding to national popular vote should encourage voter turnout even in districts where a small political party is unlikely to succeed. However, the application judge concluded, 'The quality and vigor of Canadian democracy suffers because such a threshold effectively discourage[s] individuals who do not support one of the larger parties from participating in the electoral process.'[87]

The Ontario Court of Appeal overturned the application judge's decision in *Longley*. The Court of Appeal concluded that the purpose of the funding thresholds was to prevent the misuse of public funds. Misuse must be prevented, according to Justice Blair, to protect public confidence in the electoral system, not because the government is unable to afford the payments.[88] The Court explained that Parliament's 'reasoned apprehension of harm' justified the infringement of the rights of small political parties who did not misuse public funds.[89] The Court concluded that 'The goal of upholding the integrity of [the electoral] regime overshadows the value of absolute equality in the treatment of all political parties in terms of access to public funding.'[90]

Despite the Court of Appeal's apparent contradiction of *Figueroa* and despite the seeming public importance of the subject matter of the case, the Supreme Court of Canada did not grant leave to appeal.[91] The result of the Supreme Court's decision is that differential treatment of political parties remains entrenched in the CEA and it is unclear whether *Figueroa*'s promise of equal treatment will be realised.

Emerging issues in Canadian political finance

Regulation of the 'election period'

Political party and candidate expenses are only regulated during an election period. Traditionally, political parties raise and conserve money between elections and spend money during election periods. As a result, there has been little interest in or need to regulate political party and candidate expenses between elections. Similarly, there has been little discussion about the regulation of third party political advocacy outside the election period. Two changes introduced to the CEA in 2003 and reinforced in 2006 changed the political game in Canada. Contribution limits were adopted in the wake of the Sponsorship Scandal to reassure the public that politicians could not be corrupted by contributions.[92] The government recognised that contribution limits would have an adverse effect on political fundraising. As a result, public funding for political parties was enhanced through the institution of quarterly allowances. The quarterly allowances were intended to replace the funds lost by reason of the imposition of contribution limits.

The contribution limits, however, affected political parties differently. Political parties with effective grassroots fundraising, most notably the Conservative Party, experienced little impact. By contrast, political parties heavily dependent on large corporate contributions, principally the Liberal Party, suffered. Despite progress by the other political parties, six years after the adoption of contribution limits, the Conservative Party remains the most consistent and effective fundraising organisation.

The Conservative Party's success in fundraising, combined with funding through quarterly allowances has created a situation where the Conservative Party often has more money than it can spend during an election period where expenses are limited.[93] The Conservative Party has adopted a strategy of television advertising outside election periods. In 2006, shortly after Stephane Dion's selection as Liberal leader, the Conservative Party ran a negative advertising campaign against him. This tactic was repeated in 2009 against Michael Ignatieff who replaced Dion as leader of the Liberal Party. Both of the advertising campaigns were effective. The Liberal Party, despite not enjoying the same financial resources as the Conservative Party, responded in 2009 with a negative

Table 12.2 Annual allowances paid to major political parties 2004–2009

Party	*2004*	*2005*	*2006*	*2007*	*2008*	*2009*
BQ	$2,733,868	$3,064,864	$2,950,984	$2,953,218	$3,017,092	$2,742,215
Con.	$7,913,512	$7,331,172	$9,388,357	$10,218,123	$10,439,132	$10,351,071
Lib.	$9,141,408	$9,087,333	$8,572,965	$8,517,049	$8,701,263	$7,219,593
NDP	$2,883,919	$3,879,817	$4,611,140	$4,923,795	$5,030,293	$4,998,192

Source: Elections Canada. Online. Available HTTP: www.elections.ca.

Table 12.3 Contributions to major political parties 2004–2009

Party	*2004*	*2005*	*2006*	*2007*	*2008*	*2009*
BQ	$858,746	$734,729	$529,513	$429,971	$713,085	$621,526
Cons.	$10,949,559	$17,847,451	$18,641,306	$16,983,630	$21,179,483	$17,707,846
Lib.	$4,719,388	$8,344,162	$9,063,126.36	$4,471,903	$5,811,492	$9,564,677
NDP	$5,194,170	$5,120,827	$3,972,762.57	$3,959,451	$5,412,940	$4,035,492

Source: Data compiled from political party annual returns filed with Elections Canada. Online. Available HTTP: www.elections.ca. 2009 data was taken from political party quarterly returns because annual returns were not available at the time of writing.

television advertising campaign targeting Conservative Prime Minister Stephen Harper.

The appearance of political advertising outside the election period raises the question of whether political expenses outside the election period should be regulated. For example, the UK Political Parties, Elections and Referendums Act 2000[94] (PPERA), defines the 'relevant period' for the regulation of campaign expenditures to be 365 days prior to election day. While the question of the regulation of expenditures on political advocacy outside the election period remains hypothetical in the context of federal political parties, it is a reality in British Columbia for third parties.

British Columbia Teachers' Federation v. *British Columbia (Attorney General)* revisits third party spending limit issues decided in *Harper* and poses a new and important question about the regulation of third party spending outside the election period.[95] The British Columbia (BC) provincial election in 2005 was marked by a significant increase in third party spending. The BC government reacted by adopting third party spending restrictions that mirrored the federal restrictions considered in *Harper*. The key difference between the federal restrictions on third party spending considered in *Harper* and the BC restrictions on third party spending is that the BC restrictions extend into the pre-writ period, whereas the federal limits apply only to the post-writ election period.

The British Columbia Teachers Federation (BCTF) challenged the BC third party spending restrictions on a number of grounds. Many of these grounds were issues already decided in *Harper*. The BCTF questioned the legislative objective asserted by the BC government and submitted that the real purpose of the legislation was to target unions and protect the government. The BCTF challenged the definition of 'election advertising' on the grounds of vagueness and overbreadth and introduced a better factual record than was before the Supreme Court of Canada in *Harper* to show that the spending limits did not permit third parties to conduct an effective informational campaign.

At trial, the BC Supreme Court was reluctant to revisit issues from *Harper*, even though it was clear that the BCTF put forward a more compelling case on the facts. Instead, the Court focussed on the extension of third party spending limits into the period before an election writ is issued. The third party spending limits were an obvious violation of s. 2(b) of the Charter guarantee of freedom of expression, so the Court proceeded to analyse the justification for the infringement under s. 1 of the Charter. The principal justification offered was that the extended period was necessary to prevent third parties from circumventing post-writ spending restrictions by advertising immediately pre-writ.[96]

The Court found that the justification did not outweigh the infringement on freedom of expression. The spending limits were found to be overbroad. The Court distinguished the BC third party spending limits from the national spending limits considered by the Supreme Court of Canada in *Harper* in two respects. First, the spending limits in *Harper* pertained only to the election period when Parliament is not in session. As such, the federal limits on third party speech do not constrain public debate on issues before Parliament. Second, the 'temporal proximity' to the election ensures that the shorter federal period catches little non-election advocacy.[97] Indeed, it is reasonable to assume that political communications during the period immediately preceding an election have an electoral character. The evidence before the Court indicated that most spending on election advocacy occurs late in an election period because that is viewed as the most effective time to advertise. The Court inferred from this evidence that the farther away from an election the third party advocacy took place, the less pressing need to regulate became.[98]

The constitutionality of contribution limits and spending limits

Contribution limits are a clear violation of the s. 2(b) guarantee of freedom of expression and s. 2(d) freedom of association. The question of constitutionality hinges on whether the infringement of Charter rights is justified. Contribution limits serve two of the principles of political finance regulation: equality and anti-corruption. Contribution limits address corruption and promote equality by reducing the influence that an individual may have by limiting the amount of money that may be contributed. The less money contributed, the less the sense of debt or obligation to the donor. Political parties and candidates subject to contribution limits wishing to raise money are forced to seek larger numbers of smaller donations than in the pre-contribution limit era. The result is that donor influence is more diffuse and democratic. There can be little doubt that contribution limits address a pressing and substantial objective.

The more difficult question is whether contribution limits pass the proportionality aspects of the s. 1 analysis, especially the minimal impairment test. Courts frequently defer to Parliament when considering specific limits or thresholds. If a court is satisfied that contribution limits are necessary to promote equality and combat corruption, the court may be inclined to defer to Parliament's judgment in setting the monetary limit.[99] Another view is that the minimal impairment test should be strictly applied in cases involving the political process, where the rule in question is motivated by partisan bias or has an incumbent protecting effect.[100]

The contribution data in Table 12.3 show that the contribution limits have created a persistent funding advantage for the Conservative Party. This would be useful evidence to mount a partisan bias argument if it were not for the fact that the contribution limits were passed by the Liberal Party when it had majority control of Parliament in 2003. Certainly, the tightening of the contribution limit by the Conservative Party in 2006 is open to the charge of partisan bias, but the data in Table 12.3 suggest that most of the Conservative Party's advantage resulted from the introduction of contribution limits in 2003. Some US academics have argued that contribution limits have an incumbent protecting effect, but the weight of evidence now suggests that contribution limits promote electoral competition rather than protect incumbents.[101] Whether or not contribution limits protect incumbents in the US context, there is no evidence yet that contribution limits have had an incumbent protecting effect in Canadian elections.

The prohibition on union and corporate contributions raises an additional constitutional issue. Unions have long been active in Canadian politics. Indeed, the Supreme Court of Canada has commented favourably on the tradition of political involvement of unions in a challenge to the use of union dues for political activities.[102] Union and corporate contribution to political parties are clearly expressive and associational activities. While corporate involvement in the political domain has not been the subject of favourable judicial comment, it has an equally long history. The Supreme Court of Canada in *Libman* held that third party spending limits denied the right to jointly exercise the Charter right of freedom of expression and thereby constituted an infringement of freedom of association.[103] Even if the prohibition on union and corporate contributions was found to be a Charter violation, given the deference to Parliament's concerns about third party advocacy in *Harper*, it is likely that a Court would find corporate and union contribution limits to be justified.

A final and unintended consequence of the introduction of contribution limits is that the justification for political party and candidate spending limits has been undermined. Since *Libman* and *Harper*, it has been widely assumed that the spending limits that form the core of the political finance regime are constitutional. Candidate and political party spending limits are intended to promote equality of influence and to mitigate the distorting effects of wealth. Spending limits accomplish these objectives indirectly by reducing the cost of campaigns and reducing the demand for funds. Of course, spending limits are of limited effect because they do not prevent an individual from making large donations or even underwriting the entire cost of a candidate's or political party's campaign. Contribution limits are a much more efficient and effective tool for promoting equality of influence and mitigating the distorting effects of wealth than spending limits. Contribution limits constrain the influence of donors by limiting the amount of money that can be provided. The US Supreme Court in *Randall* v. *Sorrell* considered both spending limits and contribution limits.[104] Justice Breyer, writing for himself and Chief Justice Roberts, affirmed the conclusion in *Buckley* v. *Valeo* that 'The Government's primary justification for expenditure limitations, preventing corruption and its appearance, was adequately addressed by the Act's contribution limitations and disclosure requirements.'[105] Similarly, in Canada it could be argued that contribution limits are a less drastic means of achieving objectives that have traditionally supported spending limits.

Conclusion

The shape of Canada's political finance regime is the product of a dialogue between Parliament and the courts.[106] Parliament has significantly expanded the scope of the CEA in response to real scandals and perceived threats. The political finance regime today regulates all participants in the democratic process and places significant constraints on raising, spending, and transferring political funds. The courts have recognised that expanded regulation of political finance is necessary despite some infringement of Charter rights. Indeed, the Supreme Court of Canada in *Harper* and *Libman* endorsed the egalitarian model of election regulation pursued by Parliament describing it as highly laudable.[107] For the most part, courts have only invalidated political finance measures where participatory rights of citizens have been undermined as in the case of unequal access to political funding for small political parties in *Figueroa*, the denial of the right to purchase broadcast time in *Reform Party*, and effective bans on third party spending in *Libman*. The limitation of participatory rights in each of these cases was not justified by the principles that underlie the political finance regime and instead appeared to be at least in part aimed at protecting the *status quo* from challenge or criticism. Whether or not the courts will continue to foster the democratisation of the political finance regime depends on the extent to which courts defer to Parliament.

Notes

1 Part I of the Constitution Act, 1982, being Schedule B to the Canada Act 1982 (UK), 1982, c. 11 (Charter).
2 The political finance regime is, for the most part, contained in the Canada Elections Act S.C. 2000, c.9, as amended (CEA).
3 For a more detailed discussion, see C. Feasby, 'Constitutional Questions About Canada's New Political Finance Regime' *Osgoode Hall Law Journal* 45, 2007, 513, at pp. 519–521.
4 S.C. 1874, c. 9 (DEA).
5 17 & 18 Vict. C. 102.
6 An Act to amend the Dominion Elections Act S.C. 1908, c. 26. Contributions by corporations incorporated for political purposes were still permitted.
7 An Act respecting the Election of Members of the House of Commons and the Electoral Franchise S.C. 1920, c. 46.
8 Report of the Committee on Election Expenses, Ottawa: Queen's Printer, 1966, 19–21 ('Barbeau Committee Report').
9 Report of the Committee on Election Expenses. Canada, House of Commons. Committee on Election Expenses. 1971a. *Journals*. Vol. 117, no. 146, 4 June, 605–617.
10 S.C. 1974, c. 51.
11 For a more detailed account of Canada's political finance regime, see C. Feasby, 'Canada' in T.D. Grant (ed.), *Lobbying, Government Relations, and Campaign Finance Worldwide: Navigating the Laws, Regulations and Practices of National Regimes*, New York: Oceana Publications, 2005, p. 57.
12 Canada, Royal Commission on Electoral Reform and Party Financing, *Reforming Electoral Democracy*, vol. 1, Toronto: Dundurn Press, 1991, pp. 11–13 (Chair: Pierre Lortie).

13 Royal Commission on Electoral Reform and Party Financing, Reforming *Electoral Democracy*, 326.
14 Royal Commission on Electoral Reform and Party Financing, *Reforming Electoral Democracy*, 326.
15 See Barbeau Commitee Report at pp. 13–22 discussing the role of political corruption scandals in the adoption and development of Canadian political finance controls.
16 *Harper* v. *Canada (Attorney General)*, [2004] 1 S.C.R. 827 at para. 62.
17 See, for example, *Buckley* v. *Valeo*, (1976) 424 U.S. 1 at p. 59 where equality is branded as 'foreign to the First Amendment'. For a more recent example, see *Citizens United* v. *Federal Election Commission*, (2010) 130 S. Ct. 876 per Chief Justice Roberts concurring at p. 921 emphasising that equality is not a relevant consideration and Justice Stevens dissenting at p. 958 attempting to justify the impugned legislation on terms other than equality. Note that C. Manfredi and M. Rush disagree with this view and instead emphasise the common elements of the Canadian and US approaches to adjudicating political finance issues: C. Manfredi and M. Rush, *Judging Democracy*, Broadview Press: Peterborough, ON, 2008.
18 CEA, s. 2.
19 CEA, s. 407(1).
20 CEA, s. 422.
21 CEA, s. 429(3).
22 www.elections.ca (accessed 25 May 2010).
23 CEA, s. 2.
24 CEA, s. 404.2(1).
25 CEA, s. 404.1.
26 CEA, s. 405.3.
27 CEA, s. 451(2)(h), 424(1)(b).
28 An Act to amend the CEA and the Income Tax Act (political financing) S.C. 2003, c. 19.
29 An Act to amend the CEA and the Income Tax Act (political financing), s. 24 amending s. 404.1(1).
30 An Act to amend the CEA and the Income Tax Act (political financing), s. 25 amending s. 405(1).
31 Federal Accountability Act S.C. 2006, c. 9.
32 CEA, s. 465(2).
33 CEA, s. 435.
34 CEA, s. 435.01(1).
35 For a discussion of the origins of the regulation of political broadcasting in Canada, see J. Lacalamita, 'The Equitable Campaign: Party Political Broadcasting Regulation in Canada', *Osgoode Hall Law Journal* 22, 1984, 543.
36 CEA, s. 345. The amount of free time is not specified in the CEA but it has been 214 minutes in recent elections.
37 CEA, s. 335.
38 CEA, s. 338.
39 CEA, s. 345.
40 For a comprehensive explanation of the Canadian Constitution, see P. Hogg, *Constitutional Law of Canada* (5th ed.), Toronto: Carswell, 2007.
41 Constitution Act 1867 (UK), 30 and 31 Vict., c. 3.
42 This aspect of the Charter is similar to the European Convention for the Protection of Human Rights and Fundamental Freedoms (4 November 1950) 213 UNTS 221.
43 *R.* v. *Oakes*, [1986] 1 S.C.R. 153 and *Dagenais* v. *Canadian Broadcasting Corporation*, [1994] 3 S.C.R. 835.
44 *National Citizens' Coalition Inc.* v. *Canada (Attorney General)* (1984), 11 D.L.R. (4th) 481 (Alta. Q.B.) (*National Citizens' Coalition*).

45 Ibid., para. 5.
46 Ibid., para. 54.
47 Ibid.
48 Ibid., para. 69.
49 Ibid., para. 76.
50 [1997] 3 S.C.R. 569. For a more detailed analysis of *Libman*, see C. Feasby, '*Libman* v. *Quebec (A.G.)* and the Administration of the Process of Democracy under the *Charter*: The Emerging Egalitarian Model', *McGill Law Journal* 44, 1999, 5.
51 Feasby, '*Libman* v. *Quebec* (A.G.) and the Administration of the Process of Democracy', para. 56.
52 CEA, s. 350.
53 *Harper* v. *Canada (Attorney General)*, [2004] 1 S.C.R. 827. For a more detailed discussion of *Harper*, see C. Feasby, 'Freedom of Expression and the Law of the Democratic Process', *SCLR* (2d) 29, 2005, 238 and A. Geddis, 'Liberté, Egalité, Argent: Third Party Election Spending and the *Charter*', *Alberta Law Review* 42, 2004, 429.
54 [2004] 1 S.C.R. 827, para. 77.
55 Ibid., paras. 34, 39.
56 Ibid., para. 35.
57 Ibid., para. 115.
58 Ibid., para. 112.
59 *Reform Party of Canada* v. *Canada (Attorney General)* (1995) 123 D.L.R. (4th) 366 (Alta. C.A.).
60 S 15(1) of the Charter prohibits discrimination on enumerated grounds and courts have found s. 15(1) to also apply to discrimination on analogous grounds.
61 *Reform Party of Canada*, (1995), 123 D.L.R. (4th) 366 (Alta. C.A.), para. 59.
62 Ibid., para. 54.
63 Ibid., para. 54.
64 Ibid., para. 84.
65 Ibid., para. 83.
66 Ibid., para. 86.
67 Ibid., para. 90.
68 Ibid., para.136.
69 Ibid., para. 158.
70 Broadcast Arbitrator, *Reasons for Decision: 1992 Allocation of Paid Time*, December 31, 1992, at pp. 27–30.
71 *Longley* v. *Canada (Attorney General)*, [2007] O.J. No. 4758 (C.A.) ('*Longley (C.A.)*'), para. 13.
72 *Figueroa* v. *Canada (Attorney General)*, [2003] 1 S.C.R. 912.
73 Ibid., para. 26
74 Ibid., para. 29.
75 Ibid., para. 39.
76 Ibid., para. 48.
77 Ibid., paras 68–69.
78 Ibid., para. 68.
79 Ibid., para. 76.
80 Ibid., paras 86–87.
81 Ibid., para. 91.
82 *Longley* v. *Canada (Attorney General)* (2006), 82 O.R. (3d) 481 (*Longley (Sup. Ct.)*). An earlier challenge to candidate thresholds was unsuccessful: *Barrette* v. *Canada (Attorney General)* (1994), 113 D.L.R. (4th) 623 (Q.C.A.).
83 (2006) 82 O.R. (3d) 481, paras. 20–22.
84 Ibid., para. 23.
85 Ibid., para. 24.

86 Ibid., para. 25.
87 Ibid., para. 25.
88 Ibid., para. 49.
89 Ibid., para. 78.
90 Ibid., para. 83.
91 *Longley* v. *Canada (Attorney General)*, [2008] S.C.C.A. No. 41.
92 The Sponsorship Scandal involved the direction of government advertising to advertising firms associated with the governing Liberal Party. It was alleged that these advertising firms maintained Liberal Party organisers on staff and contributed money to the Liberal Party.
93 The Conservative Party election expense limit in 2008 federal general election was CAD$19,999,230.62.
94 (UK), 2000, c. 41.
95 2009 BCSC 436.
96 Ibid., para. 199.
97 Ibid., para. 256.
98 Ibid., para. 263.
99 *Harper* v. *Canada*, [2004] 1 S.C.R. 827.
100 Feasby, 'Constitutional Questions', at p. 555.
101 See T. Stratmann, 'Do Low Contribution Limits Insulate Incumbents from Competition?', 2010, *Election Law Journal*, vol. 9, 125. See also: T. Stratmann and F.J. Aparicio-Castillo, 'Competition policy for elections: Do campaign contributions matter?', 2006, *Public Choice*, 127, 17.
102 *Lavigne* v. *Ontario Public Service Employees Union*, [1991] 2 S.C.R. 211 at para. 270.
103 *Libman*, [1997] 3 S.C.R. 569, at paras 35–37.
104 548 U.S. 230 (2006).
105 Ibid., p. 242. See also, *Buckley* v. *Valeo*, 424 U.S. 1 at 59 (1976), at p. 17.
106 P. Hogg and A. Bushell, 'The *Charter* Dialogue Between Courts and Legislatures (Or Perhaps the Charter of Rights Isn't Such a Bad Thing After All)', *Osgoode Hall Law Journal* 35, 1997, 75.
107 *Libman*, [1997] 3 S.C.R. 569, at para. 56.

13 The transformation of the campaign financing regime for US presidential elections

Richard L. Hasen

Since the mid-1970s, the United States system for the financing of presidential election campaigns has been a mixture of private fundraising by candidates, parties, and outside groups,[1] and optional public financing for candidates (and for political party conventions). The 2008 presidential election – with its record-breaking $1.8 billion campaign (including an astounding $745.7 million raised by then-Democratic candidate Barack Obama)[2] – demonstrated that the current system is in the midst of a major transformation. This chapter explains how the system is changing, offers possible reasons for the transformation, and evaluates the transformation normatively.

The first part of this chapter shows how the system is changing in four ways.

1 The voluntary presidential public financing system is no longer viable; candidates who opt in do so out of weakness, not strength.
2 A major share of private campaign contributions to presidential candidates in 2008 came through campaign finance 'bundlers' and from micro-donors giving very small amounts via the Internet.
3 Thanks to a US federal law, Bipartisan Campaign Reform Act of 2002 (BCRA), political parties can no longer accept very large campaign contributions (soft money) from wealthy individuals, corporations, and labor unions to pay for political advertising.
4 Wealthy individuals, corporations, and labor unions have shifted some, though not necessarily all, of the money that used to go to political parties and to 'issue advocacy' into outside groups (including so-called '527 organisations').

The second part explains that these four changes have likely arisen from a number of factors including:

- the failure of the US Congress to update the presidential public financing system, first enacted in 1974;
- enactment of BCRA and the US Supreme Court's shifting interpretation of the constitutionality of campaign finance law;
- the rise of cheap political speech via the Internet; and
- continued political polarisation.

The third part explores normative implications. The potential for *quid pro quo* corruption of candidates appears to remain low, thanks to a series of laws imposing contribution limits. Sale of access to candidates, however, remains a feature of US presidential elections even post-BCRA. From the standpoint of political equality, the transformation offers a mixed bag with somewhat offsetting effects. Thus, the collapse of the public financing system may have anti-egalitarian effects, but those effects are somewhat militated by the rise of micro-donors. The end of soft money and the rise of outside non-party political organisations in theory could lead to weakened political parties, but continued polarisation of the electorate have kept parties thriving even under BCRA and the shifting constitutional ground rules of the US Supreme Court.

The transformation[3]

The rules

Presidents of the United States are elected every four years (on the first Tuesday in November) in national elections.[4] Before those national elections (which take place during what is termed the 'general election' season), the two major political parties, the Democrats and Republicans, hold a series of state-by-state elections (primaries or caucuses) to determine each party's nominees for president (this period is known as the 'primary' season). Each party sets its own rules for choosing nominees based upon state results during the primary season; party nominees are formally chosen in party conventions held the summer before the general presidential election.

The rules for financing presidential elections are set by Congress (the US national legislative body) and the Federal Election Commission (or FEC, a regulatory body whose rules are secondary to those of Congress).[5] Congressional laws and FEC regulations are subject to review by an independent judiciary headed by the United States Supreme Court, which has held that some, but not all, campaign finance laws and regulations violate the First Amendment to the United States Constitution guaranteeing freedom of speech and association.

Under the Federal Election Campaign Act (FECA) passed by Congress in 1974, individuals could donate up to $1,000 during the primary season and another $1,000 for the general election to presidential candidates. BCRA, more commonly known as the 'McCain–Feingold law' for its two US Senate sponsors, raised the FECA limits to $2,000 for each election, and the figure was $2,300 per election for 2008, thanks to an inflation adjustment mechanism built into BCRA. Federal law also imposes source limitations on contributions: corporations, labour unions, most foreign citizens, and some other entities are barred from contributing to federal candidates. Candidates may contribute unlimited sums of their own money to their campaigns.

Political parties may solicit contributions and spend set amounts in coordination with presidential candidates; independent party spending is unlimited. FECA also allows for the establishment of independent political committees (or PACs). These groups may accept contributions from individuals of up to $5,000 per year. PACs in turn can contribute up to $5,000 to presidential candidates directly, and spend unlimited amounts independently supporting or opposing presidential candidates. As explained below, other political groups – not registering as PACs – also have emerged in recent years to engage in presidential election activity. Candidates, parties, PACs, and at least some of these other political groups must report information about contributions and spending to the FEC (or in some cases another agency) in periodic reports.

Presidential candidates also may decide to opt into a public financing system created by FECA. Candidates during the nomination season who opt in become eligible for public financing by raising $5,000 or more in contributions of $250 or more in at least 20 states. The government then matches the first $250 of additional contributions raised by participating candidates. In exchange, participating candidates agree to cap their overall total spending in the primary election season. The amount of the cap is set by a formula in FECA that Congress did not touch in BCRA. In 2004, the cap was $50.4 million; in 2008 the cap was about $52 million.[6]

Major party nominees may choose whether or not to participate in a separate public financing system for the general election period, a choice not dependent upon whether they participated as publicly financed candidates during the nomination process. Under the general election plan, the party nominee agrees not to raise any funds for his own campaign (though fundraising is allowed for the nominee's party organisations). In exchange, the nominee receives a flat grant from the government.

Except for a handful of self-financed candidates, all serious major party candidates accepted public financing during the primary season until the 2000 election.[7] In that election, George W. Bush, the eventual Republican nominee, opted out of the system, raising $95.6 million in privately funded donations. Al Gore, the eventual Democratic nominee in that election, accepted matching funds and raised contributions up to the public financing spending cap of $49.4 million (which included $15.5 million in public financing).[8] In 2004, both of the parties' eventual nominees opted out of public financing during the primary season. Each raised contributions many times the $50.4 million cap that would have applied to publicly financed candidates. Kerry raised $234.6 million; Bush raised $269.6 million.[9]

In the 2008 election, neither John McCain, the eventual Republican nominee, nor Barack Obama, the eventual Democratic nominee, took public financing during the primary season. Once he received his party nomination, Obama became the first major party nominee to opt for private financing during the general election season. McCain, once he became the Republican nominee, accepted the public financing grant of $84.1 million.[10] Despite opting in, McCain was permitted under federal law to continue fundraising for various Republican Party entities.[11]

The demise in presidential public financing

By 2008 it was clear that the public financing system, with its relatively paltry spending limits, was a luxury no serious candidate could afford, at least in the primary season. Indeed, in 2008, the only candidates opting for public financing were the weak ones who could not raise funds well on their own. John Edwards agreed to take public financing as his personal fundraising collapsed,[12] and McCain agreed to take it when he too was written off as having no chance at securing the Republican nomination. Once McCain became the front-runner, he backed out of his commitment to take public financing in the primary election season.[13] Obama too suggested he would participate in the public financing system in the general election, but backed away from this pledge given his unprecedented success at private fundraising during the primary season.

During the primary season (up to each party's national convention), Obama raised $414.2 million through private contributions,[14] McCain raised $216.3 million.[15] In one month alone, July 2008, Obama raised $50 million and spent $55 million, spending more in one month than he would have been able to spend *for the entire primary campaign season* had he opted for public financing and its accompanying $52 million spending cap.[16]

Looking at the fundraising by major party candidates during the primary seasons, the story is one of a dramatic rise in the ability of candidates to raise money. See Figure 13.1.

It is not only the presidential candidates who have been raising a great deal of money. Looking at total receipts for presidential campaign spending for both the primary and general election periods reported to the FEC (including public financing grants), and adjusting for inflation, spending has nearly tripled since 1996 (from $655.8 million (adjusted to 2008 dollars) in 1996 to $1,834.4 million in 2008). See Figure 13.2.

As the second part of this chapter details, it is no surprise that candidates' use of the public financing system has declined; the opportunity cost of opting in (in terms of foregone private contributions thanks to the system's concomitant spending limits) is just too high.

The rise of bundling and micro-donors

An evolution in fundraising strategies fuelled the dramatic rise in fundraising by the presidential candidates. Candidates learn from one another, emulating and

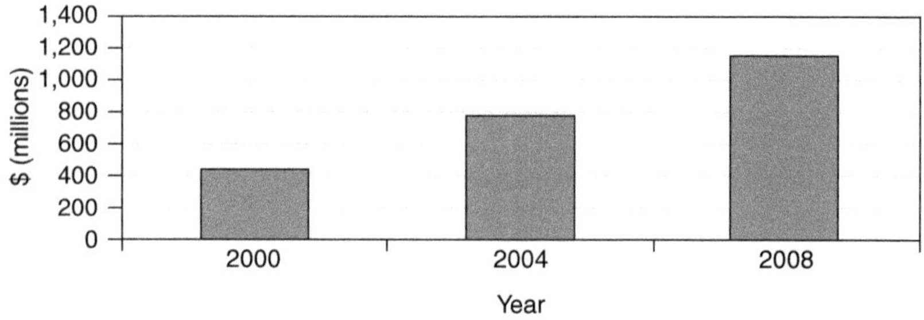

Figure 13.1 Total (inflation-adjusted) dollars raised by candidates in major party primary contests, 2000–2008.

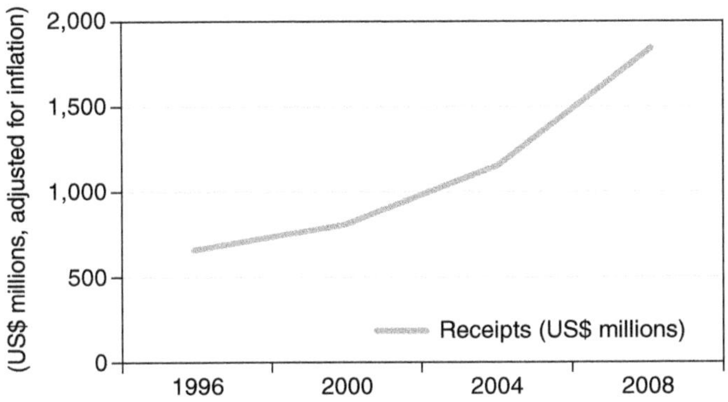

Figure 13.2 Presidential campaign receipts by election year (US$ millions, adjusted for inflation).

building upon new fundraising strategies. In recent years, the strategies of bundling and micro-donor targeting have emerged as the most important financing innovations.

Bundling. Though the practice of 'bundling' has been around since the 1980s, it really took off beginning with George W. Bush's 2000 campaign; bundling occurs when candidates begin asking some of their contributors to solicit their friends, acquaintances, and business associates to donate to the candidate.[17] These volunteers, who usually ask for the maximum legal individual donation, then 'bundle' cheques from their circle. Those bundlers reaching a certain fundraising threshold receive access to the candidate and other perquisites from the campaign. In 2000, 226 Bush 'Pioneers' each raised at least $100,000 for the campaign (in $1,000 maximum individual contributions), giving Bush over $22 million in bundled funds.[18] In 2004, when the individual contribution limits doubled from $1,000 to $2,000, Bush raised at least $77 million through bundling, about 30 per cent of his total donations.[19] Kerry, the Democratic nominee, raised at least $41.5 million through bundling, about 18 per cent of his total donations.[20] In the 2008 campaign, as of August 18, 2008, 560 bundlers raised at least $76,500,000 for McCain, and 560 bundlers raised at least $63,100,000 for Obama.[21]

Micro-Donations and Micro-Donors. The other notable campaign finance trend in the campaign finance process is a dramatic increase in both the total amount of donations given to campaigns in amounts under $200 ('micro-donations') and the number of donors giving $200 or less to a presidential primary campaign in the aggregate.

Micro-donations have made up an ever larger share of presidential nomination process fundraising in the last three elections. Micro-donations accounted for 25 per cent of the total contributions to major party candidates seeking their parties' nomination the 2000 election season. The figure rose to 34 per cent in 2004 and 38 per cent in 2008.[22]

While micro-donors and micro-donations were especially important to the Obama campaign, bundling was very important to the McCain campaign (during the primary season, before the campaign took the public grant and raised money only for the party). It is unclear if there is an emerging party divide on leading candidates' reliance on micro-donations and bundling. In 2000, Al Gore raised 20 per cent of his total primary funds and George W. Bush raised 16 per cent of his total primary funds from micro-donations. In 2004, John Kerry raised 37 per cent of his total primary funds from micro-donations. George W. Bush raised 31 per cent of his total primary funds in this manner.[23] Thus, before 2008 there appeared to be some parity in the reliance of the major party candidates on micro-donations. In 2008, however, Barack Obama raised more than half (53 per cent) of his primary funds from micro-donations. In contrast, John McCain raised 31 per cent of his funds (over $62 million) from micro-donations.[24]

Though Obama raised much more in micro-donations in 2008 than Bush did in 2004, there was much more parity when it came to the *number* of micro-donors, that is, people who gave no more than $200 *in the aggregate* to the primary campaign. The range of reliance on micro-donors among the top major party candidates in the last two presidential primary election seasons ranged from 20–26 per cent, with Obama coming in at 26 per cent, compared to Bush (2004) at 25 per cent, McCain at 21 per cent and Kerry at 20 per cent.[25]

Yet because Obama's overall fundraising was so much greater than other candidates, he raised a much larger *total amount* of money in the primary period from micro-donors than Kerry (2004), Bush (2004), or McCain (2008). Obama raised $117.7 million from micro-donors in the primary, compared to $64 million for Bush, $43.1 million for Kerry, and $42.9 million for McCain.[26]

The decline in party 'soft money' and unregulated issue advocacy, and spending

Figure 13.2's description of the amounts spent on presidential election activity for the 1996 and 2000 election season underestimates actual spending in those elections, because these figures do not include largely unregulated money spent in those elections by political parties and other organisations.

Since the passage of FECA, individuals have been limited in the amount that they are allowed contribute to political parties for federal election activity. In the 2008 period, individuals could give up to $28,500 in contributions to the national political parties (with additional amounts to state, district and local party committees for federal election activity).[27] This is a so-called 'hard money' limit.

Thanks to a narrow United States Supreme Court interpretation of what constituted election activity for purposes of the FECA, parties began collecting very large contributions from individuals as well as corporations and unions (usually prohibited sources for campaign contributions) to use to influence the outcome of presidential and congressional elections. These sums came to be known as 'soft money', and the amounts of soft money spent by the two major parties was $272 million in 1996 and $498 million in 2000.[28]

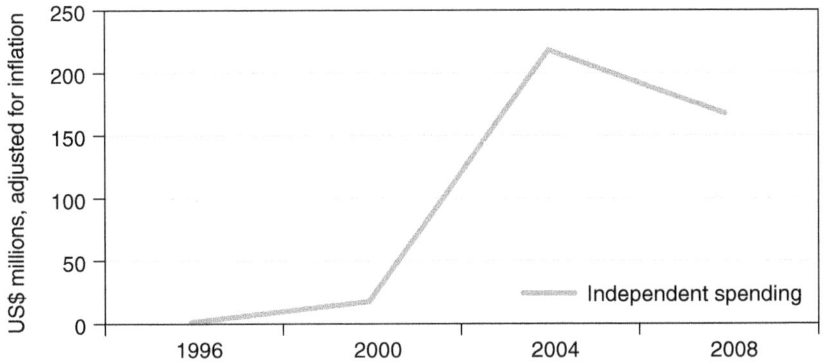

Figure 13.3 Independent expenditure spending related to presidential campaigns by election year (US$ millions, adjusted for inflation).

In addition, corporations, unions, and wealthy individuals spent unregulated sums on election-related advertising that, by avoiding words of express advocacy (such as 'Vote for Smith' or 'Vote against Jones'), skirted FECA restrictions. This spending came to be known as 'issue advocacy'. The amount spent on federal issue advocacy (for both presidential and Congressional elections) reached as much as $150 million in 1996 and $509 million in 2000.[29]

BCRA, passed in 2003, banned the parties from collecting soft money and changed the definition of relevant election activity so that more election activity came to be under federal regulation (and therefore not count as unregulated 'issue advocacy'). Though parties were banned from collecting soft money, beginning with the 2004 election, the national political parties collected more in hard money alone in 2004 than they collected in hard and soft money combined in the 2000 election.[30] In addition, thanks to other Supreme Court cases interpreting constitutional limits on political party activity,[31] parties began running significant campaigns supporting their presidential candidates *independent of* their candidate's own campaigns. Figure 13.3 shows the inflation-adjusted rise in independent expenditures (by parties and others) in the last four presidential election cycles.

The rise of '527 organisations', and the future of independent political committees

It is commonplace to observe (sometimes with reference to the game of whack-a-mole or the 'hydraulic' nature of campaign financing) that campaign finance regulations intended to stem the flow of money into electoral activity often lead to the money emerging through different forms or groups. The recent US experience validates this observation, at least to some extent.

Under current US law, an individual wishing to influence the outcome of a presidential campaign has three options: donating to a presidential campaign or political party; independently spending money supporting or opposing a presidential candidate; or contributing that money to an independent group that in turn supports or opposes presidential candidates. The third option – contributions to an independent group – offers three primary advantages to the contributor. First, though contributions to such groups are (usually) subject to disclosure, the disclosure is less transparent. Thus, instead of an advertisement opposing the President running for reelection ending with 'Paid for by John Smith', it could end with 'Paid for by Americans for American Values'. Only those who research the group's finances (through data released by the FEC or another source) will learn of Smith's contributions. Second, independent groups often have more expertise than individuals in running successful campaigns: thus, it may be more efficient for a person to contribute to another, rather than to spend the money directly. Finally, individuals with common political goals may use groups to pool their money to take advantage of economies of scale when it comes to candidate advertising, thereby magnifying the value of the money.

The main disadvantage of using such groups is that the groups may face contribution and source limitations. As noted in the introduction to this chapter, PACs may receive contributions of no greater than $5,000 per year, and cannot accept contributions from the general treasuries of corporations or labour unions.

For this reason, a number of groups formed during the 2004 elections with the goal of influencing the outcome of the presidential election without being characterised by the FEC as a political committee (and therefore subject to these limitations). These so-called '527 organisations' (named after a provision of the US Internal Revenue Code) argued that because they did not expressly advocate the election or defeat of candidates, and because they did not have the 'major purpose' of electing or defeating candidates, they were not required to register as political committees. The 527 organisations, therefore, took the position they could take contributions larger than $5,000 (and they ended up taking contributions in the millions) and could take money from corporations and labour unions.[32]

These 527 organisations played a major role in the 2004 presidential election, but their legal status was uncertain. After the 2004 election, the FEC fined a number of these groups for failing to register as political committees. Perhaps because of the legal uncertainty (and perhaps for other reasons, such as both candidates' professed dislike of these groups), 527 organisations played a less important role in the 2008 presidential election. Excluding state-focused 527s, the amount of 527 spending (to influence both presidential and congressional races) fell from $432 million in 2004 to $241 million in 2008.[33]

Going forward, the legal environment of campaign finance regulation remains uncertain. There has been considerable ideological disagreement at the FEC among its six partisan commissioners (three from each party),[34] and it is not clear how aggressively the FEC will move to regulate 527s and other political organisations, such as so-called '501(c) organisations',[35] as political committees.

More provocatively, the constitutionality of the $5,000 contribution limitation and source limitations on contributions to political committees that engage only in independent spending activity is now in question.[36] It could well be that, by the 2012 presidential elections, the United States Supreme Court will have struck down these limits, thereby immediately increasing the importance of political committees in presidential campaign financing. At the time of writing, however, the legal regime related to group campaign finance limits is one of considerable uncertainty.

Explaining the transformation

In this section, I consider why the patterns of campaign financing in US presidential elections have changed. I trace the changes to four factors:

1 the failure of the US Congress to update the presidential public financing system, first enacted in 1974;
2 enactment of BCRA and the reactions to the US Supreme Court's shifting interpretation of the constitutionality of campaign finance law in the wake of BCRA;
3 the rise of cheap political speech via the Internet; and
4 continued political polarisation in the US.

The public financing system for presidential candidates collapsed, primarily because of a combination of legal and market forces. First, the public financing system enacted first in 1976 imposed a spending cap that has not kept up with the ability of candidates to raise money on the private market. Bush's fundraising during the primary season in his first election, in 2000, showed that private fundraising efforts could almost double the amount available to candidates during the primary season. Bush raised $95.6 million privately, while Gore's spending was capped at $49.6 million.[37] Bush's innovation increased candidates' demand for political money during the primary season. Knowing that the sky was now the limit, candidates had an ever-increasing need for funds, if only not to be outspent by an opponent.

But the supply of money has expanded as well. In 2002, Congress (through BCRA) doubled the amount that an individual could give to federal candidates. In 2004, one-third of all contributions to presidential primary candidates came from donors giving at least $2,000. Bush, the eventual Republican nominee, received 44 per cent of his contributions from this group; Kerry, the eventual Democratic nominee, received 24 per cent from this group. [38] In the 2008 primary season, 37 per cent of contributions came from contributors giving at least $2,300 (the new maximum, thanks to BCRA's inflation adjustment). McCain, the eventual Republican nominee, received 38 per cent of his contributions from this group. Obama, the eventual Democratic nominee, received 32 per cent from $2,300 donors during the primary and general election season (up to October 15, 2008).[39]

Once Bush in 2000 showed how much more money he could raise beyond the low spending caps, the arms race began, and it received extra impetus from the increased supply of larger money that wealthier donors could now give thanks to BCRA. Though the Democrats had something of an ideological commitment to the public financing system, in 2004, both the eventual Democratic nominee, Kerry, and the early front-runner, Howard Dean, opted out; in 2008, both the eventual Democratic nominee, Obama, and the early front-runner, Hillary Clinton, opted out. On the Republican side, McCain appears to have shifted his decision on opting in and opting out with his political fortunes; only when it looked like his campaign was failing did he express an interest in opting in, a position he reversed when he recovered politically. At this point, the public financing system is dead for presidential primaries unless it is reformulated by Congress.

Bundling, micro-donations, and micro-donors have replaced the central role of public financing in presidential campaigns. Candidates seeking the presidency have always pursued multiple fundraising routes, with one of the most lucrative being the $1,000-per-plate (or now $2,300 per plate) dinner with the candidate. With 500 attendees, such a dinner can now clear $1 million. But as presidential candidates need to raise ever more money and to travel across the country in search of primary votes, not just money, other means of raising money have become attractive as well.

In this environment, the use of campaign bundlers has become central. Bundling shifts some of the onus of fundraising from the candidate to the candidate's supporters. Campaign bundlers likely are motivated by a number of reasons, including the desire to help elect a candidate of choice. But some bundlers likely are looking to curry influence with the candidate, securing prerequisites such as access to the candidate at special events. Bundling became more attractive to individuals looking for access after the 2002 passage of BCRA, which outlawed the giving of six- and seven-figure 'soft money' donations to the political parties. Soft money used to be the entry price for access to presidential candidates; bundling to some degree has replaced that activity.

Not everyone is capable of being a bundler. Only those people with a circle of friends or associates who can cough up maximum individual contributions (currently $2,300) can raise funds in this way. Bundling also creates a sense of competition; the publication of bundling activities likely spurs some competitiveness among bundlers for the same candidate, with different levels of participation for those who reach higher bundling levels.[40]

Micro-donation targeting arose out of a combination of candidates' increased demand for money and the reduction in fundraising costs thanks to the Internet and, in the 2008 election, text messaging. Internet campaigning was already important in the 2004 election.[41] But its use appears to be accelerating rapidly. The rise of 'cheap' political speech has increased the ability of voters to exchange political messages via email, instant messaging, amateur videos posted on YouTube and related sites, and, more frequently, social networking sites such as MySpace and Facebook.[42] Text messaging is the next frontier. The Obama campaign sent 2.9 million text messages in one day to supporters, who signed up to be 'among the first' to hear of Obama's vice presidential pick.[43] The campaign then used the collected email addresses and cell phone numbers to follow up with potential contributors.

Most importantly for our purposes, the cheap speech of the Internet allows the candidate to quickly and cheaply communicate with supporters, asking many people to give small amounts of money. Once the campaign invests in the fixed costs of Internet communication, the marginal cost of sending out numerous solicitation emails are small. And supporters can be hit over again. One donor interviewed by the *Los Angeles Times* gave $700 to Obama over a period of months in $25 increments.[44]

Repeaters were a critical part of the Obama fundraising strategy in 2008. The Campaign Finance Institute (CFI) reports that over 200,000 Obama donors started off giving contributions of $200 or less and then crossed the reporting threshold by giving more.[45] According to CFI, 'About 93,000 of these repeaters gave in cumulative amounts of no more than $400 for the full primary season. Another 106,000 repeaters ended up between $401 and $999'.[46] Future studies should consider why these donors gave *repeatedly*. How much was due to enthusiasm for the candidate, how much to the long campaign, and how much to the lower transaction costs of repeat giving over the Internet with saved account information?

The Obama story is useful in seeing how campaign fundraising techniques are additive rather than substitutionary. Obama did not choose to replace bundling with Internet-based small fundraising; he aggressively pursued both.

For parties, political committees, and outside groups, shifting laws, court interpretations, and FEC enforcement decisions have influenced the collecting and spending of political money. Strictures on PACs and BCRA-imposed limits on party soft money and issue advocacy caused donors and existing groups to shift to new organisations, such as 527 organisations. When the legality of the 527 organisational form came into question in 2008, money shifted away from such organisations. Now, with the expected move at the United States Supreme Court toward constitutionally mandated deregulation,[47] it seems quite likely that money will shift back to these groups, and potentially to political parties as well. Indeed, it is conceivable that within one or two more presidential elections, the Court will strike down all limits on contributions to political candidates and parties.[48] If the Court took that step, expect to see candidates shifting at least some of their fundraising attention to 'super-donors' giving six- and seven-figure donations. This strategy might not completely displace bundling and the targeting of micro-donors, but it would play a central role in major campaigns.

One final factor in the explosion of US fundraising is the continued high levels of party polarisation among the US population.[49] Even if the courts completely deregulate US presidential campaign financing, the amount of presidential candidate private fundraising is naturally limited by the candidates' popular support. So long as Democrats and Republicans in the United States remain firmly at odds with one another over the direction of US policy, it is likely that the supply of money for presidential candidates, parties, and outside groups will remain high. At this point, there seems little prospect that the intense polarisation which has characterised recent US presidential elections will soon diminish.

A normative evaluation of the transformation

The earlier parts of this chapter established that the campaign finance system for US presidential elections has undergone significant changes in recent elections and that both law and market forces have caused these changes. I turn now to the normative question of whether these changes are positive or negative.

Asking the normative question requires a baseline. For example, if one is concerned with the total amount of money spent on politics, then the trends emerging from the most recent presidential election nominating contests is especially bad: the total spent on presidential elections are rising dramatically (see Figure 13.2). From my normative standpoint, however, *total* money spent on elections is not a good measure of the health of the campaign process (despite the fact that media reports often focus on it because of the shock value of a $1.8 billion presidential campaign season). Beyond an argument that such spending is 'wasteful' – which raises a 'compared to what' question – primary concerns about the role of money in politics usually depend not on *total* spending, but upon some feature of the donors or the donors' relationship to candidates. That is, the real issues are those of undue influence, unequal access, or other underlying policy concerns emanating from the private financing of public elections. It is to these other policy issues that I now turn.

Corruption. Limits on contributions to presidential candidates – and later limits on 'soft money' contributions to political parties – have made it more difficult for individuals to attempt to buy influence over candidates through large campaign contributions. To this extent, the amount of potential corruption in the system remains low, especially as candidates can come to rely on a larger amount of micro-donors, none of whom contribute enough money to raise the danger of a presidential candidate *quid pro quo*. Large spending through independent groups also poses minimal possibilities of *quid pro quo* corruption, so long as those engaged in spending (and the contributors to the entity doing the spending) act independently of candidates.

Sale of access. Whether or not the sale of access to presidential candidates counts as 'corruption', sale of access has been a regular feature of the modern presidential campaign. The recent transformation of the presidential funding system described earlier in this chapter has shifted, but not ended, the sale of access. Before the enactment of BCRA, it was common for the national political parties to condition access to presidential candidates on the giving of large amounts of 'soft money'.[50] Since BCRA and the soft money ban, access sales have shifted to campaign finance bundlers. Such bundlers achieve their access not by donating their own wealth, but by tapping a large network of people they know who are wealthy enough to contribute the maximum $2,300 to the candidate. Whether the shift from soft money donors to bundlers lessens the extent to which campaigns sell access to presidential candidates is a difficult question to answer absent good empirical evidence about practices that campaigns rarely advertise to the general public.

Major contributors to outside independent political groups also may gain special access to presidential candidates after the election. Presidential candidates likely notice and appreciate when an individual spends millions of dollars supporting or opposing the candidate through an independent effort.

Political equality. Is the current campaign finance regime more or less egalitarian than the past? This question too is difficult to answer, because of cross-currents: the demise of public financing has harmed the goal of political equality, while the rise of micro-donors has helped it.

The public financing system, when it still worked, marginally promoted 'barometer equality'.[51] Under this concept, campaign spending should roughly mirror public support for the candidate's political ideas.[52] The presidential public financing matching fund programme for primaries followed this model to some extent by matching the first $250 of each campaign contribution received by a candidate. It made small donations twice as attractive as they otherwise would be and in that way created an incentive for campaigns to go after donors contributing relatively small amounts of money. Of course, the system's effects on political equality were limited: still only a small pool of people give money to presidential candidates, and those donors tended to be wealthier than the general population.

The legal and market forces described in the last part of this chapter caused the public financing system in the primaries to become obsolete. Moreover, the doubling of individual contribution limits in 2002 has since attracted campaigns to relatively wealthy contributors who could max out their contributions at over $2,000 each. Both of these forces have the tendency to make the system less egalitarian, making larger donations more important and smaller donations less important.

However, these factors have been counteracted by the meteoric rise of micro-donors. Micro-donors promote barometer equality: the greater the number of micro-donors supporting a candidate and the more intensely they do so, the greater the funding for the candidate to get out his or her message to the people. It is astounding that between the primary and general election Obama was able to raise $150 million from over one million individuals giving no more than $200.[53] Though Obama's fundraising may be unique to the enthusiasm surrounding his candidacy, he is not the only presidential candidate who has had impressive micro-donor fundraising. George W. Bush in 2004 raised $64 million from micro-donors. Even McCain, whose fundraising generally has lagged behind the other eventual nominees since 2000, raised about $43 million in 2008 from micro-donors.[54] These trends are promising from the point of view of more Americans getting involved and helping to support their preferred candidates for president in a meaningful way.

This is not to say that the current system is a fully egalitarian one. Even in 2008, more than one-quarter of all money raised by presidential primary candidates came from $2,300 maxed-out donors. Moreover, most eligible Americans still have not donated to political campaigns, and many are too poor to give even modest amounts to campaigns. If the class of donors differs in important ways from non-donors, then the campaign finance system might not be promoting political equality but instead may be skewed in one direction or another.

The concern that donors are unrepresentative of most Americans is one that merits further consideration. A study of donors in the 2004 presidential election found that donors who gave more than $200 were 'more highly educated, older and much wealthier than most Americans'.[55] However,

> [t]he small donors [i.e., micro-donors, giving under $200] stand somewhere between the large donors and the general public in many respects. Small donors were neither as wealthy nor as highly educated as large donors, although they were more so than the general population'.[56]

There is also an age skew: micro-donors 'were older, on average, than young donors, but there were also eight times as many young people among small donors as there were in the top group'.[57] Both large and micro-donors tend to be motivated by ideological considerations, but the 2004 study found 'little evidence to support the concern that small donors tend to be more polarized and more negative than large donors'.[58] We will have to see if these trends hold up in future studies of the much larger pool of micro-donors in the 2008 presidential election.

In sum, though micro-donors are not perfectly representative of the American voting population, they are more representative of the American population than large donors, who have dominated the system in the past. Moreover, the rise of micro-donors shows that a candidate with broad appeal (such as Obama or McCain) or a candidate with narrow or intense appeal (such as Paul or Kucinich) can raise enough money from people with modest means to get out the candidate's message and make the candidate a credible one if there is some popular support for the candidate's ideas. It is harder for big money to 'drown out' the voices of the many. This is political equality that 'levels up' the field rather than 'levelling down' with spending limits.[59]

Indeed, the amounts of money that a popular candidate is able to raise from micro-donors can allow the candidate to compete effectively even against self-funded wealthy candidates. Contrast the size of micro-donations raised by Obama and McCain to Mitt Romney's failed 2008 candidacy. Romney donated $44.6 million to his campaign, a bit more than McCain's micro-donations and not even a quarter of Obama's. The possibility of a wealthy candidate scaring away less wealthy competitors is less credible than in the past.

Political parties. Finally, some have feared that the transformation of the campaign finance system for US presidential elections will hurt political parties. So far, the end of soft money has not hurt the parties' fundraising abilities. At least in the current politically polarised climate, and with the rise of cheap speech and the ability of presidential candidates (even those participating in the public financing system) to jointly fundraise for the parties, political parties do not seem to be in great danger. However, parties may be weakened if the United States Supreme Court lifts limits on outside groups' fundraising ability but keeps the party 'soft money' limitations in place.

Conclusion

At least in the United States, campaign finance systems are dynamic, not static. Changes in law, technology, and strategy interact to alter the nature of fundraising. In US presidential elections, the most recent transformation has been marked by the demise of the public financing system and its replacement with bundling and micro-donations.

Though Obama's unprecedented fundraising success in the 2008 election may not soon be matched, surely other campaigns will try to replicate his success in both cultivating micro-donors and in building bundling networks (the latter an innovation pioneered by the George W. Bush campaign). The largest question mark for the near future about the financing of presidential campaigns is the legal regime. It is not clear how quickly, or how far, the United States Supreme Court will move in the deregulation of campaign financing. Should the Court move sharply in the deregulatory direction, candidates, parties, and outside groups will no doubt adapt, finding new ways to raise and spend maximum amounts of money to influence the outcome of the presidential vote. Outside groups will also be looking for new ways to influence the new president through strategic fundraising and spending.

Postscript

After this chapter went to press, the US Supreme Court took the deregulatory turn many of us expected. It held in *Citizens United* v. *Federal Election Commission* (2010) that corporations and labor unions have a constitutional right to spend directly (but without coordination with candidates) to help presidential and congressional candidates get elected. Following *Citizens United*, a host of other restrictions fell as well, including the contribution limits on contributions to PACs and other associations that engage in independent spending. Disclosure rules too became more porous, as the Federal Election Commission deadlocked along party lines over the scope of disclosure rules. As the US approaches the 2012 elections, a brave new world of campaign financing awaits.

Notes

1 Outside the US, such groups often are referred to as 'third parties'. In the US, that term typically refers to minor parties (aside from Democrats and Republicans) who run candidates in some elections. For this reason, I use the term 'outside groups'.

2 Federal Election Commission, '2008 Presidential Campaign Financial Activity Summarized: Receipts Nearly Double 2004 Total' (8 June 2009), available at www.fec.gov/press/press2009/20090608PresStat.shtml.

3 This chapter considers only campaign financing for major party (Democratic and Republican) presidential candidates. It does not consider

   1 minor party candidates for president;
   2 congressional campaign financing; or
   3 state and local campaign financing issues.

4 Though the election is national, results are tallied within each of the 50 states. Each state is allocated a number of electoral votes based on the number of House and

Senate seats each state holds. Most states award all of the state's electoral votes to the candidate who receives the most votes within the state, but there are a few states that allocate some of their electoral votes based upon certain sub-state results. The president must receive a majority of the electoral votes; otherwise the choice goes to Congress under a set of complex rules. The details of this process are beyond the scope of this Chapter. For details and a critique, see R.W. Bennett, *Taming the Electoral College*, Chicago: Stanford University Press, 2006.

5 For more details on the law described in this introduction, see D.H. Lowenstein, R.L. Hasen and D.P. Tokaji, *Election Law: Cases and Materials*, Durham: Carolina Academic Press, 4th ed., 2008, pp. 792–793, 889–892.

6 J.C. Green, 'Financing the 2004 Presidential Nomination Campaigns', in D.B. Magleby, A. Corrado and K.D. Patterson (eds), *Financing the 2004 Elections*, Washington: Brookings Institution, 2006, p. 93; Federal Election Commission, *Public Funding of Presidential Elections*, August 1996 (updated February 2008), available at www.fec.gov/pages/brochures/pubfund.shtml.

7 Lowenstein, Hasen and Tokaji, above, p. 890.

8 M.J. Malbin, 'A Public Funding System in Jeopardy: Lessons from the Presidential Nomination Contest of 2004', in M. Malbin (ed.), *The Election After Reform: Money, Politics and the Bipartisan Campaign Reform Act*, Lanham: Rowman & Littlefield Publishers, 2006, p. 219, tbl 11.1.

9 Ibid.

10 J. Kuhnhenn, 'Obama Spends $55 Million in July, McCain $32M', *USA Today*, 20 August 2008, available at: www.usatoday.com/news/politics/2008-08-20-1571558437_x.html.

11 M. Luo, 'McCain's Camp Tests Fundraising Limits', *New York Times*, 20 September 2008, available at: www.nytimes.com/2008/09/20/us/politics/20donate.html.

12 D.D. Kirkpatrick, 'Edwards Embrace of Public Money May Be Limited', *New York Times*, 29 September 2007, available at: www.nytimes.com/2007/09/29/us/politics/29edwards.html.

13 M. Mosk, 'McCain Got Loan By Pledging to Seek Public Funds', *Washington Post*, 16 February 2010, available at: www.washingtonpost.com/wp-dyn/content/article/2008/02/15/AR2008021503639.html.

14 During that same period, Senator Obama raised an addition $41.9 million to be used for the general election campaign: Campaign Finance Institute, CFI Release, 'After Holding Financial Advantage in Primaries, Obama Likely to Achieve Only Parity with McCain in General Election', 26 September 2008a, available at: www.cfinst.org/pr/prRelease.aspx?ReleaseID=205.

15 Ibid., tbl. 2.

16 Kuhnhenn, above; Daily Kos, 'Public Financing in the Primary is Dead', 21 August 2008, available at: www.dailykos.com/storyonly/2008/8/21/1589/49028.

17 A. Corrado, 'Fund-raising Strategies in the 2008 Presidential Campaign', in J.A. Thurber and C.J. Nelson (eds), *Campaigns and Elections American Style*, 3rd ed., Boulder: Westview Press, 2010, p. 105.

18 J.C. Green and N.S. Bigelow, 'The 2000 Presidential Nominations: The Costs of Innovation', in David B. Magleby (ed.), *Financing the 2000 Elections*, Washington: Brookings Institution, 2002, p. 59.

19 Green, above, p. 104.

20 Ibid., p. 105.

21 Center for Responsive Politics, *Bundlers* (2008) (accessed 12 October 2009), available at: www.opensecrets.org/pres08/bundlers.php?id=N00006424.

22 Malbin, above, tbl 11.1; Campaign Finance Institute, above, tbl. 2.

23 Malbin, above, tbl. 11.1.

24 Campaign Finance Institute, above, tbl. 2.

25 Campaign Finance Institute, CFI Release, 'Reality Check: Obama Received About the

Same Percentage from Small Donors in 2008 as Bush in 2004; Obama Also Raised 80% More from Large Donors than Small, Outstripping All Rivals and Predecessors', 24 November 2008, available at: www.cfinst.org/pr/prRelease.aspx?ReleaseID=216. See also M. Mosk and S. Cohen (2008), 'Big Donors Drive Obama's Money Edge', *Washington Post*, 22 October 2008, A1, available at: www.washingtonpost.com/wp-dyn/content/article/2008/10/21/AR2008102102996.html?sid=ST2008102103028&s_pos=, and S. Cohen, 'Small Donations Create Big Obama Donors', The Trail Blog, *Washington Post*, 23 October 2008, available at: http://voices.washingtonpost.com/the-trail/2008/10/23/small_donations_creating_big_d.html.

26 Campaign Finance Institute, CFI Release, 'Reality Check: Obama Received About the Same Percentage from Small Donors in 2008 as Bush in 2004; Obama Also Raised 80% More from Large Donors than Small, Outstripping All Rivals and Predecessors', above.

27 Lowenstein, Hasen and Tokaji, above, p. 793.

28 *McConnell* v. *Federal Election Commission*, 540 US 93 (2003).

29 Lowenstein, Hasen and Tokaji, above, p. 851.

30 A. Corrado, 'Party Finance in the Wake of BCRA: An Overview', in M. Malbin (ed.), above, p. 25.

31 See Lowenstein, Hasen and Tokaji, above, pp. 770–774.

32 R. Briffault, 'The 527 Problem ... and the Buckley Problem' *George Washington Law Review*, vol. 73, 2005, 949.

33 Center for Responsive Politics, *527s: Advocacy Spending in the 2010 Elections*, 2009 (accessed 14 October 2009), available at: www.opensecrets.org/527s/index.php.

34 B. Becker, 'Election Commission Decisions Deadlocking on Party Lines', *New York Times*, 26 September 2009, available at: www.nytimes.com/2009/09/27/us/politics/27elect.html.

35 Campaign Finance Institute, New CFI Report, 'Soft Money Political Spending by 501(c) Nonprofits Tripled in 2008', 25 February 2009, available at: www.cfinst.org/pr/prRelease.aspx?ReleaseID=221.

36 *EMILY's List* v. *Federal Election Commission*, 581 F 3d 1 (DC Cir) (2009).

37 Malbin, above, tbl. 11.1. Note that the 'primary season' runs until the summer nominating convention, so that once a party candidate becomes the presumptive nominee, he or she may continue to raise funds and then spend them attacking the other party's candidate(s) during that period.

38 Malbin, ibid.

39 Campaign Finance Institute, CFI Release, 'Reality Check: Obama Received About the Same Percentage from Small Donors in 2008 as Bush in 2004; Obama Also Raised 80% More from Large Donors than Small, Outstripping All Rivals and Predecessors', above, tbl. 1.

40 Corrado, 'Fund-raising Strategies in the 2008 Presidential Campaign', above, p. 122.

41 D. Magleby, and K.D. Patterson, 'Stepping Out of the Shadows? Ground-War Activity in 2004', in M. Malbin (ed.), above, p. 169; A.W. Corrado, 'Party Finance in the Wake of BCRA: An Overview', above, pp. 28–29.

42 E. Volokh, 'Cheap Speech and What It Will Do', *Yale Law Journal*, vol. 104, 1995, 1805; Pew Research Center for People and the Press, 'Internet's Broader Role in Campaign 2008; Social Networking and Online Videos Take Off', 11 January 2008, available at: http://people-press.org/reports/display.php3?ReportID=384.

43 A. Schatz, 'Nielsen: About Three Million Got Obama Text', *Wall Street Journal*, Washington Wire, 25 August 2008, available at: http://blogs.wsj.com/washwire/2008/08/25/nielsen-about-three-million-got-obama-text/.

44 D. Morain, 'From Small Donors Come Big Rewards', *Los Angeles Times*, 14 February 2008, available at: www.latimes.com/news/politics/la-na-money14feb14,0,5629421,full.story.

45 Campaign Finance Institute, CFI Release, 'Reality Check: Obama Received About

the Same Percentage from Small Donors in 2008 as Bush in 2004; Obama Also Raised 80% More from Large Donors than Small, Outstripping All Rivals and Predecessors', above.

46 Ibid.

47 R.L. Hasen, 'Beyond Incoherence: The Roberts Court's Deregulatory Turn in *FEC* v. *Wisconsin Right to Life', Minnesota Law Review*, vol. 92, 2008, 1064.

48 Ibid.

49 G. Jacobson, *Divider, Not a Uniter: George W. Bush and the American People, the 2006 Election and Beyond*, Pearson, 2007.

50 *McConnell* v. *Federal Election Commission*, 540 US 93 (2003).

51 R.L. Hasen, The Supreme Court and Election Law: Judging Equality from *Baker* v. *Carr* to *Bush* v. *Gore*, New York: New York University Press, 2003, p. 211.

52 R.L. Hasen, 'Political Equality, the Internet, and Campaign Finance Regulation' *The Forum*, vol. 6, 2008 available at: http://electionlawblog.org/archives/hasen-forum-final.pdf.

53 Obama eventually reached at least 2 million total donors: Political Intelligence, 'Obama Reaches 2 Million Donors', *Boston Globe*, 14 August 2008, available at: www.boston.com/news/politics/politicalintelligence/2008/08/obama_reaches_2.html.

54 Campaign Finance Institute, CFI Release, 'Reality Check: Obama Received About the Same Percentage from Small Donors in 2008 as Bush in 2004; Obama Also Raised 80% More from Large Donors than Small, Outstripping All Rivals and Predecessors', above, tbls. 1, 2.

55 Institute for Politics Democracy and The Internet, *Small Donors and Online Giving: A Study of Donors to the 2004 Presidential Campaigns*, 2006, p. 15, available at: www.ipdi.org/News/DocumentSingle.aspx?DocumentID=13860.

56 Ibid., pp. 15–16.

57 Ibid., p. 16.

58 Ibid., p. 27.

59 J.L. Fleishman, and Pope McCorkle, 'Level-Up Rather than Level-Down: Toward a New Theory of Campaign Finance Reform', *Journal of Law and Politics*, vol. 1, 1984, 211.

Part V

State funding and party autonomy

14 Justifications for regulating party affairs

Competition not public funding

Graeme Orr

Overview

The regulation of the internal affairs of political parties varies between electoral and legal cultures, finding different balances between party autonomy and freedom of association, and other regulatory goals such as transparency, accountability and internal democracy.[1] This chapter seeks to contribute to the broad debate about the degree to which regulation of the internal affairs of political parties is justified. Its specific topic is whether public funding – and its administrative concomitant, party registration – legitimates such regulation.

My argument is 'no'. Public funding, also known as state aid, state subsidy or state subvention, is no justification for regulating party affairs, except aspects of their financial accountability. This is *not* an abstentionist position. Regulation of party affairs may be entirely justified, despite its effect on freedom of association. But such regulation must be a response to particular concerns in particular jurisdictions, such as the degree of power that parties wield, or the level of corruption or ossification in the party system.

Explicit appeals to the fact of public funding do not justify treating parties as quasi-public entities and hence susceptible to regulation. Such an instinct appeals to a tendency for taxpayers to resent public funding. It draws on the language of share-holding, as if there were rights which taxpayers and the state may acquire in return for their 'investment' in parties (Johns 2001: 291). It risks eliding party autonomy as an important principle.

Similarly, the tendency of regulators to 'juridify' civic entities when they assume a tangible legal form is a form of regulatory slippage. In the case of politics, this may occur when parties move from being mere civic associations engaged in the electoral sphere, to being formally 'registered' to contest elections. Registration is merely an administrative process, useful to streamline systems of public funding and ballot labelling, and to minimise confusion between party names. Yet the act of registration forms a 'peg' on which regulators feel freer to hang regulation than would be the case if the party remained an unincorporated association, its form not captured by law.

My ultimate claim is that public funding and party regulation should harmonise around a shared goal, namely the promotion of diverse, robust and fair electoral competition. Understood that way, party autonomy and freedom of association ought not be sacrificed because of public funding. On the contrary, the law's fundamental interest in its dealings with parties, whether through public funding or direct regulation of them, is in maximising electoral competition, to promote electoral choice and representation.

Viewed against the goal of competitive elections, whether parties follow one or more models of internal democracy or, conversely, are internally hierarchical or even elitist and discriminatory, becomes a second-order issue. The law's main interest in parties' internal affairs is to require sufficient transparency so that electors and potential members alike can take any concerns they have about parties' internal machinations into account in their decisions about who to vote for or associate with.

Of course, in practice not all public funding regimes promote the goal of greater electoral competition.[2] Sometimes public funding achieves something of the reverse, helping entrench the make-up of the existing party system. In any event, the underlying structure of the voting system and its level of proportionality typically have a greater impact on competition than funding mechanisms. But the answer to any anti-competitive effects thereby created is to revisit the mechanics of the public funding or voting systems, rather than to unnecessarily regulate parties' internal affairs.

The role of parties and electoral regulation

It is not easy to generalise about political parties, as they can play quite distinctive roles across electoral cultures and systems. In some they are transitory vehicles for charismatic political leaders; in others they are stable entities. In some they are broad churches, straddling contradictory positions; in others they are tight ideological repositories. In some, they are messy mass movements, mobilising participation and turnout; in others they are wealthy, elite machines, gate-keepers of advertising war-chests and of candidate selection. In some they are subordinate to individual candidacies; in others they are well-structured hierarchies.

Indeed, even within a jurisdiction, the party system may vary, depending on factors such as party size, voting system (whether by party list or single-member constituencies or both) and level of government (with candidate centricity being more common in smaller electorates). However, one function of parties is invariable across systems: parties exist to compete for and win elective office, as rivals rather than as enemies.[3]

Many functions are adduced for elections themselves. They legitimate (or turn over) the elites which tend to make up representative governments. They provide the seminal form of political participation – voting – from which other democratic rights and accountabilities, such as free speech and open government flow. And they help shape the political community, through both the definition of the franchise and through the rituals of campaigning and polling. Throughout this, and across cultures, one bedrock purpose of free electoral regulation is to achieve diverse, fair and robust inter-party competition.

In making this claim, I do *not* mean a necessarily free-market form of political competition that would be inimical to regulation. What I mean is a broader conception of competition, embracing such a balance of political equality and liberty as will encourage diversity by creating a relatively level playing field between political aspirants and minimising undue barriers to new entrants. Enabling such diversity and competitiveness in turn feeds into those other functions of electoral legitimacy, turnover, participation and ritual.

Increasingly, in both jurisprudence and political commentary, there is a tendency to call for greater regulation of parties' internal affairs. In part this is an understandable response to unflattering episodes of malfeasance within and by parties. In part it comes from a jaded – if somewhat ahistorical – perception that parties are less and less mass movements than vehicles captured by castes of elite political professionals. In part it comes from a fear that there is insufficient competition between parties, and hence that internal selection of candidates, especially by the major parties, is where the real competition and hence public interest lies.[4] Indeed, in the two-party duopoly of the United States (a jurisdiction otherwise loathe to interfere with freedom of association) this fear is the central justification for state regulation of candidate selection in the form of primary elections.

It also comes from a tendency to regulate for regulation's sake. I label this tendency 'juridification'.[5] It is the natural instinct of regulators and academic lawyers alike: a diagnosis of a pathological case or injustice appears to *demand* some kind of regulatory response. These responses accrete over time, creating a tangled overlay of regulation of civil society that is not always coherent, let alone productive.

This is not, I should stress, an argument from a public choice position. That is, the argument does not rest on any claim for the existence of a 'market' for electoral regulation. There may well be such a market. If so, the obvious traders are parties themselves, whose parliamentary wings are the ultimate arbiters of at least legislative (as opposed to judicial or administrative agency) regulation. If such a market exists, we should be wary of the risk of both under-regulation – since party machines may prefer light regulation – and over-regulation – since parties may seek rent or partisan benefit, by imposing costs on rivals who are less able to bear such costs.

Rather, in coining the term 'juridification' I mean there is a well-meaning but typically piecemeal call for legislative regulation whenever a scandal appears, involving parties and electoral politics. This response can come from across the ideological spectrum, and from the media, academics and politicians alike. When politicians engage in it, the self-interest can be reactive rather than partisan. That is, the political motivation may be to buy short-term respite from an ethical controversy by appearing to 'do something'. Of course, there may be countervailing tendencies, either in a tradition of deference to freedom of association or in the party machines influencing legislators against imposing new regulations on them. But absent such other mechanisms encouraging legislative reticence, there is a bias or instinct towards regulation.[6]

Judicial contributions to party juridification are a secondary form of regulation. They typically bypass the filters of political debate and process altogether. Being case-driven, regulation by courts is inherently piecemeal. When rooted in constitutional norms, it may evade political review altogether.

Public funding as an argument for party regulation

Under the heading 'Promoting Democracy: A Quid Pro Quo', Professor Ewing[7] put the argument for public funding as a justification for regulating parties' internal affairs, as a set of questions:

> If the State is to support the parties in these ways, is the community entitled to expect something even more in return? In particular, if public money is being used to support political parties because political parties play an indispensable role in the democratic process, is the public not entitled to expect that the bodies that spend its money themselves meet some basic democratic criteria…?[8]

Gary Johns, a former Australian government minister and now researcher, put the argument more directly:

> The present parties are brand names with a nominal membership presence in the electorate [and] they are heavily supported by the state. Gary Gray (1997), the former national Secretary of the Australian Labor Party, estimates a third of all funds available to the ALP comes from taxpayers. *The new status of registered parties is semi-public. Ideally then, they should be beholden to the public, both electorally and in a more direct proprietorial way*, as well as to their membership. The issue is to decide the regulatory mix that would preserve free political association and *satisfy the taxpayer's investment* [emphasis added].[9]

To be fair, Johns is sceptical about the desirability of anything but reasonably light regulation of parties. But that a sceptic of regulation would concede that public funding might be a justification for regulation shows just how superficially appealing that premise is.

To many it may seem intuitively correct that if parties receive public subsidies, they should be subject to public controls. Johns' language of 'the taxpayer's investment' equates to a suggestion that public funding buys a state interest in the management of parties. At a minimum, then, should parties not be subject to such limitations on their autonomy as might be founded in a public consensus on fair and democratic processes?

There is certainly a compelling analogy between public funding and financial accountability. A party or candidate who receives public subsidies of any substance should be subject to accountability in at least two forms. One is disclosure of sources, categories and amounts of political revenues and expenditure. The second is audit requirements and good faith obligations on the accounting and expenditure of moneys in the party or campaign's interests.

Such measures are justified in principle, given the state and public interest in knowing that money is not misspent. They are also justified pragmatically, given the fungible nature of money: it is not usually feasible to corral public funding to avoid it mixing with the party's 'own' revenues, and attempts to do so are likely to raise significant problems for freedom of association. But it is practical and reasonable to allow parties to run a single set of accounts into which public funding is assimilated, whilst then opening their books to public scrutiny.

An example of the explicit tying of public funding to financial accountability is the Japanese Law Establishing Public Funding for Political Parties of 1994. Articles 14 to 20 of this law, which aim to ensure that public funding is used for political activities, require an audited annual report itemising all expenditures over ¥50 000 (around US$500).[10] Similarly, the 'opt-in' US Presidential public financing scheme requires participants 'to use public funds only for legitimate campaign-related expenses, to keep financial records and to permit extensive campaign audits'.[11]

Outside such formal accountability, however, the fact of public funding does not justify further intrusions on party autonomy. Even strong disclosure laws (which I support) are not primarily justified by the presence of state aid, although in some countries, such as Australia, disclosure was introduced alongside, and sold as a 'quid pro quo' for, public funding. Instead, disclosure is justified by concerns with undue influence and corruption by private donors. Indeed, disclosure is most needed in systems with little or no state aid, because in them, parties will be heavily reliant on donations from corporate organisations.

Proponents of regulating the internal affairs of parties understand that the real arguments for such regulation must draw on the role and power of the parties in the electoral system under debate. No one is silly enough to mount an argument from the fact of public funding (or registration) alone. For example, a long-time and articulate advocate of regulating party affairs in Australia, Senator Andrew Murray,[12] concluded his contribution to a parliamentary report with an appeal to multiple justifications for regulation:

> *Given the public funding*, the immense power of political parties (at least of some parties), and their vital role in our government and our democracy, it is proper to insist that [party] standards be met.... Greater regulation would offer political parties better protection from internal malpractice and corruption, and the public better protection from its consequences, and *it would reduce the opportunity for public funds being used for improper purposes* [emphasis added].

And similarly, two years later: '*Political parties have to be more accountable because of the public funding and resources they enjoy*, and because of their powerful public role.'[13]

Senator Murray's interest in regulation is genuine, but his assertion that public funding is a justification for regulation is essentially populist. Although public funding is not a justification for regulation there remains another justification, parties powerful public role. Conversely, Johns was wrong to suggest that '[a]n obvious way for the parties to escape the recent enhanced scrutiny of their operations is to reverse the acceptance of public funding'.[14] All that would achieve is to play to a populist sense that public funding buys regulatory rights over the parties, without addressing the underlying challenge of ensuring a truly competitive party system that, as far as possible, can be self-regulating.

Public funding, of course, varies in manner or degree from system to system. It ranges from direct electoral funding – e.g. payments per vote received – to indirect support – e.g. tax credits for donations. On one view, it includes provisions outside campaign finance, such as parliamentary support. Amongst key liberal democracies, there is a diversity of forms and mixes of public funding.[15] Germany pioneered public funding and with France has the most developed system. Currently, in Australia, there is even debate about the viability of moving to a full public funding system.

Such state support requires administrative recognition, which usually means a system of legal definition and registration of parties.[16] Such administrative systems become a peg on which the hat of regulation can be hung. As two Australian professors (approvingly) put it, in the context of pre-selecting candidates: 'The introduction of laws governing party registration has opened the doors for laying down the procedures a party must use to choose [its] candidates' (Hughes and Costar 2006: 88). Similarly, in Japan, parties did not have legal status until the reforms of 1994, which introduced public funding and, as a concomitant, required parties to seek 'the status of a legal person, according to the Political Party Legal Status Law'.[17]

Of course, regulation of parties' internal affairs can arise regardless of public funding, although a system of registration is typically a prerequisite. For example, in New Zealand, section 71 of the Electoral Act 1993 (NZ), which is entitled 'Requirement for Registered Parties to follow Democratic Procedures in Candidate Selection', was justified to temper the extra power that party elites achieved with the introduction of an electoral list system. (The provision's title was overstated – at most, it requires that party members have some direct, or indirect, participation rights in candidate pre-selection.)[18]

Similar provisions introduced in Queensland, Australia were explicitly linked to registration and access to public funding (Queensland Legislative Assembly 2002: 275). The Electoral Act 1992 (Qld), sections 73A and 75(2) (cancellation of registration if constitution is not compliant) and Part 8A (commission oversight of preselection ballots), require parties' constitutions to address certain issues, including 'that a preselection ballot must satisfy the general principles of free and democratic elections'. (Preselection is another term for the choice of endorsed candidates by a party).

But it is fallacious to assume that simply because state aid is given to parties and that, for regulatory convenience, a register of parties is opened, there is therefore a state interest – let alone a compelling one – in regulating parties' internal affairs.

In arguing that public funding is no justification for regulating parties' non-financial internal affairs, I am *not* making a radical case against any regulation of such affairs. Rather, any such regulation should be justified free of any appeal to the fact of public funding. Even a measure as unobtrusive and welcome as requiring parties to publish their constitutions and rules is not made any more compelling by the fact of public funding (or registration for that matter). It is justified by a mix of the legitimate interest of prospective members, researchers, and of voters and the media in understanding the structure and decision-making processes of the parties.

It might be objected that public finances are commonly employed to achieve disparate social goals. For instance, taxation is not simply a means to raise revenue, but is also often used to encourage beneficial behaviour – like charitable donating – and to discourage destructive behaviour – like smoking. How much more so with public subsidies, which are naturally and directly used to promote socially preferred activities, such as certain types of agriculture? Why shouldn't public subsidisation of political activity come with strings attached?

But to state this analogy is to expose its flaws. The aim of public funding ought be a healthy diversity of inter-party competition, and the ill to be discouraged is excessive reliance on wealthy or corrupting private and lobby group money. To introduce unrelated, secondary criteria for funding, such as mandating models of internal party governance, would be a categorical slippage.

State aid is also routinely given to encourage the flourishing of aspects of civil society, without it being desirable to conceive of its recipients as quasi-public entities. Obvious examples include support for charities or trade unions. Indeed, in such cases it is crucial to maintain the independence of those bodies, else the aim of bolstering civil society will be undermined, rather than supported.

Instead, arguments for the regulation of parties must rest on their public roles and power, not the source of their funding. The analogy with trade unions is helpful, not least because unions are inherently political entities. Regulation of unions ought be independent of state support (in fact, it often inversely correlates with it, under conservative governments). Regulation of internal affairs of unions is only justified where in law or fact they wield some monopoly power in an industry or have power over access to employment.

To see the flaw in the reasoning that, because public money is used to support a non-governmental body, the public can therefore 'expect' a certain internal structure or behaviours from that body, imagine the argument being applied across all realms of civic association in a plural society. Environmental, literary and artistic groups, to name a few, rely heavily on public subvention. The purpose of such grants should be to encourage their flourishing. The grants themselves do not justify imposing models of regulation or conduct over their affairs, beyond financial accountability.

It might be said that the examples given are of charitable bodies that do not wield public power in the way parties do. But some of them do wield public power, albeit not so directly as political parties. Any charity with any kind of social mission will engage in lobbying, both covert and overt. Provided the state funding of these bodies and hence their voices is not unduly partisan, such support may be desirable for the very reason that it encourages a pluralism of public discourse. This reflects the ultimate goal I suggest for party regulation and funding: diversity of electoral competition.

The main reason one would regulate to intervene in the internal affairs of a non-state organisation is to protect the participative rights of their members or to make the organisation more accessible to outsiders, such as potential members. In relation to outsiders, access should not be linked to the status of the organisation concerned. The law might wish to maintain access to an otherwise private organisation such as a trade union or an educational institution, because in the union's case, it may have an occupational monopoly on worker representation in an industry, and in the educational institution's case, because education is a universal necessity and a right. But whether the union or educational institution receives public funding is irrelevant to whether such regulation is justified.

Analogising with political parties, whilst it is true to say that some parties can assume quasi-monopolistic, or at least duopolistic status, any regulation of such parties (e.g. to ensure access for potential candidates) must be justified because of the peculiar power of those parties, regardless of whether they receive public funding or not. And whilst there is a universal right of political participation, the ultimate purpose of regulation is not so that every citizen has equal access to membership or a say in every party at all times. Parties need solidarity; they are not a smorgasbord to be sampled in the way a consumer may pick and choose from the stock of one high street retailer after another.

The ultimate point of party regulation should be to allow competitive parties to flourish. One aspect of such flourishing competition is not simply to have a variety of ideologies reflected between the parties on offer, but to allow them to experiment with different constitutions and forms of internal management.

The question of the participation rights of members of political parties is something of a furphy. At first glance it might seem odd to deny that, in a democracy, parties should be compelled to be internally democratic. For many observers, internal democracy must mean one member, one vote. Yet that is a superficial view.

Different ideologies may have different notions of what 'democratic' might mean, especially within the context of an organisation whose overriding purpose is to propagate its ideology and policies and have its endorsed candidates elected. The classic instances are the various Labour parties, which were built on trade unions as representatives of working people, rather than a principle of one-member, one-vote. Ideological bodies can be respectful of democracy as the best means of allocating public power, yet still insist that their organisations be run on hierarchical and even anti-democratic lines. They may believe that their version of the truth is best promulgated that way (e.g. churches) or, especially in the case of groups on the margin of electoral politics, they may believe in strict internal solidarity (e.g. most communist and some socialist parties). Finally, an organisation may find that structures which outsiders and regulators could see as less than democratic are simply efficient, especially at different stages of the organisation's development.

Justiciability of party affairs

Court oversight of party constitutions

Justiciability refers to the power of a court to intervene in a party's internal affairs. This can involve disputes about membership status and rights, candidate selection, executive and delegate positions, rights over money and other resources, grievance processes and even policy-making. Invariably such disputes are factionally driven. In the common law at least, such disputes typically confront a court in an application alleging a breach of party rules or customs, or some implied right to natural justice. But they can also arise collaterally in attempted review of the party's registration.[19]

By tradition, parties in the anglosphere, in particular, have been unincorporated (or voluntary) associations. In the common-law mind frame, this rendered their internal affairs immune from justiciability: their rules did not form a binding contract between members. Thus, their internal organisational and political affairs were immune from court jurisdiction, although disputes about property or employment rights involving parties could be litigated under the general law (*Cameron* v. *Hogan* (1934) 51 CLR 338).

In the second half of the twentieth century, this analogy between political organisations and amateur sporting clubs came to be untenable. Parties undoubtedly play significant public roles. As much as some judges might not enjoy having to resolve the politicised morass of party disputes, it seemed indefensible that their constitutions be treated as 'gentlemen's agreements'.

Australia had an early breakthrough in this approach to justiciability. The seminal case of *Baldwin* v. *Everingham* (1993) 1 Qd R 10 at page 17 gave the modern view that, 'where an albeit voluntary organisation fulfils a substantial public function in society, it may appear indefensible that questions of construction of its constitution should be beyond judicial resolution'.[20]

In truth, parties had long played such public functions or roles. Hence, the judge in *Baldwin* v. *Everingham* had to find a more legalistic justification for avoiding the old, non-interventionist precedent. He found it in the introduction of a formal system of party registration. This accorded parties such 'statutory recognition' as to justify treating them as quasi-public entities. The issue of public funding was mentioned, although not given prominence. In a list of justifications for judicial intervention, the judge commented: 'and of course parties are now entitled to receive public funds' (*Baldwin* v. *Everingham* (1993) 1 Qd R 10 at p. 20).

Within a few years however, another Australian judge was stressing the 'large amounts of money [that are] paid to the major political parties', in his finding that public funding was a 'significant matter' justifying court involvement in party affairs (*Clarke* v. *ALP (SA Branch)* (1999) 74 SASR 109 at paras 81–91).

It did not even seem to matter that the dispute involved a state parliamentarian and his branch, yet the only public support involved was federal electoral funds. The logic of parties as quasi-public entities transcended such legalistic niceties as whether the law of the *particular* parliament or jurisdiction accorded parties statutory recognition or benefits.

The outcome of these cases was laudable – the ability, within the discretionary remedies of the law of equity, to intervene at the suit of party members to insist that party rules are abided by. But the reasoning was not strong. Party registration in Australia was meant to be no more than an administrative measure, to efficiently manage two electoral rights and obligations:

- Ballot labelling (that is, abbreviations of party names on ballot papers). Whilst this can be seen as a benefit to parties, it is merely a consequential benefit. The purpose is to aid voters, rather than to give parties intellectual property rights in their names.
- Bureaucratic oversight of party finances, particularly payment of public funding and disclosure of donations. Registration of a party or one of its sub-divisions defines an accounting unit and identifies a responsible official as the party's agent.

The best justification for courts accepting the call to intervene in internal party affairs is, as Caroline Morris argues in surveying recent UK and NZ decisions, 'the recognition of the ultimate importance of the outcome of the selection process ... for both parties and potential candidates'.[21] From there, however, the question becomes how deeply the courts answer calls to intervene, calls which invariably come from factional struggles within each party.

In theory, if a court is to intervene to enforce a part of the constitution and rules of a party, it should intervene to enforce the whole. But that creates the problem of a recursive loop, if the party's constitution sets up an internal grievance procedure from which no appeal is said to lie. Should the court strictly enforce such an ouster clause, or should it uphold the public interest asserted in enforcing the substantive rules of the party?[22]

Further, the history of administrative law suggests that once judges start basing their justifications for intervention on reasoning about power and the quasi-public status of non-governmental bodies, then there is a strong urge to import substantive, judicially constructed rights and obligations, such as principles of natural justice. This may sound fine in principle, but it may impose unreasonable obligations on people working, in most cases, as volunteers in a party hierarchy. Further, such a move amounts to judicial legislation. For all their independence, judges may not be ideally placed to understand the practicalities of party machinery, or to balance the policy arguments and consequences of their attempts to regulate that machinery.

Justiciability and anti-discrimination law

Justiciability merely through court enforcement of a party's own rules is, in substance, not particularly contentious. A more piquant illustration of the debate over whether the law should intervene in party affairs is whether and to what degree anti-discrimination law should bind parties in their internal processes.[23] Whilst anti-discrimination law is primarily statute-based, as opposed to being generated by case law, it is relevant to justiciability. The issue is whether courts should enforce this branch of the general law in relation to parties' internal political affairs, for anti-discrimination law is not drafted with parties particularly in mind. (I use the qualification 'political' because, undoubtedly, in their ordinary commercial or employment dealings, parties should be bound by anti-discrimination law).

To a proponent of the idea that public funding generates a state interest in parties, anti-discrimination law is fertile terrain. After all, how can a liberal state justify giving resources to support a discriminatory organisation? A publicly funded body – especially one in a plural society – should be open to all. It should not be funded if it is in any way closed through invidious forms of discrimination such as age, race, religion or gender bias.

Unsurprisingly, the litigation generated in this area has tended to involve the preselection of candidates by parties, although it could equally concern access to other positions of power within a party, such as delegations to conferences or executive offices. Differing outcomes have occurred in the UK and Australia. Ostensibly, the differing outcomes reflect uncertainty in interpreting the scope of anti-discrimination provisions, particularly whether the rule forbidding discrimination in access to 'employment' or 'qualifications', applies to selection of political positions within parties (as opposed to clerical positions). But, more substantively, the decisions reflect tension between the values of anti-discrimination and freedom of association.

Thus, in the litigation culminating in *Watt* v. *Ahsan* [2008] 2 WLR 17 (House of Lords), the UK courts eventually held that preselection as a candidate for elective office was neither a profession or occupation, nor a necessary authorisation or qualification for a profession or occupation. As a result, the prohibition on racial discrimination did not apply.[24] This came only after lower courts had in effect held the opposite (*Jepson* v. *The Labour Party* [1996] IRLR 116). A similar result was reached in an earlier Australian Human Rights Commission ruling in a case of alleged marital and gender bias in candidate preselection (*Scott* v. *Gray* [1999] HREOCA 15). This abstentionist view arises from orthodox reasoning that elective office is not 'employment'. This is coupled with the argument that selection by a particular party is not a formal requirement to be a candidate for general election, even if in practice one may need major party endorsement to have a reasonable chance of being elected.

The substantive problem, of enforcing upon political parties a one-size-fits-all anti-discrimination principle designed to ensure access to goods and services in a marketplace, can be most clearly seen in relation to groups that historically have been under-represented in electoral politics. These groups include racial, ethnic and national minorities and, in most societies, women. In some cases, specialist parties have formed to raise awareness and mobilise activists, but also to promote slates of candidates for general election. Examples from recent Australian history include the Australian Indigenous Peoples' Party, the Senior's Party, and the What Women Want party. Many countries have ethnic equivalents, e.g. Plaid Cymru (the Welsh nationalist party). Sometimes the constitutions of such parties are explicitly discriminatory, in the sense that they promote the interests of the minority concerned. In other cases, the party informally practices 'positive discrimination' in preselection of candidates and selection of office bearers. After all, such positive discrimination is the *raison d'etre* of the party. Even within major parties, similar efforts are sometimes made, such as mandating a minimum percentage of women in electable seats.

It might be argued that anti-discrimination law should prima facie apply to a party's internal affairs, but with a defence for affirmative action measures. The alternative might be to apply anti-discrimination law only to the major parties, or those likely to be in a position to form government. This would be anathema to the rule of law principle that all parties be treated formally equally, but it would recognise the reality that the real evil of discrimination is where it occurs in powerful parties, with a seat in government, particularly those who otherwise purport to be 'broad churches'.

The ultimate point I wish to make is that any justification for requiring parties' internal affairs to meet anti-discrimination law lies in the power they wield, not whether they receive any public funding. Indeed, in some circumstances encouraging sectional parties (e.g. the Indigenous Peoples' Party) through public funding may be an entirely good thing in promoting diversity of electoral choice and candidate opportunities precisely *because* that party advances the cause of a group that has been marginalised from mainstream electoral politics.

The proper purposes of public funding

The purpose of state aid is not, strictly, to give benefits to parties, although that certainly occurs since the classic mechanism is the provision of tangibles, usually cash, support to the party. Rather, the ultimate aim of state aid can be compendiously described under the rubric of 'clean elections'. Unpacked, this means recognising and helping meet:

1 the need for organised, resourced political activity. Parties require resources for their bureaucratic maintenance, policy development and membership or community participation, and above all, the cost of public communication and campaigning; whilst:
2 enhancing equality of electoral opportunity by minimising undue disparities in wealth and resources between parties; and
3 minimising reliance on large scale private funding. Such donations distort both political equality and competition, and carry the risk of corruption

> (including the sale of access and unproductive fawning that goes with soliciting such donations).[25]

Ewing describes the anti-corruption rationale as 'one of the principal reasons for introducing State funding: to release the parties from the thrall of the large donors'. His other rationale is 'electoral equality and fair electoral competition … [whereby] the State ensures that the parties are able to communicate with electors, and reduces the income differences that might otherwise exist between them'.[26]

Of course, this 'clean elections' rationale for public funding is not infallible. Opponents of public funding invariably raise twin objections. The first is an in-principle objection. Such funding may amount to conscripting taxpayers to support competitive, private associations. The second is more pragmatic. Public funding may have consequential disbenefits, such as distorting the playing field, entrenching incumbents or creating lazy parties with atrophied grass-roots.

The usual response to the first objection is to note that, whilst they are not charities, parties play vital public roles, and then to design funding to follow electoral support to ensure it is democratic. The usual answer to the second objection is to experiment with the design and mix of the funding system, whilst admitting that the system will always be an imperfect balance.

My overall argument is that the ultimate purpose of any public funding system should be to promote a vibrant level of diversity and competition between parties. This purpose relates clearly to the second element of the 'clean elections' rationale, identified above, but is a deeper goal for the electoral system as a whole.

Reliance on large-scale donations is not, on a day-to-day basis, a question of corruption as such (although it occasionally can be, even with a good disclosure scheme and a vigilant media). The concern with quid pro quo corruption, or its appearance, focuses too heavily on the subjective intentions accompanying particular donations or relationships.

The more common 'corruption' is the softer form of systemic undue influence, whose ultimate corrosive effect is on diversity and competition. The major parties, because they are vying for government, attract the lion's share of self-interested money.[27] Through a slow and inevitable process, the major parties come to blend together, around the world-views of the same donor bases. This process can also occur independently, if the electoral system itself encourages an undue focus on the median voter. But it is exacerbated where private funding dominates, reinforcing this dampening down of vibrant political competition. Ideally, public funding should free parties to be truer to their ideological roots, or at least to be more willing to find positions of genuine difference.

A key question for the design of any form of public funding is how to distribute it between major, minor and even new parties. This is not just a question of political equality. It is more deeply a question of promoting diversity and competition, rather than ossifying the parties who happen to be powerful at the time the scheme is enacted.

Understood this way, public funding exists in *harmony* with the ultimate purpose of electoral law, namely to foster competitive elections. Public funding should thus focus on the orderly proliferation of parties, reflecting the diversity of social and economic ideas and interests in any polity. By 'orderly', I mean that whilst funding should be liberally spread, so that minor parties are encouraged and not locked out, it is legitimate for public funding rules to make normative judgments about the 'genuineness' of a party, even if that means indirectly taking an interest in the structuring of parties. For example, as Australian experience shows, it is legitimate to mandate a minimum number of members to register a party (*Mulholland* v. *AEC* (2004) 220 CLR 181).[28] Depending on the voting system, this may be essential to ensure a minimum level of legitimacy and avoid the swamping of ballot papers with micro-parties. It also may be necessary to deter 'gaming' of the system: for example, to prevent profiteering by celebrity candidates, funding may require proof of actual expenses rather than be a pure grant. But public funding and registration should not be linked to any drive to regulate the internal affairs of parties, let alone mandate particular forms of democratic behaviour within parties.

Conclusion

My argument has been that neither public funding nor registration of parties gives any justification for regulating their internal affairs. The only exception to this is the necessary correlation between public funding and reasonable regulation for financial transparency. For example, the public is entitled to know that party funds, if significantly reliant on public sources, are applied to lawful political purposes, through audited, published accounts. Similarly, it is reasonable to require publication of audited membership figures.

Outside that narrow correlation of public funding and financial accountability, the appeals to public funding as a rationale for regulating parties has been described and criticised in this paper as resting ultimately on populism. It is understandable that reformers wishing to make a case for regulating party internal affairs should resort to such appeals. But, however expensive public funding is, the argument is a cheap one. The case for regulating party affairs must rest, not on some sense of quid pro quo for taxpayer or state 'investment' in parties, but on arguments about the (mis)use of the power that parties wield. Ultimately, the aim of any scheme of public funding and party regulation should be that of electoral law generally, namely supporting a competitive electoral system to ensure genuine electoral choice.

Notes

1 For a recent comparison of constitutional and legislative regimes amongst different nations, see A. Gauja, *Enforcing Democracy? Towards a Regulatory Regime for the Implementation of Intra-Party Democracy*, Canberra: Democratic Audit, Australian National University, 2006, Online, Available http://democratic.audit.anu.edu.au/papers/20060424_gauja_enf_dem.pdf (accessed 21 July 2009).

2 See, for example, the discussion of thresholds in A. Geddis, 'Towards a System of Taxpayer Funding for New Zealand Elections?', *Otago Law Review*, 2002, vol. 10, 199–202.

3 M. Schudson, *The Good Citizen: A History of American Civil Life*, New York: The Free Press, 1998, pp. 110–111.

4 G. Johns, 'Party Democracy: an Audit of Australian Parties', *Australian Journal of Political Science*, 2000, vol. 35, 401.

5 G. Orr, 'The Law Comes to the Party: the Continuing Juridification of Political Parties in Australia', *Constitutional Law & Policy Review*, 2000, vol. 3, 41.

6 Similarly, Johns counsels against a 'de facto shift of control [from internal party processes] to external bodies', see G. Johns, 'Political Parties: from Public to Private' *Journal of Commonwealth and Comparative Politics*, 1999, vol. 37, 89.

7 K.D. Ewing, *The Cost of Democracy: Party Funding in Modern British Politics*, Oxford: Hart Publishing, 2007, p. 244.

8 Ewing's own position is equivocal – much of his recent book *The Cost of Democracy: Party Funding in Modern British Politics*, especially Chapter 4, is a recognition of the importance of party autonomy in the British tradition, especially given the 'asymmetry' in the historical ethos and structure of its parties. Ewing is particularly protective of the Labour Party's trade union base, see K.D. Ewing, *The Funding of Political Parties – the Trade Union Case for Reform*, London: Trade Union and Labour Party Liaison Organisation'/Amicus, 2006.

9 G. Johns, 'Desirability of Regulating Political Parties', *Agenda*, 2001, vol. 8, 291.

10 See V. Blechinger-Talcott and Y. Hasebe, 'Japan' in T.D. Grant (ed.), *Lobbying, Government Relations and Campaign Finance Worldwide*, New York, Oceana Publishing, 2005, p. 305.

11 T. Potter and P.S. Ryan, 'United States' in T.D. Grant (ed.), *Lobbying, Government Relations and Campaign Finance Worldwide*, New York: Oceana Publishing, 2005.

12 Joint Standing Committee on Electoral Matters, *The 2001 Federal Election: Report of the Inquiry into the Conduct of the 2001 Federal Election, and Matters Related Thereto*, Canberra: Parliament of the Commonwealth of Australia, 2003, p. 275.

13 Joint Standing Committee on Electoral Matters (Sept 2005) *The 2004 Federal Election: Report of the Inquiry into the Conduct of the 2004 Federal Election and Matters Related Thereto*, Canberra: Parliament of the Commonwealth of Australia, 2005, p. 388 [emphasis added].

14 G. Johns, 'Desirability of Regulating Political Parties', p. 300.

15 T.D. Grant (ed.), *Lobbying, Government Relations and Campaign Finance Worldwide*, New York: Oceana Publishing, 2005, provides a good reference source on comparative party funding.

16 For example, registration was introduced in Australian federal elections in 1983. To be eligible to register and thus 'earn' public funding, a body must be a 'political party', meaning 'an organisation … one of the objects or activities of which is the promotion of the election … of … candidates endorsed by it' (*Commonwealth Electoral Act 1918* (Cth) s. 4). Similarly, Canada registers political parties, which are defined as organisations 'one of whose fundamental purposes is to participate in public affairs by endorsing one or more of its members as candidates' (*Canada Elections Act 2000* (Canada) s. 2).

17 V. Blechinger-Talcott and Y. Hasebe, 'Japan', p. 304.

18 For judicial consideration, see *Payne* v. *New Zealand National Party* (Unreported, High Court of New Zealand, Panckhurst J, 1 May 2008).

19 For example, *Re Williams and the Australian Electoral Commission* (1995) 21 AAR 467 (administrative review of party's nominated officer effectively attempt to review officer's appointment) and *Sharples* v. *O'Shea* [1999] QSC 190 (review of party registration for alleged fraud, effectively a case about internal management of party).

20 See also *Coleman* v. *Liberal Party of Australia, NSW Division (No 2)* [2007] NSWSC 736, para. 33.
21 C. Morris, 'Candidate Selection in the Courts: where to after *Watt* v. *Ahsan*?', 2008, *Public Law*, 415.
22 In Australia, the answer so far is 'do not enforce the ouster clause', although relief still remains discretionary (*Coleman* v. *Liberal Party of Australia, NSW Division*, ibid., paras 45–47, rejecting an argument that by failing to accept internal procedures as final, the disgruntled candidate/plaintiff was himself in breach of the party rules.)
23 See further G. Orr, 'Legal Conceptions of Political Parties: through the Lens of Anti-Discrimination Law', in J.-C. Tham *et al.* (eds), *Electoral Democracy: Australian Prospects*, Melbourne: Melbourne University Press, 2011.
24 See also *McDonagh* v. *Ali* [2003] ICR 88 (House of Lords, refusing leave to appeal). For more, see Morris (2008) arguing that in relation to preselection disputes, courts should not use an employment law framework, importing anti-discrimination law, but a less interventionist model of enforcing the party's rules. Nonetheless *Watt* v. *Ahsan* recognised that a preselection could amount to a 'benefit or service' provided by a party to its members, in which case the party may have to act non-discriminatorily.
25 Compare Geddis's five aims to balance in designing public funding ('Towards a System of Taxpayer Funding for New Zealand Elections?', 186). My argument is that the ultimate goal of both public funding in particular, but of electoral law generally, boils down to item 4 in Geddis's list, namely electoral competitiveness.
26 K.D. Ewing, *The Cost of Democracy*, p. 52.
27 I. McMeniman, I, 'Business, Politics and Money in Australia: Testing Economic, Political and Ideological Explanations', *Australian Journal of Political Science*, 2008, 43: 377–393.
28 Compare *Figueroa* v. *Canada* [2003] 1 SCR 912 (striking down rule requiring parties to field 50 candidates at a national election to maintain registration).

Index